WORD ALIVE!

52 SELECTED SERMONS BY DALE A. MEYER

DALE A. MEYER

Tri-Pillar Publishing

WORD ALIVE!

Copyright © 2017 by Dale A. Meyer

Tri-Pillar Publishing
Anaheim Hills, California
Website: www.TriPillarPublishing.com
Email: tripillarpublishing@cox.net

International Standard Book Number --13:   978-1-942654-06-3

International Standard Book Number --10:   1-942654-06-5

Library of Congress Control Number: 2017960343

First edition, November, 2017
Printed in the United States of America

Front cover tulip photo taken at Concordia Seminary by Mark Polege
    (www.PhotographyofMarkPolege.com)
Front cover inset photo of Dr. Meyer courtesy of Concordia Seminary, St. Louis
Back cover photographs of Dr. Meyer: Seminary graduation (1973); with grandsons
    Christian, Connor, Andrew, Jacob, and Nicholas (2015)
Cover design: Peter Dibble, Wilsonville, Oregon

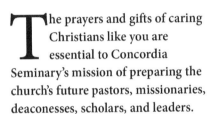

YOU CAN BLESS
PRESENT AND FUTURE GENERATIONS

The prayers and gifts of caring Christians like you are essential to Concordia Seminary's mission of preparing the church's future pastors, missionaries, deaconesses, scholars, and leaders.

With your partnership, Concordia Seminary will continue to prepare servants of Christ who are rock solid in their theology and fully prepared to lead and serve congregations now and for generations to come. You are providing faithful pastors just as sainted Christians supported Concordia Seminary to prepare the pastors who blessed you.

To give by phone or ask questions
1-800-822-5287

For more information
www.csl.edu

To give now
www.csl.edu/give

...tell to the coming generation the glorious deeds of the LORD, and his might, and the wonders that he has done.

(PSALM 78:4)

Concordia Seminary
801 Seminary Place
St. Louis, MO 63105
1-800-822-5287
www.csl.edu

To our parents,

Arthur and Norma Meyer
James and Jeanette Ermler

Your selfless love raised us in the ways of godliness. We are forever grateful.

Dale and Diane
Psalm 145:4

Contents

Acknowledgments

When you hear or read the word "you" in the Bible, chances are "you" is plural, not singular. Western culture is focused on the individual, and America today is individualism on steroids. The Church is countercultural; the Body of Christ has many individual members but we are all together in our Head, Jesus Christ. That uniqueness of the Church in today's society gives added texture to the people who helped make *Word Alive!* possible.

Rev. Dr. Gregory Seltz, I've always appreciated your adventurous spirit in ministry. New York, California, *The Lutheran Hour*, and now Washington D.C.! Those experiences, combined with your Ph.D. from Concordia Seminary, including our graduate seminar in D.C., have well prepared you for your service as Executive Director of the Lutheran Center for Religious Liberty. Thank you for the foreword, and blessings!

Thank you to LWML President Patti Ross, Mrs. Karen Shimkus, Rev. Dr. Thomas Ahlersmeyer, and Rev. Craig Reiter for your endorsements. Each of you, in your own graced way, reflects the Word of Christ alive in your heart and in your service to others:

- Patti, how great is the LWML! Thank you for your inspired and inspiring leadership, and for your ready smile.

- Karen, you've led the music at our church for many years, always with total commitment and a positive attitude. Your ministry has been dear to our family. Thank you!

- Tom, your enthusiasm is contagious! Your care for students as an educational leader and your pastoral love for congregational ministry are the mark of a churchman. Thank you!

- Craig, I'm truly proud of you! You and your classmates are the new leaders the Lord is raising up for our congregations in this new century. It's a great time to see you in ministry!

Thank you to student workers Casey Kegley and Matthew Berry for putting in many hours tracking down references and citations for the endnotes. I hope the work has in some small way furthered your appreciation for documented scholarship. The Lord will provide blessings to His Church through you. Thank you to Dr. Beth Hoeltke of the Kristine Kay Hasse Memorial Library of Concordia Seminary. In your always-helpful way, you too have helped generously with citations. We learn so much from what better minds have written; thank you for helping credit them.

Thanks to Concordia Seminary's Senior Vice President for Advancement, Vicki Biggs, and your excellent team for helping get this book to as many people as possible. In the team is Kim Braddy, who handles all the details of my heavy travel. Those trips you manage so well help shape much that I learn and write. And to my executive assistant, Pam Davitz, whose calm management of the president's office keeps things on even keel, my sincerest thanks. You keep the chaos at bay!

Deepest gratitude to Josephine and Andy Dibble. Founding Tri-Pillar and publishing books of practical service to the Church, you and your team model selfless devotion to our Lord's mission. Authors are not always easy to work with, but your grace and patience with me have made *Word Alive!* a pleasure. The Body of Christ is enriched by who you are and what you do. Now that another book is out, may you lean back, relax, and enjoy well-earned satisfaction!

Thanks are due to "you," both singular and plural, who sat in the pews while I preached. To the members of St. Peter, St. Salvator, and Holy Cross, the congregations I served as pastor, and to the people of the vacancies I served: You listened, affirmed, criticized, and helped me grow as a preacher. Churches that receive graduates from the Seminary serve the wider Church in an important way by helping their freshly-minted pastor toward maturity. And to the hundreds of thousands of worshipers who have been in the pews these 40+ years that I've been an itinerant preacher, thank you! Every time I visit and preach in a congregation, I feel a tug on my heart that I'm no longer a parish pastor.

The International Lutheran Laymen's League, Lutheran Hour Ministries, and Concordia Seminary have given me incredible opportunities to grow, in professional competence but especially in personal faith and devotion to the Gospel. Working for both organizations has been a humbling honor and has convinced me in a special way of the worldwide and eternal work of the Holy

Spirit through the Gospel. Thank you to *The Lutheran Hour* and to Concordia Seminary, St. Louis, and I thank the supporters of these two outstanding institutions.

Thank you Diane, Elizabeth, and Catharine for bearing with a husband and father who so often was away from home because of church work. Since I love to preach and have trouble turning down invitations, you bore more burdens than usual. I pray eternity shows that you were holding up the prophet's arms. My love for you is profound.

And regarding family…

Countless sermon books have been published. What motivated me to add to the long list? Partly to share what I've learned. Partly to let my flaws and weaknesses be seen so seminarians can feel comfortable in their own skin, striving for excellence but not obsessing over perfection, truly knowing themselves and therefore charitable in viewing fellow pastors. But more than anything else, I wrote *Word Alive!* so my grandchildren can reflect years from now on what Opa believed and how Opa looked at his work. I want to be in heaven with you. Together with all the members of the Body of Christ, we will marvel at our amazing God and Savior. Christian, Connor, Andrew, Jacob, and Nicholas, you are my legacy more than any book.

16

Foreword

Word Alive! is exactly that. It is the Word of God, alive in the life and teachings of Dr. Dale Meyer. His more than 40 years of service to the Church encompass work as a pastor, a professor, a theologian, the Speaker of *The Lutheran Hour*, and the president of Concordia Seminary, St. Louis. In each of these vocations, though, the key is the power of the Word, *alive* in Dr. Meyer's ministry and service to God's people. When picking up a book like this, one hopes to find well-written, engaging messages of the Gospel, preached in a variety of mission and ministry contexts. And that's what you'll find in this work. But, you will find much more than that.

Word Alive! is a devotional book, one that brings the power of God's Word to a variety of situations and issues. Titles like "Send up the Balloons," "The Flowers of Forgiveness," and "Baseball, Hot Dogs, Apple Pie, and Chevrolet" are all provocative and inviting because you know that the essence of the Gospel – "By Grace Alone, Grace in His Son" – will be delivered to the reader with a style that's all Meyer's own. If you have ever heard Pastor Meyer speak… you can actually hear his voice in the words on every page.

And that voice of the Gospel is one that is sure to bless all who read the book. In fact, *Word Alive!* is a faith-enlivening, faith-strengthening resource for anyone who opens these pages and takes these words to heart. In a funeral sermon entitled "Schedule Hope," one sees the powerful potential of these pastoral words for the lives of everyday folks. Meyer says:

> *Scheduling hope is not only for the bereaved. This big hope* [resurrection hope in Jesus!] *fills us with smaller hopes for every day. Are you struggling with unemployment or under-employment? Schedule hope into your struggles. Are you contending with physical problems? Schedule hope into your pain and weakness. Are you anxious? Are you worried? Schedule hope. Are you lonely? Schedule hope. "Blessed be the God and Father of our Lord Jesus Christ! According to his great mercy, he has caused us to be born again to a living hope through the resurrection of Jesus Christ from the dead, to an inheritance that is imperishable, undefiled, and*

unfading, kept in heaven for you" (1 Peter 1:3-4). Schedule that big hope into all that you experience and suffer in your daily life.

But *Word Alive!* is no ordinary devotional book, not at all. This is a book that also allows a person to dig deeper into God's Word by extending the sermon into one's personal life as well. Helpful to that end is the section following each sermon, entitled "For Further Reflection." There the reader can put themselves into the text, into the sermon in a more personal way, deepening their connection and knowledge of God's Word for daily life. If, when listening to a sermon, you've ever wondered, *What if I were actually there in person, listening to Jesus when He first said these words? –* well, then, this section will put that question to work for your faith life in Christ. It's powerful stuff, because digging into God's Word roots His enlivening Gospel into your daily and eternal lives by faith!

Word Alive! is also a teaching resource. Every pastor, every teacher of God's Word, is always looking for works that inspire their own ability to preach and teach the Word of God winsomely. This resource has so much to offer in that regard. Many of the sermons are relevant for particular holidays and events (such as Ash Wednesday, Thanksgiving, Lutheran Schools Week, etc.) and there are several for special occasions (including a funeral, a wedding, an installation, and a church sanctuary dedication). The back portion of the book contains a topical index and Scripture passage index for readers who want to search for encouragement on a particular subject or passage. In these pages, one sees the value of this work as a good resource for pastors who are interested in finding new ideas and inspiration for their preaching.

As a teaching resource, this book demonstrates a variety of methods, literary techniques, and homiletical models with good sermons – good preaching – on every page. Putting the book to work is sure to make any pastor, teacher, or Bible study leader a better proclaimer of the Word. There are stories that you'll never forget. There are illustrations that will not only draw you into the sermon but into the very text of the Bible as well. And there are many examples of skillful rhetorical techniques that will challenge any preacher to work harder at being up to the task of preaching God's Word so that others might indeed hear it for themselves.

But what makes this volume unique? What makes it one that should be on the shelf of every layperson, teacher, and pastor? It is the "Retrospective" section following each sermon. In these sections, Dr. Meyer reflects back on the occasion of when the sermon was preached, and adds a reflective, pastoral commentary about the sermon – one that brings the wisdom of over 40 years of preaching and ministry to bear upon what was said, and how it might be preached even better today.

You'll hear personal, practical retrospective reflections like this one from "The Triumph Song." Here, Meyer is commenting on the necessity for proclaimers of the Word, even for the best among us, to remember first and foremost one's absolute need for the very Word they are sharing. Talking about a very personal moment with our shared mentor, Dr. Oswald C.J. Hoffmann, Meyer says:

> *I was no Ozzie Hoffmann; he was incomparable. At any rate, one day Dr. Hoffmann was telling me about a friend and then, eyes down, said quietly, "He's gone too." He paused, only for a few seconds, but he was thinking about his narrowing circle of friends.*
>
> *The things of faith get personal for us ministers too. A preacher has to know personally the human feelings that come with the narrowing circle and the prospect of his own death, and a preacher has to let people know that he knows. ...*
>
> *Shortly before he died, Martin Luther wrote, "We are all beggars. That is true."[1] The narrowing circle of friends and family should not lead us to despair but to a buoyant, lively hope in Christ, who promises to lead us through the valley of death to join the Church Triumphant.*

That vulnerability to the preached Word, that mature, critiquing wisdom from a pastoral heart is seen throughout the retrospective sections in the book. In the retrospective section of another sermon, "Word Alive! Connections and Conversations," Meyer gets even more personal, saying:

> *As I age and watch, I am more and more acutely aware that unspoken assumptions about how things are, or how we imagine things are, hurt the Church. This sermon, originally delivered for the opening of*

Concordia Seminary's 177th academic year, identifies three popular but insidious assumptions: that fear of God is an outmoded religious concept, that the Church is simply an institution, and that the Word of God is bound in the Bible. Here's another one. When you read the word "you" in the Bible, you probably think it's singular. That's because our western culture is individualistic, and our current American ways of thinking are hyper-individualistic. But more often than not, "you" in the Bible is plural, not singular; the inspired writer is speaking to the whole Church, the whole Body of Christ. I'm convinced these false assumptions and others slow the growth of the Church. They seduce us into the conventional wisdom of the dominant culture around us, sapping the challenge that's in the scriptural and Reformation principles: Grace Alone, Faith Alone, Word Alone. "Having eyes do you not see, and having ears do you not hear?" (Mark 8:18). It's the task of theology professors and pastors to study, observe culture, and get all of us reflecting on our assumptions about life on the basis of the Word of God.

"The Triumph Song," "Schedule Hope," "Word Alive! Connections and Conversations" … good news indeed for every moment for every person. And in these retrospective sections of deep, pastoral reflection, Meyer demonstrates his own dependence (and ours too) on the Word. These sections bring to fruition, devotionally and prayerfully, the Scripture reading for the week, a topical prayer, and the message itself. That's what makes this book a resource that will not only devotionally warm your heart and strengthen your faith, but also make you a better preacher and teacher as well.

Dr. Meyer and I share a few things in ministry. We both have been parish pastors. We both have been professors. And yes, we are part of a small group of pastors who have been the Speaker of *The Lutheran Hour*, a calling whose whole identity is rooted in preaching the Word to people coast to coast and around the world. But, having said that, my favorite shared ministry experience with Dr. Meyer occurred when I was his teaching assistant during my residency for my Ph.D. I was privileged to teach an advanced homiletics course with him at Concordia Seminary, St. Louis. What a joy that was! I remember seeing many of the ideas displayed in this book come "alive" in the classroom as he sought to teach students to be better proclaimers of God's powerful Word. I remember him telling the students that you have to faithfully attend to the words of the text, *yes!* You have to do your exegesis, your in-depth study of the Scriptures, *yes!* But, you also have to attend to the work of constructing the sermon for the sake of your hearers. You have to ask the questions that they are asking. You have to know, or do your best to know, their point of view. Why? So that you can most effectively deliver the text to their ears, their minds, and their hearts by the power of the Holy Spirit. Yes, it is the power of the Word. But the pastor should be a man of the Word, a man skilled in words, and one who knows how to communicate so that his hearers might not only understand what was said but remember it and retain it. After all, there is nothing more important in life than being a bearer of God's "Word Alive" to others. It is, as St. Paul says, "the power of God for salvation to everyone who believes" (Romans 1:16). So many of the ideas from that very class are found within the sermons and the retrospectives of this devotional, homiletical work. They are ideas that will bless the lay reader, but they will also bless the preaching practitioner as well. I know, because I still use many of these helpful ideas in my preaching and teaching to this day.

There aren't many books today that "stay with you." But this book is one that will. It reflects the thoughts of a man whose ministry has served the Church for over four decades. But even more importantly, it lays out before our eyes the very gift of ministry for ministry, the powerful Word of God, which lives in our preaching of the Gospel and enlivens our people – because Jesus, the Word Alive, is just that kind of Savior. If you want a resource that will give your life a devotional focus, then the 52 sermons in this book will happily guide you through the year. If you want a resource that will help you become a better preacher of the Gospel, this volume will be one that does all that with flair. But, if you want to see the heart of what makes the Bible a unique Word, and the message of Jesus Christ an enduring reality still today, you'll see it in the simple, compelling *Word Alive!* sermons of a pastor who has spent his life trying to speak that Word for you.

Word Alive! is for believers and seekers, pastors and teachers, because it's God's Word *alive* for you.

Gregory Seltz, M.Div., S.T.M., Ph.D.
Executive Director, Lutheran Center for Religious Liberty
Speaker Emeritus, *The Lutheran Hour*
Washington, D.C.

Introduction

Confidence in the Gospel

Every minister has preached some lousy sermons, and I have too. Obviously we tried to keep them out of this book! This collection is eclectic – no pretension that these are the best I've preached. There's a lot of subjectivity in evaluating sermons anyway. Every pastor knows that some sermons we think are great turn out to be duds with the congregation, and vice versa. Some of the sermons in this book come from typewriter days, when I was a student or young pastor and typed out my sermons word for word, memorized them almost verbatim, and then filed them away in three-ring binders – two shelves full of three-ring binders, now with yellowed paper. Others come from my 12 years as *Lutheran Hour* Speaker. Again, randomly chosen. With the advent of computers, I started to store my work electronically, but those files are all over kingdom come. A final trove was handwritten manuscripts, often written while I was on an airplane traveling someplace to speak. The sermons you'll read – and I thank you for reading them – were altered minimally. In some of the retrospectives that follow each of the 52 sermons, you'll find my more mature comments about how I'd improve the given sermon were I writing it today. Professors of homiletics (preaching) and pastors will find things here that will prompt them to say, "That's not how I would do it." I'm fine with that – comfortable in my own skin. The great orator Cicero said in his *De Oratore* that a speaker should not be judged on any individual speech but rather on the whole body of his work.[1] The Bible covers our flaws when it reminds us, "We have this treasure in jars of clay, to show that the surpassing power belongs to God and not to us" (2 Corinthians 4:7).

I've lived through a transition from "Christian America" – churched America – to today, post-churched America. Is it bad or good that the church has lost its privilege? The decades have taught me an answer. Born and baptized in January, 1947, I was raised in a God-fearing and loving home. Weekly worship, Lutheran grade school, and Sunday school… It was "Christian America." I went to a big public high school but it was part of the fabric of "Christian America," church and public culture complementing one another. In 1965, I went off to college. First to Concordia College in Milwaukee, then to Concordia Senior College in

Fort Wayne, and on to Concordia Seminary, which had been my goal since grade school. Those were all church schools, so I didn't realize "Christian" America was going away. Working on a Master's degree at Washington University in St. Louis, and later earning a Ph.D. in Greek and Latin, started showing me different worldviews. Diane and I married in 1973, and the next year I was ordained and installed in the dual parish of Venedy and New Memphis, Illinois. It was still "Christian" America. Most people went to church, or at least knew they should go to church. Most people knew about the Bible and its main characters. Most people knew what the church taught about Jesus. Whether they truly believed in Him or not is another question. And the morality of America was still publicly based on the Ten Commandments, often displayed on government grounds and buildings. But things were changing. Liberalism in universities and media was undermining how America believed and thought, and the changes were also slipping into the heads and hearts of parishioners.

In 1981, I was called to teach at Concordia Seminary, St. Louis, but after three years took a call to Holy Cross Lutheran Church in Collinsville, Illinois. I was just too young to be talking about God and Church and not doing congregational ministry. With 2,400 members and a school of over 400, Holy Cross was different than Venedy and New Memphis. The pastoral office has basic duties, but how they are carried out varies by congregation and context. When *The Lutheran Hour* tapped me in October 1988, I began to experience firsthand what I had theoretically known, that the mission is bigger than the confines of a congregation or denomination. Church people are like butterflies in cocoons. Some see scary changes happening and pull back in. Others see changes and have confidence in the Gospel to venture forth in service and witness. I think that's a great divide for the institutional church in America today. My experiences at the Seminary have confirmed this divide. When President John Johnson invited me back to teach at Concordia Seminary, I had no clue I'd be appointed interim president in 2004 – and in 2005, Concordia's tenth president. It's been the hardest job I've ever had; no doubt part of God's plan to humble me. I'm thankful for the experience of being president because, grueling as it is, it has refined my personal faith and taught me that the public way forward for the institutional church is following the Word centered on Jesus – period. Martin Luther: "Faith is a living, daring confidence in God's grace, so sure and certain that the believer would stake his life on it a thousand times."[2] Get that? You and

I are staking our life on the unmerited grace God gives us in Jesus. In the institutional church today, I don't sense a desperation for Jesus. Desperation grows out of the sense that nothing in us merits God's grace, our religious works included. Jesus is all we have. Too many are pulling back into the cocoon, "having the appearance of godliness, but denying its power" (2 Timothy 3:5).

Older people grieve what's been lost. In "Christian America," the things of God and the things of public society easily became mixed together. Christian life and public life were homogenized, the clear differences blurred. Thereby the distinctiveness of following Jesus could get lost. But now "Christian" America is gone. That makes this new time an opportunity, a strange blessing to understand anew – or understand for the first time – the radical nature of faith in Jesus. Peggy Noonan, speech writer for President Reagan and now an insightful weekly columnist for the *The Wall Street Journal*, reflected on all the changes around us after she reread a book by Dean Acheson, Secretary of State under President Harry Truman. "Everyone's in the dark looking for the switch," she wrote. Isn't that a great description of our society today? "Everyone's in the dark looking for the switch," she wrote. "When you're in the middle of history the meaning of things is usually unclear... In real time most things are obscure..." And then she quotes Dean Acheson. "Only slowly did it dawn upon us that the whole world structure and order that we had inherited from the nineteenth century was gone."[3] Our seminarians and young church workers get it. They know that Jesus is the Light of the world (John 8:12), that we have been called out of darkness into His marvelous light (1 Peter 2:9), to let our light shine in this society (Matthew 5:16). They do not grieve what has been lost in American culture and church life; they haven't lived through it. They do look forward with hope and anticipation for their ministries and the mission of the Church in these new times. I pray that we older church people will fully welcome and bring younger generations, pastors and lay alike, into the corporate life and leadership of the Church, not making them sit at the children's card table.

More Life!

The 52 sermons in *Word Alive!* are like snapshots. The focus is supposed to be on the Word, but in the background you catch hints of America's changing cultural context. In the "Retrospective" following each sermon, I look back in three ways. In some entries, I share some preaching/rhetorical insights, sometimes critiquing how I wrote the sermon. As my dad told me, "Someone can always do it better." In other retrospectives, I look back wistfully at how the context for church and ministry has changed. And in still others, I get devotional, prompted to musings of faith by something in the sermon. I hope the retrospectives will stimulate your own thoughts, your own looking back, as you find your faithful place and His peace in this new America. Thanks to a great suggestion by the editors, we've also added some images and illustrations throughout the book. I enjoyed writing the text accompanying each image. Again, some are wistfully looking back; others have some teaching.

The "For Further Reflection" sections give you an opportunity to think about some doctrinal point in the sermon, with short teachings, questions, Bible readings, and a hymn verse or two, all grouped under a quotation from one of the Six Chief Parts of Christian doctrine. You'll find that a thread running through the reflections is the fear and love of God. As the Reformer said in explaining all the commandments, "We should fear and love God."[4] If the Church today doesn't seem desperate for Jesus, it may be because we've stopped talking about the fear of God. Without the fear of God, why would we love our only Savior? I hope reading the passages suggested in the reflections will add to the conviction of your confession, "I believe."

The Recommended Reading List gathers some book titles mentioned throughout *Word Alive!* as well as some others that I've found stimulating, especially about the changes I've seen in America and the institutional church during my lifetime. When you go to that section of *Word Alive!* you'll see I've tried to tell you why each suggested book is helpful. Some are must-reads for pastors and seminarians.

The topical and Scripture passage indexes give you an easy way to access whatever *Word Alive!* says about some topic or text that has your interest. Indexes are one of the most frequent places I go when I pull a book off the shelf searching for helpful information.

Word Alive! can be used personally or in small groups. Used personally, each week has more material than can be digested in one or two sittings. When you come upon something that gets you thinking deeper into the Word, spend time there. Don't feel you have to rush on! Used for study groups, the leader might assign the reading of a sermon, and then the group comes together to discuss the

For Further Reflection section. Feel free to quote from the book (credit is appreciated!) and to take ideas and develop them further… and better!

I've been blessed to live through the great transition from churched to post-churched America. In some ways we've let the changes, the losses, in America and in the institutional church scare us from our confidence in the Gospel. C.F.W. Walther, the first president of Concordia Seminary, told his seminarians, "I wish to talk the Christian doctrine into your very heart, enabling you to come forward as living witnesses with a demonstration of the Spirit and of power. I do not want you to be standing in your pulpits like lifeless statues, but to speak with confidence and cheerful courage, offering help where help is needed."[5] I pray Concordia Seminary's graduates will bring that "confidence and cheerful courage" into your congregation. The great devotional writer Oswald Chambers wrote, "Anything that savors of dejection spiritually is always wrong."[6] Let the Word not be bound but be the Word alive! It's a great time to be the Church!

Rev. Dale A. Meyer, Ph.D.
St. Louis, Missouri
November, 2017

List of Images

Word Alive!

Week 1 – Touching the Heart of Uncle Me

The Baptism of Our Lord
Broadcast on The Lutheran Hour
January 11, 1998

Text – Matthew 3:13-17

Then Jesus came from Galilee to the Jordan to John, to be baptized by him. John would have prevented him, saying, "I need to be baptized by you, and do you come to me?" But Jesus answered him, "Let it be so now, for thus it is fitting for us to fulfill all righteousness." Then he consented. And when Jesus was baptized, immediately he went up from the water, and behold, the heavens were opened to him, and he saw the Spirit of God descending like a dove and coming to rest on him; and behold, a voice from heaven said, "This is my beloved Son, with whom I am well pleased."

Prayer

Dear God, there's much in my life that depresses and hurts me. I need encouragement. Too often I'm down in the dumps; too often I despair and think that life stinks. I know firsthand the pain of sin and its consequences. O God, send Your Spirit through the story of Jesus' baptism to teach me that I have a Savior who wants to be with me and help me. My heart needs a gentle touch from You. Amen.

"Life stinks, and then you die." That was on a church's outdoor sign in York Center, Illinois – presumably an enticement to interest people in church. Have you ever felt that way? I've had down-in-the-dump moments when I felt like that. I'm sure you have, too. Sometimes those moments turn into hours, the hours can turn into days, the days into weeks and months and even years. There are many people whose honest evaluation of their own life is "Life stinks, and then you die." When you have those down-in-the-dump moments, or if your permanent address is Down in the Dumps, I hope you'll listen carefully to the story of Uncle Me.

Uncle Me lives in Thailand. His fellow Thais call him "Uncle," as a title of affection and respect for his age. Uncle Me is in his late 50s. One day in 1994, Uncle Me's wife sent him to the store. She needed some rice and sugar. So, Uncle Me walked to the closest store – and that meant a seven-mile walk. While he was in that store, he heard a radio program playing loudly enough for all the customers to hear. The program was called *Heart Encouraging*. As Uncle Me was checking out, he asked the shopkeeper if he could come back and listen to that program again. You see, Uncle Me had no radio in his home. The shopkeeper said "Yes," so the next day Uncle Me again walked those seven miles to the store. This time, he didn't have to buy any rice or sugar; he just wanted to hear the program. He did this for many, many days in succession.

One day, that radio program carried an announcement that there would be a meeting in the province where Uncle Me lived. The gathering was sponsored by the people who produced the program *Heart Encouraging*. And wouldn't you know it, those are the people of the Thailand office of Lutheran Hour Ministries! That is one of the many programs Lutheran Hour Ministries produces around the world. Now, when Uncle Me heard that the people who produced *Heart Encouraging* were coming to his province, he decided that he'd attend the gathering.

That's precisely what he did. When the appointed day came, Uncle Me was at the gathering place long before the meeting was to begin. He stayed throughout the entire program, and even lingered after adjournment because he wanted to learn more about Jesus. That's who had drawn him to walk those long miles, day after day after day. That's who drew him to come to the meeting. And that's who touched Uncle Me's heart with encouragement. After the meeting, Uncle Me started going to church. Six months later, he was baptized. Today, even as you and I are visiting, Uncle Me is a member of a local congregation in his province in Thailand. In fact, he's even an elder of his church.

Uncle Me's story teaches the point that no one can touch the heart like Jesus. There are many people and things that reach out and touch our hearts. Sometimes they touch our hearts for good. But sometimes their touch is not good; sometimes their touch is painful. But no one touches a heart like Jesus. When you have those down-in-the-dump moments, those "Life stinks, and then you die" thoughts, then let Jesus touch your heart with His encouragement.

I pray, and I invite you to pray with me: *Dear God, there's much in my life that depresses and hurts me. I need encouragement for my heart. Please touch my heart for good, for this moment and for all the days ahead. Amen.*

Jesus did not come to lay another guilt trip on us. The fact is that we've got plenty of laws and rules and regulations, and we are not able to live up to all of them. We don't always do our duty to our family members, to our neighbors, and to others we meet each day. We don't always do right by God. His commandments and laws make that painfully clear. We really don't need another guilt trip. We've got enough people – preachers among them – pointing out our shortcomings and our sins. Our hearts are often touched by pain and guilt. We need someone to stand with us – someone to be there for you, to be there for me, to be with us when we're feeling great and to be with us when we're down in the dumps.

Last May, I spent some time answering the telephones at Lutheran Hour Ministries. If you've listened to our programs before, you know that we invite viewers and listeners to call in for spiritual help and counsel. While my usual workload doesn't permit me to do this, last May I did have some spare time, so I answered the phones. I took four phone calls: one from Texas, one from California, one from Oregon, and the fourth from suburban Chicago. I asked each caller if they had someone, a counselor or a minister, who could be with them during their tough times. Many of the callers on that day were living with cancer. Three of the four callers said that they did have someone to be with them, but the fourth caller, the one from suburban Chicago, said that she did not. When I asked if she would be willing to let our staff put her in touch with a minister in her area, she answered, "Yes."

You see, she appreciated our broadcast, but what she really wanted was someone to be there for her. Aren't we all like that? We don't simply want someone telling us what we ought to do, as good as the advice may be. We want someone to be there for us – someone to be there *with* us – and best of all, someone to touch our heart with encouragement.

No one does that like Jesus. That's what the story of His baptism is all about. On the first Sunday after Epiphany, many Christian churches focus on the story of Jesus' baptism. In that story, we learn that Jesus is there for you. He's not there holding your hand but with nothing to say. He's with you and able to touch your heart with encouraging words, just as he touched the heart of Uncle Me.

Dear God, we pray again, teach us how Jesus' baptism can encourage our hearts. So often we're down in the dumps, so often we despair and think that life stinks. We're painfully aware of many of our sins and their consequences. We need encouragement. Our hearts need a gentle touch from You. Amen.

Listen to the story of Jesus' baptism from Matthew 3:13-17.

> Then Jesus came from Galilee to the Jordan to John, to be baptized by him. John would have prevented him, saying, "I need to be baptized by you, and do you come to me?" But Jesus answered him, "Let it be so now, for thus it is fitting for us to fulfill all righteousness." Then he consented. And when Jesus was baptized, immediately he went up from the water, and behold, the heavens were opened to him, and he saw the Spirit of God descending like a dove and coming to rest on him; and behold, a voice from heaven said, "This is my beloved Son, with whom I am well pleased."

This story of Jesus' baptism has sometimes perplexed Christians. Why, they wonder, was Jesus baptized? The Bible clearly teaches that Jesus has no sin. You and I have our sins. The Law accuses us and rightly so, but no divine Law from God could ever be used against Jesus. John the Baptizer knew that. John once called Jesus "the Lamb of God" (John 1:29), a reference to Jesus' purity and innocence. Now that being so, John the Baptizer said, "I need to be baptized by you" (Matthew 3:14). So, why was Jesus baptized?

The answer to that question is found right in Jesus' own words. He says, "This is the way it has to be now. This is the proper way to do everything that God requires of us" (Matthew 3:15 GW). Jesus was not baptized for the forgiveness of His sins. As I said, He doesn't have any. Jesus was baptized to show His solidarity with us sinners. He came to be with us. But Jesus had more in mind than only showing that He wants to be with us in all the ups and downs of life. By His baptism, Jesus not only demonstrated His solidarity with us, He also showed that He is with us as our Savior. "This," He said, "is the proper way to do everything that God requires of us." You and I don't do everything that God requires of us. Jesus was baptized to demonstrate that He came to do for us everything that we sinners haven't been able to do for ourselves before God.

He did that for you by His active obedience to God. Throughout the 30-some years of His life in the land of Israel, Jesus actively kept all the commandments of God. He did that in your place and in mine. When this Good News draws you to faith in Jesus, God looks at you and sees Jesus' perfect obedience. When your faith is in Jesus, God does not see your sins but He sees Jesus' perfect obedience. Doesn't that give encouragement to your heart, especially when your heart is grieved because of the things you have done wrong?

Jesus also was obedient to God in a passive way. That is, He was a victim upon the cross. There, He suffered for all that you and I have done wrong. He suffered for our disobedience to God's Law. He suffered for your sins. When this Gospel draws you to faith in Jesus, God forgives what you have done wrong. God remembers your sins no more. Instead of laying a new guilt trip on you for what you've done wrong, Jesus' Word touches your heart with the forgiveness that He earned at the cross. Doesn't that also give you encouragement? That's why the Heavenly Father told us to listen to Jesus. That Good News drew Uncle Me back to that store, day after day after day, to listen to the program *Heart Encouraging*. Jesus was touching Uncle Me's heart with forgiveness and with hope. When Jesus was baptized, He also had His eyes set on the future. Now, when Jesus touches you with forgiveness, He also wants to encourage you with hope. Jeremiah 29:11 says, "I know the plans I have for you, declares the LORD, plans for welfare and not for evil, to give you a future and a hope." That hope can fill your heart because of the resurrection of Jesus Christ. God the Father was so pleased with the life and the sacrifice of His Son, that he raised Him to life on Easter morning. That's the guarantee that Jesus' kindly touch is true, and this hope for your future is real. "Blessed be the God and Father of our Lord Jesus Christ! According to his great mercy, he has caused us to be born again to a living hope through the resurrection of Jesus Christ from the dead" (1 Peter 1:3).

Today, there are millions and millions of people who are being touched by Jesus through His kindly words of forgiveness and hope. Uncle Me is one of those millions. A woman named Laverne is another. She lives in Colorado, and has listened to this program for several years. When the doctor told her that she had cancer, she called our toll-free, 800 number. When Laverne was asked if she was interested in talking with a local pastor, she said "Yes," and our staff contacted a local minister. He visited with her many times, just as Uncle Me listened to *Heart Encouraging* many times. Laverne has now been taught the Good News in detail. She has been baptized, and now she communes at the Lord's altar. She's among the millions whose hearts are being touched by Jesus through His Word of forgiveness and hope.

And yet, many millions remain who would say, "Life stinks, and then you die." Pastor Roosevelt Gray told me about the rainy day he was in his office in Houston, Texas. He heard the sound of the church door closing, so he went into the sanctuary to investigate. There he met a woman. He assumed that she was seeking refuge from the rain, but she was not. "I can't stand any more abuse," she cried out. "I can't stand any more abuse."

Pastor Gray invited her to sit down to regain her composure. She did and told him that she had been abused as a child. She then had been abused by her husband. When she left her husband to seek refuge in a shelter, she was abused again. Fleeing that shelter, she shacked up with a boyfriend, and he abused her. Now on this dreary, rainy day, she had had enough. She fled into the church and said, "I can't stand any more abuse."

Referring to the Savior, Pastor Gray said, "There is One who will never abuse you." She snapped back, "Don't tell me about Jesus." Roosevelt backed off, but every now and then would speak some words of faith. Every time he did, she said, "Yeah, I know that." Well, maybe she did know some things about Jesus in her head, but her heart had not yet been touched with Jesus' kindness.

In time, she regained her composure and got up to leave. She had not shared her name with Pastor Gray. He told me that he never saw her again. But she is out there. She left the sanctuary to return to the only world she had ever known – a world of pain and hurt. Is her story like your story? Have you heard about Jesus but still have a broken, hurting heart? Life doesn't have to stink. Your future doesn't have to be dark and dismal death. You don't have to live in despair. Jesus wants to touch you with His words of forgiveness and hope. As He touched Uncle Me's heart, as He touched Laverne's heart, your Savior wants to give you help and hope.

Dear God, may Jesus' baptism teach every one of us that we have a Savior who wants to be with us and help us. May this Good News touch our hearts and draw us to Jesus. Amen.

For Further Reflection

According to Wikipedia, there are 31,102 verses in the Bible. Because that much information can be confusing, theologians have culled out the Bible's main teachings, and in the Lutheran Church they're known as the Six Chief Parts of Christian Doctrine. These Six Chief Parts are a practical way to keep "Thus says the Lord" in mind and heart. One of the Six Chief Parts is Baptism.

"Go therefore and make disciples of all nations, baptizing them in the name of the Father and of the Son and of the Holy Spirit." (Matthew 28:19)

- Jesus was baptized to "fulfill all righteousness" (Matthew 3:15). When you were baptized, God touched your heart and life with all Jesus has done and continues to do for you. Read John 3:1-18 and put yourself in the story. Would you have marveled?
- A thread throughout this book is fear and love of God. See how natural fear was transformed into the fear of God that is awe at His saving love for us – Acts 16:25-34; Acts 2:37-41.
- The blessings of Baptism – Titus 3:5-8; Romans 6:1-4; 1 Corinthians 6:11; Galatians 3:26-27

> *I bind this day to me forever,*
> *By pow'r of faith, Christ's incarnation,*
> *His Baptism in the Jordan River,*
> *His cross of death for my salvation,*
> *His bursting from the spiced tomb,*
> *His riding up the heav'nly way,*
> *His coming at the day of doom,*
> *I bind unto myself today.*[1]

Retrospective

Looking back at my old sermons has been interesting – something like the Ghost of Christmas Past taking Scrooge back to his younger years. This sermon highlighted for me the importance of emotions. When the faculty of Concordia Seminary was revising its curriculum, a counselor told us that he entered the ministry thinking that his job was to be the answer man. After all, he had spent four years at the Seminary learning theology, so he assumed his job as a pastor was to dispense answers. Or was it not an assumption? Maybe he was taught that's what a pastor does. Our counselor friend quickly found out that ministry is head and heart, and that's been a lesson for me, too, over my decades. Today's graduates from the Seminary know it's head and heart – "holistic" is the popular word. Emotions often show our distance from God, even our rebellion. The challenge is to go from subjective feelings to the objective, revealed, living Word of God. That's what Pastor Gray was trying to do with the woman who wandered into his church. That's what did happen with Uncle Me. Christian life is a constant back-and-forth, from what we feel to our dependable God, always with us in Jesus. It's the work of His Holy Spirit, and it began when we were baptized. The ghosts put fear into Scrooge. God's Spirit gives the baptized lives of joy in the true fear and love of God.

The Lord has led me into unique and very different places of service. There are a number of apt passages as I look back, but one certainly has to be Luke 17:10 – "So you also, when you have done all that you were commanded, say, 'We are unworthy servants; we have only done what was our duty.'"

I served as Speaker of The Lutheran Hour from 1989 until 2001. Each broadcast sermon was made available in print to anyone who contacted us by mail or phone. The internet had not yet become the dominant presence it is today. The radio tower on the cover of this sermon reminds us how media has changed. Back in the time of Walter A. Maier, founder of The Lutheran Hour, radio towers broadcast the program to your home, and that was pretty much it. The mailman came to your house with letters and magazines. The paper boy delivered the newspaper, but no television, no computers or tablets or cell phones. Back then, a program like The Lutheran Hour was "broadcast," the signals from hundreds of towers reaching a broad audience. Today, media has multiplied and no one program can command as large a proportion of public attention as decades ago. "Narrowcast" is today's more appropriate word. The market is fragmented. People have hundreds of TV or radio stations to choose from. On the internet, they click onto whatever suits them. It's "narrow" – harder to get your message out.

Many older church people with whom I talk long for the old days, when a program like The Lutheran Hour had a much larger share of the market than today: Can we come up with a new program? The closest thing I know to a "silver bullet" to reach as many people as possible is something old, older than radio and towers, tested and true. It's the people in the local congregation. With so much impersonal media today, people yearn for the human touch. They want human interactions that are genuine, that give relief from the pressures of hectic daily life, that are based on Christ's forgiving love and acceptance rather than the societal standard of using one another. They want people who embody the saying, "Don't tell me what a friend I have in Jesus until I see what a friend I have in you." Through radio towers and PC towers, through print and people, Lutheran Hour Ministries serves the caring and practical Word of God with the people who make up communities of faith – congregations. And the design is that they, you, take the Gospel to people who still don't know Jesus. It's flesh-and-blood broadcasting for our narrowcast society.

Dr. Dale Meyer
Lutheran Hour Speaker
International Lutheran Laymen's League
Artwork Copyright © 1989

"Touching the Heart of Uncle Me"

"The Lutheran Hour" January 11, 1998

Copyright © 1997,
International Lutheran Laymen's League

TEXT: Matthew 3:13-17

"Life stinks, and then you die." That was on a church bulletin board in York Center, Ill.,—presumably an enticement to interest people in church. Have you ever felt that way? I've had down-in-the-dump moments when I felt like that. I'm sure you have, too. Sometimes those moments turn into hours, the hours can turn into days, the days into weeks and months and even years. There are many people whose honest evaluation of their own life is, "Life stinks, and then you die." When you have those down-in-the-dump moments or if your permanent address is down-in-the dumps, I hope you'll listen carefully to the story of Uncle Me.

Uncle Me lives in Thailand. His fellow Thais call him "uncle" as a title of affection and respect for his age.

Week 2 – My Best Two Paragraphs

Broadcast on The Lutheran Hour
January 14, 1996

Text – John 1:29-34

The next day he saw Jesus coming toward him, and said, "Behold, the Lamb of God, who takes away the sin of the world! This is he of whom I said, 'After me comes a man who ranks before me, because he was before me.' I myself did not know him, but for this purpose I came baptizing with water, that he might be revealed to Israel." And John bore witness: "I saw the Spirit descend from heaven like a dove, and it remained on him. I myself did not know him, but he who sent me to baptize with water said to me, 'He on whom you see the Spirit descend and remain, this is he who baptizes with the Holy Spirit.' And I have seen and have borne witness that this is the Son of God."

Prayer

Almighty God, lead us by Your Word to think deeply about our sin, but even more touch our guilt with Your Word of forgiveness – forgiveness complete for all we've done wrong and forgiveness completely unmerited, given to us only by Your grace. As Your Spirit lifts from our hearts the load of guilt with the Word of forgiveness, motivate us to show our gratitude with a life of good works. In Jesus' name, Amen.

Last October, I spoke at a rally in Waterloo, Iowa. At the conclusion of that rally, there was an opportunity for people in the audience to ask me questions.

One of the questions was this: "Do you write your own sermons?" The answer is yes. For better or for worse, the messages that you hear on *The Lutheran Hour* have been written by me, and when I travel and speak in front of crowds, as I did in Waterloo, I deliver messages that I, myself, have prepared.

Now when I speak in front of an audience in a church or an auditorium, it's very interesting to watch the faces in the crowd. Do the people seem interested in what I'm saying? Are their eyes on me, or are they looking around? Does their body language indicate that they're with me, or that I've lost their attention? Of the millions of words that I've addressed to crowds, there have been two paragraphs that have especially held the attention of audiences. And those two paragraphs – my best two paragraphs – are about the forgiveness of sins.

I first noticed this in January of 1992, when I was speaking at a church in Wheaton, Illinois. I was delivering those two paragraphs (and, by the way, I'll rehearse those paragraphs for you a little later) when it struck me how attentively the congregation was listening. While I was preaching, part of my brain was saying: *Look at them, Dale. They're really, really listening to what you're saying.* Indeed, they were. You could have heard a pin drop. In fact, there was one woman in the back of the church who strained her neck so that she could see me as I was talking about the forgiveness of sins.

Why is the forgiveness of sins such a riveting subject? I should tell you that I tell no jokes in those two paragraphs. I have no story or illustration to keep the crowd interested. As you'll hear later, it's just straight religious talk about forgiveness. Why is that such a riveting subject? I'm convinced that the answer is that forgiveness addresses the most basic, fundamental, heartrending problem we all have – which is guilt over what we've done wrong. To put it a little more religiously, forgiveness addresses the guilt you feel because of your sin. "O almighty God, merciful Father," go the well-known words of confession, "I, a poor, miserable sinner, confess to You all my sins and iniquities with which I have ever offended You and justly deserved Your punishment now and forever."[1]

Not everyone, however, feels guilty about sin. Not everyone is willing to say those words of confession. Some people avoid heartfelt confession of their sin by changing the definition of sin. I've often been told, "Reverend, I know I'm not perfect; I'm a sinner. But I try my best." 1 John 3:4 (GW) tells us that "Sin is disobedience" to God's laws, and James 2:10 (GW) says that "If someone obeys all of God's laws except one, that person is guilty of breaking all of them."

Imperfection is only the tip of sin's iceberg. Just because you change the definition of sin doesn't mean that God has.

Other people deal with sin by ignoring it. King David seems to have done that. He knew that God forbids murder and adultery. Still, he murdered Uriah and committed adultery with Bathsheba (2 Samuel 11), ignoring God's clear commandments.

Still others go further and deny that they're sinners. We remind them that 1 John 1:8 says, "If we say we have no sin, we deceive ourselves, and the truth is not in us."

Still others deal with sin by rationalizing it. *Sure, I did wrong, but there were factors pushing me to it.* Adam rationalized his sin against God by saying, "The woman whom you gave to be with me, she gave me fruit of the tree, and I ate" (Genesis 3:12). Eve, in turn, blamed the snake (Genesis 3:13). The same rationalization happens today when people blame crime on poverty, as if the criminal had no responsibility for his actions.

Finally, you can marginalize sin. *Sin is an issue*, you might admit, *but it's only one of our many relationships to God. Don't exaggerate it.* True, we do have many points of contact with God. God gives us food, shelter, friends, and family, and the like. He gives this to us whether we're godly or not. However, that does not mean that sin is only a marginal issue between us and God. "The wages of sin is death" says Romans 6:23, and death certainly is not a peripheral issue. Sin isn't peripheral, either.

The only acceptable way to deal with sin is to acknowledge it, to realize its terrible impact upon your life, and to confess your sin to God. King David finally came to realize this. He said in Psalm 32:

> When I kept silent about my sins,
>   my bones began to weaken because of my groaning all day long.
> Day and night your hand laid heavily on me.
> My strength shriveled in the summer heat.   *Selah*

> I made my sins known to you, and I did not cover up my guilt.
> I decided to confess them to you, O LORD.
>   Then you forgave all my sins.   *Selah* (Psalm 32:3-5 GW)

That's why the forgiveness of sins is such a compelling message. Throughout the history of the Bible, sermons about forgiveness have been welcomed by people who owned up to their sins. I've just mentioned King David, the murderer and adulterer who confessed his sin and heard a great message of forgiveness from the prophet Nathan (2 Samuel 12:13). John the Baptizer also preached messages of sin and forgiveness that commanded the attention of his listeners. In Matthew 3:1-2 (GW) we read that "John the Baptizer appeared in the desert of Judea. His message was, 'Turn to God and change the way you think and act, because the kingdom of heaven is near.'"

In other words, he preached that sinners should repent and confess their sins. People turned out to hear him preach. Matthew 3:5 (GW) says, "Jerusalem, all Judea, and the whole Jordan Valley went to him." But John also pointed sinners to the Savior. In John 1:29 (GW) we read that "John saw Jesus coming toward him … and said, 'Look! This is the Lamb of God who takes away the sin of the world.'"

What an appropriate picture John used to describe Jesus. Just like a sacrificial lamb, Jesus was sacrificed on Calvary's cross to pay the price for all your sins. Because the Lamb of God paid the price by His death and was restored to life on Easter morning, the forgiveness of your sins has been accomplished. Because of Jesus' death and resurrection, your every sin has been forgiven. Now, listener, I'm giving you the first of my best two paragraphs. Because of Jesus' death and resurrection, your every sin has been forgiven. Yes, He is the Lamb of God who takes away the sin of the whole world, but it is especially *your* sin that has been forgiven by Jesus. The guilt that you feel because of your sin can be overcome by Christ's forgiveness. If your conscience is anything like mine, it has a very long finger. That finger of conscience points at you and says, *Look at what you've done. That can never be made right again!* And that may well be true. Consider your failures and your sins. Maybe your marriage failed because you sinned against your spouse. Maybe you feel guilty because you failed to meet your obligations as a father or a mother. Perhaps sin has destroyed your relationships with friends or neighbors or coworkers. I'm sure you'd like to turn the clock back to a certain time in your life and do something over and this time do it right, but the fact of the matter is that you cannot go back and do it over. Your conscience is correct: *Look at what you've done. That can never be made right.* Now, that may well be true. But because Jesus died and rose again for you, your every sin has been forgiven. That especially includes the sin that keeps you awake at night, the sin that causes you so much guilt, the sin that your conscience hurls against you. "Behold, the Lamb of God, who takes away the sin of the world" (John 1:29) and, dearest of all, who takes away *your* sin.

Because Jesus died and rose again for the forgiveness of your sin – and now this is the second of my best two paragraphs – it is not necessary for you to do good works to earn your forgiveness. Because Jesus died and rose again for the forgiveness of your sin, it is not necessary that you pray and be pious to earn the forgiveness of your sins. Because Jesus died and rose for your sin, it is not necessary that you give money to the church or tell others about Him in order to earn your forgiveness. Because Jesus died and rose for your sin, it is not necessary that you go to church to earn the forgiveness of your sins.

Are those things necessary? Yes, I mean to tell you that they are very necessary. What's more necessary, in this crumbling Western culture, than that we Christians do good works to help others, and do these good works like we've never done them before? What's more necessary, in this time when so many youth and adults are looking for spiritual answers, than that you and I pray and be pious examples of what life in Christ is all about? What's more necessary than that we freely give of our money to spread the Word of the Gospel, and that we be bold to tell others of all that Jesus has done for us? And finally, what could be more necessary than that we sinners, with all our problems, go to church on Sunday and let God's Word of forgiveness speak to our guilt, and let the Sacrament of Christ's body and blood assure us of forgiveness? Yes, these things are all necessary – but must you do them so that you will earn your forgiveness? No! Because Jesus died and rose again, your sin, especially the sin that troubles you the most, has been forgiven. All you need to do is believe it. Just believe it and you're forgiven.

That's the great difference between the Law and the Gospel. God's Law, His commandments, make wonderful promises to us. "Do this, and you will live" (Luke 10:28). The big problem is that the promises of the Law depend upon our perfect obedience. No human being, except for Christ Himself, has perfectly kept the Law. So instead of the Law being the way to blessings, it becomes our accuser. *You haven't done all God's commands*, the Law says, *and therefore you shall not live but shall die.*

On the other hand, the promises of the Gospel are unconditional. The forgiveness and life that God promises in the Good News of Jesus Christ depend upon nothing, save that you come to Him, confess your sins, and believe that for Jesus' sake you are forgiven.

> *Just as I am, without one plea,*
> *But that Thy blood was shed for me*
> *And that Thou bidd'st me come to Thee,*
> *O Lamb of God, I come, I come.*[2]

About 15 years ago, I met a young man named Dan Rowe. Dan and I engaged in typical small talk when we first met. "Where are you from?" I asked.

"A suburb of Chicago," he said. "A place called Country Club Hills."

"Oh, I know that place. I grew up in the next town, Chicago Heights. When I was small, Country Club Hills was known as Cooper's Grove. Dan, did you go to St. John's Church?" I asked.

"Yes, I did," Dan said.

"My Uncle Henry was the pastor of that church," I was proud to say, "the Rev. Henry Meyer."

"Dale," Dan said, "I want to tell you something about your Uncle Henry. I didn't grow up as a member of the church. As a teenager I visited a number of churches – church-shopping, as we call it today. One day a friend of mine, Brian Schilling, invited me to go with him to his church, St. John's. So the next Sunday I went and I heard your uncle preach. You know… his sermon had no 'but.'"

"What do you mean, the sermon had no 'but'?" I asked.

Dan explained, "Well, like I said, I had visited a lot of churches and the messages always seemed to have a 'but.' 'Jesus died and rose, *but* you have to …' and then the minister would add whatever was on his mind that week. Jesus died and rose, *but* you have to stop cussin' and swearing, or you have to stop drinking and gambling, or you have to start praying and praising, or whatever it happened to be. Those things aren't necessarily bad, but your uncle never made them a condition of the Gospel. His sermon that Sunday had no ifs, ands, or buts. Jesus died and rose for your sins – period."

Dan told me that his curiosity had been aroused. He hadn't heard such a simple, unconditional Gospel before, and he suspected that Uncle Henry was probably holding something back. So he went back another Sunday, expecting to hear an if, and, or but added to the Gospel, but there wasn't any. He went back a third time, a fourth time, a fifth time, and it was always the same Good News. Jesus died and rose again for your sins – period. Now, I'm sure Uncle Henry did talk about other things, but it's obvious that he didn't give the impression that you're saved by doing those other things. Whatever those other things happen to be, they are just grateful responses that we gladly give to God because of the Gospel.

Oh my! I didn't tell you where I met Dan Rowe. It was at Concordia Seminary in St. Louis. He had been so impressed with the pure preaching of forgiveness that he decided to become a pastor. Today, Dan is preaching that same sweet message with no ifs, ands, or buts to the people of Trinity Lutheran Church in Redding, California.

My two paragraphs aren't really mine. They weren't original with Uncle Henry either. The message of forgiveness by grace through faith comes from God. It comes to sinners through prophets like Nathan, through John the Baptist, and through modern ministers who direct sinners to Jesus. "Behold, the Lamb of God, who takes away the sin of the world!" (John 1:29).

Amen.

For Further Reflection

All of the Six Chief Parts are based on our sin and God's forgiveness. One Chief Part that does so in a special way is the Sacrament of the Altar, also known as the Lord's Supper, the Eucharist, or Holy Communion.

"Take and eat; this is my body, which is given for you. ... Drink from it, all of you; this is my blood of the new covenant, which is poured out for you for the forgiveness of sins."[3]

- Put yourself in the story – Matthew 26:26-29 (parallels in Mark 14:22-25; Luke 22:18-20). See also 1 Corinthians 11:23-24.

- The fear of God is a rich topic throughout the Bible, and it's woven through the "For Further Reflection" sections in this book. We all have our fears, the feeling that something is about to overwhelm us. Guilt can bring fear that we're going to get what we deserve, but – here's the awesome thing – because of His love for us, God comes to forgive and save us. That is what the Bible means when it talks about the fear of God. It's a Wow! See Psalm 130.
- We do have things to feel guilty about – James 4:17; Galatians 5:19-21; Ephesians 2:1
- Jesus takes God's just punishment for our sins upon Himself – Galatians 3:10-14; Colossians 1:13-14
- Take heart from these passages about the forgiveness of sins – Isaiah 1:18; 1 John 1:7-9; Romans 8:31-34. "Where there is forgiveness of sins, there is also life and salvation."[4]

> *My sins assail me sore,*
> *But I despair no more.*
> *I build on Christ, who loves me;*
> *From this Rock nothing moves me.*
> *To Him I all surrender,*
> *To Him, my soul's Defender.*
>
> *O Jesus Christ, my Lord,*
> *So meek in deed and word,*
> *Thou once didst die to save us*
> *Because Thy love would have us*
> *Be heirs of heavenly gladness*
> *When ends this life of sadness.*[5]

Retrospective

I'm glad the editors put this sermon at the front of the book. Forgiveness for our sins is the most important fact of the Bible. From it flow all the other blessings of life following Jesus. Every sermon in this book is based explicitly or implicitly on the forgiveness of sins, or should be. As I've gotten older, I've come to learn that we often speak of sin and guilt as the same thing, but they're not. Sin is what we do or fail to do, in disobedience to God's commandments. A sensitive conscience then feels guilty about the sin. Unfortunately, there are people who don't feel guilty. The 16th-century theologian Phillip Melanchthon said some people have Pharisaic pride: "I have nothing to feel guilty about" – or Epicurean indifference: "So what?"[6] After Jesus died to pay the price for our sins, the Father raised Jesus to show the sacrifice for sin was accepted. Jesus "was delivered up for our trespasses and raised for our justification" (Romans 4:25). God does not hold your sins against you. However, you and I still can feel guilty about what we've done wrong. We've heard Sunday after Sunday that we're forgiven and we believe it, but between Sundays we often start feeling guilty again. Then doubts set in: Am I a hypocrite? Do I not truly believe? Hang onto God's Word that you're forgiven, and don't be too hard on yourself for feeling guilty. That's the way we humans are wired on this troubled side of eternity. The way to deal with recurring feelings of guilt is to hear God's many words of forgiveness, to remember that you are baptized, and to receive Jesus' body and blood "for the forgiveness of sins." It's one of many practical reasons for going to church every Sunday!

Week 3 – Send up the Balloons!

National Lutheran Schools Week
Broadcast on The Lutheran Hour
March 4, 1990

Text – Genesis 4:1-10

Now Adam knew Eve his wife, and she conceived and bore Cain, saying, "I have gotten a man with the help of the LORD." And again, she bore his brother Abel. Now Abel was a keeper of sheep, and Cain a worker of the ground. In the course of time Cain brought to the LORD an offering of the fruit of the ground, and Abel also brought of the firstborn of his flock and of their fat portions. And the LORD had regard for Abel and his offering, but for Cain and his offering he had no regard. So Cain was very angry, and his face fell. The LORD said to Cain, "Why are you angry, and why has your face fallen? If you do well, will you not be accepted? And if you do not do well, sin is crouching at the door. Its desire is contrary to you, but you must rule over it."

Cain spoke to Abel his brother. And when they were in the field, Cain rose up against his brother Abel and killed him. Then the LORD said to Cain, "Where is Abel your brother?" He said, "I do not know; am I my brother's keeper?" And the LORD said, "What have you done? The voice of your brother's blood is crying to me from the ground."

Prayer

O Lord God, You gave Your Son Jesus Christ for the salvation of all people. We ask You to bless all the schools of our land. May teachers, students, parents, and all citizens strive with Your grace to fulfill the words of the apostle:

"Whatever is true, whatever is honorable, whatever is just, whatever is pure, whatever is lovely, whatever is commendable, if there is any excellence, if there is anything worthy of praise, think about these things" (Philippians 4:8). By the Christ-centered use and proclamation of Scripture, fulfill those words among us, O Lord! Amen.

God is good! Even with the problems that you and I have in our lives, God is good. Today's message is entitled, "Send up the Balloons." Many Christians will be doing that this week to witness God's goodness to all people through the existence of Christian schools. The presence of church-related schools is a reminder that we can celebrate God's goodness in the midst of our problems. Sending up balloons is a joyous thing to do. A joyous look to heaven is always helpful.

Television and radio so often suggest that the most important thing in life is to feel good. That leaves the false notion in the minds of many people that life is supposed to be a paradise. If you don't feel carefree and happy today, well, you deserve paradise tomorrow. The Bible doesn't tell it that way. The only paradise that ever existed on earth was the Garden of Eden. When Adam and Eve fell to the temptations of the devil, they were expelled from that perfect paradise on earth, and we've been living on the other side ever since.

The troubles with life on this side of paradise begin right away with Genesis chapter four. That's the story of Cain and Abel. Cain was jealous of his brother Abel, killed him, and tried to dodge responsibility by telling God, "Am I my brother's keeper?" (Genesis 4:9).

How accurately the story of Cain and Abel describes life on this side of paradise! People today have varied jobs. Cain was a farmer, and Abel was a shepherd. People today have varied moods and feelings. Cain was angry and hateful. Abel, presumably, was not. People today have conflicts. Cain and Abel certainly did. People today are tempted to sin. Cain gave in to anger and murder. People today try to repress their guilt. Cain denied that he had sinned. People today – like Cain, and Abel too – live and work, sin and worship before a holy God who calls us to account for what we do in this life. How accurately the story of Cain and Abel describes our society!

How good God is to us on our side of paradise! With all the conflicts and problems we experience in modern society, God comes to help you. He comes to you in the Good News of Jesus Christ. God comes to help you guide your feelings, your anger and joy, your desires and passions. His Word can govern your emotions. God comes to help you master sin. As with Cain, sin lies at your door. God's Word can help you overcome it. Best of all, God forgives you because of His Son's death and resurrection. All those times when sin not only sat at the door but came in to rule your head and heart, your thoughts and feelings – all those times are forgiven because of Jesus Christ. One of my favorite hymns says it this way:

> *Abel's blood for vengeance*
> *Pleaded to the skies;*
> *But the blood of Jesus*
> *For our pardon cries.*
>
> *Grace and life eternal*
> *In that blood I find;*
> *Blest be His compassion,*
> *Infinitely kind!*[1]

Today's *Lutheran Hour* is a celebration of the goodness of God. You really can experience the joy of faith, a gift well-symbolized by a soaring balloon. This uplifting goodness of God is not just for me, and not just for you – you, who I pray have come to the cross of God's Son Jesus Christ for the full forgiveness of all your sins and the certain hope of eternal life in heaven. No, the goodness of God is not just given to you and to me. It is offered to *all*. St. Paul tells us that "God our Savior … desires all people to be saved and to come to the knowledge of the truth" (1 Timothy 2:3-4). God wants all people to take a joyous look to heaven!

As I said, many Christian schools are going to send up balloons this week to celebrate that goodness of God. Church-affiliated schools are one important place where God's salvation and truth can be presented to all people. Dr. Carl Moser, Marilyn Beccue, and Cindy Davis are with me in the studio today. Miss Davis is a Lutheran school teacher in Collinsville, Illinois. Mrs. Beccue and Dr.

Moser are with the educational department of The Lutheran Church–Missouri Synod. I've asked them to be with me so we can hear of God's goodness to our society through church-related schools. Remember, our society today is no paradise. Society today is filled with many of the same thoughts and emotions present in the story of Cain and Abel.

Meyer: *Let me begin with a question to you, Dr. Moser: What do we mean when we speak of Christian schools, church-affiliated schools? Are we talking about private schools? And who pays for these schools? What are we talking about?*

Moser: *First of all, they are a very special kind of school operated by congregations – sometimes groups of congregations and sometimes individual congregations. There is a group of schools that we call private schools that are rather independent. They are secular, non-religious, non-public schools. Christian schools really aren't that type of school. They are more of a public school in that they are for the general public. But they are Christian schools in that they teach about the faith in Jesus Christ that we hold so dearly. They're open to the public, but what's private about them is that they are funded by private funds – funds from the congregations, funds from donations, funds from tuition and fees. And so they are really schools from a Christian point of view that are open to the public, operated by private funds.*

Meyer: *Why do denominations like The Lutheran Church–Missouri Synod, the Roman Catholic Church, and others, have schools? Is there something wrong with public education? Mrs. Beccue?*

Beccue: *I think the answer has to do with the phrase you used at the very beginning – "Christian schools." Churches have schools for Christian education. I would hope that they don't begin schools because they say there is something wrong with the public school. I believe the Lord has given the directive to parents for the Christian education and the spiritual nurture of their children. But I believe the church is there to help parents. And so they are helping them as they give children a Christian education.*

Meyer: *Miss Davis, what does your full-time school offer that a part-time agency of the church couldn't offer just as well? Why couldn't we send all our children to a public school and then tack on some hours of religious instruction in the evening or on weekends?*

Davis: *Our religious instruction not only includes 45 minutes of a religion class, but also we incorporate our faith and our knowledge of God into all areas of our academic learning.*

Meyer: *Is the instruction in secular subjects comparable in quality to that offered by our public schools?*

Moser: *We've done some studies with Lutheran schools across the country based on achievement test scores, and we've found that our Lutheran school students – and this is probably true of most other Christian schools, also – achieve at a 75th percentile level. Now, the average of achievement test scores is a 50th percentile. But our schools, on the average, achieve at the 75th percentile. Obviously, the education is a very quality educational program.*

Cain and Abel had conflict. Today we often hear of conflicts over religion or the lack of religion in our tax-supported, nonsectarian public schools. Some things don't change. Cain and Abel's conflict had a religious side. They both brought offerings to God, but God was pleased with only one of the worshipers. He was not pleased with Cain – and that caused conflict between the two brothers. The Bible tells us the same is true in today's society. Not every life, not every act of worship, is acceptable to God. Hebrews says, "Without faith it is impossible to please God" (Hebrews 11:6 NIV). The faith that pleases God is faith that totally trusts the blood of Jesus. Such God-pleasing people are present in both public schools and in church-affiliated schools.

Meyer: *I wonder, Dr. Moser, won't a Christian whose life is centered on Jesus Christ sometimes be uneasy with the teachings of our public, nonsectarian schools?*

Moser: *Values education is a very important part of public education. In the literature, you'll find them discussing it quite at depth and in quite many articles. However, the type of values that are taught in public school – because the United States has required that we cannot mix religion in the public schools – is quite a different kind of value education than we provide in Christian schools. For example, in the public schools they teach a lot of reliance on self, and they talk about things happening by themselves or with an individual's emphasis – nothing spiritual, nothing given to God or to indicate that there is a God. I guess the bottom line is that we object more about what they don't teach rather than what they do teach. They, for example, teach some morals, but they don't teach the biblical morals that we're so acquainted with, and which we Christians follow. Morality, we believe, is based on what God says. Morality taught in the public schools is based on what people think is appropriate at the given time based on what most people are doing. For example, sexual intercourse outside of marriage is fairly acceptable in our society today, but according to Holy Scripture it is unacceptable.*

Yes, indeed, society on this side of paradise has its tensions! Jesus said in Matthew:

> Do not think that I have come to bring peace to the earth. I have not come to bring peace, but a sword. For I have come to set a man against his father, and a daughter against her mother, and a daughter-in-law against her mother-in-law. And a person's enemies will be those of his own household. Whoever loves father or mother more than me is not worthy of me, and whoever loves son or daughter more than me is not worthy of me. And whoever does not take his cross and follow me is not worthy of me. Whoever finds his life will lose it, and whoever loses his life for my sake will find it. (Matthew 10:34-39)

Yes, Jesus says there will be tensions in society on this side of paradise. It's inevitable that we who love the Savior more than our own life will find ourselves at odds with those who value themselves more than God. Rather than run away from these struggles, instead of thinking that these conflicts of faith and values are an intrusion upon our peaceful existence, we Christians should thank our good God that we have the opportunity to witness to His truth in our day and age. We Christians have friends and family members associated with both public and Christian schools. In both school systems, there are countless Christians whose faith and values are based upon what the good God has taught us in the Christ-centered Scriptures. On this side of paradise, conflict over faith and values is inevitable, especially in education. Thank God that in these conflicts His Holy Spirit can use us Christians to testify to the truth of Christ and the values of Scripture!

Meyer: *My final question for our guests today is this: How does our society – Christian and non-Christian alike – benefit from the existence of church-related schools?*

Davis: *Our school serves as a place not only for us as teachers to witness, but also to train the children to witness to others, too. And if we can raise concerned and caring children, then, hopefully, we will have caring and concerned adults. And if they live their life as little Christs and show their faith, then, hopefully, society as a whole will benefit from that.*

Meyer: *Mrs. Beccue?*

Beccue: *I believe if you look at Christians in society today, we do benefit because there is an alternative that is offered to us, and the alternative is Christian education for our children. Actually, the entire society benefits monetarily, when you think that one-fourth of our schools are non-public schools. If we did not have these non-public schools, our entire society would have to add that one-fourth, and it would be an increase in our tax dollar. We also think in Christian schools that we are not just educating a child intellectually, but we are educating the whole child so that the child is growing emotionally, socially, and spiritually – and I believe that is a citizen well prepared to contribute to society.*

Meyer: *Dr. Moser?*

Moser: *Our Lutheran schools and other Christian schools provide educated, moral children who become educated, moral citizens with allegiance to God and to country as part of their Christian faith. These are the kinds of people that benefit our country greatly, and it's on that foundation that our country is based. And so, producing more and more students like this, who become citizens who are adult producers in our economy, is extremely important to our country. Besides, Christian schools provide excellent models for public schools, models of local control of morality, models of quality education, models of expressing Christian love throughout the day, which is a very special kind of caring and love that occurs in Christian schools. Our Christian schools have a lot to offer to the public.*

Isn't that the truth? You and I have so much to offer! We have this great message that the blood of Jesus Christ cleanses us from all sins. We have the power of God's Holy Spirit working through Word and Sacrament to conquer sin, which is still lurking at every door in contemporary society. We have hope – hope that redeemed men, women, and children who are painfully aware that we're not in paradise will one day enter a heavenly paradise because of the passion and resurrection of Jesus Christ. Of course, there will be conflicts over the values that are taught or not taught in our schools. That's part of carrying the cross, something that Jesus bid us disciples to do on this side of paradise (Luke 9:23). Would you avoid a conflict so you can have an uneasy peace with the world? No! Would you deny the Lord and His Bible in our society, only to have Him look at you the way He looked at Peter when Peter denied Him (Luke 22:61)? Would you pass up the opportunity to witness to God's goodness because you wanted to avoid discussions of values and morals in society? No, I trust you are not that kind of a Christian.

Send up the balloons! This week, many of our almost 2,000 Lutheran schools will be sending up balloons to celebrate the goodness of God. Whether you're involved with a Christian school or your local public school, think of those soaring balloons and thank our good God who raises up saving faith on this side of paradise! It's a joy to look to heaven!

Amen.

For Further Reflection

"Our Father who art in heaven" (Lord's Prayer, Introduction)

- No age discrimination; we are all *"Children of the heav'nly Father."*[2] "With these words God tenderly invites us to believe that he is our true Father and that we are his true children, so that we may pray to him boldly and confidently as dear children ask their dear father" (Martin Luther, Small Catechism).[3]
- As an adult, watch the story; see a youth after God's heart – 1 Samuel 16:1-13
- Why it's "Christian" education – Luke 2:39-52; John 1:12-17; 1 John 2:28-29
- Education in His Word – John 10:11-16, 27-28; Psalm 119:9-16; 2 Timothy 3:14-17
- Christian education is reverential fear and love of God – Ecclesiastes 12:1, 13-14; Psalm 103:13-18; Proverbs 3:1-8; Psalm 145:1-5, 17-21

> *O ever be our guide,*
> *Our shepherd, and our pride,*
> *Our staff and song.*
> *Jesus, O Christ of God,*
> *By Your enduring Word*
> *Lead us where You have trod;*
> *Make our faith strong.*
>
> *So now, and till we die,*
> *Sound we Your praises high*
> *And joyful sing:*
> *Infants and all the throng,*
> *Who to the Church belong,*
> *Unite to swell the song*
> *To Christ, our King!*[4]

Retrospective

I recall with a smile a letter I got after this message was broadcast. A listener complained that the balloons would land, be bad for the environment, and maybe even kill birds who ate them. Thanks for listening!

A theme threaded through this book of sermons is how the world has drastically changed in my lifetime, maybe yours too. One place the change is seen is in the decline of parochial grade schools. Between the years 2008 and 2013, congregations in my denomination, The Lutheran Church–Missouri Synod (LCMS), closed one out of ten of their elementary schools. During the same years, there's been an increase in the numbers of LCMS preschools and high schools. What are the reasons for these changes? I'm sure there are many, but that's not my driving concern. I often quote a friend who says, "Complaining is not a strategy." I personally grieve the closing of grade schools, am glad to see growth in preschools and high schools, but am most interested in the commanding need for Christian education in the future, whatever shape it will take.

The strategy going forward has to be a more intense focus on education in God's Word of faith for application to personal, church, and community life in this challenging new day and age. A Barna survey shows, to give you only one example of the need, that the large majority of Americans believe that Jesus was a true historical person, but only 56 percent believe in His divinity, and 52 percent believe He committed sins. Barna has found that many people in the church believe they will go to heaven because of their good works![5] It's not simply that American culture is no longer nominally "Christian." The Barna surveys indicate an erosion of effective Christian education among people of the church. Strengthening existing schools and establishing new ones can be part of the way forward. A thorough congregational emphasis and participation in Christian learning for all ages will be necessary. The internet must become a vehicle for delivering faith-growing education to church members and non-members in ways convenient to their busy schedules. It's not enough to have a website! Sunday Schools, Vacation Bible Schools, camps, and servant projects play an important role in the desired future. With today's public culture threatening the salvation of souls for whom Jesus died – yes, that is what's at stake – Christian education cannot be thought of as one aspect among many of congregational life. The Bible is our story, and we all need to be living in His story. "If you abide in my word," said Jesus, "you are truly my disciples, and you will know the truth, and the truth will set you free" (John 8:31-32).

I'm wishing I were younger and could give more decades of my life to Christian education! Rather than grieve what's been lost, let's work toward a future of well-taught Christians of every age. "One generation shall commend your works to another, and shall declare your mighty acts" (Psalm 145:4). Send up the balloons!

Week 4 – "In All Good Works Increasing"

Delivered at the Chapel of St. Timothy and St. Titus
Concordia Seminary, St. Louis, Missouri
September 2, 2007

Text – Luke 14:1-14

One Sabbath, when he went to dine at the house of a ruler of the Pharisees, they were watching him carefully. And behold, there was a man before him who had dropsy. And Jesus responded to the lawyers and Pharisees, saying, "Is it lawful to heal on the Sabbath, or not?" But they remained silent. Then he took him and healed him and sent him away. And he said to them, "Which of you, having a son or an ox that has fallen into a well on a Sabbath day, will not immediately pull him out?" And they could not reply to these things.

Now he told a parable to those who were invited, when he noticed how they chose the places of honor, saying to them, "When you are invited by someone to a wedding feast, do not sit down in a place of honor, lest someone more distinguished than you be invited by him, and he who invited you both will come and say to you, 'Give your place to this person,' and then you will begin with shame to take the lowest place. But when you are invited, go and sit in the lowest place, so that when your host comes he may say to you, 'Friend, move up higher.' Then you will be honored in the presence of all who sit at table with you. For everyone who exalts himself will be humbled, and he who humbles himself will be exalted."

He said also to the man who had invited him, "When you give a dinner or a banquet, do not invite your friends or your brothers or your relatives or rich neighbors, lest they also invite you in return and you be repaid. But when you give a feast, invite the poor, the crippled, the lame, the blind, and you will be blessed, because they cannot repay you. For you will be repaid at the resurrection of the just."

Prayer

Dear God, it seems many people don't care very much about the truth in Your Word. They think, You have your opinion; I have mine. *So I pray You to inspire Your faithful people not only to speak Your truth but also to show Your love to others, especially to those who are on the edges, snubbed by the self-righteous and sanctimonious. As Your Spirit increases good works through us, prompt people in our neighborhoods and communities to ask us about the hope that is in us. Make us thoroughly selfless in our love, just like our Lord Jesus, with no thought of reward save to anticipate hearing Your welcome, "Well done, good and faithful servant" (Matthew 25:23). Amen.*

It's 2:00 A.M. Diane and I are sound asleep in the parsonage. The phone rings. I go into the study, pick up the receiver, and at the other end I only hear gasps. I know what's happening. It's Lori [name changed], and when she is able to get her breath she will tell me that she's about to slit her wrists. Because this has happened more than once, I know the drill. Rub my eyes to wake up, lean back in my chair, put my feet up on the desk, and settle in for 30 minutes or so. First I talk to her – a monologue. As she becomes more composed, we have a conversation. When she is ready – only when she is ready – she tells me it is OK and we end the conversation. The last I heard, Lori is doing well, and I'm glad. You'll have opportunities like this too – and I know you'll be glad when you're able to bring some help and hope.

Richard Lischer graduated from Concordia Seminary in the 1960s and was assigned to a congregation in southern Illinois. In his book *Open Secrets*, he writes about Regina.[1] Regina was the single mother of a toddler named Darwin. Regina's mother lived with them. Dr. Lischer doesn't tell how it came to be a single-parent home, but it was. Broken families happen and maybe you are part of one. One day Pastor Lischer got a phone call from the nurse in the emergency room of the Alton Hospital. Little Darwin had toddled off, fallen into a farm pond, and drowned. No one was there at the hospital except mother Regina and grandmother Rhoda, going through the most profound grief imaginable. The nurse told the pastor, "Somebody else ought to be here." *Somebody else ought to be here.* People are hurting more than you and I can imagine. That includes people in the church and at the Seminary. The mission of God's people, our mission, is to be there – to be there with the help and the hope that are in Christ Jesus.

You are at Concordia Seminary so the Spirit of God can get deep down into your heart, and to form you fully after the attitude of the Lord Jesus Christ. There is a strain in the church that says it is enough for pastors to state the doctrine of the Gospel correctly, to conduct the Divine Service faithfully, and to administer the Means of Grace properly. I said there is a "strain" of this thinking in the church. It is a strain, as in disease. It is true that only the Gospel through the Means of Grace alone delivers the grace that saves us through faith. "For by grace you have been saved through faith. And this is not your own doing; it is the gift of God, not a result of works, so that no one may boast" (Ephesians 2:8-9). But let us here be formed fully by the whole Scripture. After Ephesians 2:8-9 we are taught in verse 10, "For we are his workmanship, created in Christ Jesus for good works, which God prepared beforehand, that we should walk in them." In his commentary on 1 Peter, Martin Luther asks why God left us here after Baptism. His answer is that God has left you and me here to be doing good works.[2] And so the title of my sermon is "In All Good Works Increasing." This comes from Luther's hymn, "May God Bestow on Us His Grace." Stanza three says,

> *O let the people praise Thy worth,*
> *In all good works increasing.*[3]

Our Savior abounds in good works. He came in word and deed. Today's Gospel lesson took place on a Sabbath. Jesus faithfully kept the Sabbath and communed with the word of His Father. When a man with dropsy presented himself, Jesus questioned the self-righteous legalism of the Pharisees by demonstrating that it is always in season to do good works to save life. He healed the man with dropsy – word and deed. When Jesus was with the sick in body, He often healed them. When He was with the sick in mind, He often restored them to calm. When He was with those who were spiritually confused, He showed them the way to the Father. When He was with the hungry, He fed them. When He encountered the homeless, He often restored them to society. He went to the dead and raised them. And when He was with the religious, as He was at the feast in our text, He strove to turn them from self-righteousness to a humble and penitent reception of the Father's grace.

And He did it selflessly with no thought of repayment. What a contrast – His purity in helping people contrasted to our mixed, not-always-pure, often calculating motives. A man in my first congregation volunteered to do a maintenance project at church. One afternoon when I was out making my calls, I stopped by their house to thank him for what he had done. He wasn't home, but his wife was – and she was in a foul mood. "I just stopped by to thank Richard [name changed] for what he did at church," I said. "Well, you can thank him all you want," she grumbled, "but we can't put your thanks into the bank." When we practice the daily repentance that should flow from our baptism, we see how impure and calculating our motives often are… and how pure and selfless the Savior is toward us. What recompense would suffice for His selfless coming into the world for us and our salvation? What could we ever do to repay Him for the agonies of the cross that alone brings forgiveness for our sins? Can we somehow repay Him for bursting the bonds of death and promising, "Because I live, you also will live" (John 14:19)? Our Savior abounds in good works toward you and me. What folly to think we could repay Him for coming to us in His Gospel, in Baptism, and in His meal! Here He will feed you during this year. What are you going to do, invite Jesus over for a pizza and think you've repaid Him? His words and works to us are pure and selfless. The most we can do is to receive His Word with obedient faith and let His Word be enlarged in the world by our increase in good works.

"For everyone who exalts himself will be humbled, and he who humbles himself will be exalted."

He said also to the man who had invited him, "When you give a dinner or a banquet, do not invite your friends or your brothers or your relatives or rich neighbors, lest they also invite you in return and you be repaid. But when you give a feast, invite the poor, the crippled, the lame, the blind, and you will be blessed, because they cannot repay you. For you will be repaid at the resurrection of the just." (Luke 14:11-14)

Last week, I attended a men's prayer breakfast. Mr. Larry Carlson was the speaker. He is the director of Youth Haven, a Christian nonprofit organization that operates two ranches, one in Arizona and the other in Michigan – and, by the way, they take no government money. At these ranches, the staff ministers to children ages 7 to 12 who come from the worst imaginable family situations. One child, after hearing Larry Carlson talk about Jesus, came up and asked, "Why did Jesus' parents give Him a swear word for a name?" Don't laugh. We religious people are tempted to be smug in our beliefs and to look down on others. Pharisees are not extinct. What does Jesus say? "For everyone who exalts himself will be humbled, and he who humbles himself will be exalted." When Mr. Carlson shared that story, he went on to explain to us that everything in the young lives of these children has been damned. In so many families, Jesus Christ has been misused to cuss out the wife, to cuss out the husband, to cuss out the police, the company, the neighbor – and Jesus Christ was used to cuss out the young, impressionable child. Youth Haven is serving seriously disadvantaged children who will never be able to repay them. *Serving people who will never be able to repay us.* Get it? The promise of the resurrection at the end of time, the promise of the heavenly banquet where we unworthy sinners will be guests – that is repayment enough.

What did the nurse at the Alton Hospital say when she called the pastor? "Somebody else ought to be here." My plea to you today is this: If you seminarians choose to wear a clerical collar, fine. Just don't let it choke off the flow of blood from the heart of Christ to your attitudes and actions. Don't be like the priest or the Levite who passed by on the other side when a man had been mugged by robbers (Luke 10:23-37). *Don't be the seminarian or professor who is so absorbed in theology that you forget that the whole theological enterprise is to be incarnational.* The mission of Concordia Seminary is to be there and to send there, always in the service of our Lord Jesus Christ. And when Martin Luther says that we are left here to do good works, he says that the greatest good work is to share Jesus.[4] Oh, let *these* people *"praise Thy worth, / In all good works increasing."* Amen.

O let the people praise Thy worth,
In all good works increasing;
The land shall plenteous fruit bring forth,
Thy Word is rich in blessing.
May God the Father, God the Son,
And God the Spirit bless us!
Let all the world praise Him alone,
Let solemn awe possess us.
Now let our hearts say, "Amen!"[3]

For Further Reflection

"You shall …" (Ten Commandments)

- Whether the commandment begins "You shall" or "You shall not," every commandment about our duty to others has a positive side, good works that you should do to others because you fear and love God above all things, the First Commandment
- Good works under the Fourth Commandment – Leviticus 19:32; Colossians 3:20; 1 Peter 2:18
- Good works under the Fifth Commandment – Matthew 5:5-9; Romans 12:20; Ephesians 4:32
- Good works under the Sixth Commandment – Philippians 4:8; 1 Corinthians 6:19; 1 Peter 2:11
- Good works under the Seventh Commandment – Exodus 23:4; Matthew 5:42; Luke 19:8
- Good works under the Eighth Commandment – Proverbs 11:13; Ephesians 4:25; 1 Peter 4:8
- Martin Luther: "Christians live not in themselves but in Christ and their neighbor. Otherwise they are not Christian. They live in Christ through faith, in their neighbor through love. By faith they are caught up beyond themselves into God. By love they descend beneath themselves into their neighbor."[2]

Teach us the lesson Thou hast taught:
To feel for those Thy blood hath bought,
That ev'ry word and deed and thought
May work a work for Thee.

In sickness, sorrow, want, or care,
May we each other's burdens share;
May we, where help is needed, there
Give help as unto Thee![5]

Retrospective

> *Practicing Christians are more concerned about and engaged with*
> *global poverty than the broader American public. ... Christians*
> *also donate more than non-Christians to poverty related causes,*
> *but overall giving is quite low among all adults, regardless of faith.*
> *... It may come as no surprise that Christians focus their volunteer*
> *work toward their local church. ... All [Christians] are more likely*
> *than the general population to have volunteered some of their free*
> *time to help a nonprofit organization beyond church. ... It appears,*
> *within and beyond the walls of their churches, Christians of all*
> *stripes are leading the charge and actively seeking the welfare and*
> *flourishing of their communities through volunteering and service.*[6]

That's encouraging! Historically, the Church has always been active
in works of mercy to those in need. In "Christian America" of the 20th
century, in the era many of us grew up, governmental agencies and non-
governmental charities also participated in fulfilling the Golden Rule
(Matthew 7:12). Back then, the public culture and the ethos of practicing
Christians complemented one other. Today, there continues to be concern
among many Americans for those who need help, but often it's only human

altruism. Of course that helps people, but the truest reason to "love your neighbor as yourself" grows out of the mercies we ourselves have received from God (Matthew 22:36-40; 2 Corinthians 1:3-4). If your congregation disappeared today, would your community notice? Ours is a time to heed the modern proverb, "Don't tell me what a friend I have in Jesus until I see what a friend I have in you."

Week 5 – The Flowers of Forgiveness

Valentine's Day
Broadcast on The Lutheran Hour
February 14, 1999

Text – Colossians 3:12-14 (NIV)

Therefore, as God's chosen people, holy and dearly loved, clothe yourselves with compassion, kindness, humility, gentleness and patience. Bear with each other and forgive one another if any of you has a grievance against someone. Forgive as the Lord forgave you. And over all these virtues put on love, which binds them all together in perfect unity.

Prayer

Loving God, our Creator and Redeemer, give compassion, kindness, humility, gentleness, and patience to us, Your people. Let the mercies You have demonstrated to us in Jesus Christ be reflected most winsomely by us, to our families and friends, and indeed to all whom we meet. Keep our faith and hope in You, and by our honest demonstrations of love, let Your love be known, through Jesus Christ our Savior and Lord. Amen.

Two months ago, almost to the day, I met new friends Kevin and Sandy. They were my hosts for a weekend in Northern California, and they kindly let me stay in a guesthouse on their ranch – a house they've named the Hummingbird House. As you'd expect, that house is decorated with the motif of hummingbirds. It was in that guesthouse that I came across the book entitled *Hummingbird Gardens* by Nancy Newfield and Barbara Nielsen.

From the book's introduction:

> One May afternoon more than 20 years ago, Robert Raether planted
> sultan's turban, turk's cap, and flowering maple in my South Louisiana
> garden, showing me the basics of using natural nectar sources to attract
> hummingbirds. In Louisiana's rich soil and subtropical climate, the plants
> flourished. As if by magic, a hummingbird arrived almost as soon as the
> first bud unfurled, although I had tried unsuccessfully to attract the birds
> with a feeder for more than a year. To my delight, that first hummer, a
> female ruby-throat, was followed by a succession of others that darted
> from blossom to blossom, twittering from dawn to dusk.[1]

This Valentine's Day, that image of hummingbirds attracted to garden
flowers is the picture I'd like you to hold in your mind. God's forgiveness for
you and me shows how much He loves us. We, in turn, should reflect His love
to others. When God's love blooms in your life, people will notice. "See how
they love one another," was what people noticed about the early Christians.[2] Is it
that way today? That's a question you'll have to answer for yourself. My aim in
these next minutes is to share God's love with you so that you, filled with thanks,
will desire His help to make your personality more inviting to others. Just as a
hummingbird is attracted to the flowers in a garden, life is better for all when the
flowers of forgiveness are blooming in your life and mine.

The Bible passage upon which today's message is based is Colossians 3:12-
14 (NIV):

> Therefore, as God's chosen people, holy and dearly loved, clothe
> yourselves with compassion, kindness, humility, gentleness and patience.
> Bear with each other and forgive one another if any of you has a grievance
> against someone. Forgive as the Lord forgave you. And over all these
> virtues put on love, which binds them all together in perfect unity.

Those words, written by St. Paul, describe attractive Christian qualities as if
they were clothes you put on. On Valentine's Day, we're reminded how flowers
gladden the heart and beautify the home. There are five flowers of forgiveness
that should characterize your life.

The first is compassion. Compassion starts with a deep inner feeling, but it doesn't stay a feeling. It shows itself in acts of caring. *"If you're in love, show me!"* sang Eliza Doolittle to Henry Higgins in *My Fair Lady*.[3] Sometimes men just don't get it, but we should – we must. In a religious vein, someone said, "Don't tell me what a friend I have in Jesus until I see what a friend I have in you."

The second flower is kindness. Romans 11:22 says, "Note then the kindness and the severity of God: severity toward those who have fallen, but God's kindness to you, provided you continue in his kindness. Otherwise you too will be cut off." Since God has been kind to you, the Bible says being kind to others is not optional. Again, don't tell me what a friend I have in Jesus until I see what a friend, what a kind friend, I have in you.

The third flower is humility. When someone remarked about Clement Attlee's humility, Winston Churchill responded, "Attlee is a very modest man. And with reason."[4] You and I have much to be humble about, don't we? Would you want your inmost thoughts known by all? Are you proud of everything you've done? Once again, don't tell me what a friend I have in Jesus until I see what a friend, what a sincerely humble friend, I have in you.

Gentleness is the fourth flower. The most attractive quality of a Christian wife is an "unfading beauty of a gentle and quiet spirit" (1 Peter 3:4 NIV). Have you been so frustrated that you've given up on gentleness and, instead, you nag? And Peter immediately adds that a Christian husband should be gentle: "Likewise, husbands, live with your wives in an understanding way, showing honor to the woman as the weaker vessel, since they are heirs with you of the grace of life" (1 Peter 3:7). Again, the refrain: Don't tell me what a friend I have in Jesus until I see what a friend, what a gentle friend, I have in you.

The fifth flower from today's Bible passage is patience. Did God strike you down last time you sinned? No, because He is patient. Shouldn't you be patient, too? James 5:7 says, "Be patient until the Lord comes again." If you are a patient friend, bearing with another's oddities and even forgiving their sins "seventy times seven" (Matthew 18:22 GW), then the message *"What a friend we have in Jesus"*[5] will be heard more readily.

Ah, you may be thinking. *That's all nice, but it doesn't fit my situation. I'm trying to make this relationship work, but he's not. This clown I'm living with is no beautiful hummingbird. He's a vulture, tearing at my soul, killing the joy of life*. Or a husband might think that about his wife, or you might be thinking that about some family member – a father, a mother, a stepparent, or whomever. You'll admit you're not perfect, but that other person is the problem.

"Lead us not into temptation" (Matthew 6:13), we pray in the Lord's Prayer. It's so easy to be deceived in relationships. True, your marriage and family may not be a beautiful garden right now, but it can be. If your spouse seems to be a vulture, not a hummingbird, then your own changes, your own personality improvements, your blooming with Christian characteristics, can start to change your spouse. The Bible teaches in 1 Peter 3:1-2 that a husband can be changed by the behavior of his wife, and that change can be accomplished without words. That can happen in other relationships, too. Honey is more attractive than vinegar. The more your attractive Christian qualities come into full bloom, the more change can happen in your marriage, family, friendships, and work relationships.

At the root of this potential change is one central fact. St. Paul says, "Bear with each other and forgive one another if any of you has a grievance against someone. Forgive as the Lord forgave you" (Colossians 3:13 NIV). All the attractive characteristics of Christian living that I've shared with you become possible because of one essential fact. And I stress the word *essential*. Without this fundamental fact, Christianity has been gutted to nothing more than a self-improvement system. But with this fact, the power of God is unleashed in your life in a way that is unlike any contemporary, generic self-help program. This essential fact is that the Father in heaven has forgiven you.

Forgiven me for what? you might be thinking. *The problem is with him or her.* God has forgiven you for your own lack of compassion, lack of kindness, lack of humility, lack of gentleness, and lack of patience. These are more than just excusable shortcomings: *Oh, I know I'm not perfect but...* No, these failures are sins against the way God wants you to live. Remember, these qualities are not optional. Not doing them is sinful. Forget that person who keeps troubling your relationship. These are *your* sins. What I say now is the Good News of God for you – your sins have been forgiven by the death of Jesus Christ on the cross. Colossians 1:13-14 says that God the Father "has delivered us from the domain of darkness and transferred us to the kingdom of his beloved Son, in whom we have redemption, the forgiveness of sins."

So, what is most important in any relationship you have – such as marriage, parenting, friendships, work – is your relationship with God, your relationship with your eternal Judge whose anger at your sins has been set aside by His forgiving love given to you in Jesus Christ. So, savor that forgiveness, and let your thankfulness for salvation show as you develop more and more the qualities of Christian life that Paul describes in Colossians. And do not let them bloom only on Valentine's Day, or in spring, or whenever the mood strikes you. Let them bloom always, every day, everywhere, in every relationship you have.

Always, every day, everywhere. The famous naturalist John Audubon said, "The hummingbird does not shun mankind so much as other birds generally do. Frequently, it approaches flowers in windows, or even flies inside rooms when the windows are kept open during the extreme heat of the day. It returns, if not interrupted, as long as the flowers remain fresh and unfaded."[6]

How can these qualities (compassion, kindness, humility, gentleness, and patience) remain fresh and unfading in your life? St. Paul tells us, "Let the word of Christ dwell in you richly, teaching and admonishing one another in all wisdom, singing psalms and hymns and spiritual songs, with thankfulness in your hearts to God. And whatever you do, in word or deed, do everything in the name of the Lord Jesus, giving thanks to God the Father through him" (Colossians 3:16-17).

Now here's an example of that blooming – fresh and unfaded. Hyun Kyung Kim came from Korea to live in Michigan. She says:

> Bible study was just like studying mathematics, history, geography, or the sciences. I missed, however, the most important part, Jesus Christ. Last Easter I believe the Holy Spirit inspired and helped me to meet Jesus. After I met Him, the goal of my life, my attitude toward others… was changed. Wherever I am, wherever I go, whomever I meet, I'd like to introduce them to Jesus Christ.[7]

"Let the word of Christ dwell in you richly."

Flowers do not exist for themselves. The beauty of flowers is for others, for hummingbirds and especially for people. When I stayed in the Hummingbird House on Kevin and Sandy's ranch, I spent much of my time at the kitchen table writing. I worked on my messages for this program, on articles, and the like. On that table, Sandy had placed a vase that she filled with flowers, with snapdragons and daisies. I remember thinking, *These flowers were put here just for me!* What an impact that had on my thoughts. How it made me treasure that place. That's what can begin to happen in the lives of others when they experience Christian qualities blooming in your life. Love seeks not its own (cf. 1 Corinthians 13:5). Compassion, kindness, humility, gentleness, and patience are not to be put on display for your own selfish advancement. They are to be developed and used in love for others. "And over all these virtues," St. Paul writes, "put on love, which binds them all together in perfect unity" (Colossians 3:14).

Writing in 1877, Robert Ridgway said:

> As we chanced, while hunting in the mountains, to pass through the haunts of this hummer, it frequently happened that one of the little creatures, prompted apparently by curiosity, would approach close to us and remain poised in one spot, its wings vibrating so rapidly as to appear as a mere haze around the body; now and then it would shift from one side to another, its little black eyes sparkling as it eyed us intently.[8]

"They'll know we are Christians by our love."[9] Let the flowers of forgiveness bloom in your life so others might share the mercies of God which you have received. "Let your light shine before others," Jesus said, "so that they may see your good works and give glory to your Father who is in heaven" (Matthew 5:16). In conclusion, remember, "Don't tell me what a friend I have in Jesus until I see what a friend I have in you."

Amen.

For Further Reflection

"Forgive us our trespasses as we forgive those who trespass against us." (Lord's Prayer, Fifth Petition)

- Put yourself in the story. With whom do you most identify? Luke 7:36-50.

- God's love brings our forgiveness – Romans 5:1-8. God's love casts out fear, dread – 1 John 4:16-19. Therefore, we respond with the fear of God that is reverence and love for Him – Psalm 130:3-4.
- God's selfless love, active through us – 1 Corinthians 13:1-13
- Another story: Forgiveness frees us to love those who have hurt us – Genesis 50:15-21

> *Love divine, all loves excelling,*
> *Joy of heav'n, to earth come down!*
> *Fix in us Thy humble dwelling,*
> *All Thy faithful mercies crown.*
> *Jesus, Thou art all compassion,*
> *Pure, unbounded love Thou art;*
> *Visit us with Thy salvation,*
> *Enter ev'ry trembling heart.*
>
> *Breathe, O breathe Thy loving Spirit*
> *Into ev'ry troubled breast;*
> *Let us all in Thee inherit;*
> *Let us find Thy promised rest.*
> *Take away the love of sinning;*
> *Alpha and Omega be;*
> *End of faith, as its beginning,*
> *Set our hearts at liberty.*[10]

Retrospective

We have great workers here at Concordia Seminary, and Gayle Zollmann is one of the best. Gayle is in charge of our grounds, and with Diane they're a dynamic duo who have led making the Seminary grounds a beautiful place of flowers, vegetables, herbs, shrubs, and various types of trees. Early in our time on campus, Diane was talking with Gayle, and being a husband who knows his place, I listened but kept quiet. It was fall; Diane suggested that we should plant tulips for spring. Gayle put her head down and said, "We don't have the money." Dale broke his husbandly silence: "How much do tulips cost, really? We can do that." Well, Gayle and her crew of student workers (many seminarians have part-time jobs on campus, helping them earn some money while contributing to our close community of faculty, staff, and students) planted the tulips, and they were spectacular. In the years since, more tulips, more perennials, more annuals, more beauty. This is your invitation to come visit the campus, and see God's creation in this Seminary garden! In fact, the front cover of this book features our beautiful tulips gracing the entrance of the chapel.

I tell this story because it demonstrates the importance of culture. Your congregation is more than the worship, the bulletin, the bylaws, the budget, and meetings. There's a spirit to your congregation, a culture that people sense... and judge. It's the same way with the Seminary. We have our buildings, our chapel services, our curricula, our publications, but come onto campus and you sense there's something more. There's a culture here, the assumptions and attitudes that are revealed in what our campus community does. Tulips and plantings don't make a culture, but they contribute. As a pastor and now president, I've come to put high value on the importance of culture, be it in a congregation or seminary. I teach my students to pay attention to the culture of the congregations they will be privileged to serve. It's something they'll have to pick up quietly: a question here and there, but generally listening, almost sniffing the air to find out what kind of place this church really is. Then, teaching and modeling the qualities of our text from Colossians, they quietly and patiently lead the people to reflect the "flowers of forgiveness" in us. That's true in the congregations they'll serve, in your congregation, in our Seminary, and it's true in your family and home life as well.

Week 6 – Baseball, Hot Dogs, Apple Pie, and Chevrolet

The Transfiguration of Our Lord
Delivered at St. Salvator Lutheran Church, Venedy, Illinois
and St. Peter Lutheran Church, New Memphis, Illinois
February 5, 1978

Text – Luke 9:28-36

Now about eight days after these sayings he took with him Peter and John and James and went up on the mountain to pray. And as he was praying, the appearance of his face was altered, and his clothing became dazzling white. And behold, two men were talking with him, Moses and Elijah, who appeared in glory and spoke of his departure, which he was about to accomplish at Jerusalem. Now Peter and those who were with him were heavy with sleep, but when they became fully awake they saw his glory and the two men who stood with him. And as the men were parting from him, Peter said to Jesus, "Master, it is good that we are here. Let us make three tents, one for you and one for Moses and one for Elijah" – not knowing what he said. As he was saying these things, a cloud came and overshadowed them, and they were afraid as they entered the cloud. And a voice came out of the cloud, saying, "This is my Son, my Chosen One; listen to him!" And when the voice had spoken, Jesus was found alone. And they kept silent and told no one in those days anything of what they had seen.

Prayer

O God, as Your Scriptures put us in the story of the Transfiguration, You give us a glimpse of the coming glory. As You reveal the glory of Your Son, increase godly fear in us. As we hear Jesus talk with Moses and Elijah about the coming passion, increase our thankfulness for Your unbounded grace in giving Your Son to be our Savior. And as we leave the mountain of worship to go down to the common things of our lives, let us see and hear only Jesus. Amen.

The Bible story that we will study this morning is called the Transfiguration of our Lord. The moral of this morning's story is about baseball, hot dogs, apple pie, and Chevrolet – or whatever kind of car you happen to drive.

Now, the Transfiguration happened this way. Jesus went out one day with His three closest disciples. They were Peter, James, and John. They went up a mountain. Perhaps it was Mt. Tabor, but we don't know for sure. They went there, though. Not in a Chevrolet either. They *walked* up the mountain. That was the standard way to travel in those days – you walked.

Once they got up on the mountain, Jesus went off a little bit by Himself to pray. What did the three disciples, Peter, James, and John, do? They were no different than some church people today. As soon as the sermon begins, some church people doze off. As soon as Jesus began praying, these three disciples went to sleep. I get a kick out of watching some of you dozing off during the sermon. Especially when your wife gives you an elbow. If only you could see what you look like when you wake up! Well, Peter, James, and John up there on Mt. Tabor didn't have their wives with them. No elbow woke them up. But there *was* something that woke them up. It was the strangest sight they had ever seen.

They woke up and saw the Transfiguration of our Lord. The Bible says, "The appearance of his face was altered, and his clothing became dazzling white." You are familiar with pictures of Jesus. In most of them, His clothing is usually white or cream-colored – always perfectly clean. These pictures of Jesus show no dirty smudges or sweat on His clothes. And you know these pictures… His clothes are always perfectly pressed, aren't they? Even though they didn't have permanent press in those days. Common sense will tell you that Jesus probably didn't look that picture-perfect on a normal day. His clothes weren't perfectly clean. They certainly had their wrinkles. But the Bible says that on this particular day, "His clothing became dazzling white." Not only was Jesus perfectly dressed, but His clothes dazzled. They were so bright, it was almost like looking at the sun. Our Lord Jesus was transfigured in front of Peter, James, and John.

As if that weren't strange enough, two men appeared with Jesus – two men who had been dead for hundreds and hundreds of years. This Transfiguration story is more like a Halloween story, isn't it? The first dead man who appeared was Moses. You remember Moses. He lived back in the Old Testament times. He led the children of Israel out of Egypt and to the Promised Land. Perhaps the greatest thing that happened to Moses was that he received the Law. Moses went up Mt. Sinai and God gave him the two tables of the Ten Commandments (Exodus 31:18). Moses was the first great prophet of Israel.

The second dead man who appeared was also a great prophet of Old Testament times. His name was Elijah. Sometimes they called him Elias. There are many stories told about this Elijah. For example, he was fed by ravens at the brook Cherith (1 Kings 17:1-7). He also raised to life the dead son of a widow who had befriended him (1 Kings 17:8-24). He battled the prophets of Baal on Mt. Carmel (1 Kings 18:17-40). Finally, this Elijah went to heaven (2 Kings 2:1-14). I mean, he literally went to heaven. Not the way you and I go. We die and our souls are taken to heaven to await the Last Day when our bodies will be raised. But Elijah was walking one day and fiery chariots swooped down out of the sky, snatched him up, and took him to heaven. That's a better way to travel than a Rolls-Royce or a Mercedes-Benz, let alone a Chevrolet!

These three – Elijah, Moses, and Jesus – talked. They talked about Jesus' approaching death. His death on the cross for you and me. His death for our sins. That's the death that you and I will remember in Lent. They talked about that. In the midst of all the glory… the dazzling clothing, the altered faces, the light as bright as the sun… they talked about Jesus' death on the cross.

Then Peter – remember, he woke up without a nudge from his wife – Peter said to Jesus, *This is great! Wait a minute. I'll put up three tents, and you and Moses and Elijah can stay here forever! And we'll just enjoy looking at your glory.* Peter thought that such glory was great. If you're going to go, go first class.

And what better way to go than with all the glory of the Son of God and the glory of two great saints like Moses and Elijah all around you? Man, that's living, and that's glory! And Peter wanted to settle in and enjoy that life of glory right away. St. Luke was the man who recorded the story of the Transfiguration. Luke tells about Peter this way: "Peter said to Jesus, 'Master, it is good that we are here. Let us make three tents, one for you and one for Moses and one for Elijah.'" And then Luke adds this: "not knowing what he said" (Luke 9:33). Peter wanted to settle in and enjoy the life of glory right then and there, but Luke says that Peter really didn't know what he was talking about.

That brings us to the moral of this strange story of the Transfiguration. The moral is about baseball, hot dogs, apple pie, and Chevrolet. My wife gave me strict orders *not* to sing this.[1] We'll see… At any rate, sung or spoken, the moral of the Transfiguration is about baseball, hot dogs, apple pie, and Chevrolet. If a person is going to travel first class in this world – if you're going to be the cream of society, be first among your friends and relatives, and really enjoy a life of glory – then you're not going to use baseball, hot dogs… *whoops, sorry Diane!*… baseball, hot dogs, apple pie, and Chevrolet. You're not, because those things aren't very glorious. Baseball is a great game, but it's not a high-class game like polo or going to the Alps to ski. Hot dogs are OK, but they don't serve them at Fischer's or Tony's in Belleville. Apple pie is great, but it is not as ritzy as cherries jubilee. And Chevrolet – for that matter, we could say Pontiac, Oldsmobile, Buick, Chrysler, whatever – they are good cars, but they are not in a class with Rolls-Royce or Mercedes-Benz. Baseball, hot dogs, apple pie, and Chevrolet. That's the way you and I common people live. It's not polo, filet mignon, cherries jubilee, and Mercedes-Benz.

There *is* a life of glory. A great and heavenly life of glory awaits you, if you make Jesus Christ your own… if you know Him to be God's own dear Son… if you agree with the Gospel message that He came to die and rise again for you… if you trust in Him with your whole heart… then there is a life of glory awaiting you. A life far more glorious than any filet mignon or Mercedes-Benz – more glorious than anything the richest people in this world enjoy. It is the glory of an eternity with God and all the saints in heaven.

Peter understood that there is a life of glory. That's why he wanted to put up three tents – so they could settle in and enjoy the glory, right then and there. But Luke writes that Peter didn't know what he was saying. For the moral of this strange Transfiguration story is that although there is a life of glory awaiting you and me, *now* – on earth – we carry the cross. You have to carry your cross in *this* world before you live a life of glory in the world to come.

Jesus and Moses and Elijah appeared in all the glory of God, but they talked about the cross – the gory, painful death that Jesus was about to die. There is a life of glory for you, but now the cross. A Christian who accepts Christ as Savior will have the glory of heaven, but now the cross. Now we Christians must contend with sin. We must suffer with illness. We must put up with cranky people. We must pay taxes, grow older. Parents worry about children, and children don't know what is ahead of them in life. You might get tired of carrying your crosses year in and year out. The story of the Transfiguration tells you how you can keep going – how you can make the most of your daily common life, how you can enrich your daily fare. When Moses and Elijah had disappeared, the three disciples, Peter, James, and John, saw Jesus alone. They saw *Jesus alone.* When there is trouble… when there is sickness… when Mom or Dad or children cause you worry… when someone puts you down… when someone makes light of the Church… anytime you carry your cross, look to *Jesus alone.* Jesus alone gives you the strength to carry your cross. Jesus alone hears your prayers and supports you with His spirit. Jesus alone strengthens you through Word and Sacrament. Jesus alone is your Savior. He saved you by the cross, not by the glory.

There *is* a life of glory, but now, on earth, we carry the cross – the cross of Jesus Christ.

Amen.

For Further Reflection

**"Jesus Christ … was conceived by the Holy Spirit, born of the virgin Mary, suffered under Pontius Pilate, was crucified, died and was buried. He descended into hell. The third day He rose again from the dead. He ascended into heaven and sits at the right hand of God the Father Almighty. From thence He will come to judge the living and the dead." (Apostles' Creed, Second Article)

- Put yourself in awe and reverence before the Suffering Servant: true fear and love of God – Isaiah 52:13 - 53:12
- The time from Jesus' conception to burial is called "the state of humiliation." As True God and True Man, Jesus did not always, and did not fully, use His divine attributes. Read Matthew 1:18-25; John 19:1-3, 16-18; Hebrews 2:14-18; Philippians 2:5-8.
- From Jesus' descent into hell to proclaim His victory and to all eternity, Jesus is now in "the state of exaltation." As True God and True Man, Jesus does use all His divine attributes. Read 1 Peter 3:18-22; Acts 1:3; Ephesians 4:7-10; Acts 17:30-31; Philippians 2:9-11.
- Therefore – 2 Corinthians 4:13-18; Revelation 2:10

Alleluia cannot always
Be our song while here below;
Alleluia, our transgressions
Make us for a while forgo;
For the solemn time is coming
When our tears for sin must flow.

Therefore in our hymns we pray Thee,
Grant us, blessed Trinity,
At the last to keep Thine Easter
With Thy faithful saints on high;
There to Thee forever singing
Alleluia joyfully.[2]

Retrospective

Looking back at this early sermon shows me how my organization of sermon content has changed. Every preacher wants the congregation interested in what he's saying, and that's why many often start with an illustration or some attempted humor. In this sermon, I tried to get their attention with the popular car commercial from the 1970s, and I suspect they thought, "Interesting. What's he going to do with this?" Eventually I got to the point – that seeing Jesus blesses our humdrum lives because we live now with "the hope of glory" (Colossians 1:27).

Here's how the decades have changed me. If I were outlining the sermon today, I'd start right off with a heart problem – what I mean is emotion, soul, something gnawing deep down in their being – rather than delay it. "Are you tired of the grind, tired of carrying your cross? Want more glory? Yearning for some things better than 'baseball, hot dogs, apple pie, and Chevrolet'?" I'd try to get them to think about their dissatisfaction with their less than glorious lives. "Get into the hearer's heart as soon as you can," I tell my students. "Make the hearer think, 'He's going to talk about something I need to hear.'" That means, thinking now about how you outline the sermon, you don't need your best illustration at the beginning. People will listen to the preacher at the beginning; it's midway through the sermon when minds start to wander. That's where you need to place your best illustration.

However a sermon is outlined, the first job is getting into the hearer's heart – or if you're in the pews, to internalize what the pastor says at the outset. The ultimate goal is to speak or hear a good Word from God, moving from emotions to His objective and transforming Word.

What a trip for me to look back at this old bulletin (pp. 92-93)! I see emphases that have continued with me. "Good Morning!" In many ways the pastor sets the tone for congregational life. At New Memphis and Collinsville, I greeted people before worship, welcoming them. Not so at Venedy because, being a dual parish with New Memphis, the people were already in church waiting for me. "Today's Worship" reflects my desire to get people oriented toward the theme of the day as soon as they sit down. That's a reason why I also include the sermon title in the bulletin. Along with "Today's Worship," the title starts guiding the worshipers toward hearing the sermon: I wonder what this will be about? I listed sermon questions not only to help the hearing, but also because I would ask the children for the answers at the end of the service. Today, people call that "catechesis," or at least one small part of overall catechesis, teaching the faith. Other things included in that week's bulletin were "This Week at Church" (Doesn't look like I was overworked!), the special song (supplementing The Lutheran Hymnal), "Film Night" (I can't remember that at all. Abbott and Costello! Obviously that was a different time.), and President Preus coming (which was quite an honor for our little churches).

On the subject of bulletins, my mother had a habit that has stuck with me. When we were growing up, many people carried their own hymnals to worship. Mom would stick the bulletin into her Lutheran Hymnal, and put it on an end table when she came home. The bulletin was there all week, in the hymnal, in the home, for reference. What's going on at church? Let me check the bulletin. What was that hymn we sang? What was the sermon about? I've always thought of the bulletin as a little devotional aid that should be taken home. I have never – will never – encourage recycling the bulletins as you leave worship! Recycle it at home, after you've referred to it during the week. To this day, when I leave daily chapel at Concordia Seminary, I stick the order of worship in my pocket. We all have our eccentricities!

BASEBALL, HOT DOGS, APPLE PIE & CHEVROLET

Luke 9:28-36
Transfiguration
February 5, 1978
New Memphis and Venedy, Illinois

The Bible story that we will study this morning is called
the "Transfiguration of Our Lord." The moral of this morning's
story is about baseball, hot dogs, apple pie & chevrolet... or
whatever kind of car you happen to drive.

Now, the transfiguration happened this way. Jesus went
out one day with his three closest disciples. They were Peter,
James, and John. They went up to a mountain. Perhaps a mountain called Mt. Tabor, although we don't know for sure. They
went there, though. Not in a Chevrolet either. They walked
up the mountain. That was the standard way to travel in those
days. You walked.

Once they got up into the mountain, Jesus went off a little
bit by himself to pray. What did the three disciples, Peter,
James and John, do? They were no different than some church
people today. As soon as the sermon begins, some church people
doze off. As soon as Jesus began praying, these three disciples
went to sleep. I get a kick from watching some of you dozing
off during the sermon. Especially when your wife gives you an
elbow. If only you could see what you look like when you wake
up! Well, Peter, James, and John up there on Mt. Tabor didn't
have their wives with them. No elbow woke them up. But there
was something that woke them up. It was the strangest sight
that they had ever seen.

They woke up and saw the Transfiguration of our Lord. The
Bible says that the appearance of Jesus' countenance was altered.

GOOD MORNING! It is good to have you with us this morning. We want you to feel welcome at our church and hope that you will join us again next Sunday morning.

TODAY'S WORSHIP The Transfiguration of our Lord is an exciting story because it gives us a glimpse of a life of glory. Further, it is also realistic because it shows that the life of glory is preceded by the way of the cross. May your worship help you to glimpse the glory and bear the cross.

THE ORDER OF WORSHIP
    The Hymn: "How Lovely Shines the MOrning Star"   TLH 343
    We confess our sins and hear God's forgiveness   pp. 15-16
    Pastor reads the Introit and we sing the Gloria Patri and the
      Kyrie and the Gloria in Excelsis   pp. 16-19
    Pastor and members greet one another and pray
    The Collect for The Transfiguration of Our Lord
    God speaks to us through the Bible readings   Back Cover
    We state our beliefs in speaking the Nicene Creed   p. 22
    The Sermon Hymn: "Tis Good, Lord, to be Here"   TLH 135
    The Sermon: "Hot Dogs, Apple Pie and Chevrolet" Luke 9:28-36
    The Offertory (p.22), Offering and Prayer
    The Sacrament of Holy Communion   pp. 24-31
    Communicant members of the congregation are invited to examine
    their faith and life and receive the Savior's body and blood.
    During the distribution we shall sing "Sons of God"
    The Closing Hymn: "Wondrous King, All Glorious"   TLH 41

THIS WEEK AT CHURCH
    Monday at 7:30 at Venedy - Film Nite
    Wednesday at 7:30 at Venedy - Ash Wednesday Service
    Thursday at 2:00 at Venedy - Ladies Aid
    Thursday at 7:30 at Venedy - Dorcas
    Friday at 1:00 at Hoffman - LWML Prayer Service

Sons of God, hear His holy Word! Gather 'round the table of the Lord! Eat His body, drink His blood, and we'll sing a song of love: Allelu, allelu, allelu, Alleluia!

1. Brothers, sisters, we are one, And our life has just begun;
   In the Spirit we are young; We can live forever. Sons of God...
2. Shout together to the Lord Who has promised our reward:
   Happiness a hundredfold, and we'll live forever. Sons of God...
3. Jesus gave a new command That we love our fellowman
   Till we reach the promised land Where we'll live forever.
   Sons of God...
4. If we want to live with Him, We must also die with Him,
   Die to selfishness and sin, And we'll rise forever.
   Sons of God...
5. Make the world a unity, Make all men one family
   Till we meet the Trinity And live with them forever.
   Sons of God...
6. With the Church we celebrate, Jesus' coming we await;
   So we make a holiday, So we'll live forever. Sons of God...

SERMON QUESTIONS
1. What happened on the Mount of Transfiguration?
2. There is a life of glory, but now the _____.
3. How can you enrich your daily fare?

FILM NITE Our young people are offering the congregation a free
    film nite, Monday, February 6 at 7:30. We'll be watching an
    Abbott and Costello film. Refreshments will be served.

J.A.O. PREUS, President of The Lutheran Church-Missouri Synod
    will preach in both services February 26. Please publicize
    this among your friends and acquaintances.

Week 7 – Yearning for Home

Ash Wednesday
From "Calling Us Home: A Lenten Sermon Series on 1 Peter,"[1]
Concordia Seminary, St. Louis, 2015

Text – 1 Peter 1:8-12

Though you have not seen him, you love him. Though you do not now see him, you believe in him and rejoice with joy that is inexpressible and filled with glory, obtaining the outcome of your faith, the salvation of your souls.

Concerning this salvation, the prophets who prophesied about the grace that was to be yours searched and inquired carefully, inquiring what person or time the Spirit of Christ in them was indicating when he predicted the sufferings of Christ and the subsequent glories. It was revealed to them that they were serving not themselves but you, in the things that have now been announced to you through those who preached the good news to you by the Holy Spirit sent from heaven, things into which angels long to look.

Prayer

"Lord, Thee I love with all my heart." Lord Jesus, that's the way an old hymn begins, but I confess sometimes my heart is lured away from You. That's why I'm thankful for another Lent, for this opportunity to have my love for You renewed. Give Your Spirit to my worship. Grow my love through more intense devotion. Make me yearn more and more for my true home with You. "Lord, Thee I love with all my heart; / I pray Thee, ne'er from me depart"![2] Amen.

Lent is about Jesus Christ. Our sermon text is 1 Peter 1:8-12, and it begins this way: "Though you have not seen him, you love him." Is that true? Do you love Him? I don't mean do you know about Him in your head. Of course you do. I'm not asking if you know things about His life. Sure you do. No, the question is this: *Do you love Him?* Years ago, I heard a story about a married couple going someplace in the car. The husband was driving. The wife was lamenting that the romance of their youth had gone out of their marriage. I wonder how the husband took that! Anyway, the wife recalled that when they were first married, they used to sit close together in the front seat of the car. The husband smiled and said, "I haven't moved away."

Do you love Jesus? I can't answer for you, but can only answer for myself. Yes, I love Him, but I certainly don't love Him the way I ought. Sometimes I move away from Him. You will probably admit that you do, too. I need – we *all* need – this penitential season of Lent. Lent gives you and me the opportunity to reflect on our journey – not just our journey from this Ash Wednesday to Easter, but our bigger journey through life to our eternal home with God. If you take this Lent seriously, and I pray that you will, you'll see that life is not just *"ashes to ashes and dust to dust."*[3] Take this Lenten journey seriously, and you'll see that it's Lent to Easter, it's ashes to glory, and it's dust to glorified bodies in our heavenly home. Here's the promise: Take this Lenten journey seriously and you'll love Jesus more and more – because you'll appreciate more than ever that Jesus is the way to your true home.

Have you ever yearned to go home to the people you love? Sure you have; we all have. A young person goes off to college, filled with excitement and apprehension. If that brand-new college student came from a good home, there's a yearning for the holidays when she can get back home. If you have served in the military, especially if you served overseas or even have been in combat, you know the yearning for home! When you go on a vacation, as enjoyable as it might be, you eventually say, "It'll be good to get back home." And that yearning for home is true on a daily basis as well. We go to work and look forward to the end of the day, to going home and to rest. We all know the feeling of yearning for home – the feeling of yearning to be at peace with the people we love. So I'll say it again: *Lent reminds us that we're on a journey, a journey to our eternal home with God.* We love Jesus because He's our way home.

St. Peter wrote this passage to people who yearned for home in a way we can't really relate to. The recipients of his letter didn't have an earthly home and earthly country the way you and I have our homes and our country. They lived in what we today call Turkey. They were legal aliens, not citizens as you and I are. They tended to be poor. They were have-nots who wished they could have more. Some of them were slaves, despised and subject to beatings. They were a small minority in society, unlike us Christians, who are common in America. They yearned for a home like we can't imagine. St. Peter couldn't change their status, but he did invite them to see their lives as a journey to their true home. Peter told them – and tells us – how blessed we are that Jesus is leading us on our journey to our true home.

"Though you do not now see him, you believe in him and rejoice with joy that is inexpressible and filled with glory, obtaining the outcome of your faith, the salvation of your souls" (1 Peter 1:8-9). Our journey is toward salvation. Although our circumstances are different from those of the recipients of Peter's letter long ago, we're yearning for deliverance just like them. The troubles we have, the ills that beset us, all the unwanted stuff that sin causes in our lives… we're journeying toward our full salvation when the former things will be no more (cf. Revelation 21:4). Who can imagine what our true home will be like? "No eye has seen, nor ear heard, nor the heart of man imagined, / what God has prepared for those who love him" (1 Corinthians 2:9). Keep yearning for home!

Peter continues, "Concerning this salvation, the prophets who prophesied about the grace that was to be yours searched and inquired carefully" (1 Peter 1:10). The Scriptures, the Old and New Testaments, tell us about the great gift – the grace, as Peter says – that God is giving to you and to me. Peter says the ages have focused on what we hear in Lent. Specifically, he says that the prophets were "inquiring what person or time the Spirit of Christ in them was indicating when he predicted the sufferings of Christ and the subsequent glories" (1 Peter 1:11). Lent is about Jesus. Christian life is all about Jesus. This Lent we will rehearse again what the Scriptures say about His suffering to save us from our sins. In Lent, we figuratively put on sackcloth and figuratively get down into ashes to repent for our sins – but our blessing is that Jesus lifts us up with forgiveness. It's the old, old story, as the Gospel hymn says, *"For those who know it best / Seem hungering and thirsting / To hear it like the rest."*[4] And this Lent, we won't forget that Easter is coming. Without Easter, our journey toward eternity is a literal dead end. With Easter, there is life and the salvation of our souls. Scriptures radiate His resurrection and His ascension, what Peter calls "the subsequent glories." If you and I take this Lent seriously, how can we not grow in our love of Jesus? How can we not yearn more and more for our true home?

Peter concludes this section by saying, "It was revealed to them [that is, to the Old Testament prophets] that they were serving not themselves but you, in the things that have now been announced to you through those who preached the good news to you by the Holy Spirit sent from heaven, things into which angels long to look" (1 Peter 1:12). All of this – all this in the Bible, all Lent, all the Church does – it's all God's grace to you. This is so precious that Peter says even the angels long to look into the things we hear in church. *Shhhh!* Can you hear their wings fluttering as they hover here, unseen, listening to the Good News of Jesus Christ? Hear it again: "It was revealed to them that they were serving not themselves but you, in the things that have now been announced to you through those who preached the good news to you by the Holy Spirit sent from heaven, things into which angels long to look."

So let's use this Lent to love Jesus more and more, because His passion and resurrection are leading us to our true home. God didn't want the people in ancient Turkey to settle in too much. He doesn't want us to settle into our present lives too much either. A little discontent – a desire for something better, a desire for our true home – is good. It makes us appreciate how blessed we are. The psalmist says, "Whom have I in heaven but you? And there is nothing on earth that I desire besides you. / My flesh and my heart may fail, but God is the strength of my heart and my portion forever" (Psalm 73:25-26). We're not there yet, but we are yearning. *Jesus, we love You. You're leading us home. Don't let us move away!*

Amen.

For Further Reflection

"I believe in the Holy Spirit … and the life everlasting." (Apostles' Creed, Third Article)

- "On the whole, America is still committed to Jesus. More than six in ten Americans say they have made a personal commitment to Jesus."[5] That said, about half think He was only a man and He committed sins.[6] Are you going to heaven? "I hope so" doesn't show confidence in Jesus. It actually reflects some anxiety. Read Mark 9:24.
- The Holy Spirit works through the Word of God to give certainty of eternal life, now and forever – Isaiah 55:10-11; John 6:63-69; John 20:31; Romans 10:6-13; 2 Timothy 3:14-15
- Instead of fearing because we're not certain, we reverently take His Word to heart. That is true fear of God, and so we love Him – Romans 8:28-30; 2 Timothy 1:12.
- Martin Luther: "Faith is a living, daring confidence in God's grace, so sure and certain that the believer would stake his life on it a thousand times."[7]

> *My walk is heav'nward all the way;*
> *Await, my soul, the morrow,*
> *When God's good healing shall allay*
> *All suff'ring, sin, and sorrow.*
> *Then, worldly pomp, begone!*
> *To heav'n I now press on.*
> *For all the world I would not stay;*
> *My walk is heav'nward all the way.*[8]

Retrospective

One valuable contribution that sermons can make to the lives of people is putting today's issues into eternal perspective. Our communication devices are amazing in so many ways but also bring spiritual jeopardy. We can lose our eternal perspective in this ASAP world. In his book, *Thank You for Being Late*, Thomas Friedman describes his own experience with instantaneous life:

> On April 13, 2016, I wrote a column from Niger that quoted (government official Adamou) Chaifou. It moved on NYTimes.com at 3:20 a.m. Eastern Standard Time, or 8:20 a.m. Niger time. I was departing the country that afternoon and went to the airport around 1:00 p.m. Chaifou came out to say goodbye to me and I took the opportunity to be the first to tell him, "I quoted you in my column in The New York Times today. It's up on the Web on NYTimes.com." "I know," he responded. "My kids are studying in China and they already sent it to me!" So today, a minister in Niger is telling me his kids studying in a remote university in China have e-mailed him my column from Niger before my wife had woken up and read it in Bethesda.[9]

Who can keep up with this pace? Friedman titled his chapter, "Just Too Damned Fast."

People gesture, and pastors study – or should study – how they gesture. One of my dearest pastoral and preaching gestures is to put out both hands, palms out to slow things down, and then deliberately say, "It's OK. Be calm." Next I try to take whatever the problem of the moment is and put it in a long-term perspective. That's what this sermon tried to do. Thomas Friedman shows how life has accelerated beyond our ability to keep up. Perhaps more than any time in history, a pastor has the opportunity calm harried people with eternal perspective. *"So we do not lose heart ... as we look not to the things that are seen but to the things that are unseen. For the things that are seen are transient, but the things that are unseen are eternal" (2 Corinthians 4:16, 18).*

> *Jesus, lead Thou on*
> *Till our rest is won.*
> *Heav'nly leader, still direct us,*
> *Still support, console, protect us,*
> *Till we safely stand*
> *In our fatherland.*[10]

Week 8 – Graced Toward Glory

From "Calling Us Home: A Lenten Sermon Series on 1 Peter,"[1]
Concordia Seminary, St. Louis, 2015

Text – 1 Peter 5:6-11

Humble yourselves, therefore, under the mighty hand of God so that at the proper time he may exalt you, casting all your anxieties on him, because he cares for you. Be sober-minded; be watchful. Your adversary the devil prowls around like a roaring lion, seeking someone to devour. Resist him, firm in your faith, knowing that the same kinds of suffering are being experienced by your brotherhood throughout the world. And after you have suffered a little while, the God of all grace, who has called you to his eternal glory in Christ, will himself restore, confirm, strengthen, and establish you. To him be the dominion forever and ever. Amen.

Prayer

God of all grace, as we continue to follow Jesus to our true home, let us learn the lesson of Lent – first the cross, then the crown. Teach us humbly to rely on You, always making our journey toward glory watching against the wiles of Satan and encouraged by our fellowship with other Christians around the world. By Your grace restore, confirm, strengthen, and establish us until we pass through earthly sufferings to Your eternal glory. In Jesus' name, Amen.

You've caught it, I'm sure. Our midweek Lenten services have a clear theme – God is calling us home. Sometimes in life we hear that call loud and clear. Other times, maybe most times, the call home seems distant, but we still hear it. Since we hear God's call, we know there's a goal before us, a goal to reach in the future. St. Peter says that the goal is the salvation of our souls (1 Peter 1:9). Now, the word "salvation" is church jargon. It's one of those words we throw around in church, but what does it really mean? Salvation simply means being rescued and brought safely home. One day, church services and hearing the call will be over. Through faith we know that Jesus rescues us, saves us. So, one day we'll arrive safely home, safe with God for all eternity. *Are we there yet?* No, kids, not yet! So, we think of these days as – here's some more jargon – the "time of grace." Time of grace simply means we need all the help, all the grace, we can get from our God and Savior if we're going to arrive safely in our true home. As this evening's sermon title puts it, we are "Graced Toward Glory."

To arrive safely home, we need all the grace we can get! Grace is the favor that God gives you and me because of Jesus Christ. It's the opposite of works, which, as you've heard many times, cannot save you. Grace is the favor that God gives sorry, repentant sinners because of all that our Savior has done for us. Peter talked about grace several times as he wrote to encourage Christians on their way home. "Grace and peace be multiplied to you," we read in 1 Peter 1:2. Multiplied, he said; he prayed lots and lots of grace upon them, and upon us. The Old Testament prophets prophesied about the grace you and I hear (1 Peter 1:10). God's great favor, His grace, will be manifest when Jesus Christ comes at the end of time (1 Peter 1:13). When we endure unjust suffering, that's also a grace from God. He enables us to bear suffering for being Christian, and not to retaliate (1 Peter 2:19–20). In 1 Peter 3:7, Peter says husbands and wives are heirs of "the grace of life." In 1 Peter 4:10, the various ways we serve in church demonstrate "God's varied grace." God "gives grace to the humble" (1 Peter 5:5), and in tonight's text, God is called "the God of all grace." Peter is big on grace! Through Jesus Christ, God has lots of grace for you and me, and, as I said, *we need it!* We really are living in a time of grace.

Our text this evening lists four qualities for you and me to develop as we are graced toward glory. The first is humility. God shows His favor upon the humble; Peter says, "Humble yourselves, therefore, under the mighty hand of God so that at the proper time he may exalt you" (1 Peter 5:6). The world doesn't consider humility to be sophisticated. Peter often struggled with humility. When Jesus predicted that all His disciples would leave Him on the night of his betrayal (Matthew 26:31), Peter boasted that he would never abandon Jesus (Matthew 26:33). How did that turn out (Matthew 26:69-75)? But at other times, Peter was humbly dependent on Jesus. When many people left Jesus (John 6:66), Peter said, "Lord, to whom shall we go? You have the words of eternal life" (John 6:68). *Heavenly Father, give us Your favor so we see ourselves as You see us – sinners more than we know, but graced toward eternal glory more than we can ever imagine.*

Second, our text says cast "all your anxieties on him, because he cares for you" (1 Peter 5:7). The world doesn't encourage us to admit our weaknesses and worries. Peter struggled with prayer; many of us struggle, but Jesus was tight in prayer with His Father. We see that most clearly in the Garden of Gethsemane. But Peter? Jesus told Peter and the other disciples to watch and pray – but they fell asleep. "The spirit indeed is willing, but the flesh is weak" (Matthew 26:41). Jesus said, "Sleep and take your rest later on" (Matthew 26:45). *Heavenly Father, grace us with a spirit of unceasing prayer so every anxiety prompts us to pray to You.*

Third, our text warns us, "Be sober-minded; be watchful. Your adversary the devil prowls around like a roaring lion, seeking someone to devour. Resist him, firm in your faith" (1 Peter 5:8-9). The sophisticates of American culture don't believe in the devil. No doubt that's just what the devil wants people to believe. Peter learned that the devil is insidiously real. When Jesus predicted His suffering and crucifixion, Peter, the Bible tells us, "took him aside and began to rebuke him" (Mark 8:32). Jesus said, "Get behind me, Satan! For you are not setting your mind on the things of God, but on the things of man" (Mark 8:33). *Heavenly Father, help us to know that the old wily foe now means deadly woe.[2] Give us grace to resist him firm in faith so we soon will arrive safely in glory.*

Fourth and finally from tonight's text comes a jab against American individualism. "Resist him [the devil], firm in your faith [I just talked about that], knowing that the same kinds of suffering are being experienced by your brotherhood throughout the world" (1 Peter 5:9). American individualism is not all bad, but I'm *not* the center of the universe, and neither are you. We are together, we are the Church, and we are members of the Body of Christ journeying toward salvation. Peter knew that. He was probably in Rome when he wrote this epistle, but his mind was on the whole Christian Church – especially those brothers and sisters in Asia Minor, what we now call Turkey. They were being shunned and slandered for following Jesus. *Heavenly Father, grace us with a sense of the worldwide Church, its joys and sufferings, as You call us all toward glory.*

In our passion reading this evening, we heard of Jesus' crucifixion, death, and burial. We heard that passion history, knowing that glory was going to break forth from the tomb three days later. That's our life. We died with Christ by Baptism into death, now we daily rise to newness of life in this time of grace, and we believe that one day we will be resurrected with Jesus (cf. Romans 6:1-11). Until that day, until the goal of salvation is achieved and we are brought safely home, until then, we need all the grace we can get!

> *I need Thy presence ev'ry passing hour;*
> *What but Thy grace can foil the tempter's pow'r?*
> *Who like Thyself my guide and stay can be?*
> *Through cloud and sunshine, O abide with me.*[3]

Rev. Arnold Kunz, a retired pastor, once put it this way: "Life narrows down." Don't you know that's the truth! "Life narrows down … and there in the narrow place stands Jesus."[4] "To him be the dominion forever and ever. Amen" (1 Peter 5:11).

For Further Reflection

The Sacrament of the Altar

- Instituted by our Lord Jesus – Matthew 26:26-29; Mark 14:22-25; Luke 22:19-20; 1 Corinthians 11:23-28. See also 1 Corinthians 10:16.
- "Do this, as often as you drink it, in remembrance of me" (1 Corinthians 11:25). Martin Luther wrote his Small Catechism in 1529. In a 1551 edition, "Christian Questions with Their Answers" first appeared. Questions 19 and 20 encourage us to use the "time of grace":

- ○ Question 19: What admonishes and moves you to receive Holy Communion frequently?
    - ▪ The command and the promise of Christ my Lord admonishes and moves me. Also, the burden of sin that lies heavy upon me causes me to feel a hunger and thirst for Holy Communion.[5]
- ○ Question 20: But what can a person do if he is not aware of the burden of sin and does not feel hunger and thirst for Holy Communion?
    - ▪ To such a person no better advice can be given than that, in the first place, he put his hand into his bosom and feel whether he still has flesh and blood, and that he by all means believes what the Scriptures say about this (Galatians 5:17, 19-21; Isaiah 64:6; Romans 7:18).

        Secondly, that he look around to see whether he is still in the world and keep in mind that there will be no lack of sin and trouble, as the Scriptures say (John 15:18-25; Matthew 24:9-13; Acts 14:22).

        Thirdly, that person will certainly have the devil also about him. With his lying and murdering, day and night, the devil will let him have no peace. So the Scriptures picture the devil (John 8:44; 1 Peter 5:8; Ephesians 6:10-12; 2 Timothy 2:26).[5]

O Holy Spirit, grant us grace
That we our Lord and Savior
In faith and fervent love embrace
And truly serve Him ever.
The hour of death cannot bring loss
When we are sheltered by the cross
That canceled our transgressions.

Help us that we Thy saving Word
In faithful hearts may treasure;
Let e'er that Bread of Life afford
New grace in richest measure.
O make us die to ev'ry sin,
Each day create new life within,
That fruits of faith may flourish.[6]

Retrospective

I once asked my Grandpa Meyer, it must have been in the late 1960s, what it was like for him to go to the English service. Grandpa and Grandma spoke German at home and attended our church's German service. Grandpa said he had to translate the English into German in order to understand better. Church jargon, those theological words we hear over and over, also need to be translated. We may think we know these words, like the words that lead off this sermon, "salvation" and "grace," but we should never be too sure. Jargon words have a function. They are catchwords for rich theological concepts, but they need to be understood.

To that end, a concordance is one helpful tool. A concordance is a listing of all the places in the Bible where a given word occurs. There are Greek and Hebrew concordances that some pastors use, but also English concordances everyone will find helpful. Some Bibles have short concordances in the back of the book. It was the concordance that gave me all the occurrences of the word "grace" in 1 Peter that I listed in this sermon. Concordances help us learn the rich nuances of "grace" and "salvation" and other words of theological jargon. They help us better understand the Word of God for our lives. I have included one concordance in the recommended reading section in the back of this book. Here's an idea for your personal study or for a Bible class: Write down a list of common church words you're not sure you truly understand. Be honest! Besides a concordance, where else can you go to get a better understanding?

I was a college student studying the biblical languages when I asked Grandpa that question. I was translating Greek and Latin because I had to – school assignments. He was translating to understand words for his eternal life. When life narrows down, we want to understand the words we've heard so that we'll see Jesus. It's one way of making the most of this "time of grace."

Week 9 – The Lonely Battles of Jesus

Broadcast on The Lutheran Hour
August 2, 1992

Text – Matthew 27:46

And about the ninth hour Jesus cried out with a loud voice, saying, "Eli, Eli, lema sabachthani?" that is, "My God, my God, why have you forsaken me?"

Prayer

Almighty God, whose Son had nowhere to lay His head: Grant that those who are alone may not be lonely in their solitude, but may know the comfort of Your presence and the confidence that comes from Your promise to hear prayer; through Jesus Christ, our crucified and living Savior. Amen.

Oh my God! I wish I had someone to talk to! You do – He's your heavenly Father. We all battle loneliness. You and I cry out to talk to someone – anyone! Your husband or wife died; you cry because you miss talking with your companion of so many years. You're young, and you have multiple sclerosis; you're surrounded by people who live the fast-paced life that you used to live, and you feel so lonely. You're in a nursing home, alone; the family is hundreds of miles away, or only blocks away – doesn't make any difference – they don't visit you often enough. You're single, and just had a baby; you chose adoption rather than abortion or raising the child by yourself, but now that the baby is gone, the pain of loneliness strikes deep. You work all day in a crowded office; you carpool or take the bus home, then you walk into an empty apartment and you think, *Dear God! I wish I had someone to talk to!* In three weeks, Diane and

I will take our oldest daughter to college. I'm already feeling the pain of her coming absence.

We all battle loneliness. It's not a physical battle. There can be thousands of people around, and you still feel alone. Loneliness is a spiritual battle. And there's a spiritual way for you to confront and conquer loneliness – and that way is Jesus.

Now, Jesus often was in lonely places. Do you remember the early days of His public ministry? Can you imagine how lonely it was when He spent forty days in the wilderness, fasting and being tempted by Satan (Matthew 4:1-11)? Do you remember when Jesus went to Nazareth, His home town, and preached a sermon (Luke 4:16-30)? Another lonely battle for Jesus. The people taunted Him about His parentage and tried to throw Him off a cliff. Jesus went from Nazareth to Capernaum, and made that town the home base of His ministry, but He had to stay in Peter's house (Matthew 8:14-15) because Jesus never had a home of His own. Homeless people know loneliness.

Or how about the hours before Jesus was crucified? Just before His passion, Jesus said to His disciples, "Behold, the hour is coming, indeed it has come, when you will be scattered, each to his own home, and will leave me alone" (John 16:32). Can't you picture Jesus' loneliness as He prayed in Gethsemane, and His disciples slept (Matthew 26:36-46)? Can't you feel the loneliness, the helplessness, when Judas Iscariot led the thugs into the Garden and they arrested Jesus – and His disciples scattered as far and as fast as they could (Matthew 26:47-56)? And I know you can feel the lonely pain as the Roman soldiers pounded the nails through Jesus' hands and feet and raised Him on the cross (John 19:17-18). You're not the only one to battle loneliness. Your Savior knows all about being in lonely places.

Now, I'm not going to give you religious drivel that says, *Buck up! Make the best of it!* I have no patience with positive thinking that is rooted in our own natural abilities. You know how that positive thinking line could be applied to loneliness: *Jesus had His lonely battles, and therefore you should buck up and make the best of your lonely times!*

This is an important spot in today's message. Yes, of course – Jesus is an example for living, but Jesus is more. First and foremost, Jesus is your Savior! It's a fact that He saves people who know that their natural abilities and their own positive thoughts aren't enough. He saves people who are at the end of their rope. When you're feeling all the pain and helplessness of being alone, what do you want? Someone who says "Buck up"? No! You want a Savior who comes to you, who is with you, and who Himself will help you confront and conquer loneliness. So now, I'm going to tell you about your Savior.

Jesus was often in lonely places. But do you realize that with one exception, He was never really alone? When He was in the wilderness being tempted, when He was almost thrown out of Nazareth, when He was in the Garden of Gethsemane, and so many other times when He seemed to be alone, He really wasn't. His Father was always with Him. I'm not aware that Jesus ever cried out and said, *Oh my God! I wish I had someone to talk to!* Jesus knew that His Father was always with Him – with one exception. There was one time when the Father was not with Jesus. Matthew 27:46 says that when Jesus was on the cross, He cried out, "My God, my God, why have you forsaken me?" Jesus often was in lonely places, but this was the only time when He was *really* alone.

My daughter Elizabeth, the one going to college in a few weeks, took journalism last year at Collinsville [Illinois] High School. Reporters are supposed to ask questions like *Who? What? Where? When? Why?* and *How?* We can apply these questions to this truly lonely person on the cross. *Who* was it that cried, "My God, my God, why have you forsaken me?" It's Jesus, totally. It's the Son of God and the Son of Man in that one person, hanging on the cross. Some people think that the God part of Jesus left Him, and so only the human part was left – and it was only that human part that cried out, "My God, my God, why have you forsaken me?" No, Jesus Christ is one person – one real person who cannot be divided. He doesn't come apart into a human half and a divine half. That's what the incarnation means: God has become flesh. It was one Christ – True God and True Man – who was abandoned. The reporter asks *where* did the God-Man cry out, "My God, my God, why have you forsaken me?" The *where* was on Calvary's cross, just outside the city wall of Jerusalem. There, Jesus hung for about six hours. The reporter asks *when* was the Savior abandoned by God? Not for the whole six hours when He hung on the cross, for early on Jesus said, "Father, forgive them, for they know not what they do" (Luke 23:34). And at the very end He said, "Father, into your hands I commit my spirit!" (Luke 23:46). It was sometime between these times when Jesus spoke His "fourth word" from the cross – "My God, my God, why have you forsaken me?" *What really happened?* The reporter asks this to get to the truth. This answer is awesome. The Son of

God and the Son of Man was forsaken by God. In His profound loneliness, Jesus called out to God. Jesus cried out with the words of Psalm 22:1-2:

> My God, my God, why have you forsaken me?
>> Why are you so far from saving me, from the words of my groaning?
> O my God, I cry by day, but you do not answer,
>> and by night, but I find no rest.

The Son of God, and the Son of Man, forsaken by God! You and I can identify with the other lonely times in Jesus' life – the hometown folks turn on Him, the disciples flee – ah, but this is totally different. How can we humans comprehend what was happening when the good and loving God forsook His own Son? How could such an awesome event come to pass? The answer is that God, who is holy and just, punished Jesus for your sins. The loneliness that you and I feel, the pain that cuts into our hearts, the helplessness that can make us feel so worthless – this is real! It's not simply the result of how you perceive reality. Loneliness *is* reality for sinners. Sin leads people away from God and away from each other. God created us for an intimate fellowship with one another and with Him, but when we go against His will and against His ways, we make our lot a lonely one.

Isaiah 53:6 says, "All we like sheep have gone astray; we have turned – every one – to his own way." *How* did Jesus' abandonment come to pass? Isaiah 53:6 also says, "and the LORD has laid on him the iniquity of us all."

> Surely he has borne our griefs
>> and carried our sorrows;
> yet we esteemed him stricken,
>> smitten by God, and afflicted.
> But he was pierced for our transgressions;
>> he was crushed for our iniquities;
> upon him was the chastisement that brought us peace,
>> and with his wounds we are healed. (Isaiah 53:4-5)

The reporter asks, *Why?* Why did God do this? Here the truth of the Savior comes home to your life. God did this so when you find yourself in lonely situations, you can know that you're not alone. God punished Jesus to bring you back to intimate fellowship with Him and with others. St. Paul says in Ephesians:

> Remember that you were at that time separated from Christ, alienated from the commonwealth of Israel and strangers to the covenants of promise, having no hope and without God in the world. But now in Christ Jesus you who once were far off have been brought near by the blood of Christ. ... And he came and preached peace to you who were far off and peace to those who were near. For through him we both have access in one Spirit to the Father. So then you are no longer strangers and aliens, but you are fellow citizens with the saints and members of the household of God. (Ephesians 2:12-13, 17-19)

When you're battling loneliness, you're not alone. Because Jesus was alone – truly alone – that one time on the cross, you need not face the lonely circumstances of your life as if you were truly all alone. Listen to some Bible passages where God promises that He is with you:

- Psalm 9:9-10 – "The LORD is a stronghold for the oppressed, a stronghold in times of trouble. / And those who know your name put their trust in you, for you, O LORD, have not forsaken those who seek you."

- Hebrews 13:5 – "Keep your life free from love of money, and be content with what you have, for he has said, 'I will never leave you nor forsake you.'"

- Deuteronomy 31:6 – "Be strong and courageous. Do not fear or be in dread of them, for it is the LORD your God who goes with you. He will not leave you or forsake you."

- And in Matthew 28:20, the crucified and resurrected Christ – the One who was abandoned for your sake, and who now lives – this Savior says, "Behold, I am with you always."

Now, because your God and Savior is with you, you have a dependable friend to talk to. When you want to cry out, *Oh my God! I wish I had someone to talk to!* – you do. He's God, your heavenly Father. He wants you to pray to Him.

Writer Sharleen Scott tells of her friend who's confined to a wheelchair. "Well, dear," the friend wrote Ms. Scott, "when the Fourth of July rolls around, it always makes me think of you. You were the last person I got to celebrate the Fourth with. I believe it was '84. I'll always remember our swim at the park pool and the fireworks. From then on, the best I've been able to celebrate is watching the Fourth festivities on TV." That prompted Ms. Scott to reflect: "The length of time she's been housebound hit me after I received that letter. Since 1984, I've visited seven Latin American countries during three different trips, and all that time, my friend has sat, day after day, month after month, in the same chair beside her window, looking out at the changing seasons as her body grows more fragile and feeble."

"Are there any spiritual benefits to her loneliness?" Ms. Scott asks. The answer comes from her friend's letter: "I'm doing good just to get through each day taking care of myself. We just do the best with what comes our way in life, and that's that. I literally pray myself through each day."[1]

When you think you're alone, you're really not. Because Jesus reconciled the holy and just God to you, you have a heavenly Father who is close, and who invites you to talk with Him.

Dr. Luther comments on the first words of the Lord's Prayer. He says, "With these words God tenderly invites us to believe that he is our true Father and that we are his true children, so that we may pray to him as boldly and confidently as dear children ask their dear father."[2]

How many battles with loneliness do we fight – and lose – because we forget we have a Father who is close and waiting to hear our prayers? How many times when loneliness strikes a deep and painful blow to our hearts do we fail to tend to our hurt with the Gospel of what our Savior has done for us? How many times do we feel so alone and so helpless that we forget that "God is our refuge and strength, / a very present help in trouble" (Psalm 46:1)?

> *Oh, what peace we often forfeit;*
> *Oh, what needless pain we bear –*

All because we do not carry
Ev'rything to God in prayer![3]

Amen.

For Further Reflection

"You shall have no other gods before Me." (First Commandment)

- Put yourself in the lonely story of Psalm 22. Jesus is the Person of that psalm – Matthew 27:46.
- Amidst fearful things, fear the Lord – Psalm 22:23-26
- "In the midst of the congregation I will praise you" (Psalm 22:22)

"I believe in the Holy Spirit, the Holy Christian Church." (Apostles' Creed, Third Article)

- What is the Church? Romans 12:4-5; 1 Corinthians 12:12-14, 26-27
- What does the Church do? Matthew 18:18-20; Acts 2:42-47; Acts 6:1-7; 2 Corinthians 1:1-4; 2 Corinthians 9:6-12; Galatians 6:9-10
- Dietrich Bonhoeffer: "Christianity means community through Jesus Christ and in Jesus Christ. … Whether it be a brief, single encounter or the daily fellowship of years, Christian community is only this. We belong to one another only through and in Jesus Christ."[4]

Jesus, whelmed in fears unknown,
With our evil left alone,
While no light from heav'n is shown:
Hear us, holy Jesus.

When we seem in vain to pray
And our hope seems far away,

In the darkness be our stay:
Hear us, holy Jesus.

Though no Father seem to hear,
Though no light our spirits cheer,
May we know that God is near:
Hear us, holy Jesus.[5]

Retrospective

The purpose of this sermon was to give godly encouragement to people struggling with their "lonely battles." Loneliness is not the same thing as solitude. You can be alone but all is well with your soul, but you can also be lonely, crying on the inside for help, even amidst a crowd. Just as he did tempting Jesus, the devil seizes onto our loneliness. If he can convince us we are really alone – "Nobody knows the trouble I've seen"[6] – then he's prying us away from God and from fellow believers, members of the Body of Christ whom God provides to be there with us, around us, and uphold us in our lonely struggles.

American culture today is hyper-individualistic, and it's making our loneliness worse. Entertainment celebrities, star athletes, and newsmakers are shoved in our face, day-in and day-out. Without thinking things through, we react by comparing ourselves to these media-created images and are tempted to think less of our lives. All this comes at us 24/7 in a tsunami from the electronic devices that, yes, on the one hand bring us togetherness, but on the other hand bring us only virtual togetherness. Our devices don't give us intimacy with family, friends, and fellow believers. We phone, we text, we FaceTime and Facebook, but the cold devices don't substitute for true human presence, for listening ears, warm hugs, and a real place to open up safely. In fact, our devices can seduce us into voyeurism, peeking into the lives of people who themselves often post because they are not at peace being alone. Our culture is characterized by isolating individualism on steroids.

Jesus had His "lonely battles," struggles He was called to face but, best I can tell, He was never in despair when He was alone. When He began His ministry, He was alone and tempted, but relied on God's Word. In His ministry, He spent time with others. When some stopped following Him, He asked His first disciples, "Do you want to go away as well?" (John 6:67). His intimacy with the Father filled His feelings toward His brothers and sisters (Mark 3:31-35). When He knew death was coming, He asked His disciples to watch with Him in Gethsemane while He went to pray to His Father. Alone on the cross, He was totally focused on God His Father, even in this text known as "the cry of dereliction." In all this, Jesus loved His Father with His whole being, and He loved His neighbor as Himself. He fulfilled both the First and the Second Table of the Commandments. More than just the model for our lonely battles, Jesus is with us, Immanuel, just as He was with His first disciples. Want help in your lonely battles? Fellow believers, He's with us in the members of His body, the people with whom you worship.

Every day brings to the Christian many hours in which he will be alone in an unchristian environment. These are the times of testing. This is the test of true meditation and true Christian community. Has the fellowship ... transported him for a moment into a spiritual ecstasy that vanishes when everyday life returns, or has it lodged the Word of God so securely and deeply in his heart that it holds and fortifies him?[7]

Nobody knows the trouble I've seen
Nobody knows but Jesus.[6]

People often asked how much time I was given for a Lutheran Hour message. The answer was, still is, that the program was built around the Speaker's message. That didn't mean a blank check, but did mean that the whole program was intended to support the key point from the Word of God presented in the message. When the message had been prepared, it was, still is, reviewed by a professor to make sure that the teaching is true to the Bible and Lutheran confessions. Then it's into the studio to record. When I first started recording in 1989, I found studio time frustrating. Every effort was made to make sure the recording was the best possible, including clear pronunciation. For example, being from Chicagoland, I would say "fer" instead of "for," and "ken" instead of "can." "Dale, you dropped the consonant at the end of the word 'abandoned.' Let's redo it." Never had those corrections Sunday mornings in the parish pulpit! Another reason I found the studio experience harder than live preaching on Sunday morning was reading the message rather than speaking from memory without paper. Because every word had to be correct, the speakers read their sermons for the recording. I found that difficult because I preach from memory, not from paper, and thrive on the exchange of energy from live interaction with the audience. But that all demonstrates the care to make the message of The Lutheran Hour as faithful, true, and clear as possible for you. And when I walked out of the studio, my coworkers ran with the program – including preparing the print version, such as you see here, that would be sent to people who contacted us for a copy of the message. All of this was a bit more complicated than preparing a sermon in Venedy and typing the bulletin myself!

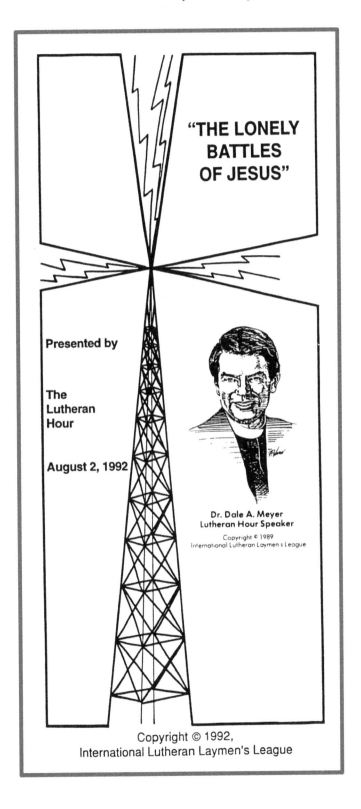

"THE LONELY BATTLES OF JESUS"

Presented by

The Lutheran Hour

August 2, 1992

Dr. Dale A. Meyer
Lutheran Hour Speaker

Copyright © 1989
International Lutheran Laymen's League

Copyright © 1992,
International Lutheran Laymen's League

Week 10 – Time, My Temple

Broadcast on The Lutheran Hour
April 13, 1997

Text – 2 Samuel 7:6

I have not lived in a house since the day I brought up the people of Israel from Egypt to this day, but I have been moving about in a tent for my dwelling.

Text – Exodus 25:15

The poles shall remain in the rings of the ark; they shall not be taken from it.

Prayer

O God, I confess that I cannot begin to understand Your greatness. How often do I look up at the tall trees, the mountains, the sun, moon, and stars, and ponder Your question, "Who created these?" (Isaiah 40:26). Not often enough! Instead, I get caught up in the things of the day: busy, busy, busy. "In returning and rest you shall be saved" (Isaiah 30:15). Help me by Your Spirit to know Your promises are true as I journey through time to eternity with You. For Jesus' sake. Amen.

My name is Dale, and I am a recovering rushaholic. Thanks to Ralph Keyes for that very descriptive word "rushaholism." Keyes wrote in his 1991 book, *Timelock: How Life Got So Hectic and What You Can Do About It*, that rushaholism is "the compulsive need to make haste and fill every spare second with activity."[1]

We rushaholics find ourselves doing everything on the run. We grab a bite of lunch on the run. We talk on the cell phone while we're driving. We do our parenting while we are driving the kids to after-school activities or soccer practice or whatever. We have trouble focusing on one task at a time because we have committed ourselves to so many other tasks. And we Christian rushaholics also catch God on the run. On Saturday evening or Sunday morning, we squeeze out an hour for God by going to church. And because we're catching God on the run, we're not always satisfied with our worship experience. Honestly now, does your weekend worship experience last you through the week?

Some time ago, I did a little creative writing and wrote a memo to God from a rushaholic:

> OK, God, I know Jesus is my personal Savior. That means I'll go to heaven someday, which is very helpful background information. But to bring You up to speed, the world is rushing at me hard and fast right here and now. FYI, Lord, everything in my life is ASAP. Someone put my life in fast forward, and I'm having trouble keeping up. Or, like someone quipped, I'm afraid I'm going to be roadkill on the information superhighway. I need more than Sunday morning talk. I need relevance. Lord, could you hurry and fax me the answer?
>
> Signed,
>
> A Rushaholic

So it is for many of us. We need more of God in the week, and we could do with less stress. If God in Christ broke our bondage to sin, death, and Satan, why are we so often living in slavery to our schedules? The Creator of time and the Savior of your soul wants you to face each day, each week, and all your time as places where He will be present with His abundant blessings. If death and the grave couldn't hold Jesus Christ our Savior, don't let your rushaholism deceive you into thinking that God is confined to a building for one hour on a weekend. My message today is entitled, "Time, My Temple."

Here's something for you to mull over. There is no command in the Bible to build church buildings. Maybe you're thinking, *What about the temple in*

Jerusalem? If you go back and read 2 Samuel 7, you'll see that the temple was David's idea, not God's. In fact, in 2 Samuel 7:6 God said, "I have not lived in a house since the day I brought up the people of Israel from Egypt to this day, but I have been moving about in a tent for my dwelling." As you may know, God did allow a temple to be built – but it was not built by David. David's son Solomon built it. Solomon, wise king that he was, knew very well that you can't confine God to a building. In his dedicatory prayer Solomon said, "Will God really dwell on earth? The heavens, even the highest heaven, cannot contain you. How much less this temple I have built!" (1 Kings 8:27 NIV). J.B. Phillips wasn't the first one to realize that we believers often imagine God to be too small.[2]

Why is it that God does not command us to build church buildings? Hebrews 13:14 says, "Here we have no lasting city, but we seek the city that is to come." God's history with His people is that He's always leading us forward. He's not going to let His redeemed people settle in until we come to our permanent home, heaven. Abraham had a settled life in Ur of the Chaldees, but God called Abraham to journey by faith to a new and unknown land. The sons of Jacob had an established life in Canaan, but God sent a famine that brought them to Egypt and to their brother Joseph. When the Hebrews had spent centuries in Egypt, God led them through the Red Sea and toward a Promised Land. God's history is that He's always leading His people forward. We who are rushaholics often rush around almost like chickens with their heads cut off. We careen from one activity to the next and wonder, *What's my purpose in life? What am I really accomplishing?* God's history with His people teaches us that, yes, we Christians do rush around, but we ought to do so with a sense that in all our activities, God is leading us.

There's a great demonstration of God's forward movement in Exodus chapter 25. When the Israelites were at Mt. Sinai, God gave them many instructions, including the instructions for building the Ark of the Covenant – the place where God chose to show His presence to His sojourning people. That ark was an ornate box with a lid. Among other things, it contained the Ten Commandments. The lid was called the mercy seat, and on the lid were statues of two angels, their faces looking toward the center of the ark. In Exodus 25:12, God said, "Cast four rings of gold for it [the ark] and put them on its four feet, two rings on the one side of it, and two rings on the other side of it." Then come two significant verses: "Put the poles through the rings on the sides of the ark in order to carry it. The poles must stay in the rings of the ark. Never remove them" (Exodus 25:14-15 GW). Why keep the poles in the rings? Just as this time of year sees many of us setting our clocks forward, so God is leading us forward. "The poles must stay in the rings of the ark." This God never falls back; He's springing forward, leading His people toward a Promised Land.

What kind of God led His ancient people and – God being an eternal God – is leading His busy people today? I said that the ark contained the Ten Commandments. Those are the commandments that ancient Israel broke and that you and I break in our thoughts, words, and deeds. Breaking the commandments often causes us to feel guilt and shame, and to experience alienation from God and from others. But here's good news. In Leviticus 16, God gave instructions for the sacrifices on the Day of Atonement. Leviticus 16:15 (GW) says, "Aaron will slaughter the goat for the people's offering for sin. He will take the blood inside … and sprinkle it on the throne of mercy and in front of it." That means the blood of the sacrificial animal covered the sins of the people against the Ten Commandments.

That propels us to a beautiful passage in the New Testament, in 1 John 1:7 – "The blood of Jesus his Son cleanses us from all sin." St. Paul also was thinking of the ark and the mercy seat (the lid of the ark) when he wrote in Romans 3:22-25,

> There is no difference between people. Because all people have sinned, they have fallen short of God's glory. They receive God's approval freely by an act of his kindness through the price Christ Jesus paid to set us free from sin. God showed that Christ is the throne of mercy where God's approval is given through faith in Christ's blood.

So what kind of God led ancient Israel and is leading His Church today? A God who offers forgiveness to all through faith in Jesus Christ.

God continues to move His people forward. The fact that you are forgiven means that your busy, rushaholic days ought to be lived in the hope of eternal life. 1 Peter 1:3 says, "Blessed be the God and Father of our Lord Jesus Christ! According to his great mercy, he has caused us to be born again to a living hope through the resurrection of Jesus Christ from the dead." That is why we have church buildings. It's not that God commanded us to build churches, but because

God commands His people to preach, teach, and hear His word. Deuteronomy 6:6 (GW) – "Take to heart these words that I give you today." Colossians 3:16 – "Let the word of Christ dwell in you richly." In John 8:47 Jesus says, "Whoever is of God hears the words of God," and then Jesus adds a sobering thought for anyone who neglects the word of forgiveness: "The reason why you do not hear them is that you are not of God." Romans 10:17 (GW) – "So faith comes from hearing the message, and the message that is heard is what Christ spoke." So, yes, we do build churches so the Word of Jesus Christ can be proclaimed. Through that Word, the Spirit of God delivers the forgiveness of sins, creates a lively hope for the future, and works saving faith in you. However, that's not the end of the story.

The ark was eventually destroyed. The temple that Solomon built was eventually destroyed. Our churches, from the most awesome cathedrals to the beloved church on the plains, will one day be no more. Remember, "Here we have no lasting city, but we seek the city that is to come" (Hebrews 13:14). When Jesus was raised from the dead, He didn't retire. He didn't say, *My work is all done; I can withdraw from the lives of My people*. When Jesus ascended, He didn't enter retirement. Today, He gives His Holy Spirit, who works faith through the Word of the Gospel. He's going to keep proclaiming that Good News until you and I see Him. And He has promised that He will come and we will see Him. The angel on the mount of ascension said, "Jesus, who was taken up from you into heaven, will come in the same way as you saw him go into heaven" (Acts 1:11). Jesus Himself earlier had said in John 14:3, "If I go and prepare a place for you, I will come again and will take you to myself, that where I am you may be also." We may be rushaholics, always on the go. We are also God's people who should be living with a sense of eternal direction. We are always springing forward toward the Promised Land, our eternal rest in heaven.

So, your life and mine is a journey through this world toward eternity. That suggests that the times of our lives – the days, the weeks, all the years – should be thought of as a temple: *time, my temple*. I'm suggesting today that you think of time as a magnificent temple, in which God meets and leads His people day by day in forgiveness and in the hope of glory. Thinking of time as a temple in which you are living is a much better concept than thinking of time as a thing. Thinking of time as a thing is the popular view, one which Christians have adopted when they talk about the "stewardship of time." But time isn't so much a thing as it is the place where we live. Things will survive your death, but when you die, time for you will be no more. Things are specifically treated by God in the commandment that says, "Thou shalt not steal" (Exodus 20:15 KJV), but time isn't mentioned there. Time has a commandment all its own. God views the times of your life as something so important that after He gave the First Commandment ("Thou shalt have no other gods before me" – Exodus 20:3 KJV), and after He gave the Second Commandment ("Thou shalt not take the name of the LORD thy God in vain" – Exodus 20:7 KJV), God next gave that commandment about how you manage your time: "Remember the sabbath day, to keep it holy" (Exodus 20:8 KJV). In a previous message about time, I taught that we Christians have a different way of telling time. Today, I'm teaching that time is not so much a thing as it is a temple in which God makes us holy by all our contacts with His Word – and we respond with all our activities throughout the week.

If you've ever visited a magnificent cathedral, you've probably not only admired the beauty and grandeur of the building but you've also wandered through all the nooks and crannies of that magnificent construction. You admired the high altar, the focal point of the whole cathedral, but you also walked in the transepts, the balcony, the smaller chapels, and all the other parts that contribute to such a great house of worship. The times of your life should be like that. The focal point of your temple of time is the altar of Christ's sacrifice on Calvary's cross for your sins. That forgiveness and the hope of His resurrection come to you each Lord's day through the preaching of His Word and the administration of the Holy Sacraments. But during the week, you go into the nooks and crannies of your life, doing all the things that you do, but always remembering that your whole life is a temple in which God is meeting and leading His people. As Paul encourages the Corinthians, so you and I want our whole week to be praise to God. 1 Corinthians 10:31 says, "So, whether you eat or drink, or whatever you do, do all to the glory of God."

Earlier in the message, I had a memo to God from a rushaholic. If God would fax a memo back, it might go something like this:

To: Rushaholic

From: God

Re: Your memo

Thanks for contacting Me. Feel free to do it more often. You want more of My goodness through the week and less of the world's stress? I can do that for you. I think I've already addressed your concerns in My book. See especially the chapter called Exodus 20. You'll notice in those commandments that I never asked for churches to be built. I do ask that the people I have redeemed will love Me with their minds and hearts, with the words of their lips, and with the way they manage their time. Give it some thought and, as I said, I hope to hear from you again.

Signed,

God

That, as I said, is just some creative writing based upon what I've learned about time from my study of the Bible. Another time, I'll talk about how important it is for you to take time off. Until then, think of time as a temple.

Amen.

For Further Reflection

"Remember the Sabbath day by keeping it holy." (Third Commandment)

- True worship is not compartmentalized to one day – Galatians 4:10-11. True worship is a totally Christ-centered life – Matthew 16:24-26; Galatians 2:20.
- The command "Remember" does teach us to distinguish the days and seasons of our heavenward journey – Exodus 20:8-11; Ecclesiastes 3:1-8; Psalm 90:12
- A negative example: Put yourself in the story of people who lost sight of their goal, the Promised Land – Hebrews 3-4; Romans 15:4
- True fear and love of God on our heavenward way: Awe before the Creator of all (Isaiah 66:1-2) and our eager waiting to see our Savior (Hebrews 9:27-28; 1 Peter 1:3-9)

- We're on the way! Psalm 46:10; Psalm 122:1; Psalm 84

> *Then let our songs abound,*
> *And ev'ry tear be dry;*
> *We're marching through Immanuel's ground,*
> *We're marching through Immanuel's ground*
> *To fairer worlds on high,*
> *To fairer worlds on high.*
>
> *We're marching to Zion,*
> *Beautiful, beautiful Zion;*
> *We're marching upward to Zion,*
> *The beautiful city of God.*[3]

Retrospective

If there seems to be lethargy in today's Church, it may be because we've lost our sense of pilgrimage. We are living in a time of immediacy, our frenetic rushaholism even greater today than 20 years ago when this sermon aired. Communication is instantaneous around the world. Credit enables me to have anything I want right now. I'm conditioned to escape unpleasant things as quickly as possible. I imagine I can pretty well manage my life with my smartphone. We've lost our sense of journeying to the eternal. Or have we willingly given it up?

To this here-and-now time in which we try to cope, couple the tendency of some preachers to talk exclusively about Jesus' death and resurrection, which was oh, so long ago. Crucial as that first-century history is, there's more. Jesus' ascension, His pouring out of the Spirit not just on Pentecost but today through Word and Sacrament, the promise that He will return as judge of living and dead and take His faithful to the eternal joys of heaven... all these should make us look forward. We tell our seminarians that we are not preparing them to become the curators of church museums. Museums are nice, but not many people want to go to a museum every Sunday morning. Church buildings are so set in one place. No, keep the poles in the rings! We're pilgrims in God's creation and the Spirit is leading us to see our Savior face to face. I want our graduates to inspire us with the indescribable heavenly future opened to us by Jesus' death and resurrection. Students, lead us to be forward-looking and hopeful! Make Jeremiah 29:11 a theme of your theology and ministry.

Christian life as pilgrimage makes more and more sense to me. I feel it in my bones, literally. Having attained "three score years and ten," as the King James puts it in Psalm 90:10, the greatest adventure of all is before me. Pastors and ministries are like the helpful people who stand alongside the course of a 10K race, offering water and encouragement. I see myself with Abraham journeying to an unknown land, with Jacob and family sojourning in Egypt and their descendants led through the wilderness by the pillar of cloud and fire... I'm in that story, and sooner or later will come to the Jordan, trusting Jesus to lead and welcome me into the Promised Land.

> *Run the straight race through God's good grace;*
> *Lift up your eyes, and seek His face.*
> *Life with its way before us lies;*
> *Christ is the path, and Christ the prize.*[4]

Week 11 – The Triumph Song

Palm Sunday
Broadcast on The Lutheran Hour
March 27, 1994

Text – 1 John 4:4

Little children, you are from God and have overcome them, for he who is in you is greater than he who is in the world.

Prayer

O Holy Spirit, help us discern the seasons of life. In unbounded times of youth and in the productivity of adult years, caution us with the eternal word, "For everything there is a season" (Ecclesiastes 3:1). When optimism and energy wane as we age, help us hear ever more clearly the ever-nearing triumph song, hosannas made eternal by the sacrifice of our Savior for our sins and for our eternal life. Amen.

Aging is like the songs of Holy Week. Palm Sunday is the beginning of Holy Week. It's the day that Jesus rode into Jerusalem. The crowds gathered; some placed their coats on the road before Jesus, and others threw palm branches before Him (Mark 11:8). They joyfully and loudly shouted "Hosanna!" (Mark 11:9), for they were expecting Jesus to do great things.

Ah, but in a few days, those hosannas were gone. Jesus hadn't reestablished an earthly kingdom. He hadn't thrown the Romans out of Jerusalem. He hadn't liberated the people. He hadn't lived up to the hype. The hosannas were gone.

Not only gone, but they gave way to other sounds. "Crucify him, crucify him!" (John 19:6) some called out. That's exactly what they did. On a hill just outside the city, a hill called Calvary or Golgotha, Christ was executed along with two criminals. No hosannas that day, which we now call Good Friday. The next day, Holy Saturday, obviously wasn't filled with hosannas, either.

The people who had hoped in Christ felt bitterly disappointed. One disciple put it this way: "We had hoped that he was the one to redeem Israel" (Luke 24:21). Their grief was understandable. After all, it seemed they had lost, and that the world had won. The only thing to do now was save their own necks by staying clear of the authorities. Beyond that, they'd get on with their lives and try to blend in with the world around them.

What those disciples didn't know on Good Friday or on Holy Saturday was that Easter was coming. On the third day, Christ rose from the dead! First some women who had followed Christ, then some men, then more and more believers, hundreds of thousands, eventually millions of Christ's people sang the song of triumph. Christ had conquered death. The Spirit of God that raised Jesus taught the Church to sing again "Hosanna!"

I said at the outset that aging is like the songs of Holy Week. Like the hosannas of Palm Sunday, we often greet age with joy. You've seen the little toddler who is proud to declare, "I'm not a baby anymore!" The adolescent wants to get older in order to drive a car. The older teen wants to get out of the teens and reach the legal drinking age. When I turned 40, someone told me that it was great. "You're old enough to have been around the block a few times," she said, "and you're young enough to still enjoy it." Most people anticipate their retirement. You can wake up in the morning and do what you want – no boss, no deadlines, only freedom. We have so many eager expectations about getting older. It's like the joyful hosannas that were in the air on the first Palm Sunday.

But the hosannas can disappear, can't they? Maybe you don't have enough dollars to do what you always dreamed about doing when you retired. Maybe your health isn't good. And certainly the circle of family and friends gets smaller. I remember a woman I used to visit during my year of internship for the ministry. She lived in Dearborn Heights, Michigan, and told me over and over again how she and her husband had looked forward to retirement. Age 65 came, and he did retire from his job in the auto industry. A few weeks later, he died. This dear woman had looked ahead with great expectation, but the hosannas disappeared all too quickly. Your health can be less than perfect and the dollars fewer than you'd like, but when your dear family and friends are taken from you, when you're increasingly alone in the world, hosannas are hard, even impossible, to sing.

At such times, however, the people of the Church have it so much better than those who are outside the Church. The Bible says, "He who is in you is greater than he who is in the world" (1 John 4:4). That "He" is the Spirit of God whom the Church confesses. "I believe in the Holy Spirit," says the Apostles' Creed. It is this same Spirit that teaches us in the Word of God that Christ had to die. It is this Spirit that teaches that Christ's death is the only way we receive forgiveness and are reconciled to God. And it is this same Holy Spirit who both raised Christ from the dead on Easter and raises faith in our hearts. When a Christian friend or family member dies, it is this Spirit in the Church who puts hosannas in our heart – and in due time, on our lips – with the promise of heaven. No wonder, then, that the people of Christ's Church can sing the triumph song. "He who is in you is greater than he who is in the world."

Pay attention to what I mean by the word "Church." When I say Church, I'm not talking about the names that are in denominational computer databases. Some of those people on church membership lists are hypocrites. In the same way, I'm not talking about countless denominations that can be filled with hypocrites and also with false teachings. There are hundreds of denominations filled with thousands of hypocrites, but there's only one Holy Christian Church, and its members are all true believers.

That's what I mean when I say Church. Again, the creed says, "I believe in the Holy Spirit, the Holy Christian Church." The members of this Church are known only to God. That's why it is sometimes called the "invisible Church." But that doesn't mean it's unreal or only a concept. Though known only to God, the Holy Christian Church is present on earth. Its members are gathered together wherever the Gospel is purely preached and the Sacraments administered according to that Gospel. Martin Luther once said, "I believe that there is on earth through the whole wide world no more than one holy common Christian Church"[1] – one Church with only true believers, not several hundred denominations with hypocrites hidden among the faithful.

Furthermore, there is *one* Holy Christian Church, and not two. There's not one Church on earth and a separate Church in heaven. No, there's only one Church, one Body of Christ, as it is often called in the Bible. Part of that Church, part of the Body of Christ, is on earth. That includes you, I hope, and it includes me. We sometimes speak of ourselves as the "Church militant" – militant because we're striving and struggling as if in battle to follow Christ. And you know how hard it can be sometimes to keep the faith.

But when a believer in this Church militant dies, his or her soul is immediately taken to heaven. The believers in heaven are often called the "Church triumphant" – triumphant because the earthly warfare of faith is over and they are eternally singing the triumph song in heaven. Revelation 7 describes the Church triumphant:

> These are the people who are coming out of the terrible suffering.
> They have washed their robes
> and made them white in the blood of the lamb.
> That is why they are in front of the throne of God.
> They serve him day and night in his temple.
> The one who sits on the throne will spread his tent over them.
> They will never be hungry or thirsty again.
> Neither the sun nor any burning heat will ever overcome them.
> The lamb in the center near the throne will be their shepherd.
> He will lead them to springs filled with the water of life,
> and God will wipe every tear from their eyes.
>   (Revelation 7:14-17 GW)

That's the triumph song of the Church.

Since there is only one Holy Christian Church – some of us on earth, many more in heaven – you and I can share with those heavenly members of the Church in singing the triumph song. That's especially encouraging when hosannas are hard to come by. A well-known Christian hymn, "For all the Saints," reminds us who struggle in the Church militant to be encouraged by the Church triumphant:

> *And when the fight is fierce, the warfare long,*
> *Steals on the ear the distant triumph song,*
> *And hearts are brave again, and arms are strong.*
> *Alleluia! Alleluia!*[2]

I was raised in a place called Chicago Heights, Illinois. I left there to go off to college almost 30 years ago. Sometimes when I go back home, I'm able to attend a worship service at our church (St. Paul's Lutheran Church) and sometimes I also visit our church cemetery. Funny thing about aging – after 30 years away from home, I recognize more names on the headstones in the church cemetery than I recognize faces in the congregation. Aging does that. Our circle of friends and family gets ever smaller.

That's sad in one way, but it also prompts me to remember that those departed Christians and I are together members of the one Holy Christian Church. Though they are gone from my sight, we are still one in the Church, together in the one Body of Christ. This Church on earth and in heaven sings the triumph song, even when some of us on earth are saddened because loved ones have been taken away from us.

My loneliness because friends and family die is especially comforted in the Sacrament of Holy Communion. In that Sacrament, Christ our Savior gives us His true body and blood. Many a time, the liturgy of Holy Communion has the pastor speaking these words: "Therefore with angels and archangels and with all the company of heaven, we laud and magnify Your glorious name, evermore praising You and saying … "[3] Do you know what happens then? The congregation breaks into song and sings: *"Holy, holy, holy Lord God of Sabaoth; heav'n and earth are full of Thy glory. Hosanna, hosanna, hosanna in the highest."*[4]

The people outside of the Church talk around death. *You have the memories of your loved one,* they say. True, but memories aren't enough. *You can celebrate the life of your loved one,* the world says. True, but it's hard to celebrate in the midst of grief. *A person dies and another is born,* the world says, trying to console us. True, but I'd rather keep the one I had. The people outside the Church talk this way, but it's not satisfactory to people who are yearning for life. This world cannot sing the song of triumph in the face of hated death. Only the Church can do that. "He who is in you is greater than he who is in the world."

So I encourage you to join with angels and archangels and all the company of heaven in singing the triumph song. Rehearse over and over again the meaning of Christ's death and resurrection. Reread over and over again the biblical words by which the Holy Spirit gives and strengthens faith in the Savior. Receive again and again the blessings of the Holy Sacrament. That's the way to sing the triumph song.

And when death breaks your heart – when it takes away a dear Christian friend and silences your hosannas – console yourself with the strains of the triumph song sung by our fellow Church members in heaven. Just as the Holy Spirit put hosannas back on the lips of the first disciples who were devastated by the death of their Lord Jesus, so the Word of the eternal triumph song will bring hosannas back to your lips.

Finally, sing the triumph song of the Church so others will hear the blessings of Christ. Many people in our society are aging without Christ. Many older adults are living with no hope of glory. Many do not know that Good Friday and Holy Saturday are followed by Easter. Many older adults are robbed of their hosannas by the death of loved ones, and they don't know the Church's song of triumph. So please, share Jesus Christ with someone who doesn't know Him and the power of His resurrection. Sing the triumph song so people who do not know Christ will be blessed by the same Spirit who turns our weeping into joy.

> *Onward, then, ye faithful,*
> *Join our happy throng,*
> *Blend with ours your voices*
> *In the triumph song.*[5]

Amen.

For Further Reflection

"I believe in the Holy Spirit, the holy Christian Church, the communion of saints." (Apostles' Creed, Third Article)

- Pick a character to identify with as you put yourself into the story – John 11:1-44
- "We should *fear* ... God."[6] A Christian living in senior housing tells me, "People want to talk about death and dying." You can feel terror as a sinner when you anticipate coming before your God (Matthew 27:3-10; Hebrews 10:26-31), but clinging only to Jesus' forgiveness, *fear* of God becomes awe

and reverence that God will bring you *through* the valley of the shadow of death *into* eternal life – Psalm 23:4, 6; John 14:2-6; 1 Corinthians 15:16-22; 2 Timothy 1:9-12.

- Growing in true *fear and love of God*: Historically, "the communion of saints" was not another way of saying "the Holy Christian Church." In early centuries, it meant the sharing, the communion, of holy things by which the Holy Spirit nurtures faith and we encourage one another – Matthew 26:26-28; Acts 2:42; 1 Corinthians 10:16-17; 1 Corinthians 11:26.
- Therefore, worshiping and talking openly about death and dying prepares us, and is our opportunity to witness to true *fear* (awe, reverence) *and love of God* – Hebrews 10:25; Romans 13:11; Psalm 73:25-26

Jerusalem, my happy home,
When shall I come to thee?
When shall my sorrows have an end?
Thy joys when shall I see?

O Christ, do Thou my soul prepare
For that bright home of love
That I may see Thee and adore
With all Thy saints above.[7]

Retrospective

The twelve years I was privileged to work at The Lutheran Hour were years of countless blessings. One was to spend time with Dr. Oswald Hoffmann, the Speaker of The Lutheran Hour from 1955 until 1988. When he retired, he kept very busy traveling around the country and world, continuing to use his unique voice and down-to-earth style in service of speaking the Good News of Jesus Christ. If he was in St. Louis when I also happened to be in town – for I traveled a lot, still do – I'd always stop by his office and pay my respects. I never acted too familiar with him; my respect for his person and work was too high. I was no Ozzie Hoffmann; he was incomparable. At any rate, one day Dr. Hoffmann was telling me about a friend and then, eyes down, said quietly, "He's gone too." He paused, only for a few seconds, but he was thinking about his narrowing circle of friends.

The things of faith get personal for us ministers too. A preacher has to know personally the human feelings that come with the narrowing circle and the prospect of his own death, and a preacher has to let people know that he knows.

> *Someone has said that <u>every preacher must try to give his people … something to feel. No great preacher was ever afraid of emotion.</u> He must give the impression that this thing matters intensely, both to him and to his hearers; that it is in literal fact a matter of life and death.*
>
> *A sermon cannot really be a pleasant and informal chat; it cannot be an innocuous moral essay; still less can it be a formality which has to be gone through. And yet it does sometimes give that impression. Rhadakrishnan, the great Indian thinker, once said of preachers and theologians of the West known to him: "Your theologians seem to me like men talking in their sleep." On the other hand, we must not forget the witness of one: "I preached what I did feel – what I smartingly did feel."*
>
> *The preacher must feel the wonder of the Christian message. Only then can he stab awake the dull and listless hearts of men and women for whom a church service has somehow become a bore rather than a thrill.*[8]

Shortly before he died, Martin Luther wrote, "We are all beggars. That is true."[9] *The narrowing circle of friends and family should not lead us to despair but to a buoyant, lively hope in Christ, who promises to lead us through the valley of death to join the Church Triumphant.*

One day, only a few years into my time at The Lutheran Hour, Dr. Hoffmann was in his office. As almost always, I stepped in to say "hello." "How ya doin'?" he asked. "Fine," I said, but added, "Sir, I've been traveling and people out in the church are talking about you." He perked up, deep voice: "Oh, what are they saying?" "They're saying that Oswald Hoffmann is no Dale Meyer." A momentary pause, and then he burst into his inimitable laugh. He loved humor because he knew life the way people live it. That made his preaching of Jesus such a blessing to millions. And now he too sings the triumph song. His familiar tag line was, "What more can I say than 'Amen'?"

Week 12 – Your Identity: Forgiven by the Holy Cross

Holy Week
Delivered at Park View Lutheran Church, Eldridge, Iowa
March 26, 2017

Text – Romans 3:21-24

But now the righteousness of God has been manifested apart from the law, although the Law and the Prophets bear witness to it – the righteousness of God through faith in Jesus Christ for all who believe. For there is no distinction: for all have sinned and fall short of the glory of God, and are justified by his grace as a gift, through the redemption that is in Christ Jesus.

Prayer

Heavenly Father, You promise me forgiveness through Your Son Jesus. In these next minutes, I pray Your Spirit will sink that wonderful truth deep into my being. My heart is not empty; it is filled with guilt and fears because I am a sinner. Fill my heart to overflowing with the assurance of forgiveness; overcome any distress hidden deep within me; and embrace me as Yours as I stand in awe before the cross of Your Son, my risen Savior. Amen.

Is there anyone here who doesn't realize that the world has changed? This is not the America that those of us with gray hair grew up in. The kids don't know that, and that's one of the blessings of being young – they don't see the changes. But a lot of us do see the changes, and we think, *Oh my goodness gracious, what's going on here?* One of the things that has happened in our very changed culture is people are starting to ask: *Who am I, really? Who are you, really?* So, I want to ask you, in light of all the changes in American culture, where do you fit in?

Several weeks ago, I googled the word "gender" and I came across a list from ABC News that identified 58 so-called genders.[1] Fifty-eight! And you thought there were only two! People are creating all sorts of ways to find out who they are. Some are searching for their identity in their ancestry. Maybe you've seen a TV commercial for a company called 23andMe. Send in a sample of your saliva, and they'll analyze your DNA and tell you where you *really* came from. People are trying to find out where they fit in. *Maybe if I knew where I really came from, then I will know who I am today.*

This Lent, we are seeking to find our identity at the holy cross of Jesus. One aspect of our identity – there are many aspects – is that you and I are forgiven by God. Now, we talk a lot about forgiveness in the church. It's in the air. But forgiveness is a tough thing. It's not as easy as merely talking and hearing about it. Forgiveness has to get deep down; this is one of the challenges of being a Christian. Following Jesus means that we get His forgiveness deep down into our being. You get it so deep down into your being that when people blame you for what you did wrong – and you may very well have done something wrong – you know that Jesus died on the cross for your sins, and you can cope with this criticism for what you did wrong.

Consider how Judas and Peter acted on Maundy Thursday and Good Friday (Matthew 26:57-75). Judas betrayed Jesus, but couldn't get it deep down into his being that Jesus came even to forgive his terrible sin of betraying the Son of God. So Judas took his life. Peter betrayed Jesus too, although not in the same way Judas did. Judas was sorry but didn't believe the promise of forgiveness. Peter also was sorry but he looked at Jesus and believed the promise of forgiveness. Judas despaired unto death; Peter repented unto life.

What have you done in your life that you deeply regret? Cheated on your spouse? That breaks the Sixth Commandment. Had an abortion or pressured someone to have an abortion? That breaks the Fifth Commandment. Given so much of yourself to your career that your family suffered, even fell apart? That breaks the Fourth Commandment. Let an addiction go untreated? That breaks the Fifth Commandment. Pocketed some money at work that wasn't rightfully yours? That breaks the Seventh Commandment. Maybe you haven't done any of these egregious things. Maybe you're sitting here and thinking, *Thank God I haven't done any of those things! I'm a little bit better than that.* Then listen to Romans 2:1 – "You have no excuse, O man, every one of you who judges. For in passing judgment on another you condemn yourself, because you, the judge, practice the very same things." You're breaking the same commandments as those people you might look down on.

So what is that thing in your life that you seriously regret? I have found from experience that when I have hurt someone else, it takes a while for it to dawn on me that I really did something wrong. It takes time. Now maybe we've stuffed that sin deep down inside, and we think it's going to go away because we've deep-sixed it. But it doesn't go away. It lays there, and every once in a while it rumbles and causes us problems. The best thing you can do is to rouse that sleeping monster, wake up that guilt, and face it once and for all, so you can deal with it before the cross of Jesus. Until you bring it up and lay it in front of the cross, it is going to continue to torment you in one way or another – sometimes obviously, sometimes secretly. When it starts to dawn on you that you've done something really wrong, you find yourself churning deep down. "God uses guilt so we feel uneasy about our wrong-doings."[2]

The best place to deal with those deep churnings of guilt is at the holy cross. When you look at Jesus on the cross, there are two things that happen. First, you face the fact that you really *are* guilty. At the start of this service, the choir sang,

> *When I survey the wondrous cross*
> *On which the Prince of Glory died,*
> *My richest gain I count but loss*
> *And pour contempt on all my pride.*[3]

I *"pour contempt on all my pride."* When you look at the cross of Jesus, you should feel more guilty. Jesus isn't dying to, say, save the whales or stop global warming. He's not doing this to give you some entertainment. He's dying because I have sinned, and because you have sinned. That thing that you've stuffed deep down inside? He's paying for that! He's paying the price for what you and I owe the holy and just God. God can't sweep your sin under the rug, the way we do with some sins. "The soul who sins shall die" (Ezekiel 18:4). That's what the Law says. The purpose of the Law is to amp up our guilt. So looking at Jesus on the cross makes us feel more guilty, like looking at someone whom we've seriously wronged. That's the first thing that happens when you look at the cross. But, here's the second thing – and this is what we call the Gospel: You look at the cross and you know that Jesus is willingly up there for *you*. He didn't have to go to the cross, but He knew that His heavenly Father wanted Him to go and set things right between us and our great God. And so you look at Jesus on the cross and think, *Wow! You're doing this for me?* And He is!

There are times when we'd like to turn the clock back and do something over again, and this time get it right. *This time*, we think, *I'm not going to blow it; I'm not going to sin, I'm not going to hurt anyone.* Sometimes these things come up in the middle of the night and they trouble us and worry us, and we toss and turn. *I've made a mess of things. What am I going to do now?* That's the sin that Jesus is paying for on the cross. He's doing it for *you*. So name it. Name that sin you've done that's churning, unresolved, deep down in your being. Bring it up and put it before the holy cross of Jesus. Lay it before the cross so you can hear, *My son, my daughter, it is for* that *sin that I died. Be of good cheer. Your sin is forgiven – period!*

One of the reasons why we should keep coming back to church is that we need to hear this over and over again. You and I are hardwired to feel guilty. Maybe you've had it happen that you've done something wrong, and you come to church and go through the ritual of confession and forgiveness; then you leave, and during the week this same guilt comes back at you. I'm sure you've experienced it. I have too. We are wired to feel guilty. So one of the reasons we keep coming back to church is that when this stuff keeps coming back up, we can lay it at the foot of the cross, Sunday after Sunday, so we keep growing in our faith. We keep growing in our confidence that, yes, we really are forgiven. We come to church every Sunday because we need to hear those words: *You are forgiven.* That's what God intends His Law to do in us – amp up our guilt so we turn to Jesus as our only hope for forgiveness and a fresh start. And that's the wonderful Gospel, the Good News. "All have sinned and fall short of the glory of God, and are justified by his grace as a gift, through the redemption that is in Christ Jesus, whom God put forward as a propitiation by his blood, to be received by faith" (Romans 3:23-25).

When you're feeling bad about something you've done wrong, someone may tell you, "Forgive yourself." Can you really do that? I wonder if that's possible.

If you've done something really bad that is churning deep down – something that hurt another person, let alone breaks God's commandments – then I don't know that you have it within your being to forgive yourself. Try as you might, you still feel guilty. Judas couldn't forgive himself because the only place that he looked was within himself. And when he looked within, he saw guilt. Peter, on the other hand, was deeply disturbed, but looked to Jesus. It is better that I say, Jesus looked to Peter. That's the wonderful thing about looking to the holy cross of Jesus for forgiveness. You're looking outside yourself to God. Forgiveness is not in you; it comes from *outside* of you, from God, from heaven, from the cross, and from Jesus looking at you and saying, *Father, forgive Dale (or Sally or Joe or you)*. So, can you forgive yourself? It all depends on how you look at it. From inside of yourself (Law), no. Judas couldn't. From the outside *into* you (Gospel), yes – just like Peter looking to Jesus – by trusting the promise of forgiveness that comes from the holy cross of Jesus. Inside of ourselves, there's only guilt. Outside of ourselves, as Paul says, "Now the righteousness of God has been manifested" (Romans 3:21). Outside of ourselves comes this blessed assurance that it is well with our soul.

Dietrich Bonhoeffer was a German Lutheran pastor who resisted Hitler and the Nazis. For that, he was put into jail and executed. While he was in jail, Bonhoeffer wrote a poem – a tortured poem. The title of the poem is "Who am I?" I'll just read the very end of the poem:

> *Am I then really that which other men tell of?*
> *Or am I only what I myself know of myself?*
> *Restless and long and sick, like a bird in a cage,*
> *Struggling for breath, as though hands were compressing my throat,*
> *Yearning for colors, for flowers, for the voices of birds,*
> *Thirsting for words of kindness, for neighborliness,*
> *Tossing in expectations of great events,*
> *Powerlessly trembling for friends at an infinite distance,*
> *Weary and empty at praying, at thinking, at making,*
> *Faint, and ready to say farewell to it all.*
>
> *Who am I? This or the other?*
> *Am I one person today and tomorrow another?*

Am I both at once? A hypocrite before others,
And before myself a contemptible woebegone weakling?
...
Who am I?
They mock me, these lonely questions of mine.
Whoever I am, Thou knowest, O God, I am thine![4]

There are many aspects to your identity, but the most important is that you are God's beloved child. Your most important identity is that, by the holy cross of Jesus, you are – deep down – forgiven.

    Amen.

For Further Reflection

"I believe in the Holy Spirit ... the forgiveness of sins." (Apostles' Creed, Third Article)

- Put yourself in the story – Luke 18:9-14. With whom do you identify? Maybe both?
- Have you made the turn of repentance? Psalm 32:1-6; Psalm 130; 1 John 1:8-10; Luke 24:44-48
- Judas' fear of God was despair over his sin rather than repentant hope in God – Matthew 27:3-10; Psalm 42:9-11
- Peter's love for Jesus came because He was forgiven – John 21:15-19
- How awesome, the fear of God in the best sense! Matthew 9:2-8; Revelation 1:4-6

Ye who think of sin but lightly
Nor suppose the evil great
Here may view its nature rightly,
Here its guilt may estimate.
Mark the sacrifice appointed,
See who bears the awful load;

'Tis the Word, the Lord's anointed,
Son of Man and Son of God.

Here we have a firm foundation;
Here the refuge of the lost;
Christ, the Rock of our salvation,
His the name of which we boast.
Lamb of God, for sinners wounded,
Sacrifice to cancel guilt!
None shall ever be confounded
Who on Him their hope have built.[5]

Retrospective

Growing up in the church and then attending seminary, I always heard about forgiveness. What I don't recall learning was how practical forgiveness is for daily living. God pronounces me innocent because of Jesus' death on the cross, but how does that change how I see myself and how I interact with others? That was taught to me by the Rev. Uwe Holmer of Germany. On one of my trips to Germany after the Berlin Wall went down in 1989, I met Pastor and Mrs. Holmer. Their story made a huge impact on my understanding of forgiveness. When Erich Honecker was deposed as leader of communist East Germany, the new regime of Egon Krenz wanted to distance itself from Honecker and his wife Margot, but didn't know what to do with them. Most ironically, the new regime contacted the church for help. The church in turn contacted Pastor Holmer who was leading a social service agency, and, long story short, the Honeckers moved into the Holmer's home for three months. The Holmers did this despite the fact that their family had suffered in many ways from the policies of old East Germany under Honecker.

"How were you able to do that?" I asked Uwe. He then laid out forgiveness in the most practical way I had ever heard. He told how he had to search his own heart daily to see his own sins that God had forgiven. How could he, a forgiven sinner, not forgive the Honeckers? He described those daily meditations as "stillness before God." He showed how not forgiving other people for the wrongs they've done can become a poison to your own soul. When a former prisoner accosted Holmer for forgiving Honecker, Uwe said, true, he hadn't been imprisoned by the East Germans but if you don't forgive, your anger will consume you. To that the former prisoner said, "Yes, you're right." My own understanding and preaching about forgiveness has never been the same since I was blessed to meet and speak with Pastor Uwe Holmer.

This is why our contemporaries, seeking to find their true identity, can only truly find it at the cross. Martin Luther says, "Where there is forgiveness of sins, there is also life and salvation."[6] And the Apology of the Augsburg Confession says that the justification of the sinner by God's grace through faith in Christ "is the most important of all Christian teachings ... without which no poor conscience can have lasting comfort or recognize properly the riches of Christ's grace."[7] Of course, to appreciate the benefits of forgiveness, you and I must know our deep-down sins and humble our hearts in confession!

Week 13 – Christ the Victor!

Easter
Broadcast on The Lutheran Hour
April 19, 1992

Text – Hebrews 2:14-15

Since therefore the children share in flesh and blood, he himself likewise partook of the same things, that through death he might destroy the one who has the power of death, that is, the devil, and deliver all those who through fear of death were subject to lifelong slavery.

Prayer

O Holy Trinity, we praise You this glorious Easter Day for the resurrection of our Savior! Heavenly Father, by raising Your Son, You assure us that atonement for our sins has been accomplished. O Son of God, You laid down Your life and took Your life up again for our eternal salvation. "Thousand, thousand thanks shall be, / Dearest Jesus, unto Thee."[1] O Spirit of the Father and of our Lord Jesus, raise us to the newness of life that flows from our baptism into Christ and assures us that the last enemy, death, has been defeated. Blest and Holy Trinity, all praise to You now and forever! Amen.

You do not have to be afraid to die. That's good news for you this Easter Day.

Quite a few years ago, there was an elderly parishioner in my congregation. A fine woman, she was well along in years and her health was failing rapidly. Everyone knew she had only a short time left to live. Since she was too ill to attend church services – something which she had always faithfully done – I visited her in her home. We'd chat and then I'd have a Bible reading, some devotional comments, and prayer. Although she was a Christian, she would not talk about death. Try as I did to get into a conversation about death, she would not talk about dying. Later on, her family told me that she always avoided the topic of death. Death scared her, and she's not alone. Death can seem terrifying. It wouldn't surprise me if you have been, or now are, afraid to die.

Let me tell you about a second parishioner. Several years ago, this church member was going to have heart bypass surgery. I visited him in the hospital the night before the procedure. We had barely begun to visit when he said, "Pastor, when this is all over, I'll be home. Either I'll be home with my family, or I'll be home in heaven with my Savior." I thought, *Wow! What a wonderful confession of faith.* He wasn't coerced into saying that. I didn't have to pry it out of him. It was a confession of confidence in the face of death. This man was not afraid to die.

You don't have to fear death either, because Jesus Christ is risen. The risen Christ is the Victor over Satan. More than anyone else, Satan wants you to fear death. Satan wants to rob you of Christian confidence in the face of your own death. By leading you into despair, Satan wants to take away from you the assurance of God's love for you. Today, we celebrate the resurrection of Jesus Christ, who – Praise God! – is Victor over Satan. Now, you put your hope and confidence in Jesus and you need not fear death. Are you afraid to die? That's natural. Death ends so many pleasant associations. No more time with your husband or wife; no more time with parents or children; the smiles and laughter, even the pain and tears that make a home – no more. The loss of loved ones can make death terrifying.

Fear death? Yes, when you also consider the pain that might come as you die. Some people are here one minute and gone the next, but many people suffer slower and more painful deaths. That's not a pleasant prospect. It's one that very understandably can make you afraid.

Fear death? Yes, there are even more reasons. You'll be experiencing something you've never experienced before. You know how you feel apprehensive when facing something unknown, such as surgery, travel, or a new job? Death is the greatest unknown you'll ever experience, and that can make you understandably afraid.

Satan knows all of this. Satan also knows something else, something with which he'll try to make you fearful and despairing. Satan knows that you're a sinner who has not always lived the way God wants you to live. Satan knows that God wants – no, it's more accurate to say *demands* – that you be perfect in your relationship to other people and to God. Satan knows the Bible. He knows that God says, "You shall be holy, for I the LORD your God am holy" (Leviticus 19:2). Satan knows that you don't have a leg to stand on before God your Maker and Judge. As it says in Psalm 143:2, "Enter not into judgment with your servant, for no one living is righteous before you." Of all the things that Satan can use to make you afraid of death, this is his greatest weapon: Your death will bring you before your holy and uncompromising Judge. Are you afraid to die? Satan knows you've got good reason to be scared.

The purpose of my Easter message is to make you a victor over any fears of death you may have. You can conquer the fear of death because – and only because – Christ is Victor over Satan. Put your confidence in Christ who died but now lives, and you can be confident that you'll survive your own death. Put your confidence in Christ of Easter and you'll be a victor over that fearmonger Satan. Put your confidence in Christ, the Victor who promises you eternal life, and you'll bash Satan in the head.

The resurrection of Jesus Christ means that the dead body of Jesus, His corpse, was made alive and is still alive today. Christ is risen indeed! The story is told in Luke 24:

> But on the first day of the week, at early dawn, they went to the tomb, taking the spices they had prepared. And they found the stone rolled away from the tomb, but when they went in they did not find the body of the Lord Jesus. While they were perplexed about this, behold, two men stood by them in dazzling apparel. And as they were frightened and bowed their faces to the ground, the men said to them, "Why do you seek the living among the dead? He is not here, but has risen. Remember how he told you, while he was still in Galilee, that the Son of Man must be delivered into the hands of sinful men and be crucified and on the third day rise." And they remembered his words. (Luke 24:1-8)

That's the Easter story. Now let me explain why it is so important as you consider your death.

Your sins have separated you from much of the love and kindness of God. The fact is, your sins made you God's enemy. Such a situation suited Satan well. Being God's chief enemy, Satan is happy when he can put as much distance between you and God as possible.

Though Satan was pleased, God wasn't. No way was God going to let Satan get the best of Him. No way was God going to let death conquer life. No way does God want you to feel forever the force of His anger against your sins. In plain words, God doesn't want you to go to hell.

So God sent His Son into this world. The eternal Son of God, the second person in the Holy Trinity, became true flesh and blood. He didn't just put on a body like an actor might put on a costume. The Son of God literally became flesh and blood.

With that true flesh and blood, the Son of God who had become also a perfect Son of Man did something that we human beings do. He died. And yes, Jesus' death was painful. Not simply because it was by crucifixion (a hideous way to die), but because Jesus suffered in his physical body the full brunt of God's anger against the sin of all people. In those few hours on the cross, Jesus suffered the full measure of hell so that you wouldn't have to. On the cross, Jesus reconciled the holy God to mankind.

How do I know that? How can you know that God is at peace with you because of Jesus' death? The answer is the resurrection! By restoring the dead body of Jesus to life, the Triune God proclaimed to the world that your sins have been paid for. By the resurrection of Jesus, the Triune God proclaims the supremacy of life over death. By the resurrection of Jesus, the Triune God gives hope instead of hopelessness, heaven instead of hell, and confidence instead of fear. Paul says that Jesus "was delivered up for our trespasses and raised for our justification" (Romans 4:25). By the resurrection, Jesus Christ is proclaimed the Victor, and through faith in Jesus Christ, you conquer death.

Do you realize what that means? Because of Christ's victory, you can be free of the fear of death. In the New Testament book of Hebrews we read this: "Since therefore the children share in flesh and blood, he himself likewise partook of the same things, that through death he might destroy the one who has the power of death, that is, the devil, and deliver all those who through fear of death were subject to lifelong slavery" (Hebrews 2:14-15). The death and resurrection of Jesus Christ means that Satan has been conquered. That old enemy who works on your fears, who wants you to throw up your hands and despair, has been conquered by Jesus Christ. Now you do not have to be afraid of death.

You're free – free from the fear of judgment. Your sins were paid for at the cross. The resurrection proves that. When you put your faith in Jesus, God sees you as a holy person.

> *Jesus, Thy blood and righteousness*
> *My beauty are, my glorious dress;*
> *Midst flaming worlds, in these arrayed,*
> *With joy shall I lift up my head.*[2]

You're free – free from the fear of judgment, and free from the fear of the unknown! Now when you think about death, when you think about your journey through the valley of the shadow of death, you know that you have a Savior who has already made the journey and who will guide you successfully into heaven.

Peter Marshall was a Presbyterian minister well known for his prayers. He once told about a mother explaining death to her child:

> You remember when you were a tiny boy how you used to play so hard all day that when night came you would be too tired even to undress and you would tumble into your mother's bed and fall asleep?
>
> That was not your bed … it was not where you belonged.
>
> And you would only stay there a little while. In the morning, much to your surprise, you would wake up and find yourself in your own bed in your own room.
>
> You were there because someone had loved you and taken care of you. Your father had come – with big strong arms – and carried you away.
>
> Kenneth, death is just like that.[3]

That's what death is, waking up in your own room. In a similar way, you can be as confident about going to heaven.

You're free – free from the fear of judgment, free from the fear of the unknown, and free to live God's life now. In his book, *Learning to Die, Learning to Live*, Robert Herhold wrote, "It's too bad that dying is the last thing we do, because it could teach us so much about living."[4] Oh, you don't have to wait to die to learn how to live. Put your repentant faith in your Savior, and you can live confidently.

That applies to all areas of daily living, including the painful things associated with death. It's possible that your death will be physically painful. Your death will separate you temporarily from Christian loved ones. Perhaps there are other things about death that bother you. Do you know what to do when those fears raise their head? The answer is not to *"whistle a happy tune, so no one will suspect I'm afraid."*[5] Oh, no! The answer is go to Jesus, crucified and risen for you! Believe in the Savior who once was dead but now lives. Meet Him in His promise, "I am the resurrection and the life. Whoever believes in me, though he die, yet shall he live" (John 11:25). Be confident! You're more than conquerors through Him who loves you (cf. Romans 8:37). No need to fear death. Jesus is Victor!

Amen.

For Further Reflection

"I believe … in Jesus Christ … The third day He rose again from the dead."
(Apostles' Creed, Second Article)

- Put yourself in the story – Matthew 27:62 - 28:10; Mark 16; Luke 24; John 20. Would you have believed it? Wow!
- Christ bids us not to fear death – Revelation 1:17-18
- "We should fear … God"[6] means awe and adoration that Christ makes us victors – Romans 8:31-39; 1 Corinthians 15:1-11; 1 Thessalonians 4:13-18
- The question – John 11:25-27
- When you answer "yes," that is the fear and love of God! Psalm 116

> *Awake, my heart, with gladness,*
> *See what today is done;*
> *Now, after gloom and sadness,*

Comes forth the glorious sun.
My Savior there was laid
Where our bed must be made
When to the realms of light
Our spirit wings its flight.

This is a sight that gladdens –
What peace it doth impart!
Now nothing ever saddens
The joy within my heart.
No gloom shall ever shake,
No foe shall ever take
The hope which God's own Son
In love for me hath won.[7]

Retrospective

At The Lutheran Hour, I learned quickly not to assume anything about people who wrote to me. Don't assume they're church-goers. Don't assume they're Lutheran. And, as I think this Easter sermon demonstrates, don't assume listeners understand basic religious words and concepts. Twenty-five years after "Christ the Victor!" aired, it's even more true. Preachers in churches and media dare not assume their audience knows the basics of the Christian faith.

The Barna Group surveys the religious beliefs and practices of Americans. In 2017, they identified five popular beliefs about Jesus:

1) Most people believe that Jesus was a true historical person.

2) Americans are divided about the divinity of Jesus: 56% say He is; the rest aren't sure or think He was just a great religious leader.

3) *People are also divided about whether Jesus committed sins: 52% say "Yes," 46% say "No," and 2% aren't sure.*

4) *Strangely, most Americans claim to have made a commitment to Jesus. I wonder what that means, given so much doubt about His divinity and sinlessness.*

5) *Finally, Americans are conflicted about the way to heaven – good works or faith.*[8]

That was such an eye-opener that I got copies of Barna Trends 2017 for the faculty and Board of Regents of Concordia Seminary. I have used it in the preaching class I teach, and I know that other professors use the information as well. Knowing your audience is key to Christian witness in any age, but is especially challenging when long-time believers ignore the changes in American religious belief. Ignoring our cultural context is a lack of Christian love for others.

So now, more than in the past, sermons need to teach in a plain style. Ancient rhetoricians said that a speech should do three things: teach, please, and persuade. Biblical knowledge and understanding of key faith concepts have eroded among church members, making teaching a more important component of preaching today than back in "Christian" America. The teaching can't be pedantic and boring, lest the people not be pleased enough to come back. And if the sermon is crafted to be persuasive – Preacher, does your sermon have a concrete goal? – the Holy Spirit can ride the words down into the heart and accomplish the conviction that comes only from the working of God. As I reread this sermon, I saw simple, plain teaching. Easter is no longer a time to chastise "Christmas and Easter" Christians, but a day to thank God that they came to church, for whatever reason they came, and to teach them with a smile and infectious joy what the resurrection means for their lives. Can't assume anything about anyone anymore!

Week 14 – Schedule Hope

Delivered at Holy Cross Lutheran Church, Collinsville, Illinois
for the funeral of Mr. James Fulton
January 30, 2015

Text – 1 Peter 1:13

Therefore, preparing your minds for action, and being sober-minded, set your hope fully on the grace that will be brought to you at the revelation of Jesus Christ.

Prayer

Our dear Lord Jesus Christ, You have died but now You live. You have promised that You will bring us through death into life, into a life that never ends – life that is everlasting. We pray, we beg Your Spirit to sink that wonderful promise deep into our hearts. Help us hold onto the hope that we shall be with Jim and one another in life everlasting. Amen.

Irmgard, Christina, Deborah, Dottie, and your families, brother Ed, and all the family and friends, once again we express our sympathies to you. My wife and I have known Jim and your family for over 30 years. He was a great guy – a great guy. What I'm going to say in these next minutes comes from something he said. About a month ago, he called the church office and asked, "What do I have to do to schedule my funeral?" The answer was that you really don't have to do much at all, just wait – and when the time comes, have your family call the funeral home. Well, Jim, the funeral has been scheduled, it is happening now, and here's what the preacher is saying. I'm asking your family and all of us to schedule hope – *schedule hope*. The basis for my remarks is 1 Peter 1:13 – "Set your hope fully on the grace that will be brought to you at the revelation of Jesus Christ."

Before we talk about hope, let's talk about why we are here. We don't know a whole lot about God but we do know some things. One thing we know is that God is the source of life. "In the beginning, God created the heavens and the earth. … And God said, 'Let there be … ' and there was … " (Genesis 1:1, 3, 6, etc.). When Adam and Eve sinned and when we sin… I'm not going to take time to pound on you that we are all sinners. How would you like to have your innermost thoughts and desires known publicly? All right, we're sinners. When Adam and Eve sinned and when we sin, we're rebelling against the God of life. That leaves us nothing but death. That's why we're here. "The wages of sin is death" (Romans 6:23a). Jesus Christ comes and reverses that. He is Son of God and Son of Man, human and divine. When He died on the cross on Good Friday, He endured God's punishment for our sin. "For Christ also suffered once for sins, the righteous for the unrighteous, that he might bring us to God, being put to death in the flesh but made alive in the spirit" (1 Peter 3:18). *But made alive in the Spirit.* At the end of that day, Good Friday, He was dead. They buried His remains, just as we bury Jim's remains. But if Jesus successfully paid the price of our sins – remember, our sins bring death – then death should give way to life. Presto! Easter! "Death is swallowed up in victory" (1 Corinthians 15:54). *Sin takes us from life into death; Jesus takes us from death into life.* "The wages of sin is death, but the free gift of God is eternal life in Christ Jesus our Lord" (Romans 6:23).

You and I are on our way to everlasting life. Let's learn how it goes from your husband and father. He believed and was baptized into Jesus Christ. Sin has taken its toll; he has died. But his soul, his being, is now with God in eternity. And on the Last Day, the day of Christ's glorious reappearance, his body will be raised, a glorified body to be reunited with the soul – and Jim Fulton will have received life without end. That's what we believe is ahead of us – ahead of us who trust that Jesus paid for our sins, who trust that Jesus leads us through death into life. That's why the Bible says, "Set your hope fully on the grace that will be brought to you at the revelation of Jesus Christ" (1 Peter 1:13). In other words, schedule hope. In your grief, you feel like your life is ended. Schedule hope. Don't just feel your emptiness; fill your emptiness with hope. Don't just remember the past; look forward to the coming heavenly reunion. *Schedule hope!*

Let me give you an illustration about hope. This will sound silly, but it will make the point. You're sleeping, but at some time your head wakes up. Sooner or later your head tells your body that it's time to get up, and you do. Your head doesn't leave your body in bed. I mean, you all seem to have brought your bodies with you, didn't you? Your heads aren't here without your bodies. With that in mind – I said it sounds silly, but here comes the point – the Bible describes us believers as the Body of Christ (1 Corinthians 12:12-31). He's the head; we're the members of the body (Ephesians 5:23). On Easter the Head rose, and sooner or later He's going to raise His members, raise us from the bed of death into life. That's the day of His return, and it enables us to live the days ahead in hope. Where our head is, there shall we be also. "Because I live, you also will live" (John 14:19). "Set your hope fully on the grace that will be brought to you at the revelation of Jesus Christ" (1 Peter 1:13). *Schedule hope!*

Scheduling hope is not only for the bereaved. This big hope fills us with smaller hopes for every day. Are you struggling with unemployment or under-employment? Schedule hope into your struggles. Are you contending with physical problems? Schedule hope into your pain and weakness. Are you anxious? Are you worried? Schedule hope. Are you lonely? Schedule hope. "Blessed be the God and Father of our Lord Jesus Christ! According to his great mercy, he has caused us to be born again to a living hope through the resurrection of Jesus Christ from the dead, to an inheritance that is imperishable, undefiled, and unfading, kept in heaven for you" (1 Peter 1:3-4). Schedule that big hope into all that you experience and suffer in your daily life.

Martin Luther said that the Gospel, the Good News, hasn't been preached unless we talk about the resurrection of Jesus Christ and our future resurrection to be with Him.[1] A poet named Martin Schalling put it this way:

Lord, Thee I love with all my heart;
I pray Thee, ne'er from me depart,
With tender mercy cheer me.
Earth has no pleasure I would share,
Yea, heav'n itself were void and bare
If Thou, Lord, were not near me.
And should my heart for sorrow break, [It has, hasn't it? Oh, so
    painfully!]

My trust in Thee no one could shake.
Thou art the portion I have sought;
Thy precious blood my soul has bought.
Lord Jesus Christ, my God and Lord, my God and Lord,
Forsake me not! I trust Thy Word.

Lord, let at last Thine angels come,
To Abram's bosom bear me home,
That I may die unfearing;
And in its narrow chamber keep
My body safe in peaceful sleep
Until Thy reappearing.
And then from death awaken me
That these mine eyes with joy may see,
O Son of God, Thy glorious face,
My Savior and my fount of grace,
Lord Jesus Christ, my prayer attend, my prayer attend,
And I will praise Thee without end.[2]

Closing Prayer

"Why are you cast down, O my soul, and why are you in turmoil within me?"
(Psalm 42:5).

My God, You know why I'm cast down! My heart has been taken from me by the death of my loved one. Cruel, merciless death! Sadness smothers my life and grief has hollowed me. The minutes seem like hours. Oh, I need hope! Give me just a spark, just a flicker to get me through this day. In the slowness of this sad time, let hope be kindled and begin to fill my empty soul. Let not my tears quench the hope that will bring me through this time.

"Hope in God; for I shall again praise him, my salvation and my God"
(Psalm 42:11).

Amen.

For Further Reflection

"I believe in … the resurrection of the body, and the life everlasting."
(Apostles' Creed, Third Article)

- The Bible teaches the resurrection of the body, but to what kind of life? Where would you want to be in this parable of Jesus? Luke 16:19-31.
- Yes, the wrong side of eternity is horrifying but it is possible – Matthew 25:34, 41; John 5:24-29; Revelation 1:5-7
- "They have Moses and the prophets; let them hear them" (Luke 16:29). Faith trusts God's Word of forgiveness for Jesus' sake. Sincerely saying, "I believe," your soul will go to the Lord at death – Luke 23:43; Revelation 14:12-13.
- Your body? It will be raised glorified on the Last Day for life everlasting – Job 19:25-27; 1 Corinthians 15:35-49; 1 Thessalonians 4:13-18
- Trusting the Gospel makes the terror of hell give way to awe, reverence, and true fear and love of God – Psalm 16:8-11; John 10:24-30; 1 Peter 1:9

> *I am content! My Jesus ever lives,*
> *In whom my heart is pleased.*
> *He has fulfilled the Law of God for me,*
> *God's wrath He hath appeased.*
> *Since He in death could perish never,*
> *I also shall not die forever.*
> *I am content! I am content!*
>
> *I am content! At length I shall be free,*
> *Awakened from the dead,*
> *Arising glorious evermore to be*
> *With You, my living head.*
> *The chains that hold my body, sever;*
> *Then shall my soul rejoice forever.*
> *I am content! I am content!*[3]

Retrospective

When the church office told me Mr. Fulton had asked how to schedule his funeral, I knew I had the title for this sermon. Over and over I stress to students how helpful a title can be for the sermon. It's helpful for hearers, especially when the title is printed in the worship folder. People sit down in church and look over the bulletin. When they see the title of the sermon, they start thinking about the sermon topic. It's like a hook on which they can begin to hang their thoughts. A title also helps focus the pastor on what he's going to say about the biblical text, especially when he disciplines himself to make sure that every paragraph relates in some direct way to the title. The theological content of the sermon comes from the Word of God but the outline should come out of the sermon's central thought, pointed to by the title. It's a discipline that helps toward clearer communication of the Word. The Greek philosopher Plato complained that public "speakers seldom define the topic of debate."[4] Now whenever I see Mrs. Fulton, I know that in some small way the title helped her set her "hope fully on the grace that will be brought to you at the revelation of Jesus Christ" (1 Peter 1:13).

Week 15 – Happy Coping

Delivered at Holy Cross Lutheran Church, Collinsville, Illinois
February 10, 1985

Text – Psalm 112

Praise the LORD!
Blessed is the man who fears the LORD,
    who greatly delights in his commandments!
His offspring will be mighty in the land;
    the generation of the upright will be blessed.
Wealth and riches are in his house,
    and his righteousness endures forever.
Light dawns in the darkness for the upright;
    he is gracious, merciful, and righteous.
It is well with the man who deals generously and lends;
    who conducts his affairs with justice.
For the righteous will never be moved;
    he will be remembered forever.
He is not afraid of bad news;
    his heart is firm, trusting in the LORD.
His heart is steady; he will not be afraid,
    until he looks in triumph on his adversaries.
He has distributed freely; he has given to the poor;
    his righteousness endures forever;
    his horn is exalted in honor.
The wicked man sees it and is angry;
    he gnashes his teeth and melts away;
    the desire of the wicked will perish!

Prayer

O Lord, my God and my Savior, I'm not the only one with problems. I'm awed by Your promise to be with me in the struggles of my life. Sometimes I'm in a bad way because of my own sin. Help me confess my sin sincerely, and with Your help amend my sinful life. Other times I have problems even though I haven't done anything wrong; it's just a sinful world. By Your Spirit, increase my confidence that You are with me in my life. You give us Jesus to forgive us and be our helper in every need. May I always be awed that You love and help me so much. Amen.

This text describes someone who has it all together, someone who is happily coping with life. That's what I want to talk about – happy coping. I don't just want to talk about coping, because everyone copes. Some do it better than others. Some sail through life without a care. Some use doctors and counselors and ministers. Everyone has a way of coping. I want to talk about Christian coping – facing the problems in your life as a redeemed child of God.

The first thing we have to admit is that *all of God's children have problems.* Yesterday morning, when I was watching cartoons with the kids, I was impressed by the cereal commercials. "It's going to be a Golden Grahams day." Or there's the one where a guy wakes up with dreams of going to McDonald's for breakfast. You get the impression that the right breakfast will eliminate all problems. Those of you with small children are familiar with Mr. Rogers. *"It's a beautiful day in this neighborhood... "*[1] Mr. Rogers never has any problems – or does he? *All of God's children have problems.* And if we look at Psalm 112, the psalm of this man who is happily coping, we see that he has problems too. Verse 2 says, "His offspring will be mighty in the land." Do you think those children ever needed their diapers changed? Do you think they ever cried in the middle of the night? Do you think they caused him some gray hairs? Sure they did. *All of God's children have problems.* Verse 4 says, "Light dawns in the darkness for the upright." That means that there were times when things got pretty dark for this man. *All of God's children have problems.* Verse 5 says, "It is well with the man who deals generously and lends." What does that mean? It means that he gave to help others. I'm sure that the devil was there, saying, "Hey, you can't afford to give to others; you need to take care of yourself!" *All of God's children have problems.* Verse 7 says, "He is not afraid of bad news." That implies that there were times in his life when he heard bad news. *All of God's children have problems.* Verse 8 says, "His heart is steady; he will not be afraid, until he looks in triumph on his adversaries." He had enemies. The psalmist had problems. Mr. Rogers must have his problems. Pastor Meyer has his problems. I'm sure you do, too. For some happy coping, let's do some free confessing: *All of God's children have problems.* You do, and so do I.

We can't leave it there, can we? Misery loves company, but no one wants to be unhappy. Some years ago, the man who was then the development director for KFUO gave me a little plastic card, the size of a credit card. It said, "Lord, there's nothing You and I can't handle together." That, friends, is not just coping. That's Christian coping. That's happy coping.

Yes, Lord, there's nothing You and I can't handle together. So, Lord, it's time for us to bring You in. Before a Christian copes with problems, we have to cope with *God.* That's what the psalmist did. Verse 1 says, "Blessed is the man who fears the LORD, who greatly delights in his commandments!" *Fear the Lord.* You shouldn't think that this just means *be scared of God.* We can all be scared of God. Some of the problems that I've got to cope with, some of the problems that you've got to cope with, come because of our sin. We deserve our problems. In "Christian Questions with Their Answers" in the Small Catechism, the very first question is this: "Do you believe that you are a sinner?" The answer is, "Yes, I believe that I am a sinner."[2] Question 4 asks, "What have you deserved from God because of your sins?" Here's the answer, the terrifying correct answer, "I deserve his wrath and displeasure, temporal death, and eternal damnation."[2] But fearing God means more than just being scared. The word for "fear" in Hebrew, *yirah* (יִרְאָה), means to have reverence or to stand in awe. Standing in awe of God is where happy coping comes from. With this big universe, I stand in awe that God knows and calls me by name. I stand in awe that He would let His own Son die for me. I'm surprised when people do me favors – but that someone should *die* for me? I stand in awe that God comes to me Sunday after Sunday after Sunday with Good News, news of love, of forgiveness, of support, of encouragement. That's what it means to fear God. Can you do that? God is saying to us: *With this big world and all its problems, I want to be with you and help you face your problems.* Man, I can cope happily!

"Blessed is the man who fears the LORD, who greatly delights in his commandments!" Happy coping means taking time each day to stand in awe of the God who loves you. We all know that no problem was ever solved simply by throwing money at it. By the same token, work alone doesn't make for happy coping. It takes delight – delight in His commandments. That means time to pause and reflect each day in devotion … coming to church and clearing your mind for worship … coming to worship regularly … praying to God without ceasing (1 Thessalonians 5:17). The more you become wrapped up in God, the smaller your problems become. That makes for happy coping.

All of God's children have problems. The way to cope happily with your problems is to remember that no matter how dark it gets, you are still God's child. You are God's child! He loves you. Take away your problems? He may not do that. But give Him time each day, stand in awe of His love each day, and He will help you to cope – cope happily.

Amen.

For Further Reflection

"Jesus Christ … conceived … born … suffered, died and was buried." (Apostles' Creed, Second Article)

- God's healing promise comes with something physical. Put yourself in the story – 2 Kings 5:1-15.
- Jesus, True God and also True Man – Matthew 1:18-20 (is conceived); Luke 2:1-20 (is born); Matthew 4:2 (is tempted); Mark 3:20 (hungers); John 19:28 (thirsts); Mark 4:38 (sleeps); John 11:35 (weeps); Matthew 27:21-26 (suffers); John 19:30 (dies)
- True God and True Man, He offers us His healing touch – Hebrews 4:14-16
- Sacraments: real things for real people from a real Savior

- The Sacrament of Holy Baptism – "What does Baptism do for us? Baptism works forgiveness of sin, delivers from death and the devil, and gives eternal salvation to all who believe this, as the words and promises of God declare" (Martin Luther, *Small Catechism*).[3]
  - God's deliverance through water commanded by the resurrected Christ – Matthew 28:19; 1 Corinthians 6:11; 1 Peter 3:18-22
- The Sacrament of the Altar – "What blessing do we receive through this eating and drinking? That is shown to us by these words: 'Given' and 'poured out for you for the forgiveness of sins.' Through these words we receive forgiveness of sins, life, and salvation in this sacrament. For where there is forgiveness of sins, there is also life and salvation" (Martin Luther, *Small Catechism*).[4]
  - God's deliverance through bread and wine, Jesus' body and blood – Matthew 26:17-30; 1 Corinthians 11:23-26

I have no help but Thine; nor do I need
Another arm but Thine to lean upon.
It is enough, my Lord, enough indeed;
My strength is in Thy might, Thy might alone.

Mine is the sin, but Thine the righteousness;
Mine is the guilt, but Thine the cleansing blood;
Here is my robe, my refuge, and my peace:
Thy blood, Thy righteousness, O Lord my God.[5]

Retrospective

Would I write this sermon differently today? In one way, yes. I'd talk more about Jesus. Jesus is present in the sermon as the One whom God sent to pay the price for our sins. That fact puts us in awe of God's love for us, which is the biblical sense of the fear of God. After that I went on to say God is with us now, and the way we can be assured of His presence is through worship and a devotional life. Nothing wrong with all of that, and reading this 30-some years later, I found the sermon helpful to me at a personal level. After all, I, like you, am one of God's children with problems.

Today I'd add stories about how Jesus coped with His problems – not problems caused by His sins, He has none, but caused by our sins, which are many. I'd tell how His life of intimate devotion with His Father enabled Him to endure all that He did for us. And I'd lay out how Jesus through His Spirit is very present here and now to help us in every need. This week's "For Further Reflection" section has added those notes of His presence. Jesus' help in time of need is a rich area for pastoral preaching – it's how God is present here and now. I have no picture of God in my mind; He's mysteriously hidden from our sight. I do have a picture of Jesus. In my mind I see His face; in my memory I see Him in all the paintings of my childhood book, One Hundred Bible Stories. My mind sees Him as True God and also True Man. Have you heard people in meetings talk about some proposal and ask, "What would that look like?" Over my years I see more and more that our faithful coping as flesh-and-blood human beings looks to Jesus and thereby we look more and more like Jesus. "I live by faith in the Son of God" (Galatians 2:20). That's what I'd add!

Week 16 – Who Is Your Hireling?

Good Shepherd Sunday
Delivered at Holy Cross Lutheran Church, Collinsville, Illinois
April 26, 2015

Text – John 10:11-18

I am the good shepherd. The good shepherd lays down his life for the sheep. He who is a hired hand and not a shepherd, who does not own the sheep, sees the wolf coming and leaves the sheep and flees, and the wolf snatches them and scatters them. He flees because he is a hired hand and cares nothing for the sheep. I am the good shepherd. I know my own and my own know me, just as the Father knows me and I know the Father; and I lay down my life for the sheep. And I have other sheep that are not of this fold. I must bring them also, and they will listen to my voice. So there will be one flock, one shepherd. For this reason the Father loves me, because I lay down my life that I may take it up again. No one takes it from me, but I lay it down of my own accord. I have authority to lay it down, and I have authority to take it up again. This charge I have received from my Father.

Prayer

Lord Jesus, thank You for being our Good Shepherd. What does that comforting image really mean in our busy adult lives? Help us contrast Your constant care with those things we imagine will see us through life. Our jobs, our families, our resources… all are gifts to us from the Father, but they are not the Good Shepherd. Only You are. Give us Your Holy Spirit so we'll know more clearly how You care for us, and thereby we will love You more deeply. Amen.

You and I have a challenge before us in this sermon. The Gospel lesson of John 10:11-18 is the beautiful and dear image of Jesus as the Good Shepherd. "I am the good shepherd," He says. Our challenge is to understand why this image should be as relevant to our daily lives as it is dear to children. It's cute for kids – *"I am Jesus' little lamb."*[1] But adults? *Church was nice today, hearing about the Good Shepherd, but where's the challenge, where's the bite, where's the truth that gets into your head and makes you think more intently about your spiritual life?* When our children were small, we'd put them to bed at night and say their bedtime prayer with them. On Sundays, I would ask them, "What was the sermon about this morning?" If they could tell me the main idea of the sermon 12 hours later, I knew they got it. That's the challenge – to get into your head why the image of the Good Shepherd is as relevant to the daily lives of adults as it is dear to children.

The English Standard Version (ESV) translates the passage this way: "I am the good shepherd. The good shepherd lays down his life for the sheep. He who is a hired hand and not a shepherd, who does not own the sheep, sees the wolf coming and leaves the sheep and flees, and the wolf snatches them and scatters them. He flees because he is a hired hand and cares nothing for the sheep." The contrast is between the Good Shepherd and a hired hand. The King James translation, 400 years old, uses the word "hireling." That's a word that's still used today – hireling. It describes a person who is paid to do a job and does it, but doesn't care all that much – someone who puts in their time and nothing more. I like that word, hireling. What I like about it is that it's different enough that it can get into our heads. So here's my question: Who is *your* hireling? Who do you look to to take care of you?

Who is your hireling? To whom do you look to take care of you? We all have our hirelings, and a little later I'll tell you about one of mine. To whom do you look to take care of you? For some of us, it's our job and career. You get into work that is satisfying, pays a good salary, and ideally pays some benefits. You look to the company to take care of you. That's changed over the years. People used to work for one company their whole working lives and then collected their pension. That's changed. You can't depend upon the hireling of job and career the way you used to. By the way, I suspect that many of our seminary students look at the job of ministry as a hireling. They'll work hard for their congregation, do their best, and expect that they will be taken care of. Any job, any career, sooner or later proves to be a hireling. Who is your hireling? Maybe it's marriage and family. We have ideal and romantic visions of marriage and family: a spouse who is my best friend and loves me unconditionally, and children who are the envy of other parents. Sooner or later you find out that as dear as marriage and family can be, it's still a hireling – and there are times when they let you down. Who is your hireling? To whom do you look to take care of you? The possibilities are endless. I made the title of this sermon "Who Is Your Hireling?" so you and I will reflect on whom we really trust to take care of us day by day.

A hireling is not necessarily bad. The hirelings I mentioned are good. A job, a career, marriage, and family are very good things: gifts from God Himself. Oh, there are also evil hirelings. If you look to drugs or alcohol to take care of you – and sadly there are many people who do – that's an evil hireling. If you're only after getting as much money as you can, that's an evil hireling. But many of the hirelings we have are actually good things – gifts, as I said, from God Himself. The challenge is to identify who is your hireling, and to get into your head that your hireling won't lay down his life for you the way Jesus did. The challenge is to get into your heart the freedom of knowing that your hireling doesn't own you. Your job, your career, marriage, and family don't own you. The Good Shepherd does. "You were bought with a price" (1 Corinthians 6:20). Identifying your hireling challenges your prayer and worship life. When the wolf comes – when the tough times come, when temptations come – the hireling may not be able to help you. The hireling might even hightail it out of your life, but the Good Shepherd truly helps you. There are some wonderful hirelings that God has given to take care of us, but only Jesus is *the* Good Shepherd. You wouldn't notice this, but that's why we make our pastors learn Greek. The Greek text puts special stress on Jesus as *the* Good Shepherd. He's not just one of many shepherds. He's not another hireling. He's *the* Good Shepherd. He laid down His life for you. He was raised from the dead for you. He knows you. He speaks to you. His Spirit and Word protect you from the wolves of life – wolves who seek to separate you from the flock so they might destroy you. No hireling, even the good ones, can do what *the* Good Shepherd does.

I'll tell you about one of my personal hirelings. I've always been a book-worm. I like books. I like to be alone and think. I especially like to think about how the big things impact our daily lives, like how our smart phones and tablets are changing the ways we act and think. Anyway, when I was younger, I thought that my book learning could teach me the truth about God. I have learned a lot about God; you don't get to be a professor of theology without having a lot of head knowledge about God. Knowledge was my hireling, but I have come to learn that knowledge can't teach me the truth about God. Knowledge doesn't teach us to know God; faith does. Only *the* Good Shepherd knows me and calls me by name. Knowledge can't die and rise for me. Jesus does.

There was one bedtime prayer that Katie said when we put her to bed. I can still hear her voice clearly:

> *I am Jesus' little lamb,*
> *Ever glad at heart I am;*
> *For my Shepherd gently guides me,*
> *Knows my need, and well* [fobides] *me,*
> *Loves me ev'ry day the same,*
> *Even calls me by my name.*[1]

That's what she said, "well *fobides* me." It was so cute and so dear to us that we couldn't bring ourselves to correct her. *"Knows my need, and well provides me."* Who are the hirelings in your life? They may be good things – gifts from God. Just sink it into your heart and daily thoughts that only *the* Good Shepherd knows your needs and well provides you.

Amen.

For Further Reflection

"Give us this day our daily bread." (Lord's Prayer, Fourth Petition)

- The Good Shepherd gave us this prayer – Matthew 6:9-13 (also Luke 11:2-4)
- "Daily bread includes everything that we need for our bodily welfare, such as food and drink, clothing and shoes, house and home, land and cattle,

money and goods, a godly spouse, godly children, godly workers, godly and faithful leaders, good government, good weather, peace and order, health, a good name, good friends, faithful neighbors, and the like" (Martin Luther, Small Catechism).[2]

- Put yourself in the story. Who was this man's hireling? Mark 10:17-22.
- Do you understand? Read Mark 8:14-21. Luther again: "God surely gives daily bread without our asking, even to all the wicked, but we pray in this petition that he would lead us to realize this and to receive our daily bread with thanksgiving."[2]
- "You shall have no other gods. … We should fear, love, and trust in God above all things" (First Commandment with Luther's explanation).[3]

Savior, like a shepherd lead us;
Much we need Your tender care.
In Your pleasant pastures feed us,
For our use Your fold prepare.
Blessed Jesus, blessed Jesus,
You have bought us; we are Yours.
Blessed Jesus, blessed Jesus,
You have bought us; we are Yours.

We are Yours; in love befriend us,
Be the guardian of our way;
Keep Your flock, from sin defend us,
Seek us when we go astray.
Blessed Jesus, blessed Jesus,
Hear us children when we pray.
Blessed Jesus, blessed Jesus,
Hear us children when we pray.[4]

Retrospective

I grew up in Chicago Heights, a suburb south of Chicago. Its population was about 25,000 people in 1950, and I recall farm fields surrounding much of the city. There were several farms in our extended family, so landing in my first charge, a dual parish in the small towns of Venedy and New Memphis, Illinois, was not shocking. True, I didn't know the day-in and day-out details of farming, but field work, milking, and equipment were not foreign to me. I was curious to know more about the lives of my parishioners and so I asked questions, plenty of questions. The work load in those two congregations wasn't heavy – by design, we usually send graduates into places where they can get their feet on the ground, gain experience and confidence – so I sometimes drove tractors and plowed for one of our farmers. That was a hoot! The people saw their pastor driving a six-bottom plow behind an Allis-Chalmers tractor. I know many of my classmates began their ministries in situations with which they had some familiarity, just as I did.

Back then, we wouldn't have thought that going to a rural congregation was cross-cultural. Going to New York City, yes, but not rural or suburban America. Today, every student goes into cross-cultural ministry. Obviously the new pastor who goes into a church-planting situation is getting into cross-cultural work. So is the grad who's sent to a church in decline and afraid this may be their last chance to survive. The candidate sent to a major metropolitan area with many ethnic communities has much to learn, questions to ask. The pastor sent to a suburban church has to learn what's unique about the culture there, not assuming that his previous experience with suburbia gives him correct knowledge of his new congregation. And everyone sent to rural America is heading into a cross-cultural experience, unlike 50 years ago. Rural America has declined in many ways, so much so that in many places it is experiencing problems that we used to associate with the inner city. Every ministry situation today is cross-cultural, not only demographically but especially theologically. People everywhere have God's Law in their hearts, put into the human heart at the creation but blurred by sin. The clear teaching of the Law to illumine sin and bring repentance and the proclamation of the forgiving and hopeful Gospel is not in people naturally; it comes from outside, and the ministry brings it. That makes ministry cross-cultural, theologically as well as demographically.

Ministry being cross-cultural has homiletical implications. Growing up in less-urban and more-rural America meant that the population generally understood much of the Bible's imagery, like sheep, shepherds, and hirelings. Today, kids in the city don't know where milk comes from, don't know the origin of bread and other foods, and have probably never been in the open spaces of the country. And wool? Comes from the store, right? Can today's preacher assume that the images of the Bible are readily understood? And if you want an eye-opening experience, ask a missionary or Bible translator about the difficulties of putting key biblical images into a different culture. All ministry is cross-cultural, and that means that all ministry is stimulating!

Week 17 – When You Raise Your Heads from Prayer

Delivered at Zion Lutheran Church, Mascoutah, Illinois
June 12, 1983

Text – Psalm 50:15

Call upon me in the day of trouble;
I will deliver you, and you shall glorify me.

Prayer

Let us bow our heads and pray. ... *Dear Father in heaven, since You have promised to hear us when we call upon You, help us not only bow our heads in prayer, but also raise our heads after prayer knowing that You have heard us. Because You so graciously hear us, we glorify You for Your deliverance in days of trouble and every day of our lives. In Jesus' name, Amen.*

OK, you can raise your heads. It turned out just as I figured. When someone says "Let us bow our heads and pray," we do it automatically. When you bow your heads, you expect certain things to follow. The minister (or whoever is praying) will address God. He or she may thank God for this, that, or the other thing. Then they may ask God for this, that, or whatever. They'll probably say something like, "In Jesus' name," or "For Jesus' sake," and then "Amen." When you bow your heads to pray, you expect certain things to happen.

What do you expect to happen when you raise your head from prayer? Maybe you never thought about it. But just as surely as you expect something to happen when you bow your head and talk to God, so you should really expect something to happen when you raise your head from prayer. Why not expect things to happen? *You've been talking to God!* There's no one who has more resources, more energy, more love, and desire to help you than God. I mean, He's really interested in you. That's why He gave you the privilege of prayer. That's why He says in today's text, "Call upon me in the day of trouble; I will deliver you, and you shall glorify me." There is no one who can help you in your life like God. Prayer is the place where we go and ask for that help. So when you bow your head to pray, call upon Him. And when you raise your head from prayer, expect great things to happen.

What kind of great things happen? Well, at least two things. The first is that you know you have been heard. He promises to hear you. "Call upon me in the day of trouble; I will deliver you." "Ask, and it will be given to you; seek, and you will find; knock, and it will be opened to you" (Matthew 7:7). "LORD, thou hast heard the desire of the humble" (Psalm 10:17 KJV). God hears.

Not everyone hears what you say. My wife asks me to take out the garbage, and sometimes I hear her and sometimes I don't. You might go to someone and ask them for help, but after you've talked for a while, you discover he's really not listening. Teenagers get frustrated with parents and say, "You're not listening to me!" Not everyone hears what you say. But God hears.

Dr. Luther talks about the word "Amen" in the Lord's Prayer. Luther says, "Why do we close our prayers with the word 'Amen'? … We can be sure that these petitions are acceptable to our Father in heaven and are heard by him, for he himself has commanded us to pray in this way and has promised to hear us. Therefore we say, 'Amen. Yes, it shall be so.'"[1]

There is something interesting about how the Lord made our bodies. We've got bones and joints in our neck that permit us to move our heads up and down. When someone says, "Let us bow our heads and pray," you are able to move your head down. When someone says, "Amen," you can move your head up. Up and down… what does it mean when you move your head up and down? It means *yes*. And that's what the word Amen means: *God has heard my prayer.* Isn't that great? When you raise your head from prayer, you're saying, *Yes, Amen, God has heard my prayer.*

When you raise your head from prayer, you know that you have been heard. And secondly, you give God glory. The text says, "Call upon me in the day of trouble; I will deliver you, and you shall glorify me." When you raise your head from prayer, you don't wag your head in disbelief. You don't wag your head in worry. But you raise your head, and give God the glory. You give God the glory because He has heard you and He is going to act on your prayer. He may do exactly what you asked Him to do. He may not – He may do something different and far better! But because He has heard you, you raise your head and give God the glory. The three lessons that I read earlier from the lectern talk about giving God the glory. In all three lessons, people give God the glory because of what He has done. Jesus Himself glorified God in prayer. In John 17:1 Jesus prayed, "Father, the hour has come; glorify your Son that the Son may glorify you." What a model of prayer! Countless times, the Savior went off by Himself to pray. Countless times, He bowed His head and poured out His heart to the Heavenly Father. Countless times, He raised His head. He raised His head knowing that God heard Him. He raised His head to live His life and give God the glory.

That's what I came here to say. What a pleasure it is for me to be here today. How good it is to know that you and your pastor are energetically doing the work of the kingdom. How good it is to see your smiling Christian faces once more. And how good it is to pray with you, and for you. Amen. That means, *Yes, God hears us!* Give God the glory.

Amen.

For Further Reflection

"Our Father who art in heaven" (Lord's Prayer, Introduction)

- Put yourself in the story: Jesus teaches us to pray to God as "Our Father" – Matthew 6:7-15. That Jesus teaches us to pray "Our Father" shows us to pray with and for one another.
- Our almighty Father (Psalm 124:8; Luke 1:37) hears our prayers for His Son's sake – John 15:7; John 16:23-24. This is why we fear and love God.
- But what does it say about you when fears take over after prayer? – James 1:6-7; Luke 18:1-8
- Instead, confidence in prayer – Isaiah 65:24; Luke 11:1-13; Hebrews 4:16; 1 John 5:13-15

- *"Almighty God, You have given us grace at this time with one accord to make our common supplication to You; and You have promised through Your most beloved Son that when two or three are gathered together in His Name you will be in the midst of them: Fulfill now, O Lord, our desires and petitions as may be best for us, granting us in this world knowledge of Your truth, and in the age to come life everlasting; through Jesus Christ our Lord. Amen."[2]*

Retrospective

This sermon seems shorter than others in the book – for example, the sermons I delivered on The Lutheran Hour. In fact, all of these sermons were of comparable length when they were preached. Lutheran Hour sermons were read and recorded word for word, with no congregation present and no ad-libbing. For sermons delivered before a congregation on Sunday, I write and memorize my sermon almost verbatim so that I can watch the audience as I preach. That way, I can read their faces and enlarge on points where I'm noticing a special reaction. In my first years of preaching, I rigorously avoided ad-libbing for fear of saying something on the spur of the moment that would be proven wrong. But as years have gone by and pulpit experience increased, I do it more, but still never too much! Or so I'd like to think. Ad-libs can make sermons too long, and I confess that I've preached some too-long sermons!

In recent years, my thoughts about prayer have been deeply influenced by Mark 11:24. "Therefore I tell you, whatever you ask in prayer, believe that you have received it, and it will be yours." Jesus says, "Believe that you have received it." Jesus doesn't say wait and worry until God gets around to answering. No, when we believing children ask something of our heavenly Father, Jesus says to believe that God is already on it, immediately answering. In the future, we'll see in hindsight what God did. So when you raise your heads from prayer, you are nodding "Yes," for God is already answering. Awesome!

Week 18 – A Pastor's Prayer for His People

Ascension
Delivered at St. Salvator Lutheran Church, Venedy, Illinois
May 4, 1978

Text – Ephesians 1:15-23 (NIV)

For this reason, ever since I heard about your faith in the Lord Jesus and your love for all God's people, I have not stopped giving thanks for you, remembering you in my prayers. I keep asking that the God of our Lord Jesus Christ, the glorious Father, may give you the Spirit of wisdom and revelation, so that you may know him better. I pray that the eyes of your heart may be enlightened in order that you may know the hope to which he has called you, the riches of his glorious inheritance in his holy people, and his incomparably great power for us who believe. That power is the same as the mighty strength he exerted when he raised Christ from the dead and seated him at his right hand in the heavenly realms, far above all rule and authority, power and dominion, and every name that is invoked, not only in the present age but also in the one to come. And God placed all things under his feet and appointed him to be head over everything for the church, which is his body, the fullness of him who fills everything in every way.

Prayer

O Spirit of God, as Paul prayed for the Ephesians, lead us also to know our Lord Jesus better, that we grow in His faith and love for all God's people. Open our eyes to live in the hope of the glorious inheritance He has gained for us. Inspire us by the blessings of the Gospel to live in the power You give by our baptism and Word of Christ. In this faith and in our love for one another, lift all our hearts heavenward until we, too, shall be with our ascended Lord Jesus in the glory of the Father. Amen.

This text is a prayer of St. Paul for the Christians in Ephesus. It is also the prayer that any pastor will pray for the Christians in his congregation. It is his prayer that you – the people of the Church – will get to know your God much better through the power of God at work among you.

God's power is indeed at work among you. You are all quite familiar with power. All the work you do uses power. It might be electrical power, or the power from diesel engines; it might be muscle power or brain power. You know from experience: the more power, the better. More power to pull bigger plows and discs to work more ground. More power in your vacuum cleaners to make your houses cleaner. More education for our young people means more brain power for their betterment. You are all familiar with power – and you know that the more power, the better.

God also has a power that is at work among you. It is the power that has taken you from death to life when your old Adam was drowned in Baptism. It is the power that helps you grow in faith toward Christ and in love toward one another as you faithfully and regularly receive the Lord's Supper. That power of God is at work in you, too, through the Scriptures, to help you walk worthy of your calling. That is, to lead a life of good works. But this power is like coal – it has to be mined and burned; this power is like solar energy – it has to be collected and converted to a form we can use. There is plenty of power there, but it has to be used, it has to be harnessed. So also God has great power to work among you Christian people, but you don't always use it. It is Paul's prayer for the Christians at Ephesus, it is my prayer for you, that this great power will go to work in your life so you might get to know your God much better than you do now.

This power of God is clearly seen in the ascension of Christ. The story of that ascension was read to you before from Acts chapter 1. Christ led his disciples out to a mountain, spoke with them briefly, and then was raised from the ground up into the sky until a cloud came and removed Him from the sight of the apostles. Now, St. Paul says that the power which is at work among you people here is the same power that raised Christ to the right hand of the Father: "That power is the same as the mighty strength he exerted when he raised Christ from the dead and seated him at his right hand in the heavenly realms" (Ephesians 1:19-20 NIV). The ascension of Christ to the right hand of the Father is a demonstration of God's power. By the way, we might explain what it means when it says Christ ascended to the right hand of the Father. That does not literally mean that Christ now sits on the right side of God. Rather, to sit at the right hand is a biblical expression meaning to be in full favor with the Father, to enjoy full privileges and power of the Godhead. The power that raised Christ to heaven is the same power Christ Himself exercises.

What does this ascended Christ do with His power? Paul tells us that Christ rules "far above all rule and authority, power and dominion, and every name that is invoked, not only in the present age but also in the one to come. And God placed all things under his feet" (vv. 21-22 NIV). God's power has made Christ Lord of all. He is the power above all other powers. His power is greater than the power of the president, Congress, dictators, the Communist Politburo. His power is greater than the powers of IBM, General Motors, and Standard Oil. His power is greater than that of union... or management. His power is greater – and here is comfort for you – than the power of the devil. For, as Paul says, all things have been placed under Christ's feet. His power is greater than all other powers. Now St. Paul prays for his friends at Ephesus, just as any pastor will pray for the people in his congregation. And what does he pray? He prays that this power above all powers, the power of God, the power that raised Christ to the right hand of the Father, might also be at work among you so you will get to know your God better than you have ever known Him before. St. Paul says:

I have not stopped giving thanks for you, remembering you in my prayers. I keep asking that the God of our Lord Jesus Christ, the glorious Father, may give you the Spirit of wisdom and revelation, so that you may know him better. I pray that the eyes of your heart may be enlightened in order that you may know the hope to which he has called you, the riches of his glorious inheritance in his holy people, and his incomparably great power for us who believe. (vv. 16-19 NIV)

With these words, St. Paul folds his hands and asks that you will get to know your God better. He asks that you will get to know three specific things about God. First, the pastor prays, *God, let these people know the hope to which You have called them*. Before God called you to be His own in Baptism, you had no hope. You had no great future spread before you. You had nothing to pull you on through those dark and difficult days that come your way. People who do not know God are people who have no eternal hope. But Pastor Paul prays that you might know you have an eternal hope.

Secondly, he prays that you might know the rich blessings God has promised you. Blessings – think of them! Forgiveness, full and free, for all you have ever done wrong. Eternal life beyond the grave. Unity with fellow Christians, unity with people you may have disliked and hated in the past. Joy, even in the midst of sorrow. Peace, that passes all understanding. Abundant blessings are yours through your faith in the ascended Lord Jesus Christ. And the pastor prays that you will get to know and embrace these blessings.

Thirdly, Paul prays that you might be amazed by the greatness of God's power at work among us. It ought to blow your mind wide open... It ought to make your eyes pop out and your mouth shut up... It ought to amaze you... this great power of God at work among us. If you would pay attention to that power, it would indeed amaze you. Like coal or solar energy, though, you've got to harness the power. Paul prays that you will put to work that great power of God.

That is the pastor's prayer for you. It is a prayer that the ascended Christ also prays to His Father for you. We know that this prayer is acceptable and according to the will of God. The only thing that needs to be done is that you – each one of you – let this power of God go to work in your life. Let the power that raised Christ to the right hand of the Father, also raise you to new and better things.

Amen.

For Further Reflection

"He ascended into heaven and sits at the right hand of God the Father Almighty." (Apostles' Creed, Second Article)

- Put yourself in the Bible story. You're there! Luke 24:51 and Acts 1:9-11.
- Wow! Read Ephesians 1:20-23 again. That's what it means to sit "at the right hand of God the Father Almighty." Are you awed before the ascended Lord Jesus Christ?
- What does our ascended Lord give us, His Church? Ephesians 4:10-12
- Therefore, let your attitude ascend – Colossians 3:1-4
- "Draw us to Thee"! John 14:2-3 and John 17:24

> *Draw us to Thee,*
> *For then shall we*
> *Walk in Thy steps forever*
> *And hasten on*
> *Where Thou art gone*
> *To be with Thee, dear Savior.*[1]

Retrospective

I smiled when I was about to review this sermon – a 31-year-old rookie preaching about a pastor praying for his people. Oh, I sure hope I didn't pontificate in my pastoral immaturity! To my relief, I didn't. What I did do – more than I realized 40 years ago – was speak about relationships on our heavenward way, although I never used the word "relationships." There's the relationship between Paul and his Ephesian congregations. Today people yearn to know and see evidence that their pastor truly cares about them. The sermon talks about spiritual relationships, no promoting church programs or institutional issues. There are times for that, but not too often, especially in the small country churches where I began my ministry. Relationships of power dominate our workaday life, and that was a convenient touch point for the power of God at work in us through the gifts of the ascended Christ. That's a power different from the power relationships that wear us down in this world. Above all, the sermon is about our ongoing relationship with our Savior, about treasuring the hope and blessings that stand us in awe of our ascended Lord. Our faith is not just that Jesus died for our sins and rose again, but the continuing "greatness of his power toward us who believe" (Ephesians 1:19). That 31-year-old wrote words this 70-something still needs to hear and take to heart! Sooner or later we all experience young pastors. As long as he grounds himself in the Word, he'll speak words beyond his years.

As a young pastor in my first call, the dual parish of New Memphis and Venedy, Illinois, I was impressed with the ministry of Rev. Hubert Temme in Centralia, Illinois. I once asked him, "What evangelism program do you use?" He laughed, and answered with his Australian accent, "I don't have one. I just try to make the people feel good about their church." That stuck with me, and I've tried to do that every place I have served. That's the reason for this drawing of St. Salvator Lutheran Church. I came across a company that sold weekly bulletins personalized with the church's name and drawing of the building on the front page, as you see here. Marketers call it "branding." I hoped it would further impress our church upon those who worshiped with us. We did the same for the church in New Memphis, as you'll see from the drawing included for Week 22.

About the name of the church in Venedy — I could never definitively trace why it was called St. Salvator. The first baptism was recorded in 1837 in nearby Johannesburg. Several years later, when they needed a pastor, they got Ottomar

Fuerbringer from the Saxons who settled in Missouri in 1839 and eventually founded The Lutheran Church–Missouri Synod. Fuerbringer was concerned about the doctrinal contents of the hymnal the congregation was using. The result was a division of the church in Johannesburg, with several families going "up the hill" to Venedy where they established a new congregation, St. Salvator. "Salvator" means savior in Latin, which most pastors knew back in that time. We had to know Latin when we were in seminary; it's no longer required today. Saint is English for the Latin "sanctus," holy, but in those days the people spoke German, not Latin. My guess is the new congregation was named Sanctus Salvator, Holy Savior, which became Saint Salvator as English become more and more common. In a similar quirk of translation history, there is a Lutheran church today in St. Louis named Saint Trinity, where saint was also the translation for holy. Rev. Fuerbringer was close to the Saxon leader, C.F.W. Walther, who thought church names should in some way reflect God, such as Trinity, Holy Cross, Zion, and so on, which happen to be the names of the new congregations in St. Louis with which Walther was associated. However the congregation in Venedy got its name, my impression is that its people have felt good about their church throughout its long history. Well, at least most of the time!

Saint Salvator Lutheran Church
Venedy, Illinois **62296**
Box 586

Rev. Dale A. Meyer,
Pastor

Pastor's Phone:
(618) 324-6366

Sunday Service:
10:00 A.M.

Sunday School:
9:00 a.m.

188

Week 19 – *"Mom!"*

Mother's Day
Broadcast on The Lutheran Hour
December 13, 1992

Text – Luke 2:19

Mary treasured up all these things, pondering them in her heart.

Prayer

Almighty God, You were so wonderful to Your servant Mary. You chose the blessed virgin to be the mother of Your dearly beloved Son, our Savior, Jesus Christ. Choosing Mary, You showed us all that You care for the poor and lowly in our world. Make us humble in heart like Mary. In the pressures of life, help us also to receive Your Word with faith and to rejoice in Jesus Christ, our only Savior. Amen.

"Mom!" You mothers have heard that thousands of times. Does your child ever go through the house and look for you? No. Do they ever stop to think that you might be doing something that can't be interrupted? No. Do they ever think you might be tired? Well, of course they don't. *"Mom!"*

I'm sure that you do your best to keep it all together. But there must be times when it all comes apart – times when you let the pent-up anger come out. Even when it looks to others like you've got it together, *you* know what you're feeling on the inside. Life is pounding you. You can't cope with the stress. Sometimes when you hear that cry of *"Mom!"* for the umpteenth time, you can't hold it in any longer. Your anger explodes.

You're not really angry at your child. The poor child didn't suspect that he or she was about to set off a nuclear explosion. Maybe you're mad at your husband. Women have been told for a long time that "you can have it all." Many of you wives and mothers now really do have it all. You've got a demanding job, and you've still got most of the chores at home. Perhaps your husband is a workaholic and seldom at home. Or maybe he's a couch potato who's insensitive to your needs. You've got it all, all right – and try as hard as you do, sometimes your anger explodes when you hear that cry, *"Mom!"*

Or, maybe you don't have a husband. You're widowed or divorced and trying to be mom and dad at the same time. Even most couch potatoes will get up and do something to help with the kids once in a while, but you're doing full-time duty as mom and dad. Can you show your son how to play football? How quickly can you change an electrical outlet? When your car dies, do you know what to look for under the hood? Well, maybe you do and can teach me a thing or two! Either way, I pray that God helps every one of you single moms to keep it all together. But there must be times when you simply can't, and your anger explodes when you hear that cry, *"Mom!"*

The shrapnel from that angry explosion hurts your child. Does that child have a clue about all the things that are churning within you? Of course not. The main thing your child knows is that you are mom, and you're there to help. When you explode, your child really feels it. I remember one time I got angry and used my strongest voice. My little daughter stood there and literally was shaking. I learned from that, and I've tried to put the lid on my anger ever since. But what happens if you don't go to your child and say, "I'm sorry I got so mad…" If you don't explain that you're worrying about something – if you keep exploding and never deal with it – your children are going to start spewing anger too. What's that scientific rule? For every action, there's an equal and opposite reaction. The shrapnel from your angry explosions is going to produce hurt and anger in your children.

No wonder that Psalm 37 says, "Refrain from anger, and forsake wrath!" (Psalm 37:8). Paul writes:

> Put on then, as God's chosen ones, holy and beloved, compassionate hearts, kindness, humility, meekness, and patience, bearing with one another and, if one has a complaint against another, forgiving each other;

as the Lord has forgiven you, so you also must forgive. And above all these put on love, which binds everything together in perfect harmony. And let the peace of Christ rule in your hearts, to which indeed you were called in one body. (Colossians 3:12-15)

You'd like to be that kind of Christian, wouldn't you? We all would. Here the example of Mary can help. The mother of the Christ Child was a mom who strove to get it all together. God helped her. Mary's child, Jesus, can help you get it together too. In fact, your Savior can make you feel like more than a conqueror (cf. Romans 8:37) in the stresses of life.

Mary must have been overwhelmed. She had no reason to expect a pregnancy. After all, she was engaged to Joseph but she wasn't yet married and living with him. Next thing she knew, an angel appears and tells her that she's been chosen to be the virgin mother of the long-awaited Messiah! Mary, a virgin, is dealing with a humanly unplanned pregnancy, but a pregnancy that was planned by God. Overwhelming!

How did Mary respond to all this? You know how you respond to stress in your life. Sometimes you come totally unglued. How did Mary react? Luke chapter one tells us that she left her hometown of Nazareth and spent three months with a relative named Elizabeth. The Bible records something that Mary said to Elizabeth – something that shows that Mary was able to get it all together. She said, "My soul magnifies the Lord, and my spirit rejoices in God my Savior, / for he has looked on the humble estate of his servant" (Luke 1:46-48).

Mary was full of joy! Mom, think about the times when you've exploded – or wanted to. Here's a woman in an overwhelming situation who's got it all together! Do you know why? Because, as she herself said, she was rejoicing "in God my Savior, / for he has looked on the humble estate of his servant."

To get it all together, first you need to believe that you have a Savior. Mary knew that she needed salvation. Many times in Luke chapter one, she speaks of herself as humble, as a servant, as a person of no account in the world. She knew she needed a Savior. We don't need a Savior simply from the annoyances of life: phones ringing at the wrong time, husbands zoning out or even deserting, bills piling up, balancing family and career, and then a child crying *"Mom!"* We need more than that. Mary – like you, like me – needed God Himself to speak to her heart and say, *I see you exactly as you are, and I love you. I forgive you. I'll help you through it all.*

God does precisely that for you in that child, Jesus. God sent Jesus specifically for you. As a child and later as an adult, Jesus did not sin. We sin and fail to meet God's demands, but Jesus is a holy person.

Jesus suffered a terrible death on Calvary's cross. His death was terrible not only because it was a painful crucifixion, but because He let Himself be punished by God, His Father, for your sins.

Jesus came back to life on Easter and is alive right now so you can take all your sins, all your anger, all your frustrations, all your hopes to Him, your Savior. As the Easter hymn says,

> *He lives to bless me with His love;*
> *He lives to plead for me above;*
> *He lives my hungry soul to feed;*
> *He lives to help in time of need.*[1]

God did all this in Jesus so you can say with Mary, "My soul magnifies the Lord, and my spirit rejoices in God my Savior, / for he has looked on the humble estate of his servant."

Getting back now to Mary's story: After staying with Elizabeth for three months, Mary returned home to Nazareth. Joseph married her. When it was almost time for the baby to be born, Joseph and Mary had to travel south to Bethlehem because of a government order. There the blessed virgin gave birth to our wonderful Savior. Shepherds near Bethlehem heard that the Savior was born. They came and worshiped Him. Wise men from the east heard that a king had been born. They, too, came and worshiped Jesus. Mary was still overwhelmed. She still had to keep on getting it together.

Luke 2:19 says, "Mary treasured up all these things, pondering them in her heart." The Greek word for "pondering" – *sumballó* (συμβάλλω) – is similar to our expression "get it together." Mary treasured the birth of her Savior, and she strove to get it all together in her mind and heart.

"Mom!" You beleaguered mothers who hear that cry a million times a day should follow Mary's example. Every one of you – female or male, adult or child – can cope by treasuring what God has given you in the Savior Jesus. Take a

moment (or two or three) – or as much time as you can get, and whenever you can get it – and treasure the Good News that you have a Savior who is present to forgive and to help.

Tell Jesus you're sorry you exploded in anger. Search your feelings and tell Jesus what it was that enraged you. Lay before Him that you feel bad that you blew up in front of your child. Then know – know for sure – what John 3:17 says: "For God did not send his Son into the world to condemn the world, but in order that the world might be saved through him." You're forgiven! God's Spirit works through that Word of forgiveness so you too can say, "My spirit rejoices in God my Savior." Now *that's* the way to get it together!

Every now and then, my computer flashes the words "Please wait" on the monitor screen. The computer is trying to sort things out. Mary spent a lot of time trying to sort it all out, trying to get it all together. You should do the same. Pause daily, hourly, and remember God's program for you. When you're building toward an explosion, please wait. Remember God has given you a Savior, and you can rejoice.

Get it together now, because you'll have less and less opportunity to do it as time passes. *"Mom!"* You're going to hear that less and less. Children come into this world dependent upon their parents. You do almost everything for them. They know it! When the child calls *"Mom!"* he or she is saying, "I'm dependent upon you!"

But that changes. That dependence upon you declines as the years go by. It was that way even for the child Jesus. Mary put the swaddling clothes on Him. Mary laid Him in the manger. The eternal Son of God had become also a true human child, dependent upon his mom.

As Jesus grew, His physical dependence upon Mary and Joseph became less, and it became obvious to them that this child was on a special mission. We have only one childhood story about Jesus. When He was 12 years old, the family went to Jerusalem to worship. When friends and family were returning home, Jesus stayed behind in the temple. Mary and Joseph became frantic when they couldn't find their boy. *Where's our child?* They finally found Him in the temple. "'Son, why have you treated us so? Behold, your father and I have been searching for you in great distress.' And he [Jesus] said to them, 'Why were you looking for me? Did you not know that I must be in my Father's house?'" (Luke 2:48-

49). As Jesus grew up, He became less and less dependent upon Mary and Joseph, and was more and more about His Father's business.

"Mom!" You're going to hear that less and less as the years go on. Your child is slowly growing more independent of you. As your child grows away from you, please, please don't send them away angry. Teach them to grow independent of you, but teach them more and more dependence upon their God and Savior. Your child says to you, "I'm not a baby anymore!" and that becomes the truth. Mom, don't let this child grow up and go away angry. When the pressure is building within you, when you're ready to explode, please wait. Like Mary, treasure the Gospel and ask God's Spirit to help you get it all together – and then thank God for helping you to respond one more time with love when your child calls, *"Mom!"*

Amen.

For Further Reflection

"And in Jesus Christ ... born of the virgin Mary" (Apostles' Creed, Second Article)

- "We should fear and love God."[2]
  - To those who fear God, blessing through mothers – Psalm 128:1-6
  - We live in the love of God because His love for us is reflected in motherhood – Isaiah 49:13-15; Psalm 113:1-9
- Put yourself in these stories:
  - Privileged to raise her child – Exodus 2:1-10
  - Praising God for her child – 1 Samuel 1:21 - 2:11
- A mother passes on her faith – 2 Timothy 1:5
- A mother models devotion – Luke 1:38; Luke 2:19
- A prayer for the harried mother: "Thy will be done on earth as it is in heaven."
- "God's will is done when he breaks and defeats every evil plan and purpose of the devil, the world, and our sinful flesh, which try to prevent us from keeping God's name holy and letting his kingdom come. And God's will is done when he strengthens and keeps us firm in his Word and in the faith as

long as we live. This is his good and gracious will" (Martin Luther, Small Catechism).[3]

O Savior, child of Mary,
Who felt our human woe;
O Savior, King of glory,
Who dost our weakness know:
Bring us at length we pray
To the bright courts of heaven,
And to the endless day.[4]

Now thank we all our God
With hearts and hands and voices,
Who wondrous things has done,
In whom His world rejoices;
Who from our mothers' arms
Has blest us on our way
With countless gifts of love
And still is ours today.[5]

Retrospective

This sermon, originally for Advent, lends itself nicely to Mother's Day. Popular assumptions about marriage have changed in the 25 years since this sermon aired. The sermon you've just read comes from a different time, and from a minister whose audience accepted the value of traditional, biblical marriage. Mother's Day has always been an opportunity to extol the virtues of godly mothers, but this is especially important in our day and age. I have heard of pastors who are so devoted to the liturgical calendar of the church that they will not take time in worship to honor godly mothers and hold them up as examples of why the Fourth Commandment commands us to honor them. Our opponents twist our observances against us. For example, the communists of old East Germany co-opted the church's rite of confirmation with "Jugendweihe," a confirmation into the communist party, and they did so with great harm to the spiritual life of the people. We should take advantage of secular observances to present the Bible's teachings about the Christian worldview and life. Mother's Day, Father's Day, Memorial Day, Labor Day, Thanksgiving, New Year's Day... these secular observances are opportunities at hand for us to teach the Christian worldview. In the middle of the last century, when traditional views of marriage and motherhood were still dominant, respected Lutheran pastor Paul Nesper, wrote:

> *The Lutheran Church, with its splendid arrangement of the church year, is loathe to observe special days of every kind. Mother's Day, however, may well be accepted, and where the arrangement of the church year does not interfere a special sermon on the beauty of motherhood, the sanctity of marriage and home life, the family altar, Christian education, and kindred subjects may well be delivered.*[6]

Paul Clayton was the morning on-air personality on radio station KFUO-AM. He taught me the acronym TOMA, "top-of-mind awareness." When people come to church with something on the top of their minds, we pastors should be aware and speak to it a Word from God. Inspired by the Virgin Mary, we thank God for you mothers!

Week 20 – Word Alive! Connections and Conversations

Pentecost
Delivered at the Chapel of St. Timothy and St. Titus
for the opening of the 177th academic year,
Concordia Seminary, St. Louis, Missouri
September 4, 2015

Text – Hebrews 4:12-13

For the word of God is living and active, sharper than any two-edged sword, piercing to the division of soul and of spirit, of joints and of marrow, and discerning the thoughts and intentions of the heart. And no creature is hidden from his sight, but all are naked and exposed to the eyes of him to whom we must give account.

Prayer

Great God, the promise of Your judgment would terrify us were it not that Your mercy reveals to us the heavenward way. Heard through our ears, seen in the pages of the Bible, we pray Your Holy Spirit take the living voice of the Gospel down into our hearts, so we live before You in reverent fear and love, and through our connections and conversations in witness to all people. For Jesus' sake! Amen.

"And no creature is hidden from his sight, but all are naked and exposed to the eyes of him to whom we must give account." Look at the people sitting around you. All creatures, especially you and I, are naked and exposed before God. That's not a pretty sight, all of us here naked and exposed; it is, as they say, "too much information." But that is the way the eternal Judge sees us – and that should put the fear of God into us all. Now, you certainly don't hear about the fear of God in contemporary American culture – our culture with its omnipresent media reinforcing our self-centered quest for happiness. But you and I are to be different. We are baptized. When you entered the chapel, you may have noticed a small square of granite in the sidewalk right before the door. That granite inlay cryptically says, "Ecclesiastes 5:1." That's code – a reminder that you and I must give an account to the eternal Judge. Ecclesiastes 5:1-2 says:

> Guard your steps when you go to the house of God. To draw near to listen is better than to offer the sacrifice of fools, for they do not know that they are doing evil. Be not rash with your mouth, nor let your heart be hasty to utter a word before God, for God is in heaven and you are on earth. Therefore let your words be few.

Honestly, I also don't hear the fear of God talked about much in church. I suspect that's why mainline American denominations are not growing. To be sure, the global Christian Church is growing. I'm told the Mekane Yesus Lutheran Church in Ethiopia is baptizing 900 people a day, but in America it's a different story. The Lutheran Church–Missouri Synod has lost 18 percent of its members in the last 40 years. Don't you think the devil has his hand in this decline? If the devil can tempt us into indifference about the coming judgment, why would we have a passionate love for the only One who can deliver us from eternal death? If we are indifferent to the fear of God, how can we truly love our God and Savior? You can be sure there will be no indifference when Jesus comes back to judge us, naked and exposed.

> *Nothing in my hand I bring;*
> *Simply to Thy cross I cling.*
> *Naked, come to Thee for dress;*
> *Helpless, look to Thee for grace;*
> *Foul, I to the fountain fly;*
> *Wash me, Savior, or I die.*[1]

There are many temptations the devil uses to make Americans indifferent to the fear and love of God. Let me identify three that *"the old evil foe"*[2] uses to our harm. The first is what I've already been talking about – indifference to the coming judgment, and therefore, no fear and love of our God and Savior. When we are indifferent or only give lip service to judgment, the result is that Jesus and the Gospel are confined to the past. That's so important; let me repeat it: *When we are indifferent or only give lip service to judgment, the result is that Jesus and the Gospel are confined to the past.* Now to be sure, what Jesus did during His visible ministry is the source and essence of our salvation, but if we only talk about it as a first-century event, we end up being curators of a museum instead of proclaimers of something awesome now and for eternity. Do you think it's possible that people may not be coming to our churches because they don't like going to museums? I do know people who like to go to museums, but most of them don't go every week. The devil doesn't mind us saying that Jesus died for our sins as long as we leave it in the past, in the museum, and are indifferent to His return in judgment. That's the devil's first way of weakening the Church.

The second temptation is the word "Church." What pops into your mind when I say the word "Church"? Maybe you think of the building. Maybe you think of a church service: *I'm going to 8 o'clock church.* Maybe you think of a congregation called Trinity Lutheran Church, with its school, its properties, its employees, its bylaws and constitution, its groups and its members. When we hear the word "Church," we tend to think of a Christian institution. Guess what? There *was* no institutional Christian Church in the decades after Jesus died, rose, and ascended – not in the way we think of it. There was no institutional Christian Church on that first Pentecost, when thousands and thousands of believers were added. In fact, the word "Christian" didn't exist at Pentecost. The word "Christian" came later, in Antioch in Acts 11:26. At Pentecost, the people who followed Jesus were known as people of "the Way" (Acts 9:2) because they followed Him who is "the way, and the truth, and the life" (John 14:6). They were a small group within Judaism. Judaism had various groups, like the Pharisees and Sadducees and Essenes, and now this little group of people who had started to follow Jesus of Nazareth – the people of the Way. It wasn't until after 70 A.D., some 40 years after Pentecost, that the Church was generally considered something separate from Judaism. Now what does this mean? That's the great Lutheran question: *What does this mean?* It means what we confess in the explanation to the Third Article of the Apostles' Creed:

> I believe that I cannot by my own thinking or choosing believe in Jesus Christ, my Lord, or come to him.
>
> But the Holy Spirit has called me by the gospel, enlightened me with his gifts, sanctified and kept me in the true faith. In the same way he calls, gathers, enlightens, and sanctifies the whole Christian church on earth, and keeps it with Jesus Christ in the one true faith.[3]

There's nothing there about the Church being buildings and budgets – institutional things. The Church in its essence is people who publicly confess and follow the One who is the way, and the truth, and the life.

> In the same way he calls, gathers, enlightens, and sanctifies the whole Christian church on earth, and keeps it with Jesus Christ in the one true faith.
>
> In this Christian church he daily and fully forgives all sins to me and all believers.
>
> On the Last Day he will raise me and all the dead and give eternal life to me and all believers in Christ.
>
> This is most certainly true.[3]

The third temptation of the devil concerns this book – the Bible. Guess what? Most people in the early Church couldn't read or write. It's estimated that only 10 percent of the people in the Roman Empire were literate.[4] John 8:6 tells us that Jesus could write. Paul was a scholar; he could read and write. Peter? I'm not so sure. They were as intelligent as we are, but most people couldn't read or write. It's interesting to watch people in worship when the Bible lessons are read. Many look down and follow along in the bulletin, or look up and follow the words on the screen. That's not the way it was back at the time of Pentecost. Why would they have a bulletin? Most of them couldn't read! The Holy Spirit got Jesus into their hearts when Church people spoke about Jesus – about who Jesus is, what Jesus did, what He does, how He fulfills the prophecies, and the wonderful promises He makes to His followers. When Paul said, "Faith comes from hearing, and hearing through the word of Christ" (Romans 10:17), he was speaking literally. And so our text from Hebrews says: "The word of God is living and active, sharper than any two-edged sword, piercing to the division of soul and of spirit, of joints and of marrow, and discerning the thoughts and intentions of the heart."

What does this mean? Martin Luther said, "God be praised, a seven-year-old child knows what the church is: holy believers and the little sheep who hear the voice of their shepherd."[5] Again, Luther says in the Small Catechism, "We should fear and love God that we do not despise preaching and his Word, but regard it as holy and gladly hear and learn it."[6] And so the devil tempts us to confine Jesus to the past, and to suppose that the Church is just another institution. We easily fall to those temptations when we forget that the Word is the *viva vox evangelii*, the living and active Word of the Gospel. Therefore we pray, "Almighty God, grant to Your Church Your Holy Spirit and the wisdom that comes down from above, that Your Word may not be bound [and put on a shelf] but have free course and be preached to the joy and edifying of Christ's holy people."[7]

All this points to the living and active Word, spoken in church by people who will soon see Jesus in judgment. All of this points to the importance of connections and conversations.[8] I love taking walks, and I love walking through Washington University. WashU is a world-class school, but people don't acknowledge you when you meet on the sidewalk. They don't have the friendly culture of Concordia Seminary. So I thought it was strange the other day when I was looking at construction at their athletic complex. A man, maybe 60, smiled and greeted me. He introduced himself as the head football coach. I said, "I'm Dale Meyer and I work at Concordia Seminary." He said, "I'm a Christian, too. I try to bring it to bear on what I do here. I'd love to talk more with you." You see, connections and conversations! A pastor needs a study where he obviously studies, but the pastor's office should be where you connect and converse with people. I've noticed that the pastors of healthy and growing churches aren't in the institutional office as much as they are out with people, out with church members, and out in the community. Their office is their feet, their car, and their cell phone. God intends His Word to be alive in connections and conversations. And about this book, the Bible? Johannes Gutenberg's invention of movable type is a great blessing. We are doubly blessed to speak, hear, and read the living voice of the Gospel. But when you open the Bible and when you study theology, take it as the Spirit intends it for you – the living and active Word of God that will transform you. When you prepare to minister to others, lift the words off the page; get your head out of the book and manuscript. Speak the living and active Word from your heart to their hearts.

The Word, alive through connections and conversations, is like fireworks. *Pop, pop, pop, pop.* Sometimes it's just one pop, and *"ah"* from the crowd. Sometimes several pops, and oh, the finale! *Pop, pop, pop, pop, ah, ah, ah, awe, awe, awe.* That's the way the Word of God should be – living and active. Sometimes simple insights. *Ah!* Other times, more insights. *Ah!* becomes increasing awe. And oh, when the finale comes! *Pop, pop, pop, living and active, living and active. Pop, pop, pop, Word alive, Word alive,* "Light from above."[9] And on that day, you and I won't appear "naked and exposed to the eyes of him to whom we must give account."

> *Jesus, Thy blood and righteousness*
> *My beauty are, my glorious dress;*
> *Midst flaming worlds, in these arrayed,*
> *With joy shall I lift up my head.*[10]

The finale is coming, and the Spirit of our Lord Jesus is getting us ready by His Word, His Word alive, living and active through connections and conversations.

Amen.

For Further Reflection

"From thence He will come to judge the living and the dead." (Apostles' Creed, Second Article)

- *That day of wrath ... / What horror must invade the mind / when the approaching Judge shall find / and sift the deeds of all mankind!*[11]
  - Read Isaiah 63:1-10; 2 Peter 1:1-14

- *Recall, dear Jesus, for my sake / you did our suffering nature take / then do not now my soul forsake!*[11]
  o Read 2 Thessalonians 2:13-17; Revelation 20:11 - 21:8; Mark 13:24-36
- *In weariness You sought for me, / and suffering upon the tree! / let not in vain such labor be.*[11]
  o Read Habakkuk 2:1-4; Mark 13:24-36

> *The Gospel shows the Father's grace,*
> *Who sent His Son to save our race,*
> *Proclaims how Jesus lived and died*
> *That we might thus be justified.*
>
> *It brings the Savior's righteousness*
> *To robe our souls in royal dress;*
> *From all our guilt it brings release*
> *And gives the troubled conscience peace.*
>
> *It is the pow'r of God to save*
> *From sin and Satan and the grave;*
> *It works the faith which firmly clings*
> *To all the treasures which it brings.*[12]

Retrospective

At Pentecost we marvel at the amazing growth of the early Church, but hidden in our wonder about the past is some lament that today's Church in America seems to be struggling. As I age and watch, I am more and more acutely aware that unspoken assumptions about how things are, or how we imagine things are, hurt the Church. This sermon, originally delivered for the opening of Concordia Seminary's 177th academic year, identifies three popular but insidious assumptions: that fear of God is an outmoded religious concept, that the Church is simply an institution, and that the Word of God is bound in the Bible. Here's another one. When you read the word "you" in the Bible, you probably think it's singular. That's because our western culture is individualistic, and our current American ways of thinking are hyper-individualistic. But more often than not, "you" in the Bible is plural, not singular; the inspired writer is speaking to the whole Church, the whole Body of Christ. I'm convinced these false assumptions and others slow the growth of the Church. They seduce us into the conventional wisdom of the dominant culture around us, sapping the challenge that's in the scriptural and Reformation principles: Grace Alone, Faith Alone, Word Alone. "Having eyes do you not see, and having ears do you not hear?" (Mark 8:18). It's the task of theology professors and pastors to study, observe culture, and get all of us reflecting on our assumptions about life on the basis of the Word of God. Where the Gospel of God is present, the Holy Spirit is present to give and strengthen faith. The Spirit's working leads us to see life in new ways with new assumptions, with the mind of Christ. In our challenging times, the living voice of the Gospel continues to be the Church's way forward.

> *O Spirit, who didst once restore*
> *Thy Church that it might be again*
> *The bringer of good news to men,*
> *Breathe on Thy cloven Church once more.*[13]

Week 21 – Your God, My God

Delivered at Holy Cross Lutheran Church, Collinsville, Illinois
for the marriage of Andrew Sidwell and Sarah Bickel
May 30, 2015

Text – Ruth 1:15-16

And she said, "See, your sister-in-law has gone back to her people and to her gods; return after your sister-in-law." But Ruth said, "Do not urge me to leave you or to return from following you. For where you go I will go, and where you lodge I will lodge. Your people shall be my people, and your God my God.

Prayer

O Spirit of the One who affirmed, "A man shall leave his father and his mother" (Genesis 2:24), Who blessed the marriage at Cana (John 2:1-12), and Who teaches us to see in marriage a reflection of His love for the Church (Ephesians 5:21-33) ... O Spirit, fill us with wisdom and patience and Your selfless love, so those with whom we live and work will want to know more about Jesus, desiring our God to be their God. Amen.

I'd like to lead you into some thoughts about the words we just heard. Ruth said to Naomi, "Your God [will be] my God." Ruth didn't say that out of the blue. She had lived closely with Naomi for ten years and was drawn to the God that Naomi worshiped. Here's the backstory. Naomi was married to a man named Elimelech; they had two sons and lived in Bethlehem. When a famine came, they moved to the country of Moab and there Elimelech died. The two boys married Moabite women, but after ten years both those sons died (Ruth 1:1-5). Naomi told her daughters-in-law, *I'm going to move back to Bethlehem. You stay here in your native land, find husbands, and have a good life* (cf. Ruth 1:6-9). The one daughter-in-law stayed, but Ruth said *no*: "Do not urge me to leave you or to return from following you. For where you go I will go, and where you lodge I will lodge. Your people shall be my people, and your God my God" (Ruth 1:16). In those ten years, Naomi had shown Ruth a God that Ruth wanted to have in her life.

Andy, as you look ahead, will you show Sarah a God that she will want in her life? Sarah, will you show Andy a God that he will want in his life? Will the way you live and build your marriage lead you to say to one another, "Your God will be my God"? I know you're both Christian. I know you both have received a Christian education. That's useless if it doesn't go from your head into your heart and into your life. Jesus says, "By their fruit you will recognize them" (Matthew 7:20 NIV). It would be hypocrisy to have this church ceremony and then for you to establish a life together where God and the Spirit of Jesus Christ are not dominant in your hearts and in your home.

Spirituality in marriage is a struggle. Andy, there is someone whom you love more than Sarah; your greatest love is Andy. Sarah, you are your greatest love. I'm saying that from experience; my greatest love is me. This is the fundamental sin that is in every one of us. For you to be the kind of person that leads your beloved to say, "Your God will be my God," you must take on an internal ongoing spiritual struggle. The struggle is to die to yourself. The struggle is to develop the spiritual disciplines of prayer and devotion and Bible reading and church attendance. That is the way the Spirit of God and the Lord Jesus get down into your heart and life. To be truly Christian is to get over yourself and be filled with Jesus Christ. St. Paul says, "I have been crucified with Christ. It is no longer I who live, but Christ who lives in me. And the life I now live in the flesh I live by faith in the Son of God, who loved me and gave himself for me" (Galatians 2:20).

Andy, look at Sarah. God has made her beautiful in body, soul, and spirit. He has created her and He has redeemed her for eternity. She is His before she is yours. God wants Sarah to be His forever. As you learn to be husband to her, remember that God wants you to take special care of this special gift. Show her the heart of Christ – compassionate, forgiving, and embracing. Inspire her to lead a life that will one day lead her to heaven.

Sarah, look at Andy. God has made him strong, outgoing, and confident. Your calling in marriage is to be the helper that is specially fit for him. He belongs to God before he belongs to you. Make faith integral to your life together, so he also will spend eternity in heaven.

"Your God will be my God." There will be many times when your self-centeredness shoves aside love of God and love for one another. At such times, I hope that the words "your God will be my God" will haunt you, prick your conscience. But far more often, and as the years progress, I pray that you will see in each other the mystery of God's love for us all in Jesus Christ. Then you will confess with a unity of heart and life and faith and worship, "Your God will be my God."

Amen.

For Further Reflection

"You shall have no other gods." (First Commandment)

- "We should fear, love, and trust in God above all things."[1]

"You shall not commit adultery." (Sixth Commandment)

- Every negative command also implies a positive command: "We should fear and love God that we lead a pure and decent life in words and actions, and that husband and wife love and honor each other" (Martin Luther, Small Catechism).[2]

- Can you see yourself in this ultimate marriage story? Revelation 21:1-8
- The fear and love of God in Christian marriage – Ephesians 5:21-33; 1 Peter 3:1-12
- A prayer for Christian marriage: "Hallowed be Thy name." (Lord's Prayer, First Petition)
- God's "name" is His revelation to us. "How is God's name kept holy? ... when his Word is taught in its truth and purity and we as children of God lead

holy lives according to it. Help us to do this, dear Father in heaven!" (Martin Luther, Small Catechism).[3]

> *My soul, now praise your Maker!*
> *Let all within me bless His name*
> *Who makes you full partaker*
> *Of mercies more than you dare claim.*
> *Forget Him not whose meekness*
> *Still bears with all your sin,*
> *Who heals your ev'ry weakness,*
> *Renews your life within;*
> *Whose grace and care are endless*
> *And saved you through the past;*
> *Who leaves no suff'rer friendless*
> *But rights the wronged at last.*
>
> *His grace remains forever,*
> *And children's children yet shall prove*
> *That God forsakes them never*
> *Who in true fear shall seek His love.*
> *In heav'n is fixed His dwelling,*
> *His rule is over all;*
> *O hosts with might excelling,*
> *With praise before Him fall.*
> *Praise Him forever reigning,*
> *All you who hear His Word –*
> *Our life and all sustaining.*
> *My soul, O praise the Lord!*[4]

Retrospective

Meeting with couples before marriage, I share my wish for them that the day will come when they can sit together and reminisce about all they've gone through together: joys and sorrows shared, hopes realized and disappointments that broke their hearts, raising the kids but still worrying about them, paying the bills and coming to some financial stability, and through all that and more, becoming the best of friends. That's the sweet spot where Diane and I now find ourselves. She texts me the latest. I text back or think: When I call or get home, I've got to tell Diane about this! In the morning before going to our tasks for the day, and again at 4:00 P.M. when it's "Triscuit time" for our Golden Retriever, Ferdie (with snacks for us too!), we sit and talk about whatever. Best friends. When we were raising Elizabeth and Catharine, our conversations were more about coping with the day's challenges: Lizzie has volleyball and Katie has cello lessons. How are we going to get each of them where they need to be? Now the girls have their own families and their own coping discussions. Been there; done that. God help you! Meanwhile Diane and I will sit in our quiet house and talk, sharing the day's events and news, but more and more sharing our feelings about issues and about faith. We're both quiet people, including convictions of faith. Faith is in our hearts, not on our sleeves; that's the way we both were raised. Other times we sit and talk only a little. We don't have to talk, because we both know we are fulfilled by being in each other's company. Over all these years of marriage, I think our experience shows that husband and wife are not two identical human beings but were made by our Creator to complement one another. I could not ask for more love than God has given me in marriage.

210

Week 22 – You and the Centurion

Delivered at St. Salvator Lutheran Church, Venedy, Illinois
and St. Peter Lutheran Church, New Memphis, Illinois
June 12, 1977

Text – Luke 7:1-10

After he had finished all his sayings in the hearing of the people, he entered Capernaum. Now a centurion had a servant who was sick and at the point of death, who was highly valued by him. When the centurion heard about Jesus, he sent to him elders of the Jews, asking him to come and heal his servant. And when they came to Jesus, they pleaded with him earnestly, saying, "He is worthy to have you do this for him, for he loves our nation, and he is the one who built us our synagogue." And Jesus went with them. When he was not far from the house, the centurion sent friends, saying to him, "Lord, do not trouble yourself, for I am not worthy to have you come under my roof. Therefore I did not presume to come to you. But say the word, and let my servant be healed. For I too am a man set under authority, with soldiers under me: and I say to one, 'Go,' and he goes; and to another, 'Come,' and he comes; and to my servant, 'Do this,' and he does it." When Jesus heard these things, he marveled at him, and turning to the crowd that followed him, said, "I tell you, not even in Israel have I found such faith." And when those who had been sent returned to the house, they found the servant well.

Prayer

Jesus, how do I approach You? Help me learn from the centurion that I should come to you humbly but confident in Your Word. Too often I'm timid in prayer and negligent in Bible study, but Your Spirit can grow my trust in You during this time of devotion. For that I pray. "Say the Word!" Amen.

It is often interesting to compare ourselves to people in the Bible. That is what we will be doing in today's sermon. You and I are going to look at the centurion from Luke chapter seven. Now, a centurion is a soldier in the Roman army. You remember that Israel was not an independent country back in the days of Jesus. It was ruled by the city of Rome and the Roman army. The centurions were the real backbone of the Roman army. Each centurion was in charge of 100 foot soldiers. It was up to the centurion to provide discipline, efficiency, and organization for his men. Usually, centurions were career army men. They were pretty important in the whole military scheme of things. This morning, we want to look at that one centurion whose story is told in Luke 7. We will compare his faith to my faith and your faith. Hopefully, the example of the centurion will strengthen and encourage us.

The Bible says, "After he had finished all his sayings in the hearing of the people, he entered Capernaum. Now a centurion had a servant who was sick and at the point of death, who was highly valued by him. When the centurion heard about Jesus, he sent to him elders of the Jews, asking him to come and heal his servant." The soldier had a problem. His servant was sick – hovering between life and death. The serious illness of his servant disturbed him greatly because he valued this servant. So, what did the centurion do? He sent word to Jesus. He asked Jesus to come and heal his servant. That's the first thing we notice this morning about the centurion – he had a problem, and he took it to Jesus.

Compare yourself to the centurion. Do you take your problems to Jesus? Several years ago here in church, we all selected our favorite hymns. If my memory serves me correctly, the most popular hymn was number 457:

> *What a friend we have in Jesus,*
> *All our sins and griefs to bear!*
> *What a privilege to carry*
> *Ev'rything to God in prayer!*

Oh, what peace we often forfeit;
Oh, what needless pain we bear –
All because we do not carry
Ev'rything to God in prayer![1]

I hope that you really do that – take everything to God in prayer. *The Lutheran Standard* is the official publication of the American Lutheran Church (ALC). It is like our *Lutheran Witness*. The last issue of *The Lutheran Standard* carried the results of a survey in which most people said that when they pray, they pray for health. That's good. That's what the centurion did. But I hope you don't limit your prayers only to medical matters. Take *everything* to God in prayer. You know how time and time again, in the course of a day, you think of your husband or wife? You know how you share big things and little things with one another? That's the same way you should take everything to God in prayer. Certainly, there is much to pray for! Pray for health. Pray for a happy family life. Pray for your church. Pray for a good harvest. Pray for rain. Farming is dangerous work; pray that our farmers will not suffer accidents with their machinery. In short, pray about anything and everything. The centurion took his problem to Jesus. Do you?

Remember, the centurion sent messengers to Jesus. The Bible says, "And when they came to Jesus, they pleaded with him earnestly, saying, 'He is worthy to have you do this for him, for he loves our nation, and he is the one who built us our synagogue'" (A synagogue is a Jewish church. This centurion must have been a rich man.) "And Jesus went with them. When he was not far from the house, the centurion sent friends, saying to him, 'Lord, do not trouble yourself, for I am not worthy to have you come under my roof.'" This centurion was a very humble man. He certainly didn't have to be humble by the standards of the world. After all, he had a hundred men under his command. He probably was very self-assured and confident. But he went to Jesus most humbly. He must have known that he was going to the Lord, the almighty Son of God.

I hope you take your problems to Jesus, but do you take them humbly? You ought to. There is a lot for you to be humble about. Think of the wrong you have done in your life. Think of your failures. Have you always put God and your church first – ahead of all else? I doubt it. We all know that there are some people in this world who come to you only when they want something from you, and the rest of the time they have no use for you. That's the way you and I often deal with God. When we desperately need something, we ask Him for it. The rest of the time, we are lukewarm toward God and His Church. For that reason, we should follow the example of the centurion. We should go to Jesus with our problems. We should go to Him often. But we should go very humbly, for He is God – and we are poor, miserable sinners.

"Lord, do not trouble yourself," he says, "for I am not worthy to have you come under my roof. Therefore I did not presume to come to you. But say the word, and let my servant be healed." *Say the word.* That's interesting. The centurion completely trusted Jesus' word. Do you? I don't think so. I don't think I do, either. And I can prove it. First, we don't know His Word all that well. When we have Bible class, an average of 20 people attend. Do the rest of you know God's Word – the Bible – cover to cover? Of course not. No one does. But how can we claim to trust His Word if we do not study it? There is a second proof that we do not trust Jesus' Word as completely as we should. How often do I see you troubled, in despair, wringing your hands and worrying yourself to death? I see it all the time. You wouldn't do that if you completely trusted God's Word. The Word tells us that God is on our side. He supports us with His power and with His grace. It is His power that placed us in this world and protects us day by day. It is His grace that gives us Jesus the Savior. His kindness tells us that nothing can trouble those who have taken refuge in the wounds of the Savior. If we know and trust His Word completely, we will have a good and pleasant life in this world. But you'll never have that unless you dig into the study of God's Word and trust it completely.

The centurion told Jesus, "Say the word, and let my servant be healed." He was completely confident that Jesus would answer his prayer. Are you? When you pray, do you know that God will answer you? Let me read to you several Bible passages that are in the catechism: "And whatever you ask in prayer, you will receive, if you have faith" (Matthew 21:22). "But let him ask in faith, with no doubting, for the one who doubts is like a wave of the sea that is driven and tossed by the wind. For that person must not suppose that he will receive anything from the Lord" (James 1:6-7). "Ask, and it will be given to you; seek, and you will find; knock, and it will be opened to you" (Matthew 7:7). When you pray, you should be completely confident that God will answer your prayer. He may not answer it exactly the way you want. But that's good – because when God doesn't answer your prayer just the way you want, that means He is going to answer your prayer in an even better way than you can imagine! That's great! So, pray with confidence. Would you buy anything from a salesman who said, "I'm selling such-and-such, but you really don't want any, do you?" Of course you wouldn't. Unfortunately, that's the same timid way a lot of us pray to God. The centurion prayed confidently. We ought to follow his example.

We all know what happened to the centurion's servant. He was healed. The prayer was answered. I'm sure that the centurion counted that miraculous recovery as a great blessing in his life. You and I, like the centurion, should find God's blessings in our lives. That blessing may not always be in the area of healing. Jesus did heal the centurion's servant. However, we remember that St. Paul prayed to be healed and he was not (2 Corinthians 12:8-10). If you ever pray to be healed from some malady, and the answer comes back *No*, then that is the blessing. When God leaves illness in your life, it is for your good. But God's blessings are not confined to medical matters. Think of all the other blessings you have in your life. There are spiritual blessings. First and most importantly, you have a Savior, Jesus Christ. He died and rose again for you. Therefore you will not be punished for your sins, but instead you are forgiven and have the wonderful hope of life everlasting. Think of the blessing of your church – this wonderful place where we believers gather and worship each Sunday. You ought to thank God every day that you have such a fine church.

Besides the spiritual blessings, there are material blessings. I'm a city boy, you know. Sometimes I get a little irritated with you country people because of all the blessings out here that you take for granted. When I delivered milk in the bad sections of Chicago, I always carried an iron hook in my hand for protection. Do you count it a blessing that here in the country, you don't have to worry about being attacked? Back home, the air isn't as fresh as it is out here. Someone once teased me and said that whenever I get homesick, all I have to do is breathe some exhaust fumes and I'll feel right at home. There's some truth to that. Every time you breathe, count it a blessing. I could go on and on. God has blessed you richly. Don't let a single day go by, but that you stop and marvel at how good God has been to you.

When the centurion's servant had been healed, Jesus said, "I tell you, not even in Israel have I found such faith." Jesus marveled at the strong faith of the centurion. How does Jesus feel about *your* faith? Is He really impressed with you? It wouldn't be a bad idea this week for you to ask the Holy Spirit to strengthen your faith. When you leave church today, follow the example of the centurion. You will certainly benefit from it.

   Amen.

For Further Reflection

"For Thine is the kingdom and the power and the glory forever and ever. Amen." (The Lord's Prayer, Conclusion)

- Whose is the kingdom, the power, and the glory?
- Put yourself in the story – John 18:28 - 19:16
- "Why are you so afraid?" Mark 4:35-41; Mark 8:14-21; Matthew 28:16-17; James 1:2-8
- Faith! Psalm 34:22; Mark 9:14-27; John 20:24-29
- The explanation to the conclusion of the Lord's Prayer: "We can be sure that these petitions are acceptable to our Father in heaven and are heard by him, for he himself has commanded us to pray in this way and has promised to hear us. Therefore we say, 'Amen. Yes, it shall be so'" (Martin Luther, Small Catechism).[2]

> *How firm a foundation, O saints of the Lord,*
> *Is laid for your faith in His excellent Word!*
> *What more can He say than to you He has said*
> *Who unto the Savior for refuge have fled?*
>
> *"Fear not! I am with you, O be not dismayed,*
> *For I am your God and will still give you aid;*
> *I'll strengthen you, help you, and cause you to stand,*
> *Upheld by My righteous, omnipotent hand.*
>
> *"The soul that on Jesus has leaned for repose*
> *I will not, I will not, desert to his foes;*

That soul, though all hell should endeavor to shake,
I'll never, no never, no never, forsake!"[3]

Retrospective

Biblical literacy has declined in the 40 years since I preached this sermon. I see that loss of memorized passages even in our seminarians, hastening to add that I don't blame them. It's the culture in which we all live. This sermon from a 30 year old took the people through the story of the centurion by quoting a section of the text, commenting, quoting another section with comment, and so on. This is called expository preaching. It's an easy way to approach a narrative text, and I'm convinced it draws people in. We all love stories. And when all went home from church, preacher and parishioners had a little more biblical literacy, a little more substance in our daily lives with Jesus.

My first call was to the dual parish of St. Peter, New Memphis, and St. Salvator, Venedy, Illinois. St. Peter was organized in 1861, and two years later built and dedicated a beautiful church building that served the congregation for almost a century. The congregation was devastated when a tornado destroyed that building in 1960, but they determined to rebuild – such was their commitment to God's church. And this line drawing from a bulletin during my time shows the new sanctuary completed in 1961.

I have many pleasant memories of this building. One that I'll share with you shows how the Gospel is passed through families from generation to generation. At the back of the church was a door that led inside to the small sacristy. Every Sunday, I'd gather outside that door with several men and we'd "chew the fat." Warren Krausz, Milton Backs, Ardel Going, Charles Krausz, Al Schirmer, Tom Schmink, Marvin Krausz, and Herb Mueller were among the regulars, as I recall. Come 8:30 A.M., Herb would look at his watch and ask, "Reverend, should I ring them in?" – meaning, should he go and ring the church bell in the tower in front of the church. "Yup," was my reply, and the group went in to join their wives for worship. Herb was the son of Rev. Almar Mueller, who had served St. Peter for 33 years until his death in 1960. With his death and the tornado, 1960 was a sad year for St. Peter! Herb's daughter JoAnn married Willis Harriss (I performed the ceremony), and their son Mark is now the faithful pastor of Zion Lutheran Church in Hillsboro, Missouri. That's just one story from this small congregation that I was privileged to serve: people who love their Lord, gather faithfully around His Word, and pass the faith on to children and grandchildren. Don't underestimate what God can do through your church, little though it may be, from generation to generation! (Psalm 145:4)

Saint Peter Lutheran Church
New Memphis, Illinois 62266

Rev. Dale A. Meyer,
Pastor

Pastor's Phone:
(618) 324-6366

Sunday Service Time:
8:30 A.M.

Sunday School:
9:45 a.m.

Week 23 – The Angels Laugh; the Devils Weep

Broadcast on The Lutheran Hour
October 31, 1999

Text – Psalm 128

Blessed is everyone who fears the LORD,
 who walks in his ways!
You shall eat the fruit of the labor of your hands;
 you shall be blessed, and it shall be well with you.

Your wife will be like a fruitful vine
 within your house;
your children will be like olive shoots
 around your table.
Behold, thus shall the man be blessed
 who fears the LORD.

The LORD bless you from Zion!
 May you see the prosperity of Jerusalem
 all the days of your life!
May you see your children's children!
 Peace be upon Israel!

Prayer

Almighty and eternal God, You are the Creator of all things, and love all that You have made. Our communities and country are blessed by Your creation of marriage for man and woman. For the sake of our common welfare, help us all honor marriage. Give grace to those who are married to live in loving and supportive companionship with one another according to Your Commandments.

Instill reverence for the holiness of marriage in those who are young and yearn to know married love. Put hope in the tears of those who have lost their spouse, and the eternal Easter in their longings. We pray in the name of Jesus, who blessed the wedding at Cana and continues to bless us all today. Amen.

It's a Saturday evening in March. Leonard Kopp is a merchant who occasionally delivers fish to the convent in Torgau, Germany. On this particular evening, the 31st, it's not what he unloads at the convent that is as important as what he takes away from the convent on his wagon. The year is 1523, and it's been five and a half years since the Reformation broke out in Europe. Some priests and nuns, influenced by the new religious teachings, have been leaving their orders. And on this night, Mr. Kopp is helping 12 nuns escape from the convent in Torgau.

Nine of those nuns ended up in Wittenberg, the center of the new teachings. Some of the leaders in that town helped find permanent positions for the nuns. That happened easily for eight of the nine. But the ninth – she was more difficult to place. For two years, she did domestic work. A well-to-do young man from Nuremberg was picked to be her husband, but he went off and married someone else. Another prospective bridegroom was found, a Dr. Glatz. But the woman said, "No, not him."[1] There was, however, an older man, 37 years old, who had caught her eye. In time, she married this man, 16 years older than she was. Yes, on June 13th, 1525, Katharina von Bora married Dr. Martin Luther.

Luther, the man whose 95 theses had initiated the Reformation, first thought it was a joke when someone suggested that he should marry Katie, or anyone for that matter. He eventually warmed up to the idea, but he had a lot to learn. He said, "There's a lot to get used to in the first year of marriage. One wakes up in the morning and finds a pair of pigtails on the pillow which were not there before."[2] But Martin came to praise marriage and to love his Katie. Just as the Reformer learned a lot about practical Christian living in marriage and family, so can you and I. Psalm 128 (GW) is a good guide. Listen:

> Blessed are all who fear the LORD
>   and live his way.

You will certainly eat what your own hands have provided.
   Blessings to you!
   May things go well for you!
Your wife will be like a fruitful vine inside your home.
Your children will be like young olive trees around your table.
   This is how the LORD will bless the person who fears him.
     May the LORD bless you from Zion
       so that you may see Jerusalem prospering
        all the days of your life.
     May you live to see your children's children.
Let there be peace in Israel!

Again, that is Psalm 128. The first verse says, "Blessed are all who fear the LORD and live his way." In my ministry, people have told me that they don't like this talk about fearing the Lord. They say that God is a God of love, not fear. Through the years, Katie and Martin learned to understand what the fear of the Lord really means.

Katie was born on January 29th, 1499, in Lippendorf, Germany. This year [1999], therefore, marks the 500th anniversary of her birth. In 1505, she was received into the cloister in Brehna. Interestingly, that was the same year that her future husband entered the monastery in Erfurt. In 1509, Katharina next entered the cloister Marienthron in the little town of Nimbschen. On October 8th, 1515, she became a nun.

Many people in those days entered convents and monasteries to calm their fear of the Lord. Back then, the common people were often taught to have a shivering, quaking fear of God. Jesus was pictured as a stern judge who was ready and eager to cast the unworthy into hell. The way to escape that destiny, many people imagined, was to enter a religious order – to become a monk or a nun. I don't know if Katie looked at God that way and entered the convent out of fear, but Martin certainly did. He became a monk and then a priest because he hoped to make peace with the God whom he feared. However, the phrase fear of God came to mean something different to both Martin and Katie. Yes, God is stern and strict, and Jesus Christ will one day come in judgment of all sinners. People today might want to ignore that teaching of the Bible, but it won't go away. But to his joy – and ours, too – Luther discovered in the Bible that God does not delight in the death of the sinner, but wants sinners to have eternal life. The Reformer was led by the Spirit of God to see that Jesus Christ is the One through whom God gives forgiveness for all sins and opens the way to eternal life. "The fear of the LORD is the beginning of wisdom," says Psalm 111:10; and 1 Corinthians 1:24 teaches that the wisdom of God is Jesus Christ. That's what it means to fear the Lord – to live your life before the holy God with faith in the Savior Jesus Christ. That was the foundation of the home that Katie and Martin established.

In that home, Katie had her hands full! Psalm 128:2 (GW) says, "You will certainly eat what your own hands have provided. Blessings to you! May things go well for you!" The Luthers ate what their hands had provided. Martin took care of the garden. I'm sure he wasn't totally dependable. His work, his writing, his travels – in short, his commitment to the truth of the Gospel – must have made him often forget the garden. I'm sure Katie had to step in. She also took care of the orchard. She caught and cleaned fish from a nearby pond. She took care of the barnyard animals and actually did the slaughtering herself. Yes, she had her hands full!

By the way, the information I'm sharing with you comes from the classic biography of Martin Luther written by historian Roland Bainton of Yale University. It's called *Here I Stand*, and it's worth reading and rereading.[3]

Katie often had her hands full of other common family problems. There were the bills. Martin was naïve when it came to money. He once said, "I do not worry about debts because when Katie pays one, another comes."[4] They took in student boarders to help pay some of those bills. More work for Katie. Martin routinely invited guests into their home. Of course, he didn't ask her about that. We men haven't changed much through the centuries! And he was often sick, requiring her attention and care. Oh yes, Katie had her hands full!

But isn't it comforting for you to hear that? That's the way life is for us too – full of problems. But it's in those troublesome situations of daily life that the blessings of God are most truly appreciated. St. Paul was Luther's favorite biblical author because he laid out so clearly the message of salvation by grace through faith. God through St. Paul says, "'My grace is sufficient for you, for my power is made perfect in weakness.' Therefore I will boast all the more gladly of my weaknesses, so that the power of Christ may rest upon me" (2 Corinthians 12:9). Yes, Katie had her hands full and so do you. But that's where the blessings come. "*Oh, blest the house, whate'er befall, / Where Jesus Christ is all in all!*"[5]

Psalm 128:3 (GW) describes another aspect of Katie and Martin's home: "Your wife will be like a fruitful vine inside your home. Your children will be like young olive trees around your table." Katie bore six children to Martin: sons John, Martin, and Paul, and daughters Elisabeth, Magdalena, and Margarethe. Young Martin became a lawyer and Paul became a doctor. You know that with the blessing of children can also come sadness. Daughter Elisabeth died at about one year of age, and Magdalena died when she was 14. When such heartbreak comes, what a refuge it is for parents to know that the tomb of Jesus Christ is empty. What comfort comes to grieving parents to know that the risen Christ not only gives abundant life here and now, when our hands are full of problems, but He who lives also gives unending life in heaven to His followers.

What great healing is available to parents' broken hearts when they look back and know that they did teach their young children to know Jesus by faith, and they did not – as so many foolish people do – let the children grow up without Jesus. Parents who do not raise their children in the nurture and admonition of the Lord are guilty of spiritual dereliction of duty, for which they will give an answer when the Judge comes.

Roland Bainton tells that when Magdalena was dying, Martin prayed, "Oh God, I love her so, but Thy will be done." Then he asked his daughter, "*Magdalenchen* [Dear little Magdalena], my little girl, you would like to stay with your father here and you would be glad to go to your Father in heaven?"

She said, "Yes, dear father, as God wills."[6]

Quoting directly from Bainton's biography, *Here I Stand*:

> Luther reproached himself because God had blessed him as no bishop had been blessed in a thousand years, and yet he could not find it in his heart to give God thanks. Katie stood off, overcome by grief; and Luther held the child in his hands as she passed on. When she was laid away, he said, "*Du liebes Lenichen* [Beloved little Lena], you will rise and shine like the stars and the sun. How strange it is to know that she is at peace and all is well, and yet be so sorrowful!"[6]

Psalm 128:4 (GW): "This is how the LORD will bless the person who fears him." Katie and Martin were blessed. As the story of Magdalena testifies, it wasn't always easy. You know that even on the normal days, marriage can be tough. "Good God, what a lot of trouble there is in marriage!" Martin once said. "Adam has made a mess of our nature. Think of all the squabbles Adam and Eve must have had in the course of their years. Eve would say, 'You ate the apple,' and Adam would retort, 'You gave it to me.'"[7]

One time at supper, Luther was regaling their guests with his theological insights, of which Katie had had enough. "Doctor," she said (she always called him "Doctor"), "why don't you stop talking and eat?" He shot back, "I wish women would repeat the Lord's Prayer before opening their mouths."[8] I don't know what happened next. Roland Bainton didn't print that! Obviously, Martin and Katie were sinners just like the rest of us. That's why they so treasured the forgiveness of sins. That's why they feared the Lord. And in that, they were so blessed.

Katie Luther died on December 20th, 1552. She was 53 years old. Her husband Martin Luther had died six years earlier. Katie was buried in St. Mary's Church in Torgau. You can still visit her grave today.

Luther, as I said, first thought it a joke that he should marry. But as he thought about it, he realized that marriage and family is a place to confess your faith. You need not retreat from the facts of the world to be a true Christian. In fact, involvement in the day-to-day things of life is the best place to demonstrate the faith, hope, and love that are ours in Christ Jesus. With that truth in mind, Luther wrote to a friend and said, "You must come to my wedding. I have made the angels laugh and the devils weep."[9]

May your marriage and family life do the same. Live in the true fear of God, place the hopes of your heart in Jesus Christ your Savior, keep your hands full by serving one another in the small things of daily life, and you will be blessed. As the 128th Psalm (GW) concludes,

> May the LORD bless you from Zion
> so that you may see Jerusalem prospering
> all the days of your life.
> May you live to see your children's children.
> Let there be peace in Israel! (vv. 5-6)

Yes, may the angels laugh and the devils weep! Amen.

For Further Reflection

"I believe in God, the Father Almighty, maker of heaven and earth."
(Apostles' Creed, First Article)

- The Creator of man and woman instituted marriage – Genesis 2:18-25
- Put yourself in the story – Genesis 24:42-61. "Where you go I will go" (Ruth 1:16).
- Because sin attacks the life-long union of a man and a woman, the Savior reaffirms the holiness of marriage – Matthew 5:27-30; Matthew 19:3-9. See also 1 Corinthians 6:12-20; Hebrews 13:4. Reverent fear of God keeps love and marriage holy.
- Psalms praising the Creator and Preserver – Psalm 103:1-18; Psalm 127:1-5; Psalm 128:1-6; Psalm 145:8-21
- *"Oh, blest the house, whate'er befall, / Where Jesus Christ is all in all!"*[10] – 2 Samuel 7:29; Proverbs 3:33; Colossians 3:12-17

> *O Father, all creating,*
> *Whose wisdom, love, and pow'r*
> *First bound two lives together*
> *In Eden's primal hour,*
> *Today to these Your children*
> *Your earliest gifts renew:*
> *A home by You made happy,*
> *A love by You kept true.*
>
> *Unless You build it, Father,*
> *The house is built in vain;*
> *Unless You, Savior, bless it,*
> *The joy will turn to pain.*
> *But nothing breaks the union*
> *Of hearts in You made one;*

The love Your Spirit hallows
Is endless love begun.[11]

Retrospective

I loved reading this sermon; the stories of Katie and Martin made me think of my own marriage. Diane and I met in the summer of 1972. I had just returned from vicarage, and she was teaching at Bloom Township High School and worshiping at my home congregation. The first time I saw her, I knew I wanted to ask her out. She says she knew immediately that she was going to marry me. She's never said if that intuition came with anticipation or foreboding! Within a few months we were thinking of marriage, and the happy day came June 16th, 1973. Loud crashes of thunder and pounding rain could be heard during the ceremony. People told us that was a sign of good luck. I don't know about signs, but I have been blessed by Diane more than I can say. I have much to be thankful for as we celebrate our 45th anniversary in 2018.

She taught some after we were married, but mainly put her energies into our home and children. When I began to work for The Lutheran Hour in 1989, I began traveling on weekends to preach all over the country and sometimes out of the country. She said at the outset that she'd stay home and keep a normal home life for our girls. She did faithfully, and I attribute the good character and faithfulness to church of our daughters Elizabeth and Catharine to Diane. Through all the years, she participated actively in church and community. She served many years on the board of the Collinsville Memorial Library, was on the civic organization "Collinsville Progress," was elected to the Collinsville City Council, and in Missouri was chair of a commission for the City of Clayton. Diane is a Proverbs 31 woman. These years we enjoy one another's company more than ever before, aware of fleeting time. I regret that I've never been a romantic – klutz is a better word – but our love has grown, and we are the best of friends.

Week 24 – A Man and His Toys

Father's Day
Broadcast on The Lutheran Hour
June 18, 2000

Text – 1 Timothy 6:6-11

But godliness with contentment is great gain, for we brought nothing into the world, and we cannot take anything out of the world. But if we have food and clothing, with these we will be content. But those who desire to be rich fall into temptation, into a snare, into many senseless and harmful desires that plunge people into ruin and destruction. For the love of money is a root of all kinds of evils. It is through this craving that some have wandered away from the faith and pierced themselves with many pangs.

But as for you, O man of God, flee these things. Pursue righteousness, godliness, faith, love, steadfastness, gentleness.

Prayer

Teach us, O Lord, to live the simpler life that comes from single-minded devotion to You. Too often we find our houses filled with possessions while our hearts are breaking with unhappiness. Whatever the cost to us may be, teach us to know Jesus as our priceless treasure. Fill our hearts with the riches of Your forgiveness through Him. We thank You for every father who has lovingly raised his children in godliness and pray their examples will inspire all fathers. For Jesus' sake. Amen.

They say the difference between men and boys is the size of their toys. I want to introduce you to a man who has had more toys than you can imagine, a man who learned what makes the real difference in life. Let me introduce you to Jorge Valdés.

Jorge Valdés was born in 1956 in Santiago de las Vegas, a small, rural town on the outskirts of Havana, Cuba. His father, Hidalgo, owned a furniture factory and his mother, Angela Teresa, took care of Jorge, his brother J.C., and their sister Maria. When Fidel Castro seized power in 1959 and began to impose a hardline communist economy, Jorge's parents knew the government would soon take all they had worked for. So, on October 11th, 1966, the Valdés family fled Cuba for Miami. Bureaucratic hassles detained mother Angela Teresa for a time in Cuba, but eventually she was able to join her husband and children in Miami.

With all their possessions left behind in Cuba, the Valdés family went from a comfortable life to living in poverty in the Little Havana section of Miami. That poverty didn't set well with Jorge, so he set his heart on toys – not childhood toys, but the toys of grownups.[1]

Jorge explained:

> Coming to the streets of Miami and suddenly seeing a 1968 GTO… "Wow, I'll be the happiest man on earth if I ever have that." Working very hard all my life, the only thing I could do since I worked full time and went to school full time was drive by all those mansions and … tell my girlfriend, "You know, Nellie, I'll be happy the day I have a house like that. I will have a house like that." And then tell my parents, "Mom, Dad, I'm going to buy you a big house one day."[2]

Those were high hopes that young Jorge had, but they were not apple-pie-in-the-sky hopes. He realized his aspirations. "When I was 20 years old, I had two Learjets, my own JetRanger [helicopter]. I had mansions in every country and city that I went to 'cause I hated to carry a suitcase where I went. I drove around in a Rolls Royce. I had a fleet of cars."[2]

He really did have a fleet of cars. Jorge told me he once went to buy a new Corvette. As he was looking at several models on the showroom floor, he didn't know which color Corvette he liked best. So, he bought them all! Young Jorge had set his heart on toys and he got them – the biggest, the best, and the most.

Are you suspicious? Do you sense he didn't acquire his wealth in a legal way? You're right. At one time, Valdés controlled over 95% of the cocaine coming into the United States. But that's not what I'm getting at with his story. As terrible as the drug trade is, my message is about something even deeper. I want you to think about what Jorge was after. Think about what we all are after. We all want to be content in our lives and – this being Father's Day – dads and moms work to pass on material happiness to their children. Unlike Jorge, most of us strive for happiness in legal ways. You take the overtime, you work the extra job, you follow the market, you use your credit wisely, you leverage your assets: You do all this to acquire happiness for yourself and the ones you love. If you would take a drive and see the big homes being built, you'd think that our booming economy is finally filling our deep need for happiness. Today, many of us have the toys, but our hearts are still aching. Toys can fill your house and your garage, but they can't fill your heart.

Jorge Valdés was not content. He continued:

> The reason I kept accumulating all this money and all this power was because I was searching for some meaning to my life … I was just the most miserable human being in the world. I tried to find the answers to my happiness in everything the world had to offer. It was always a dead end…
>
> When the world looked at me and said, "You've got it made. You're dating the prettiest women in America and you're flying around to all those wonderful places and you're miserable? Impossible!" But I was.[2]

When his bodyguard was killed, Jorge realized the bullet had been meant for him. He began to call his whole life into question. At the funeral, his bodyguard's daughter said to Jorge, "Godfather, my daddy went to be with Jesus." Jorge told me what he thought when he heard that little girl imagining that her father was in heaven. "Wow," he said, "if there is a Jesus, what we are doing is not going to get us there."[2]

As much as that bothered him, his discontent was to increase even more. Again, a child was responsible. This time it was his own daughter. One weekend,

Jorge was partying at one of his mansions. His daughter from a previous marriage was spending that weekend with him. In the middle of the night, this toddler came to her father's bedroom. Scared, she was reaching out for her father's help. *How can I help her*, he thought. He realized how filthy he had become in the life he was living. Having the biggest, best, and the most toys wasn't proving to be the answer.

> How did I allow life to lead me where I am? Why is it that my parents, who have so little in this world, have this joy they say comes through their relationship with God? Why now? I am the epitome of the American dream. I have anything an American or anybody in the world would want… I talk more about America because we're blessed with more wealth here … I have everything. Yet I am so devastated, so morally corrupt, so … empty in my life. I need something different.[2]

What he needed was Jesus Christ. You need Him too. We all do. Jesus Christ knows both riches and poverty. He knows riches we can't imagine because He is the eternal Son of God. Before the world was made, before time was reckoned, Jesus Christ existed as God along with His Father. He has riches far different than anything you or I could ever track in an account. His are the riches of the glory of God. Yet, the treasures of heaven did not keep Him from coming into our poverty.

He came into our world, born of the Virgin Mary in the poor surroundings of a stable in Bethlehem. As an adult, He once remarked that foxes have holes and birds have nests but He had no place to lay His head (Matthew 8:20). No large home, no condo, no multi-car garage: I suppose the census would have classified Jesus as homeless. One time when He had to pay a tax for the temple in Jerusalem, He did so by working a miracle. He told Peter to go catch a fish. When Peter caught the fish, he opened the fish's mouth and, just as Jesus had predicted, Peter found a coin that he could use to pay the tax (Matthew 17:24-27).

I presume Jesus did that because He didn't have the money. When He died, He had not prearranged His burial. He had no tomb. A kind and well-to-do man named Joseph from Arimathea let the body be placed in his own, newly-hewn tomb. These are samplings from the New Testament that show Jesus led a poor man's life.

Why? St. Paul answers: "You know the grace of our Lord Jesus Christ." He writes in 2 Corinthians, "Though he was rich, yet for your sake he became poor, so that you by his poverty might become rich" (2 Corinthians 8:9). For you Jesus did it. Now He offers you a wealth that all the toys in the world cannot give. He gives you His very self. In Him is the priceless glory of the eternal God. Someone has observed that the hole in your heart and in mine is a God-shaped hole. When Jesus fills your heart, you will be content whether you have few or many possessions. In fact, you'll come to understand that all those material things the commercials say you need are incidental to your well-being. Often, they are irrelevant. Sometimes they are even opposed to your true joy.

I hope all of this lies heavily upon your heart. Are you seeking contentment and happiness for yourself and your family in things that our commercial society is constantly pitching at us? A new house, a new car, a new investment, a new this, a new that? Don't misinterpret. Material possessions are not to be despised. They are, in fact, to be respected. The commandment, "Thou shalt not steal" (Exodus 20:15 KJV), shows that God places a value upon personal property. But God also says, "If riches increase, set not your heart on them" (Psalm 62:10). Again the Bible says, "Whoever trusts in his riches will fall" (Proverbs 11:28). Accumulating toys will prove to be your dead end.

I asked Jorge, "What would you say to a young person?" He replied:

> You know what I tell a young person or an old person? I start by saying, "The only way to true joy and happiness, the only way to break a bond of any addiction or break a bond of any emptiness is through a change of mind and heart that can only come through an intimate relation with Christ." And they say, "You're exclusive," and I say, "Yeah, I've tried everything else the world has to offer and I couldn't do it."[2]

Jesus Christ is the only way because He's the only One through whom you can come to the glory of God. All the riches in the world cannot buy God and His happiness. That only comes through faith in Jesus who forgives our many sins. That's the glory of God that can make a person content and happy in life.

Today, Jorge Valdés believes that Jesus Christ died on the cross to forgive his sins, as terrible as his sins were. Jesus Christ died for your sins too, whatever they may be. Among your sins and mine is the folly of seeking happiness in things rather than in God. You may not have done drugs or some other terrible crime, but we've all wandered away from the path of eternal contentment and happiness the Creator intended for us, His children. St. Peter wrote, "He himself bore our sins in his body on the tree, that we might die to sin and live to righteousness. By his wounds you have been healed. For you were straying like sheep, but have now returned to the Shepherd and Overseer of your souls" (1 Peter 2:24-25).

"For the love of money is a root of all kinds of evils. It is through this craving that some have wandered away from the faith and pierced themselves with many pangs. But as for you, O man of God, flee these things. Pursue righteousness, godliness, faith, love, steadfastness, gentleness" (1 Timothy 6:10-11).

Jorge's spiritual house is in good order now. I was curious to know if Jorge misses the things he had in the old days: the mansions, the cars, the fawning people. "Do you miss the toys?"

> I miss them all. You know, the thing about it is that people say when you have all this power, "How can you go through life now without it?" And I tell people, "I do, I go through without it." I miss it… Who doesn't miss going to the store and buying whatever you want to buy? The difference is that now the hole that… was inside my body, in my mind, in my soul, has been filled. It's filled with a relationship with Jesus.[2]

It's not true that the person who dies with the most toys wins. "Riches do not last forever; and does a crown endure to all generations?" (Proverbs 27:24). The truth is that the crown of life will be given to the person who believes in Jesus Christ. That's where God offers you the true riches of His glory. That's how He will fill the hole in your heart.

Amen.

For Further Reflection

"Give us this day our daily bread." (Lord's Prayer, Fourth Petition)

- "Daily bread includes everything that we need for our bodily welfare."[3] Can "daily bread" become your god? Put yourself in the story – Luke 12:13-31.
- We should fear God because we, mortal creatures of a day, are dependent upon Him – Psalm 145:15-16; Matthew 5:45; Ecclesiastes 1:1-11; Ecclesiastes 12:13-14. *"Silent bow before Him."*[4]
- Jesus teaches us that the gifts of "daily bread" are only a part of our Father's overall care for us – Matthew 6:11; Matthew 6:33-34
- All God's provision for us is centered in Jesus – 2 Corinthians 1:20; John 6:35; Isaiah 55:1-3
- What more do we need? 1 Timothy 6:8; Proverbs 30:7-9; Ephesians 5:20. Therefore, we love God above all things.

> *Hence, all earthly treasure! / Jesus is my pleasure,*
> *Jesus is my choice.*
> *Hence, all empty glory! / Naught to me the story*
> *Told with tempting voice.*
> *Pain or loss, / Or shame or cross*
> *Shall not from my Savior move me / Since He deigns to love me.*[5]

Retrospective

I was 53 years old when I wrote this sermon, and I think I got it right. Accumulating stuff will never give us lasting satisfaction. What I've come to believe, in the years since I wrote this, may strike you as strange. It's not something normally taught to us in church, Sunday School, or parochial school, but I'm convinced it's true. It is this: God strips away from us all the earthly things which we hold dear. God personalizes how He matures us. How Jorge came to see that it's all about Jesus is not the same way God leads – or tries to lead – us. We can be obstinate, you and I. But whatever your personal story is, the Heavenly Father disciplines us, His children, by stripping away all the things we hold dear. It may be slowly or it may come in one fell swoop, but the Father finally takes all away from us. "The Lord disciplines the one he loves, and chastises every son whom he receives" (Hebrews 12:6). Think about it. Your possessions, your friends and family, your health, and finally this life itself will be taken away from you.

I once visited a little church in the Hartz Mountains of Germany. The railing leading up to the high pulpit was decorated with the wood carving of a naked man. "What's that about?" I asked. Answer: "We brought nothing into the world, and we cannot take anything out of the world" (1 Timothy 6:7). From the pulpit comes the Word of God that the Good News of Jesus is all we finally have. The things you and I hold dear are gifts of God, not to be despised, but in the progress of life, aging, He takes them away so that more and more we come to see that Jesus is all we have. This learning has been profound to me.

I once asked my students if they hoped in their coming ministries to move their parishioners away from the bad feelings we all have in life. They said that's what they hope to do, that they want to get their hearers off the feelings of loss and into more upbeat feelings. I disagreed. In a strange way – and certainly this is not welcome to our natural feelings – the grievous losses we experience are drawing us to an ever-closer focus on Jesus. I believe that our heavenly Father, taking away bit by bit the props that support us, is drawing us to depend only on Him.

> *When ev'ry earthly prop gives way,*
> *He then is all my hope and stay.*[6]

Week 25 – Let the Lambs Leap

Nativity of St. John the Baptist
Delivered at Holy Cross Lutheran Church, Collinsville, Illinois
June 24, 1984

Text – Luke 1:39-45

In those days Mary arose and went with haste into the hill country, to a town in Judah, and she entered the house of Zechariah and greeted Elizabeth. And when Elizabeth heard the greeting of Mary, the baby leaped in her womb. And Elizabeth was filled with the Holy Spirit, and she exclaimed with a loud cry, "Blessed are you among women, and blessed is the fruit of your womb! And why is this granted to me that the mother of my Lord should come to me? For behold, when the sound of your greeting came to my ears, the baby in my womb leaped for joy. And blessed is she who believed that there would be a fulfillment of what was spoken to her from the Lord."

Prayer

Heavenly Father, already in the womb John the Baptist leaped for joy when he met Your Son Jesus. As we begin our new relationship, a new pastor for our congregation, give us joy as we come together to meet the Savior. Give us joy in introducing other people to Jesus. Bless this congregation and its organizations. Like frolicking lambs, let us leap for joy because of Jesus. Amen.

Today the Church is observing the birth of John the Baptist. Some newer translations of the Bible call him John the Baptizer. I guess they do that so we don't think he belonged to First Baptist or Meadow Heights Baptist Church. Whatever you call him, John was the forerunner of Jesus. He was the messenger God sent to preach repentance. He came to tell Baptists and Lutherans and Jews and everybody that the Messiah, the Savior, was about to come. My sermon text tells about the first time that John himself met the Savior. It was before John was even born: "When Elizabeth heard the greeting of Mary, the baby leaped in her womb."

Babies can do that, you know. They know what's going on outside the womb. When Diane was carrying our daughter Katie, we went to an Okawville Rockets basketball game. When I cheered loudly, Katie leaped in the womb. Diane said she would do the same thing in church when I preached. Katie knew the sound of her dad's voice. John knew that he was meeting the Savior. So the Bible says he leaped – he jumped in the womb. It was exciting for John to meet the Savior, to meet the One to whom his whole life was dedicated. There is something interesting about this word "leap." The word in Greek is *skirtaó* (σκιρτάω). John leaped, *skirtaó*, in the womb. That same word is used for animals frolicking joyfully. Horses and goats are said to leap with joy, *skirtaó*. The word is also used of lambs leaping for joy. John the Baptist was a little lamb who leaped for joy when he met the Savior. Today there are little lambs and big sheep, young people and old, infants and adults, rich and poor, healthy and sick, married, single, widowed, divorced – today there are all kinds of lambs who leap with joy when they meet the Savior.

A baptism, for example. What an occasion for joy! Here are children born in sin, born under the wrath of God – children who would be lost unless delivered by the Lord Jesus Christ – but in Baptism God makes them children of heaven. The spirits of those children must leap with joy. We know that the angels in heaven rejoice over one sinner, one child, who repents (Luke 15:10). Or what about someone who has gotten away from church for a while and then comes back? Maybe I'm talking about one of you. Since I'm new, I don't know all your spiritual histories. Maybe you, for whatever reason, happened to come back to church. What an occasion for joy! Joy – not because you meet the new pastor, not because it's another body in church we can count for attendance, not because it's another dollar in the plate. It's an occasion for joy because, in this church, you meet Jesus Christ, the Savior, the One who died, the One who says, *If you've gotten away from church, that's forgiven. Let me take you in My arms and bring you back to the fold, back to your Father's house.* This is an occasion for joy. I could go on and on talking about the lambs that leap every day because of what God is doing through Holy Cross: baptisms and communions, Stephen Ministers and Andrew Callers, VBS, Sunday School, Christian day school. Lambs are leaping with joy because they are meeting the Savior. If you haven't noticed the joy back here at church, then take a long look at your sins, take a long look at Jesus, and look at what God is doing here at Holy Cross.

Today we are recognizing the Ladies Aid of our church. This is a big year for the Ladies Aid – 125 years of activity, of service, lady lambs leaping for joy. I want to tell you, the ladies are a joyful group. Other organizations are, too, but today we are recognizing the Ladies Aid. One of the best times I've had lately was about ten days ago when I went with about 21 members of the Ladies Aid and toured the new synodical office building. It was fun. Our text for today sounds like a ladies meeting. Mary and Elizabeth got together to visit – the kind of thing that ladies like to do. Mary and Elizabeth come together, and what happened? Because they got together, John met the Savior. It was the ladies who arranged that joyful occasion where the sinner John met the Savior Jesus. Our Ladies Aid today – indeed all the organizations of the church, and the church itself – is in the business of arranging meetings where sinners meet their Savior. So my request today is, *let the lambs leap.*

Let the lambs leap! Do your part to introduce people to the Savior. Let your faith show. Let God and Jesus become part of your normal conversation. Invite someone to come to church. You don't have to twist their arms. You don't have to be a Jesus freak. Be yourself, but do what you can to let the lambs leap. You can do something back here at church. Join an organization, like the Ladies Aid. Volunteer for VBS or Sunday School. Get into the Stephen Ministries, the Andrew Callers. Plan to attend the Great Commission Convocation in St. Louis in October. You'll be hearing much more about that. You don't have to spend 24 hours a day at church. I'm not asking you to do that. But you can do something to let the lambs leap. Show your joy.

This is my first sermon as your pastor. I have one major goal for Holy Cross. I want the church *full* on Sundays. You fill it, and I'll show you Jesus. I'll do all I can to make you leap for joy because you have a Savior. Help bring people to Jesus. Make our visitors feel welcome. Introduce them to me. There are so many people I have to meet. Please help bring them to Jesus, so that lambs young and old may leap.

Amen.

For Further Reflection

"Remember the Sabbath day by keeping it holy." (Third Commandment)

- "We should fear and love God that we do not despise preaching and his Word, but regard it as holy and gladly hear and learn it" (Martin Luther, Small Catechism).[1]
- What kind of hearer are you? Find yourself in one of these cities – Acts 17:1-34.
- A dread, fearful prospect – Revelation 3:14-22
- True fear and love of God in His Word – John 6:60-69; Psalm 19:7-11; 1 Peter 1:8-12, 22 - 2:3

> *O Holy Spirit, enter in,*
> *And in our hearts Your work begin,*
> *Your dwelling place now make us.*
> *Sun of the soul, O Light divine,*
> *Around and in us brightly shine,*
> *To joy and gladness wake us*
> *That we may be / Truly living, / To You giving / Prayer unceasing*
> *And in love be still increasing.*
>
> *Give to Your Word impressive pow'r,*
> *That in our hearts from this good hour*
> *As fire it may be glowing,*
> *That in true Christian unity*
> *We faithful witnesses may be,*
> *Your glory ever showing.*

*Hear us, cheer us / By Your teaching; / Let our preaching / And our labor
Praise You, Lord, and serve our neighbor.*[2]

Retrospective

*The first sermon of a new pastor to his congregation is obviously im-
portant. This was my first sermon to Holy Cross in Collinsville, Illinois,
upon accepting their call to be their pastor. Writing about public speaking,
the Greek philosopher Aristotle said three things in a speech persuade
people. First is the character of the speaker. Does integrity show? Second
is identifying with hearers at an emotional level. Does the speaker feel as
we feel? Third is logical persuasion. Is his argument convincing?*[3]
*Aristotle's three are needed in sermons too, and whether the first or the
five hundredth sermon to a congregation, the pastor has to show integrity,
empathy, but most important of all, God's living and active Word. The
pastor works to open the ears and hearts of the listeners so the Holy Spirit
has ample room to do the convincing. That's why I closed this first sermon
by asking the parishioners simply to come to church. Of all the statistics a
church person can gather, the one more important than all others to me
was and still is church attendance. Are the people coming? And if not,
why? People have redefined regular church attendance. "Regular" used
to mean every Sunday; now it's coming every month or so. This reflects
America's cultural shift from a churched to a post-churched society.
However, data need not be destiny. People will come with more regularity
when they know a congregation is welcoming, the sermons are substantive
and applicable words from God, and the church's culture is something
they want to be part of. In such congregations, the Spirit has ample room
to work. I've seen it in my many travels, and experienced it in my pastoral
ministry. They come; the Spirit works. The Word did not – does not – return
void (Isaiah 55:11).*

I know I wrote this sermon in the basement of our home in Collinsville, Illinois. That's where I did my reading and writing; a church office is too busy a place for me to think. I don't remember what kind of typewriter I used, but it obviously was a typewriter, not yet a word processor or computer. The top line of the sermon page is revealing. The title and text, of course. The occasion – "Nativity of JB." JB because I didn't want to take the time to type out "John the Baptist." Similarly, you see in the second paragraph, "When Diane was carrying Katie..." I used ellipses because I knew the story so well I didn't need to type it out. An illustration you know well needs no intentional effort to memorize, will be delivered from your heart, and allows for eye contact with your hearers. When I sit down to write out a sermon, I have the goal to write it as quickly as possible, within an hour or so. I can if I've done the preparatory work, decided upon a focused title, a tight outline, key words and phrases, and relevant illustrations. It's interesting to me that I did not include on that line, "Inaugural Sermon at HC." Perhaps that was omitted because we had lived in Collinsville for three years while I was teaching at the Seminary, and the congregation of Holy Cross had heard me preach before. It wasn't the normal "reveal" of the new pastor. Various things come together in any given sermon: liturgical date, congregational emphases, and so on. The preacher in preparation will try to bring them all together under his overarching title and theme. One last observation about the first line: It gives the date and place. That's helpful looking back, such as when publishing a book of old sermons!

LET THE LAMBS LEAP   Luke 1:39-45   Nativity of JB   6-24-84   Holy Cross, Collinsville

Today the church is observing the birth of JB. Some newer translations of the Bible call him JBaptizer. I guess they do that so we don't think he belonged to the 1st Baptist or Meadow Hts Baptist church. Whatever you call him, John was the forerunner of Jesus. He was the messenger God sent to preach repentence. He came to tell Baptists and Lutherans and Jews and everybody that the Messiah, the SAvior, was about to come. My sermon text tells about the first time that John himself met the Savior. It was before John was even born.

Babies can do that, you know. They know what's going on outside the womb. When Diane was carrying Katie... Katie knew the sound of her dad's voice. John knew that he was meeting the Savior.So the Bible says he leapt, he jumped in the womb. It was exciting for John to meet the Savior, to meet the one to whom his whole life was dedicated. There is something interesting about this word "leap" The word in Greek is skirtao. John leapt, sk, in the womb. That same word is used for animals frolicking joyfully. Horses and goats are said to leap with joy, sk. The word is also used of lambs leaping for joy. JB was a little lamb who leapt for joy when he met the Savior. Today there are little lambs and big sheep, young people and old, infants and adults, rich and poor, healthy and sick, married, single, widowed, divorced - today there are all kinds of lambs who leap with joy when they meet the Savior.

A baptism, for example. What an occasion for joy! Here are children born in sin, born under the wrath of God, children who would be lost unless delivered by the Lord Jesus Christ, but in baptism God makes them children of heaven. The spirits of those children must leap with joy. We know that the angels in heaven rejoice over one sinner, one child, who repents. Or what about somebody who has gotten away from church for a while and who comes back. Maybe I'm talking about one of you. Since I'm new, I don't know all your spiritual histories. Maybe you for whatever reason happened to come back to church. What an ocaasion for joy! Joy-not because you meet the new pastor, not because its another body in church we can count for attendance, nto because its another dollar in the plate-its an oaassion of joy because in this church you meet Jesus Christ, the Savior, the one who died...the one who says, if you've gotten away from church, that's forgiven. Let me take you in my arms and bring you back to the fold, back to your Fathe's house. An occasion for joy. I could go on and on talking about the lambs/that leap everyday because of what God is doing through Holy Cross. Baptisms and communions, Stephen ministers and Andrew callers,VBS, SS, Christian day school - Lambs are leaping with joy because they are meeting the SAvior. If you haven't noticed the joy back here at church, then take a long look at your sins, take a long look at Jesus, look at what God is doing here at Holy Cross.

Today we are recognizing the Ladies Aid of our church. This is a big year for the Ladies Aid. 125 years of activity, of service, lady lambs leaping for joy. I want to tell you, the ladies are a joyful group. Other organizATIONS are, too, but today we are recognizing the ladies aid. One of the best times I've had lately was about 10 days ago when 22 I went with about 21 memebrs of the LA and tourned the next synodical office building. It was fun. Our text sounds like a ladies meeting. Mary and Elizabeth got together to visit. The kind of thing that ladies like to do. Mary and Elizabeth come together, and what hhppened? Because they got together, John met the Savior. It was the ladies who arranged that joyful occasion where the sinner John met the Savior Jesus. Our ladies aid today, indeed all the organizations of the church, the church itself, is in the business of arranging meetings where sinners meet their Savior. So my request today is "Let the lambs leap."

LLL Do your part to introduce people to the Savior. Let your faith show. Let God and Jesus become part of your normal conversation. Invite somebody to come to church. You don't have to twist their arms. You don't have to be a Jesus freak. Be yourself, but do what you can to let the lambs leap. You can do something back here at church. Join an oragination, like the la. Volunteer for VBS, SS. Get into the Stephen ministries, the Andrew callers.Plan to attend the great comm in Oct. You'l l be hearing much more about that. You don't have to spend 24 hours a day at church. Not asking you to do that. But you can do something to let the lambs leap. Show your joy. This is my first sermon

Week 26 – Cross and Country

Independence Day
Delivered at St. Salvator Lutheran Church, Venedy, Illinois
and St. Peter Lutheran Church, New Memphis, Illinois
July 3, 1977

Text – Luke 20:19-26

The scribes and the chief priests sought to lay hands on him at that very hour, for they perceived that he had told this parable against them, but they feared the people. So they watched him and sent spies, who pretended to be sincere, that they might catch him in something he said, so as to deliver him up to the authority and jurisdiction of the governor. So they asked him, "Teacher, we know that you speak and teach rightly, and show no partiality, but truly teach the way of God. Is it lawful for us to give tribute to Caesar, or not?" But he perceived their craftiness, and said to them, "Show me a denarius. Whose likeness and inscription does it have?" They said, "Caesar's." He said to them, "Then render to Caesar the things that are Caesar's, and to God the things that are God's." And they were not able in the presence of the people to catch him in what he said, but marveling at his answer they became silent.

Prayer

Great God of the nations, we thank You for our nation, our United States. Oh, the blessings we have here! Even greater are the blessings You, our heavenly Father, give us as citizens of the cross of Your Son Jesus Christ, freedom from sin, death, and the devil. Help us by Your Holy Spirit to be faithful citizens of the cross so that we might also be citizens who bless our country. In Jesus' name we pray. Amen.

The Pharisees were a group of Jews who lived in Jesus' time. They thought they knew it all when it came to religion. They were very upset with Jesus because He came and taught religion to the common people. What Jesus taught the people was far different from what the Pharisees had been peddling. You see, the Pharisees had been peddling their own notions about religion, but Jesus taught the Word of God. When spiritually discerning people hear the clear Word of God, they follow it. Such people don't come in droves to hear the intellectual opinions of ministers or professors or Pharisees. But people receptive to the truth will come in crowds to hear the clear Word of God. That is what Jesus taught. That is why the people came to Him in droves. No wonder, then, that the Pharisees were upset with Jesus. Jesus was cutting into their following.

So the Pharisees decided to trap Jesus. They wanted to trick Him into saying something that they could use against Him. They knew that if they could get Him to say the wrong thing, it would be good ammunition for them to use against Him. So, the Pharisees came to Jesus and they showed Him some money. They asked Jesus if the Bible permitted people to pay taxes to the Roman government. The trick was this: If Jesus said *No, you shouldn't pay taxes*, then He was guilty of treason against the government. If Jesus said *Yes, you should pay taxes*, then the Pharisees could accuse Jesus of shortchanging God. The Pharisees thought, *He's got to say one thing or the other, and either way we'll trap Him.* But what did Jesus say? He demolished the Pharisees! He cut right through their proud and arrogant trap. He showed them that they didn't know as much about religion as they thought they did. And, you know what Jesus said: "Render to Caesar the things that are Caesar's, and to God the things that are God's." Caesar was the title of the head man of the Roman government – like a president or king. The word Caesar is where we get the German word Kaiser. So, Jesus is saying, *Give to the government what belongs to the government, and give to God what belongs to God.*

Jesus distinguishes between two different realms: the civic and the divine. The divine realm is God's world, the world of faith, the world of the Church, the world of the cross. But the civic realm is the world of the government, the world of our country. On this weekend in July, our thoughts turn especially to the civic realm in which we live. We think of our country, the United States of America. Last year we celebrated our nation's bicentennial with much festivity and with a renewed commitment to the purposes for which our nation was founded. This Fourth of July, the festivities may be a bit less than last year, but certainly our dedication to the United States is as great as ever. Here God has blessed us richly on every side. This is a good land that brings forth bumper crops with regularity. We get so accustomed to bumper crops that if we don't happen to set a record one year, we act like there was a crop failure. Here in these United States, we have science and technology that make this country the industrial leader in the entire world. Here in this country, we have a Constitution that guides all our citizens. What is more, the Watergate scandals have shown us that even our politicians must live by the laws of our Constitution! And here, in these United States, God has given us freedoms. These are the freedoms spelled out in the Bill of Rights – the first ten amendments to the Constitution. They include the freedom that our homes will be private, not unjustifiably searched; the freedom to say what we think, without fear of punishment by the government; and of course, the freedom to worship God as we choose. With all these blessings surrounding us in our country, this Fourth of July weekend is certainly a time for you and me to stop and ask God's continued blessing upon our country. *"O Lord, stretch forth Thy mighty hand / And guard and bless our Fatherland."*[1]

As wonderful as our country is, it looks sickly and pale when we compare it to another country in which we are citizens – God's country. God's country is the country of the cross. You and I are citizens of the cross by faith in the Son of God. We have been given faith through Baptism, through the Scriptures, and through Holy Communion. Our faith is founded on the cross: the cross on which Christ died for our sins... the cross that was once a symbol of shame and punishment, but now because Christ rose from the dead, is a symbol of victory and eternal life... the cross, which is at the heart of our Church and to which you and I look every time we worship. We are citizens of the cross.

The cross gives us freedom. The Bill of Rights in our Constitution gives us some freedoms. But those freedoms are only for external practices. They do not free the heart and soul. They are temporary freedoms, which we enjoy only in this life, but not in the life to come. But the cross gives us the greatest freedom of all. Faith in the cross of Christ frees us from sin, from death, and from the devil himself.

Sin is a dictator that ruled us before our baptism. Sin is a dictator that still tries to gain control of our lives every day.

Death… Death is far more than the cessation of bodily functions. It is far more than the cause of a funeral. Following our physical death is either eternal life or eternal death. For an unbeliever, physical death is the end, once and for all – the eternal end of God's kindness.

And the devil… In this modern day and age, does anyone still believe in a devil? Does anyone believe that there is such a thing as this bad, fallen, rotten angel who goes around trying to make people sin? I'll tell you: Look at the world around you. Read your newspapers and watch the news on TV. Then try and tell me that there is not a devil. His handiwork is all about us. There is a devil! If you think not, you'll be easy pickins for him.

Sin, death, and the devil are tyrants. They oppress us. But the cross of Christ frees us from their rule. You and I are citizens of the cross.

It is important that you and I remember that there are two realms: the civic and the divine. There is the cross, and there is the country. The two are separate. Many fine things can be said about our country. But remember – there's one thing it cannot do. It cannot free you from sin, death, and the devil. The Constitution of the United States, the Declaration of Independence, and all the laws that have ever been passed in Washington or Springfield do not bring us a saving Gospel. Our United States is a nation of law. Every citizen and every politician is under the law. But the law cannot save a single soul. Citizenship in the United States of America does not make you righteous before God. You are made righteous before God only by faith in the cross of Jesus Christ. When you die, God will not let you into heaven because you are an American citizen. He will let you into heaven only because you are a citizen of the cross. It is only because in faith you have confessed your sins and asked the Savior's forgiveness that God saves you. This is the Gospel of God. It comes from the cross of Christ, not from our country.

Yet, we citizens of the cross are very interested in the welfare of our country. Psalm 122:6 says, "Pray for the peace of Jerusalem!" Jerusalem was the capital city of Israel. The Psalmist is telling the people to pray for their country. Good citizens of the cross pray for their country. We do it for many reasons. We hope that God will continue to shower upon us all the blessings we have enjoyed in the past. We pray that we will remain strong and prosperous. We also pray for our country for the sake of the Gospel. God has given us a country where the message of the cross can be proclaimed. Other messages can be proclaimed, too, of course. Just as it was with the Pharisees, so it is today: Ministers can peddle their own notions, intellectuals and professors who think they know it all can spout off their ideas. In our country, you are even free to worship the devil. And there are some who do that. But alongside all that garbage, here in the United States we have the freedom to proclaim the Gospel of Jesus Christ in terms that are loud and clear. We have the wonderful freedom here to tell the story of salvation. We preachers can preach about Christ. I have no reason to be afraid that the government will put me in jail for what I preach. I'm not going to be shot because I said earlier that the United States can't save a single soul – only the Gospel can. I can preach the truth in terms that are loud and clear. You can do the same. The story of the cross is not only for the preacher to tell. Every citizen of the cross should tell the story. You can do that by the life you lead. Don't sin. Christ freed you from sin. You should tell the story. Tell others about the cross. Bring them to church. God has blessed us with a country where we can practice our religion. We should take advantage of the opportunity!

"Render to Caesar the things that are Caesar's, and to God the things that are God's." You and I are citizens in two realms. One is our country. God bless it, so we and our children can pass our time in safety and peace. The other realm is the realm of the cross, the world of faith, the world of salvation. God help us to be good citizens in both.

Amen.

For Further Reflection

"Honor your father and your mother." (Fourth Commandment)

- "If men were angels, no government would be necessary. If angels were to govern men, neither external nor internal controls on government would be necessary. In framing a government which is to be administered by men over men, the great difficulty lies in this: you must first enable the government to control the governed; and in the next place oblige it to control itself."[2]

- Put yourself in the story. An example of ineffective government – Judges 17:1-13, especially v. 6. See also Judges 21:25. People are not angels!
- Understanding the purpose of government in the fear of God – 1 Samuel 8:1-22; 1 Samuel 12:10-15; Romans 13:1-7
- Why the Church prays for effective government – 1 Timothy 2:1-4
- "Give us today our daily bread. … What, then, is meant by daily bread? Daily bread includes everything that we need for our bodily welfare, such as … good government, good weather, peace and order, health, a good name, good friends, faithful neighbors, and the like" (Martin Luther, Small Catechism).[3]

Lord of our life and God of our salvation,
Star of our night and hope of ev'ry nation:
Hear and receive Your Church's supplication,
Lord God Almighty.

Lord, be our light when worldly darkness veils us;
Lord, be our shield when earthly armor fails us;
And in the day when hell itself assails us,
Grant us Your peace, Lord:

Peace in our hearts, where sinful thoughts are raging,
Peace in Your Church, our troubled souls assuaging,
Peace when the world its endless war is waging,
Peace in Your heaven.[4]

Retrospective

Students in my preaching classes often ask their wives to read through their sermons. Often the wife says the sermon is fine but reads too simply, not educated enough. To that I say, "Great! You want your sermons to read simply." This sermon, "Cross and Country," is a good example of the oral style. Short sentences. One thought following another. No fancy words. Writing something to be delivered orally and heard with the ears, aurally, is different than writing something to be read, the literary style. When a person is reading, she can pause whenever she wants to make sure she understands. The reader is in control. Listening is different. The preacher is in control and therefore should choose his words and construct his sentences so the listener can keep up. I have listened to many sermons that were chock-full of fine thoughts but not as effective as they might have been, simply because they were not written in the oral/aural style. Like a man racing a horse, the preacher kept galloping on, sharing his thoughts – but the audience couldn't keep up, the thoughts were coming too fast, so the listeners gave up trying to follow.

The live delivery and reception of a sermon is different than the quiet reading of words on a page. Over two thousand years ago, the Greek philosopher Aristotle observed that the speeches of the great orators "are good to hear spoken, but look amateurish enough when they pass into the hands of a reader."[5] The great motivator toward effective communication from the Christian pulpit should be love – selfless love for the people entrusted to the pastor's care – such that he disciplines himself to speak the treasures of God's good Word simply, but not simplistically.

Week 27 – Kindling the Commitment

Broadcast on The Lutheran Hour
July 7, 1996

Text – 1 Timothy 6:12-14 (GW)

Fight the good fight for the Christian faith. Take hold of everlasting life to which you were called and about which you made a good testimony in front of many witnesses. In the sight of God, who gives life to everything, and in the sight of Christ Jesus, who gave a good testimony in front of Pontius Pilate, I insist that, until our Lord Jesus Christ appears, you obey this command completely. Then you cannot be blamed for doing anything wrong.

Prayer

O God, Your love for us is greater than we can comprehend. Oh, how often we do not truly see Your loving kindnesses all around us! But when we do, when we perceive traces of Your love for us, lead us by Your Spirit to follow the trail to ever greater awe for all the love You give us. Just as we are committed to those we love in our present life, lead us more and more to live in Your perfect will, returning Your love with our love, returning Your kindness with our ever-increasing commitment to You. "Whom have I in heaven but you? And there is nothing on earth that I desire besides you" (Psalm 73:25). In Jesus' name, Amen.

If God told you that you're going to die within the next 24 hours, would you change your conduct? Perhaps so. Perhaps you would call into work and say, "I can't come into work today; I'm going to be very sick."

Perhaps you would devote your last day to prayer – to praying like you've never prayed before. Let me ask, however: Shouldn't you be praying fervently every day? Whether it's one of many days of life or your final day of earthly life, isn't prayer supposed to be one of your daily disciplines? Doesn't the Bible say, "Pray without ceasing" (1 Thessalonians 5:17)?

Perhaps you would devote your last day to reading the Bible. Like a student cramming for a final exam, you'd finally settle down and do your homework. But let me ask again: Shouldn't you be reading your Bible every day? If you haven't disciplined yourself to do this divine homework every day, how will you know what pages to turn to when death is near?

If God told you that you're going to die within the next 24 hours, wouldn't you be kind to people around you – kinder than you've ever been before? Since you're about to come before the eternal Judge, would it really matter who was at fault in the quarrels of your life? Once again, let me ask a counter question: Shouldn't you be kind every day? "Be kind to one another," says Ephesians 4:32, "tenderhearted, forgiving one another, as God in Christ forgave you."

Well, you see my point. If God told you ahead of time that today will be the last day of your earthly life, such an announcement should cause no fundamental change in the way you go about your daily business.

> Let each day begin with prayer,
> Praise, and adoration.
> On the Lord cast every care;
> He is your salvation.
> Morning, evening, and at night
> Jesus will be near you,
> Save you from the tempter's might
> With His presence cheer you.[1]

"Whether we live or whether we die, we are the Lord's" (Romans 14:8). Or at least, so it should be. The basic question is not whether you're going to live or die today. The underlying question is about your daily commitment to God. What is the level of your commitment to the God who has made you, who redeemed you, and before whom you will be required to give an account of your life? *"God be in my head and in my understanding,"* goes an old, old prayer. *"God be in my eyes and in my looking; God be in my mouth and in my speaking; God be in my heart and in my thinking; God be at my end and at my departing.*"[2] So goes the old, old prayer. But who among us prays so devotedly each day? Who among us lives such a consecrated life each day? I do not. So I must pray with some sense of shame. But I also pray with confidence and hope: *O God, my heavenly Father, help me to love You with all my heart and with all my soul and with all my mind* (cf. Matthew 22:37). Am I alone in that prayer? Or can I make the assumption that your commitment to God is not what it ought to be, and that you also will ask your heavenly Father to kindle a greater commitment in your life? That's what it's about, today and every day – kindling the commitment.

St. Paul, the old apostle and veteran of the faith, said the following to his dear young Timothy:

> Fight the good fight for the Christian faith. Take hold of everlasting life to which you were called and about which you made a good testimony in front of many witnesses. In the sight of God, who gives life to everything, and in the sight of Christ Jesus, who gave a good testimony in front of Pontius Pilate, I insist that, until our Lord Jesus Christ appears, you obey this command completely. Then you cannot be blamed for doing anything wrong. (1 Timothy 6:12-14 GW)

So says the Word of God. Although that's an inspired Word from God Himself, at first reading it doesn't seem to help with my need for greater commitment each day of my life. Now, I don't mean to be irreverent, but look at all the commands that Paul laid on Timothy, that God lays on us. Listen to the imperatives of that passage: "Fight the good fight." "Take hold of everlasting life." "Obey this command completely." Those are commands. Now, there's also a promise connected to those commands: "Then you cannot be blamed for doing anything wrong." My problem is that I'll never receive the promise if it's up to me to keep the commands. Jesus told it like it is when He said to the sleepy disciples in Gethsemane, "The spirit indeed is willing, but the flesh is weak" (Matthew 26:41). Paul, too, knew that it's not so simple to keep the commands of God. He wrote to the Romans, "For I do not do the good I want, but the evil I do not want is what I keep on doing" (Romans 7:19). Yes, I want to kindle a greater commitment to God each day of my life. I want to keep the commandments. I want to receive the promise. My problem is that day in and day out, I'm just not up to it.

Who is? No one. Psalm 143:2 (GW) tells it like it is: "[LORD,] Do not take me to court for judgment, because there is no one alive who is righteous in your presence." That inability to live up to God's commands leaves people in some pretty sorry states. It leaves some people in despair, because they realize that they cannot attain eternal life on their own. It leaves some people indifferent. *Who cares? I can't do it anyway.* Or, flying in the face of the facts, some people you know become presumptuous and falsely trust their own merits. *Sure, I can keep God's commands. Commitment to God? No problem!* Where are you? Presumptuous? Indifferent? Despairing? If the sum and substance of your religion is striving by yourself to fulfill the commands of God, you will not attain eternal life. "Not everyone who says to me, 'Lord, Lord,' will enter the kingdom of heaven, but the one who does the will of my Father who is in heaven" (Matthew 7:21).

God's will is not simply command. His commands rest upon what God has already done. You're reading the Bible wrong if you focus on the Law and ignore the Gospel. The imperatives of today's text are based upon the indicative, i.e., statements of fact. Listen: "Fight the good fight for the Christian faith." What is the Christian faith? It is those truths of salvation that God has revealed to us. The fact of God's revelation of Good News in Jesus Christ has a logical consequence, therefore: "Fight the good fight." Listen again: "Take hold of everlasting life to which you were called." What is this call? The call is God's action. By the Good News that Jesus Christ is your crucified, resurrected, and ascended Savior from sin, God has done what you could never do. He has done what our natural religious aspirations could never do, because we are by nature dead in trespasses and sins. God has redeemed you and me from sin and death and given us forgiveness and life. Listen again: Paul says, "In the sight of Christ Jesus, who gave a good testimony in front of Pontius Pilate, I insist that, until our Lord Jesus Christ appears, you obey this command completely." Again, the command is based on a preexisting fact. Jesus testified before Pilate that He is not only the King of the Jews, but the ruler of a kingdom that is not of this world (John 18:36). Because of the fact of that testimony to the truth, Paul tells Timothy and God commands us to commit ourselves completely to this Christian faith. So it is that God's action in Christ comes before our action. God's call to us in the Gospel precedes our response.

Dr. James H. McConkey describes the relationship between God's call to us through the Savior and our subsequent commitment this way:

> The highway of consecration is the first sight which greets the believer's eyes as he steps out from the crimson fountain which has cleansed his sin-stained soul. It confronts him like a great triumphal arch, opening into the pathway of his life of ministry. A pierced hand flings open its portals before his eyes. A voice from the Redeemer of his soul cries out, "I beseech you, present your body [as] a living sacrifice." Its gates are crimsoned with the blood of Him who gave Himself for you. Its archway is empurpled with the rich clusters of fruitage the hidden Vine is seeking to bear through you, His yielding branch. It echoes with the shouts of victory of those who walk its blessed path. It is resplendent with the glory of God, which shines from the lives that walk therein in the light of His face. Oh, what a highway is this! Have you entered it?[3]

Have you entered it, that highway of consecration? I have. But not because of the commands of God. His commands are good, but the sin within me prevents me from doing what God desires. It's through faith that I've laid hold of eternal life, faith in Christ – "the faithful witness," as Revelation 1:5-6 calls Him, "the firstborn of the dead, and the ruler of kings on earth … [the One] who loves us and has freed us from our sins by his blood." Martin Luther says:

> I believe that I cannot by my own thinking or choosing believe in Jesus Christ, my Lord, or come to him. But the Holy Spirit has called me by the gospel, enlightened me with his gifts, sanctified and kept me in the true faith. In the same way he calls, gathers, enlightens, and sanctifies the whole Christian church on earth, and keeps it with Jesus Christ in the one true faith.[4]

The Spirit of God and of Christ calls you and kindles your commitment by the very same Gospel that has graciously put me on that highway of consecration. Your commitment to God and Christ is not the Gospel. The Gospel is the Good News of eternal salvation from sin, death, and Satan. That is what calls us, what enlightens us, and what kindles our commitment.

This Gospel calls for your total commitment. *"Love so amazing, so divine, / Demands my soul, my life, my all!"*[5] It is said that in the early days of the Church, "the Empress Eudoxia endeavored to destroy Chrysostom, the gold-tongued and valiant preacher."[6] Chrysostom wrote to a certain Cyriacus and said,

> If the empress wants to saw me asunder, she may do so; the prophet Isaiah met with the same fate. If she desires to drown me in the sea, I shall think of Jonah. If she shall try to cast me into the fire, I shall bear in mind the three men in the fiery furnace. If she shall compel me to fight with wild beasts in the arena, I shall remember Daniel in the lions' den. If she will have me beheaded, I shall reflect on John the Baptist. If she shall have men stone me to death, I shall endure what Stephen endured. If she craves for my life and all my possessions, she is welcome to them; for naked came I from my mother's womb, naked will I depart this life.[6]

For such a commitment of heart, soul, and mind, you and I must continually pray to our heavenly Father!

Jan Hus is a timely example of another Christian's commitment even unto death. July 6th is the anniversary date of his martyrdom. Hus was born in 1373 in Bohemia. He received his education at the University of Prague, became a priest in 1402, taught at the university, and eventually became its rector. In 1411, Pope John XXIII (that's right, there was another Pope John XXIII who lived in the 15th century) promoted the sale of indulgences. That is, the people were being taught the false idea that you could lighten the punishment of your sins by buying an indulgence. Hus complained against the practice – a complaint that got him into trouble with the hierarchy who then forced him into exile. After about two years, Hus came out of exile to attend the Council of Constance. He appeared before the council in June of 1415 and refused to retract his positions. On July 6th, Jan Hus was condemned as a heretic and burned at the stake.

A foolish man, would be the verdict of many in our society. *Why give up your life for some little point of religion?* But, what is Jesus' response? "For whoever would save his life will lose it." He says in Mark chapter 8:

> For whoever would save his life will lose it, but whoever loses his life for my sake and the gospel's will save it. For what does it profit a man to

gain the whole world and forfeit his soul? For what can a man give in return for his soul? For whoever is ashamed of me and of my words in this adulterous and sinful generation, of him will the Son of Man also be ashamed when he comes in the glory of his Father with the holy angels." (Mark 8:35-38)

Jan Hus didn't really lose his life. Isaiah, John the Baptist, Stephen, and all the Christian martyrs were not foolish for their commitment to the truth. "Be faithful unto death, and I will give you the crown of life" (Revelation 2:10). The Christian martyrs wear the heavenly crown, not because of their martyrdom but because of the Gospel which they believed. That means that today and every day, whether you live or whether you are about to die, the Gospel kindles commitment to God and Christ and eternal life. Luther says:

Faith is a living, daring confidence in God's grace, so sure and certain that the believer would stake his life on it a thousand times. This knowledge of and confidence in God's grace makes men glad and bold and happy in dealing with God and with all creatures. And this is the work which the Holy Spirit performs in faith.[7]

Lord give us such a faith as this;
And then, whate'er may come,
We'll taste e'en now the hallowed bliss
Of an eternal home.[8]

Amen.

For Further Reflection

"Thy will be done on earth as it is in heaven." (Lord's Prayer, Third Petition)

- "God's will is done when he breaks and defeats every evil plan and purpose of the devil, the world, and our sinful flesh, which try to prevent us from keeping God's name holy and letting his kingdom come. And God's will is done when he strengthens and keeps us firm in his Word and in the faith as long as we live. This is his good and gracious will" (Martin Luther, Small Catechism).[9]
- Salutary fear of God in conduct (Genesis 39:6-23) and faith (Luke 18:1-8). Considering those examples, are you living in God's will?
- Jesus' example of perseverance in His Father's will – Romans 5:6-11. "God shows his love for us" (v. 8). Yes, Jesus is our example. But Jesus, someone outside us, worthy of imitation (1 Peter 2:21-25), is more – Galatians 2:20. He is in you!
- "Firm in his Word and in the faith as long as we live"[9] – Matthew 5:10; Revelation 2:10; Colossians 2:6
- Put yourself in the story – Hebrews 11; Mark 9:24

> *Cast care aside, lean on your guide;*
> *His boundless mercy will provide.*
> *Trust, and enduring faith shall prove*
> *Christ is your life, and Christ your love.*
>
> *Faint not nor fear, His arms are near;*
> *He changes not, who holds you dear;*
> *Only believe, and you will see*
> *That Christ is all eternally.*[10]

Retrospective

Monday through Friday, the bells ring at 9:25 A.M. to summon the Concordia Seminary community to chapel. If you're in the area, you are most welcome to join us. Each week on Thursday we have "communal prayers," a time when individuals can offer their own petitions. You can depend on it, every Thursday someone prays for persecuted Christians. There is discrimination in America against Bible-confessing Christians, but in other parts of the world there is out-and-out persecution, deadly persecution, torture, and beheading. What would I do?

"Faith is a living, daring confidence in God's grace, so sure and certain that the believer would stake his life on it a thousand times."[7] The stark truth: I am staking my life on Jesus Christ! That obsesses me. It troubles me because the truth is, "I believe; help my unbelief!" (Mark 9:24). Lord Jesus, kindle my commitment! But that stark reality steels my faith. Say and do what you will, criticize me, I follow Jesus. "We walk by faith, not by sight" (2 Corinthians 5:7). Thy will be done in my life!

Week 28 – Nearer God's Heart

Delivered at the Chapel of St. Timothy and St. Titus,
Concordia Seminary, St. Louis, Missouri
September 26, 2014

Text – Isaiah 5:1-7

Let me sing for my beloved
   my love song concerning his vineyard:
My beloved had a vineyard
   on a very fertile hill.
He dug it and cleared it of stones,
   and planted it with choice vines;
he built a watchtower in the midst of it,
   and hewed out a wine vat in it;
and he looked for it to yield grapes,
   but it yielded wild grapes.

And now, O inhabitants of Jerusalem
   and men of Judah,
judge between me and my vineyard.
What more was there to do for my vineyard,
   that I have not done in it?
When I looked for it to yield grapes,
   why did it yield wild grapes?

And now I will tell you
   what I will do to my vineyard.
I will remove its hedge,
   and it shall be devoured;
I will break down its wall,
   and it shall be trampled down.
I will make it a waste;

it shall not be pruned or hoed,
    and briers and thorns shall grow up;
I will also command the clouds
    that they rain no rain upon it.

For the vineyard of the LORD of hosts
    is the house of Israel,
and the men of Judah
    are his pleasant planting;
and he looked for justice,
    but behold, bloodshed;
for righteousness,
    but behold, an outcry!

Prayer

O Spirit of God and of our Lord Jesus, help my every gaze upon nature to be filled with thoughts of You. Put me in awe that I am a beloved part of Your magnificent creation. Let the varied magnificence of nature remind me of the splendors of Your people, varied but Yours in Jesus Christ. Where we have sinned and failed to delight You, forgive us for Jesus' sake. Where we do bring forth the beauties of justice and righteousness, all praise to You! Make us, we pray, a delightful planting to our God and Savior. Amen.

Maybe you've walked through a garden and seen these words on a plaque, or maybe you've seen them as you browsed in a garden store:

The kiss of the sun for pardon,
The song of the birds for mirth,
One is nearer God's heart in a garden
Than anywhere else on earth.[1]

If you enjoy gardening, as Diane and I do, you know it's not quite as idyllic as Dorothy Frances Gurney's poem suggests. Did you ever get poison ivy? I get it all the time. Did you ever get chigger bites? How about the shock of seeing a snake, despair after all your work was flattened by hail, or having your back thrown out because of the garden? This finger? I broke it in the garden. Maybe there's more to God than simply "the kiss of the sun for pardon" and "the song of the birds for mirth." Indeed, the garden teaches us about both the magnificence of creation and how sin has corrupted God's creation.

Today's text from Isaiah 5 is about a vineyard, not a garden – but the appeal of gardens and vineyards is similar. The text tells us that the LORD loved the vineyard he planted:

> Let me sing for my beloved
>   my love song concerning his vineyard:
> My beloved had a vineyard
>   on a very fertile hill.
> He dug it and cleared it of stones,
>   and planted it with choice vines;
> he built a watchtower in the midst of it,
>   and hewed out a wine vat in it (vv. 1-2)

But now comes a twist; things aren't so idyllic in the vineyard: "And he looked for it to yield grapes, but it yielded wild grapes" (v. 2). Wild grapes – weeds in the garden! Did you ever plant something in the garden that turned out so badly that you uprooted it? "And now I will tell you what I will do to my vineyard," the LORD announces beginning in verse 5:

> And now I will tell you
>   what I will do to my vineyard.
> I will remove its hedge,
>   and it shall be devoured;
> I will break down its wall,
>   and it shall be trampled down.
> I will make it a waste;
>   it shall not be pruned or hoed,

and briers and thorns shall grow up;
   I will also command the clouds
      that they rain no rain upon it. (vv. 5-6)

It makes you think twice about being "nearer God's heart in a garden"!

Jesus used the image of a vineyard in Matthew 21:33-46. A man planted a garden and rented it out to tenants. But when the owner sent servants to collect the rent, the tenants killed the servants. In exasperation, he sent his son (you know the name of that son; you love Him), but they killed the son too. Jesus asked His hearers what the owner would do. "He will put those wretches to a miserable death and let out the vineyard to other tenants who will give him the fruits in their seasons" (Matthew 21:41). Looking for grapes – precious grapes – but he got wild grapes... and they killed his son to boot.

I hope you understand that this text isn't about vineyards or gardens. It's about the people of God: ancient Israel, and you and me today.

   For the vineyard of the LORD of hosts
      is the house of Israel,
   and the men of Judah
      are his pleasant planting;
   and he looked for justice,
      but behold, bloodshed;
   for righteousness,
      but behold, an outcry! (Isaiah 5:7)

God loved His Israel, His "pleasant planting." He planted them to do good works, specifically to bring justice and righteousness to all people – but they gave him "wild grapes." Their works were bloodshed and outcries. Today, you and I are God's people, His "pleasant planting" by Baptism into our Lord Jesus and the Christian faith. Why did God plant that vineyard in Isaiah? Why did God bring you into the Church? Because He loves you. The Church is His planting, His vineyard. It's not really *our* church, *our* seminary, *our* denomination; it's His. And God does the work for His Church. Like preparing a vineyard or garden, He plants us by Baptism, and He lovingly nurtures and cultivates us by His teaching and preaching and Supper. It's His work in us, and in return He looks for us to produce "grapes," good works for His delight. He looks for us to bear the fruit of righteousness – that is, to live by faith in the Son of God who loved us and gave Himself for us. He looks for us to bear the fruit of justice – that is, the second great commandment – to love our neighbor as ourselves (cf. Matthew 22:39). Are you hearing all my references to "He" and "His"? This pleasant planting of the Church is all centered in Jesus, the beloved Son who died, rose, and gives us His Holy Spirit. Jesus says, "I am the true vine, and my Father is the vinedresser. ... Whoever abides in me and I in him, he it is that bears much fruit, for apart from me you can do nothing" (John 15:1, 5). Where are we "nearer God's heart"? When we are thankful beyond words because He has made us part of His pleasant planting through Jesus Christ.

We don't always do that, do we? Wild grapes – instead of righteousness and justice for all people. That's why God keeps sending us prophets and apostles, sermons and Bible studies, and conversations with fellow Christians. We're in the time of grace, God's goodness leading us to repentance (cf. Romans 2:4). This pleasant planting is about love, God's love to us in Jesus, and our grateful love that yields good works for Him. Jesus says, "If you love me, you will keep my commandments" (John 14:15). In the love of Jesus, Church is God's pleasant planting, and with one another we are nearer to God's heart... until He takes us home.

Amen.

For Further Reflection

"Jesus Christ ... suffered under Pontius Pilate, was crucified, died and was buried. ... He will come to judge the living and the dead." (Apostles' Creed, Second Article)

- Put yourself in the story of judgment against those whose fruits were evil – Matthew 21:33-46
- "We should *fear* ... God"[2] – James 4:17; Romans 3:20; Ecclesiastes 12:13-14; Matthew 10:28

- What does Jesus, the One killed by the workers in the vineyard but vindicated by resurrection, do for us? Galatians 3:13; Isaiah 53:4-5; Romans 5:19
- Therefore, "We ... fear and *love* God"[2] by doing good to all people – Galatians 6:10, Luke 25:13-17; Matthew 25:31-46

> *Wondrous honor You have given*
> *To our humblest charity*
> *In Your own mysterious sentence,*
> *"You have done it all to Me."*
> *Can it be, O gracious Master,*
> *That You deign for alms to sue,*
> *Saying by Your poor and needy,*
> *"Give as I have giv'n to you"?*[3]

Retrospective

"Young Christians are twice as likely as the national average to have volunteered for a church (31% compared to 15%) or for a non-profit (19% versus 11%)."[4] *I find that volunteer spirit alive and well among today's seminarians. Regarding volunteering for a church, they are obviously required to be active in a congregation, but many go beyond the minimum requirements and gladly spend more time in their churches. The same is true about volunteering in the community. When Hurricane Harvey devastated Texas in August 2017, I was delighted to hear stories about seminarians volunteering to help. They did this on their own, before we put any official program in place. They have, if I may venture, more active hearts and hands for righteousness and justice in society than many in previous generations. That's one reason my great delight as president of Concordia Seminary is our Millennial students. They encourage me, against the natural tendencies of age and cynicism, not to "grow weary of doing good, for in due season we will reap, if we do not give up" (Galatians 6:9).*

Week 29 – *Jesus, Huh?*

Delivered at Trinity Lutheran Church, Arcadia, Michigan
July 26, 2015

Text – Mark 8:14-21 (also read Mark 6:30-52 and 8:1-13)

Now they had forgotten to bring bread, and they had only one loaf with them in the boat. And he cautioned them, saying, "Watch out; beware of the leaven of the Pharisees and the leaven of Herod." And they began discussing with one another the fact that they had no bread. And Jesus, aware of this, said to them, "Why are you discussing the fact that you have no bread? Do you not yet perceive or understand? Are your hearts hardened? Having eyes do you not see, and having ears do you not hear? And do you not remember? When I broke the five loaves for the five thousand, how many baskets full of broken pieces did you take up?" They said to him, "Twelve." "And the seven for the four thousand, how many baskets full of broken pieces did you take up?" And they said to him, "Seven." And he said to them, "Do you not yet understand?"

Prayer

Beautiful Savior, Son of God and Son of Man, help me in this meditation to grow in my awe for You. How many times You have come to teach me what a great Savior You are! But how many times I have tried to confine You to my own natural way of understanding! I confess, and I ask that You interrupt my normal thoughts with awe for You.

Glory and honor, / Praise, adoration,
Now and forevermore be Thine![1] *Amen.*

You are good people. Do you get that? You are good people… good because of the supernatural grace of God. Martin Luther says we are saints and sinners at one and the same time.[2] By nature, you and I are sinners. God is supernatural, above nature. When King Solomon dedicated the temple, he prayed, "Behold, heaven and the highest heaven cannot contain you; how much less this house that I have built!" (1 Kings 8:27). This supernatural God, above nature, comes into our nature by sending Jesus, by coming to us with words – words of forgiveness and hope – by coming to us with words and water in Baptism that saves us. And the supernatural God comes into our nature with words and bread and wine in the Lord's Supper: "This is my body … this is my blood" (Matthew 26:26, 28). This is the supernatural grace of God that makes you good people, saints and sinners at one and the same time.

Most of us have heard this for a long, long time. You've heard it said in various ways and from various biblical texts. Our familiarity with the Gospel gives the devil an opportunity to pull you away from God and Jesus. As one of my fellow professors says, the temptation is that we "domesticate" Jesus. We've all seen cute little puppies. They get trained. Sometimes the cute little puppy sits on its haunches and puts up its paws. "Nice puppy. Nice puppy. Now go back into your nice little house." *Nice Jesus. Nice Jesus. You came into the world. You died for our sins. You'll take me to heaven. Nice Jesus. Now church is over. You stay here in your nice Jesus house, and I'll come and see you again.* Domesticated Jesus. And that's the natural thing for us to do because we are creatures of nature, doing, as the song says, *"Doin' what comes natur'lly."*[3] What I want to get into your heads today is that we shouldn't regard Jesus in simply a natural human way, a *nice Jesus* way. Jesus wants us to know Him as the awesome Son of God who alone can save us, and who came to do just that (cf. 2 Corinthians 5:16).

Three Bible stories will help us here. The first is from Mark 6:30-44. Jesus and the disciples had been very, very busy. So naturally – naturally (we're creatures of nature) – they were tired and needed rest. They went away to rest, but wouldn't you know it? People kept flocking to Jesus to hear Him teach. Now it's getting late. Suppertime is coming. The disciples said, "Send them away" (v. 36). Jesus says, "You give them something to eat" (v. 37). *Jesus, huh? There's no*

Schnucks or Shop 'n Save here. There's a Walmart in Capernaum, but it's not a Supercenter. Jesus, a lack of planning on their part does not constitute an emergency on our part. Jesus, huh? That's a totally natural human reaction – but the Son of God responds with a supernatural miracle. Five loaves and two small fish end up being "twelve baskets full of broken pieces and of the fish" (v. 43). The disciples must have been impressed; they remembered the miracle and eventually it was written down in the Gospels, but at the time they thought it was just something amazing. *Jesus, huh?* should have become Jesus awe, but it didn't.

The second story is from Mark 6:45-52. After feeding the 5,000, Jesus told the disciples to get into the boat and go across the lake to Bethsaida. He went by Himself to the mountain to pray. Now mind you, it's late. Recall that the 5,000 were fed in the evening, so now it's 3:00 A.M. or so. The disciples were struggling against the wind, when Jesus "came to them, walking on the sea" (v. 48). Struggling against the wind is natural; walking on the sea is supernatural. Of course, they were scared – they thought it was a ghost. Listen to this: "He spoke to them and said, 'Take heart; it is I. Do not be afraid.' And he got into the boat with them, and the wind ceased. And they were utterly astounded, for they did not understand about the loaves, but their hearts were hardened" (vv. 50-52). They were astounded because they were still regarding Jesus from a human point of view. They should have known from the feeding of the 5,000 that the One who could miraculously feed the masses is the supernatural Savior come to deliver His people. Only God gave manna from heaven (Exodus 16); only the Son of God can feed the masses. Jesus walking on water and calming the wind should have been no surprise. *Jesus, huh?* should have been Jesus awe – this is the Son of God – but the disciples didn't get it.

The third story is itself a collection of three stories, and they are found in Mark 8:1-21. Once again, a great crowd has gathered. Again, it's late. Jesus says, "If I send them away hungry to their homes, they will faint on the way. And some of them have come from far away" (v. 3). Jesus is setting His disciples up to give Him the right response, but… "His disciples answered him, 'How can one feed these people with bread here in this desolate place?'" (v. 4). *Really?* Jesus had to be thinking, *Guys, huh? Don't you get it?* So, Jesus proceeds to feed 4,000 people, and this time there are seven baskets of leftovers. Sometime later, Jesus has an argument with the Pharisees. They wanted Him to give them a sign to prove Himself to them – a sign they would accept. My, He had given so many signs, but they wanted to fit Him into their view of reality.

After that disagreement, Jesus got into the boat with His disciples:

> Now they had forgotten to bring bread, and they had only one loaf with them in the boat. And he cautioned them, saying, "Watch out; beware of the leaven of the Pharisees and the leaven of Herod." [A supernatural teaching from the Son of God! By now, they should have known that when Jesus opens His mouth, they should pay attention, but…] And they began discussing with one another the fact that they had no bread. [Jesus was thinking, *Huh? Don't you guys get it?*] And Jesus, aware of this, said to them, "Why are you discussing the fact that you have no bread? Do you not yet perceive or understand? Are your hearts hardened? Having eyes do you not see, and having ears do you not hear? And do you not remember? When I broke the five loaves for the five thousand, how many baskets full of broken pieces did you take up?" They said to him, "Twelve." "And the seven for the four thousand, how many baskets full of broken pieces did you take up?" And they said to him, "Seven." And he said to them, "Do you not yet understand?" (Mark 8:14-21)

Jesus, huh? They still didn't get it – that the One who was in many ways so like them, in so many ways natural as we are natural, is also the supernatural Savior come to deliver them (cf. Philippians 2:5-11).

The natural thing for us to do is try to understand Jesus according to our minds, to fit Jesus into our story. That's *"Doin' what comes natur'lly."*[3] I meet someone and find some natural way to relate him or her to my life. You get a bill, and figure out how you're going to fit it into your situation. You struggle with an illness – nature isn't the way it should be – and you see things in terms of your troubles. That's natural. We want Jesus to fit Himself into our story. *Nice Jesus.* But Jesus says, "Do you not yet understand?" *Understand your story by My story. Understand your life by My life. Understand the natural things in your life by My supernatural presence with you.* Don't have enough bread to live? "Take heart; it is I. Do not be afraid" (Mark 6:50). Struggling against the wind; work is too hard? "Take heart; it is I. Do not be afraid." Do not have the health you naturally want? "Take heart; it is I. Do not be afraid." Regard Jesus as a natural historical figure, and you'll forever be buffeted by natural problems; it's guaranteed. Regard Jesus as Son of God and Son of Man, and you'll be given a perspective above natural problems, a supernatural perspective, a heavenly perspective as the Spirit of God grows you more and more into full Christian maturity. Then our doubting moments – *Jesus, huh?* – will become Jesus awe moments. "Take heart; it is I. Do not be afraid."

Nice Jesus? We can't domesticate Jesus. That's why in the Gospel of Mark, Jesus is always trying to get the disciples to see – and not just see but really perceive – to hear – and not just hear but really understand – that He is the supernatural Son of God come to save us. The disciples never quite get it in Mark, but we learn from the rest of the New Testament that they did get it after the resurrection. In the resurrection, they saw our nature of sin and death transformed by forgiveness and life and immortality. They never again saw Jesus in just a human way. Listen to John's description of Jesus in Revelation chapter one:

> Then I turned to see the voice that was speaking to me, and on turning I saw seven golden lampstands, and in the midst of the lampstands one like a son of man, clothed with a long robe and with a golden sash around his chest. The hairs of his head were white, like white wool, like snow. His eyes were like a flame of fire, his feet were like burnished bronze, refined in a furnace, and his voice was like the roar of many waters. In his right hand he held seven stars, from his mouth came a sharp two-edged sword, and his face was like the sun shining in full strength.
>
> When I saw him, I fell at his feet as though dead. But he laid his right hand on me, saying, "Fear not, I am the first and the last, and the living one. I died, and behold I am alive forevermore, and I have the keys of Death and Hades." (Revelation 1:12-18)

Devotion by devotion, Bible study by Bible study, conversation about faith after conversation about faith, worship after worship after worship, the Spirit of God is making you His people, saints and sinners at one and the same time. The Spirit is taking your natural *Jesus, huh?* moments and transforming them into Jesus awe moments. "Take heart; it is I. Do not be afraid."

Amen.

Beautiful Savior,
Lord of the nations,
Son of God and Son of Man!
Glory and honor,
Praise, adoration,
Now and forevermore be Thine![1]

For Further Reflection

"I believe ... in Jesus Christ." (Apostles' Creed, Second Article)

- Put yourself into the stories of this sermon. What would have been your natural reaction? Read Jesus' parable in Matthew 25:1-13. Which group are you in? Sometimes the good group, but other times? Mark 9:24!
- "We should *fear* ... God."[4] No one can believe for you – Hebrews 10:31; Luke 23:39-43; Habakkuk 2:4; Luke 7:50.
- What Jesus, the Son of God, does for us: Fear is a natural emotion, and we should have a salutary fear of God because of our sins – Psalm 143:2. Greater than that for a believer is true fear – awe, reverence – that God comes in Christ to save us – Psalm 33:8; Psalm 96:4; Romans 8:31-39.
- Therefore, we "fear and *love* God"[4] – Deuteronomy 6:4-6; Matthew 22:34-38; Psalm 73:25-26. Why would we love God if we don't stand in fear and reverence before our only Savior?

Oh, for a faith that will not shrink
Tho' pressed by many a foe;
That will not tremble on the brink
Of poverty or woe;

That will not murmur nor complain
Beneath the chast'ning rod,
But in the hour of grief or pain
Can lean upon its God;

Lord give us such a faith as this;
And then, whate'er may come,
We'll taste e'en now the hallowed bliss
Of an eternal home.[5]

Retrospective

I like this sermon because I'm so much like the disciples – slow to get it. As a parish pastor, I'd go to one of Collinsville's nursing homes and was often greeted by a friendly man who announced he was Jesus Christ. A short conversation, but all the while I was thinking, Yeah, right. You're here in this home, just where you should be. The first disciples knew there was something special about Jesus. He commanded attention, and that's why they left their jobs to follow Him, but in the Gospel of Mark they never get that He is God's Son come into our lives. "Jesus, huh?" I've grown up in the church, learned a lot about religion, and in seminary and ministry got to know a whale of a lot about Jesus, God, and the Bible. But I'm still learning – and I repent and say I'm learning too slowly, that He's present with me day-in and day-out to correct and chasten, to guide and lead, and to forgive and give lively hope. St. Paul said he took "every thought captive to obey Christ" (2 Corinthians 10:5). That's my goal in sanctification, obedience every moment to His presence and promise, "Take heart; it is I. Do not be afraid" (Mark 6:50). To that end I fixate on the harder sayings of Jesus, the ones that make me react naturally, "Jesus, huh?" Unlike my nursing home friend, His miracles show that He is supernatural God come into the world to help and save us. The home of trusting His promises is just where I should be. He is Jesus the Christ!

Week 30 – God's Mouth House

Delivered at Peace Lutheran Church, Lemay, Missouri
for the dedication of the new sanctuary
August 24, 2014

Text – Mark 4:21-25

And he said to them, "Is a lamp brought in to be put under a basket, or under a bed, and not on a stand? For nothing is hidden except to be made manifest; nor is anything secret except to come to light. If anyone has ears to hear, let him hear." And he said to them, "Pay attention to what you hear: with the measure you use, it will be measured to you, and still more will be added to you. For to the one who has, more will be given, and from the one who has not, even what he has will be taken away."

Prayer

Dear God, You have given us Your Word to hear and follow. Lead us to immerse our daily lives in Your Scriptures and shape the lives of our earthly congregations around Your Word. Whether we worship in an ornate sanctuary or a rented space in a strip mall, there Your Word ministers forgiveness, hope, and life to us. Amidst all the words of our busy lives, guide our congregation to heed most the Word of Christ that Your Spirit speaks to us. Amen.

I thank you for the privilege of being here, and for the special honor of delivering the dedication sermon. This past Monday I stopped by, and Pastor Kastens kindly showed me this beautiful new sanctuary. My reaction was, "Wow!" I don't know if I've ever seen a new construction that is this beautiful and that has such wonderful promise for the ministry and mission of a church. Congratulations! You have done well. In preparing for this sermon, I also came up with a nickname for this sanctuary. I'll share that with you later.

I begin with a proposition. I'm going to lay something in front of you. If you take it to heart, you'll get something in return. Here's the proposition: If you pay attention to *what* you hear, then this beautiful sanctuary will be a place of ever-increasing blessings to you. Let me say that again: *If you pay attention to* what *you hear, then this beautiful sanctuary will be a place of ever-increasing blessings to you.* My text is Mark 4:21-25. In this passage Jesus is speaking. One of the striking features of this new church is the stained glass windows, and every window features Jesus. So as I give the sermon text, look at Jesus. He spoke these words to His first disciples. He speaks these words to us today:

> And he said to them, "Is a lamp brought in to be put under a basket, or under a bed, and not on a stand? For nothing is hidden except to be made manifest; nor is anything secret except to come to light. If anyone has ears to hear, let him hear." And he said to them, "Pay attention to what you hear: with the measure you use, it will be measured to you, and still more will be added to you. For to the one who has, more will be given, and from the one who has not, even what he has will be taken away."

Jesus tells us, "Pay attention to *what* you hear." Oh, we hear a lot in our lives! Our minds are overloaded with the data of this digital age. From 1970 to 2008, the number of televisions doubled. In 1990, there was one computer for every five Americans. By 2005, only one in five did not have a computer. Today, 80% of Americans are connected to the internet. In 1985, the number of telephone calls per year was 425 million. In 2006, the number of phone calls per year was 13 billion. 86% of Americans use a cell phone.[1] I could give you more numbers, but why? You know that we're swimming upstream against a torrent of images and information and data. Jesus says, "Pay attention to *what* you hear." Why shouldn't we be discriminating in what we hear and watch? You were baptized into Jesus Christ. Hundreds, thousands are yet to be baptized here in this sanctuary. You were baptized into His death for the forgiveness of your sins and into His resurrection for the sure and certain hope of everlasting life. That will be proclaimed here to hundreds of thousands in the years to come. And here you will receive His body and blood in Holy Communion. It brings you forgiveness of sins, life, and salvation. Of course, we want to be discriminating in what we hear. Your salvation depends upon it! "Pay attention to *what* you hear."

In the verses right before this passage, Jesus told the Parable of the Sower (Mark 4:1-20). In that parable, He talks about how people hear the Word of God. Some hear the Word and the devil immediately comes and snatches it away. Others hear the Word of God, receive it with joy, but they fall away because they don't get deeper into the Word. Still others hear the Word but the cares of life, the deceitfulness of riches, and desire for things choke out the Word. But the good soil – God help you and me to be that good soil – these are the people who receive the Word and it grows up and produces thirtyfold and sixtyfold and a hundredfold. The Word you will hear here produces growth! "For the word of God is living and active, sharper than any two-edged sword," says Hebrews 4:12. It lays bare our sins. It exposes our hypocrisies. But it does more. Jesus says, "The words that I have spoken to you are spirit and life" (John 6:63). Peter says, "Lord, to whom shall we go? You have the words of eternal life" (John 6:68). This is what the Spirit will do to you as you make it your business to hear the Word of God in this church. When you do, you'll be blessed more than you can imagine. "Pay attention to *what* you hear: with the measure you use, it will be measured to you, and still more will be added to you. For to the one who has, more will be given." And then Jesus adds a warning: "And from the one who has not, even what he has will be taken away."

So, congratulations! You have built exceedingly well. In closing, let me point something out. There is no command in the Bible to build church buildings. That's right – there is no command in the Bible to build church buildings. The Bible says, "For here we have no lasting city, but we seek the city that is to come" (Hebrews 13:14). We are pilgrims journeying toward our heavenly home. You and I are followers of our risen and ascended Lord Jesus Christ. Now we see Him in a glass darkly but then we shall see Him face to face (cf. 1 Corinthians 13:12). The reason we build churches is so we have a place to hear His Word, a place to put deep roots into the Gospel, and a place where the Spirit of God can multiply the faith, the hope, and the love that are in Christ Jesus.

Now, at the start of the sermon I said that I came up with a nickname for this sanctuary. The truth is, it's not a name that I came up with. Martin Luther came up with the nickname, and he talked about it in a sermon in 1522.[2] Luther said that a church is God's "mouth house," *mundhaus* in German. And that's the title of this sermon. Remember that, and we'll all be blessed. This church is God's mouth house; here we pay attention to what we hear. "He who has ears to hear, let him hear" (Mark 4:9)!

    Amen.

For Further Reflection

"Hallowed be Thy name." (Lord's Prayer, First Petition)

- God's name is not simply "Father" or "Jesus," as my name is Dale and your name is ___ . God's "name" is what He reveals to you about Himself – Psalm 103:1. Put yourself in the story – Luke 10:38-42. "Pay attention to *what* you hear."
- "We should *fear* ... God."[3] Cursing or swearing (cf. Second Commandment) is not the only reason to fear God. Any misrepresentation by clergy or laity of God's revelation in the Bible does not hallow God's name – Jeremiah 23:28; Acts 5:1-11; Revelation 22:18-19.
- God gives us His Word; how awesome is that? 2 Timothy 3:10-17; Romans 10:8-10; John 6:68-69
- Therefore, "We should fear and *love* God."[3] Look through Psalm 119. Every verse is about God's Word. "Oh how I love your law!" (Psalm 119:97).

> *I know my faith is founded*
> *On Jesus Christ, my God and Lord;*
> *And this my faith confessing,*
> *Unmoved I stand on His sure Word.*
> *Our reason cannot fathom*
> *The truth of God profound;*
> *Who trusts in human wisdom*
> *Relies on shifting ground.*
> *God's Word is all-sufficient,*
> *It makes divinely sure;*

And trusting in its wisdom,
My faith shall rest secure.[4]

Retrospective

I teach a class on Law and Gospel for concluding seminarians. I truly love the class. We go through the Ten Commandments using an old, 16th-century theological book by Martin Chemnitz. Chemnitz is called the "Second Martin" because his encyclopedic writings of theology summarized and preserved the work of the Reformer. Looking at each commandment through the lens of Law and Gospel is stimulating, but the command, "Remember the Sabbath day, to keep it holy" (Exodus 20:8), is where I tell students, "Here's a special opportunity for you in your 21st-century ministries." People today are so bombarded with information and instantaneous communication ("Why haven't you answered my email?") that the idea of shutting it off, if only for a time, and communing with the eternal God is a welcome invitation. This is far different than the years when I grew up and first served in the ministry. Life was somewhat controllable then – somewhat. Today, the new normal is a new abnormal. We're out of breath. "Remember the Sabbath day" is about hearing God's Word, and that's best done when we first slow down for times of quiet, our frantic internal engines shifted to idle, to be with the One who created us and desires to take us to heaven. "Pay attention to what you hear." Don't just do something; sit there. God's mouth house!

Week 31 – Come Ye Apart

Broadcast on The Lutheran Hour
August 4, 1991

Text – Mark 6:31 (KJV)

And he said unto them, Come ye yourselves apart into a desert place, and rest a while: for there were many coming and going, and they had no leisure so much as to eat.

Prayer

O God, there are times when we just have to get away from it all. Where better to go but to You and to our Savior! You who have created us, You who have redeemed us at Calvary – You are able to refresh our lives when we come apart to be with You. The amusements and activities of this world are often fine when properly used. Lord, don't ever let us substitute the vacations and escapes of this world for time with You. Give us Your Spirit so we might regularly come apart in heart and mind to be with You. Amen.

"Let's get out of here!" You've said that. Sometimes you've said it in desperation; you were in a bad place. Sometimes you've said it in anticipation; you're setting out on a vacation. Other times you had your wits about you and you simply knew you needed a change of scenery. "Let's get out of here!" You know who else has said that? Jesus. You might not think of Jesus as saying something like that. He's so perfect. He's such a strong personality. He's in control of everything. You probably wouldn't think of Him saying, as we do, "Let's get out of here!" But He did. "Come ye yourselves apart into a desert place, and rest a while," He told His followers.

In my message today, I'm going to tell you that Jesus understands your desire to get away – and I hope to describe what Jesus does for you when you accept His invitation, *Come ye apart.*

Jesus invites you to come apart often, especially when you're hurting. You can't always take a day off when you need it. Maybe your vacation seems endlessly far away. No matter. Your heart and mind can always take off, even if only for a few minutes at a time. Jesus appeals to your heart and mind to come apart often to be with Him, especially when life has been tough on you.

Bruce Prewer wrote the following piece entitled, "Where People Live."

> *Where people live with a bitterness of spirit which poisons and distresses those around them: Lord, Your kingdom come.*
> *Where people live greedily, without gratitude or grace, keeping a ruthless eye on the possessions of others: Your kingdom come.*
> *Where folk resort to violence, rape, terrorism, and warfare, spreading suffering and accelerating hatreds: Your kingdom come.*
> *Where people suffer disease, handicap, or savage injustice, without any faith to support them: Your kingdom come.*
> *Where communities of mixed races ache with ugly fears and hatreds, and the grief which follows repression or violence: Lord, Your kingdom come.*
> *For all who sit with the dying, make funeral arrangements, or spend tonight sleepless and grieving, we pray for the gift of divine comfort.*
> *Lord, Your kingdom come, Your will be done on earth as it is in heaven, through Jesus Christ our Lord.*[1]

As I said, that poem is entitled, "Where People Live." It describes where you and I live. You have your unique needs and feelings. You have your problems. You have your hurts.

Jesus has been there. He understands that you need to get away. Jesus wasn't some kind of phantom who came down into this world but wasn't really one of us. He's a real human being who knows what it's like where people live. A case in point is when Jesus said, "Come ye yourselves apart into a desert place, and rest a while." Jesus and His followers had just heard that John the Baptizer had been murdered. That shook them, and they needed to get away. So, yes! Jesus knows firsthand how you feel when you say, "Let's get out of here!" He's sincere when He invites you to get away, at least with heart and mind for a few minutes if you can't physically take off. "Come to me, all who labor and are heavy laden," He says, "and I will give you rest" (Matthew 11:28).

Jesus appeals to you to come apart to be with Him. *With Him* – that's not where most people today are going to get away.

Let me tell you about a homeless ten-year-old boy. No parents, no home – he fends for himself along the Sabana Grande, one of the main shopping districts in Caracas, Venezuela. I heard about this boy – I don't even know his name – from Pablo. Pablo produces television commercials in Venezuela and has a reputation for befriending young people. So, a social worker friend told Pablo about this ten-year-old boy who was absolutely impossible to deal with. Social workers and psychologists had all struck out with this ten-year-old child of the streets. "Pablo," the friend asked, "would you try to do something with him?" So Pablo tried. He let the boy sleep in his office. You could have predicted what happened. The next morning, Pablo discovered that the boy had played with all the expensive television equipment in the office. Pablo was mad, and he let that boy have a piece of his mind.

But eventually Pablo sat down and calmly talked with the boy about his life. "How do you eat?" Pablo asked. The boy answered, "Very well." He hung around the back door of fine restaurants on the Sabana Grande, and was well fed by the scraps of garbage the restaurants threw out. "Where do you sleep?" Pablo asked. The boy said he slept with about 25 other street kids in an empty house near the Sabana Grande. That was his place.

Pablo asked, "Are boys and girls in that house?" "Yes," was the answer.

"Do 'things' happen in that house?" Pablo asked.

"Things" was Pablo's polite word for sexual activities. The boy answered, "Everything. Everything happens." The boy's description fit the word "everything." And we don't need to get into that.

The boy said that many nights he was approached by prostitutes. They'd be lonely and ask him to spend the night with them. He said he often did. The boy gave them a place, away from their usual activity. Everybody looks for a place to get away.

I asked Pablo, "Has this boy become an animal?" His answer was "No, no. He has the same needs and feelings that you and everyone else have."

You have needs and feelings and hurts. Where's your place to get away? A place like the boy has – where everything happens and everything is allowed? A getaway with drugs, because so much in this world is crummy and the only way to cope is to get high? Or maybe you're more "respectable." Drugs would mess you up in too many ways, but alcohol is socially acceptable. Enough drinks and your problems go into oblivion right along with you. Where do you go? Plunge into your work? Keep yourself busy, become a perpetual-motion machine because you can't justify your existence if you're not constantly doing something? Where do you go to get away? The places to go are countless, and their deceptions are so great.

When Jesus invites, *Come ye apart*, He invites you to come to Him. "Come ye yourselves apart into a desert place, and rest a while," He says. Come away from the amusements and activities of your life. Come away from the destructive use of drugs and sex and alcohol and work. Come away from whatever lures you with its promises. And – this is important – come beyond your own needs and feelings. Come beyond yourself, and learn from Jesus.

He invites you to follow His story from the days when John the Baptizer appeared in the desert and announced Jesus' coming. Come apart from your own daily life to learn how Jesus lived life as you live life, with needs and feelings and hurts. And, oh, how it hurt when He heard that John had been murdered. Come apart, read the Bible, learn of His very real life – yes, very real. Come apart and learn how Jesus lived the life that you should have been living your whole life long. Yes, that's the marvelous thing about retreating to Jesus. We see Him doing in life what we have been unable to do. Read in the Bible about His perfect life in this evil world.

And come apart to meditate upon His death on the cross. Talk about a lonely place! Jesus cried out, "My God, my God, why have you forsaken me?" (Matthew 27:46). The answer to that question is that God was punishing Jesus for the evils of this world, including your evils and mine. God abandoned His own Son to lonely suffering so that things could be made right between you and God. When Jesus died, God brought Him back to life so that you could have a place with God. Jesus is alive now and He says to you, "Come to me, all who labor and are heavy laden, and I will give you rest" (Matthew 11:28).

This is the One who appeals to your heart and mind to get away from it all and come regularly to Him. Let the others go to their amusements, their activities,

Week 31 – Come Ye Apart

their escapes. Let others put their stock solely in days off and vacation. The Savior who said to His disciples, *Let's get out of here*, is the Savior who appeals to our hearts today, "Come ye yourselves apart." If you go to Jesus, you won't come back the same.

You'll be surprised by what you learn when you come apart from your workaday world to be with Jesus. Let me tell you another story from Pablo. Pablo's a great storyteller. And, this is about a man called "the jackal."

A Latin American mother abandoned her baby son. Apparently, she took him into the wild and just left him. Somehow or other, this baby boy survived. When he was older, he wandered into town and was befriended by a butcher. The butcher gave him some clothes and fed him. After a while, this wild young man left the butcher. In time, he took up with a woman who had four children. One day, they all went out onto an island and got drunk. They fell into an angry fight, and this wild young man killed the woman and her children.

Eventually he was captured, put in prison, tried in proceedings that lasted seven years, and finally sentenced to death. That was the first time that society had paid any attention to this so-called jackal. In his imprisonment, he was taught for the first time that many of the things he had done were wrong. He hadn't known right from wrong before that time. It reminds me of what St. Paul wrote: "Yet if it had not been for the law, I would not have known sin. For I would not have known … if the law had not said, 'You shall not … '" (Romans 7:7).

Now, maybe this surprises you, but when you accept the invitation to come apart to a lonely place with the Jesus of the Bible, you learn more about sin, and specifically about your sins. The Bible will teach you how sinful you and humanity are.

Ours is a world filled with evil. Pablo's stories of the jackal or the homeless boy in Caracas could be duplicated a million times over. Don't tell me that sin is simply our moral imperfection. Don't tell me that sins are little shortcomings that we might confess to a priest or pastor. Don't tell me that sin is an outdated religious concept. This world in which we live is filled with terrible, aggressive evil, and everyone feels the need to get away from it. And the Bible teaches that you and I are a part of that sinful humanity.

But coming to Jesus isn't like going behind the woodshed for a beating. The world beats you hard enough. That's where we live. And that's why everyone is looking for escape. No, coming apart with Jesus teaches you the greatest spiritual truth: You're forgiven. Whatever your sins, you are forgiven. The Spirit of Jesus teaches you that you are forgiven.

- *OK, so you messed up at work last month.* Because of Jesus, God forgives you.

- *OK, you're under pressure and ready to crack.* Because of Jesus, God forgives and can calm you.

- *All right, you're having trouble coping. You're having trouble living up to everyone's expectations.* Because of Jesus "The eternal God is your dwelling place, and underneath are the everlasting arms" (Deuteronomy 33:27).

That's real rest, and it's more satisfying than all the amusements and activities of the world.

Here's a demonstration of that. This letter was written to our office in Venezuela:

> I'm writing to thank you for what you have done in getting me the booklet, "Depression." It came at a very opportune moment because family problems had brought me to the edge of suicide. After reading this booklet, I've changed my way of thinking, and I see things differently. Now I can accept what is happening to me and still have hope.

This is a woman who needs to get away. Her own desperation said that the only way out was suicide. But the story of Jesus showed her the better way. Jesus said, *Come ye apart.* She came, and she was helped.

Jesus understands your need to get away. You may or may not be able to change the outward circumstances of your life, but you can get away by taking yourself to Jesus. You may not always be able to get a day off when you need it. Vacation may seem endlessly far away. When you feel the need to get away from it all, you can. Your thoughts and affections can always retreat to Jesus. Unlike so many false escapes in this world, He will help you. *Come ye apart.*

Amen.

For Further Reflection

"Thy kingdom come." (Lord's Prayer, Second Petition)

- God's kingdom is where He reigns and rules: over all creation ("kingdom of power"), in believers ("kingdom of grace"), and in heaven ("kingdom of glory"). How does God reign and rule in your life? Psalm 103:19; Mark 4:26-34; Philippians 3:20.
- "We should *fear* ... God."[2] Not coming apart with Jesus – Mark 3:5; John 6:53-67; 2 Timothy 4:10.
- What God does for us: "God's kingdom comes when our heavenly Father gives his Holy Spirit, so that by his grace we believe his holy Word and lead a godly life now on earth and forever in heaven" (Martin Luther, Small Catechism).[3] See John 3:5; 2 Timothy 4:18.
- Therefore, we "fear and *love* God"[2] – John 3:5; Colossians 1:13-14; Mark 4:20; Luke 17:15-16

> *Just as I am, without one plea*
> *But that Thy blood was shed for me*
> *And that Thou bidd'st me come to Thee,*
> *O Lamb of God, I come, I come.*

> *Just as I am, though tossed about*
> *With many a conflict, many a doubt,*
> *Fightings and fears within, without,*
> *O Lamb of God, I come, I come.*

> *Just as I am, poor, wretched, blind;*
> *Sight, riches, healing of the mind,*
> *Yea, all I need, in Thee to find,*
> *O Lamb of God, I come, I come.*[4]

Retrospective

Here's a common conversation I have with seminarians: "That was a fine sermon you preached. Good going!" The pious answer comes back, "It was God." "You mean God studied the text, outlined and wrote the sermon, and delivered it? Really?" Students' piety can sometimes confuse their theology. Paul says we are coworkers with God (1 Corinthians 3:9). Yes, we do nothing – squat – to merit our salvation. That's the realm the Bible calls "justification." But afterwards in "sanctification," we can block the Spirit's work to grow us, the justified, in grace and holiness. Over a quarter of a century after writing this sermon, I think the dynamics of justification and sanctification need more teaching than ever. Going to church is an example. Who gets you up, dresses you, drives you to church, and walks in to take a seat? Who listens attentively or, on the negative side, who gives into the distraction of your cell phone? You! *It's the same reading this sermon book, and I thank you for that. Who pulled the book off the shelf, opened it, and is reading this page? You are, because – and this is important – because the Spirit of God motivates you to come apart with Jesus in devotion. The straight and narrow of godly living has ditches on both sides. On one side is the temptation to do nothing to grow spiritually, wrongly pawning your spiritual lethargy off on God. On the other side is the temptation to let your spiritual disciplines tempt you to the heresy of synergism, that your justification is worked by you and God. The Word leads us on the sanctified way. "Work out your own salvation with fear and trembling, for it is God who works in you, both to will and to work for his good pleasure" (Philippians 2:12-13). Coming closer to the end of my journey, getting alone with Jesus is more important than ever!*

Week 32 – The Gift of Anger

Broadcast on The Lutheran Hour
August 1, 1999

Text – Psalm 32

Blessed is the one whose transgression is forgiven,
    whose sin is covered.
Blessed is the man against whom the LORD counts no iniquity,
    and in whose spirit there is no deceit.

For when I kept silent, my bones wasted away
    through my groaning all day long.
For day and night your hand was heavy upon me;
    my strength was dried up as by the heat of summer.   *Selah*

I acknowledged my sin to you,
    and I did not cover my iniquity;
I said, "I will confess my transgressions to the LORD,"
    and you forgave the iniquity of my sin.   *Selah*

Therefore let everyone who is godly
    offer prayer to you at a time when you may be found;
surely in the rush of great waters,
    they shall not reach him.
You are a hiding place for me;
    you preserve me from trouble;
    you surround me with shouts of deliverance.   *Selah*

I will instruct you and teach you in the way you should go;
    I will counsel you with my eye upon you.
Be not like a horse or a mule, without understanding,
    which must be curbed with bit and bridle,

or it will not stay near you.

Many are the sorrows of the wicked,
  but steadfast love surrounds the one who trusts in the LORD.
Be glad in the LORD, and rejoice, O righteous,
  and shout for joy, all you upright in heart!

Prayer

O Lord, life can hit us hard; it can badly beat us up. Even on the normal, un-eventful days, pressures and people can get to us and make us angry. Because of all You have done for us – coming into our world, dying for our sins, and rising to give us the hope of eternal life – we want to live our whole life in You. Teach us now through Your Word to handle the anger that occasionally wells up within us so we can grow in faith toward You and in love toward others. In Your name we pray. Amen.

Has your anger ever gotten you into trouble? It has me. When I was in about the 5th grade, an older kid said something that irritated me. I let him know it – and I ended up with a broken tooth. Many years later, I now look at that as a minor incident. Minor as it was, it was one of those times when anger has caused me problems. People who know me well would not describe me as an angry person, but anger is an occasional part of my life.

It's part of yours, too. Some of you may think you don't get angry, but psychologists say we all do. Anger is a natural human emotion. For some people, anger explodes. For others, it implodes; they bottle it up. However you handle anger, this emotion can have bad effects. You can find your relationships strained or destroyed by anger. You can be left with unnecessary guilt. Your health can deteriorate. Because of the way you handle anger, you may lose a job or get poor grades in school. You can lose money. You can get in trouble with the law. Still think anger isn't an issue? What about the news? Anger has erupted throughout our society, and it can hurt us in so many ways.

Debbie Morris knows about anger. If anyone ever had a right to be angry, she did. On May 31st, 1980, 16-year-old Debbie was out with her friend, Mark. They had bought a milkshake and drove down to the riverfront in Madisonville, Louisiana. This was not an isolated place; it was usually quite safe. But two men came at them with guns and forced their way into the car. At first the men, Robert Lee Willie and Joseph Vacarro, said they only wanted the car and the kids' money. When they got that, they said they'd drive them out of town and let them go.

Fifteen minutes later, Debbie and Mark realized these two wanted more. When they pulled off the road, they discovered that their nightmare was only beginning. They forced Mark into the trunk of the car. Robert Lee Willie forced Debbie to take her clothes off and he raped her for the first time. She would be raped two more times during this horrible ordeal. The two drove deeper into the woods where they took Mark out of the trunk, tortured him with a knife, shot him in the head, and left him for dead.

During the next 24 hours, Willie and Vacarro drove Debbie back and forth across state lines, looking for the right place to kill her and dump her body, just as they had done a few days earlier to an 18 year old named Faith Hathaway. But unlike Faith's awful outcome, Debbie's nightmarish experience took a more fortunate turn. Near Madisonville, they let her go and she walked home. Her information helped the police find Mark, who was clinging to life and did survive his wounds.

If this story sounds like something right out of a book or a Hollywood movie, you are half right. Sister Helen Prejean wrote a book called *Dead Man Walking*.[1] It focuses on the death penalty and on Sister Helen's spiritual counsel to death row inmates, including Robert Lee Willie. A popular film of the same name was made shortly after that, combining the facts and criminals from several cases, including Debbie's. As for Debbie, her release from her captors did not mean a return to normal life. Now she was living her life held hostage to her feelings of isolation, loneliness, and anger.

I was angry with Robert Willie and Joseph Vacarro for the obvious reasons – for kidnapping me and raping me and, you know, causing me to lose my trust in people and causing me to lose my normal teenage years. There was part of me that was angry with my mom. I blamed my mom's alcoholism on some of this. I was angry at my dad because my parents were divorced and my dad had moved out of state. I was angry at Sister Helen for not ever letting this go away and just, you know, be part of my past. And, I think most of all I was angry at God. You know, I trusted God the most, and my perception of Him was a loving, caretaking God. I never thought God would let something so terrible happen to me. And so I was just disappointed and angry and completely disillusioned. My whole idea of who God was just shattered.[2]

Psychologists Ron and Pat Potter-Ephron write, "Anger acts like a blinking light at a railroad crossing. It only goes on once in a while, but when it does there really is a train coming down the tracks. Anger tells you to look for the problem. It also tells you to do something to make the situation better."[3]

Debbie didn't pay attention to those flashing lights. Angry, she didn't see the train coming down the tracks. That failure caused her problems. She abused alcohol. She experienced nightmares, panic attacks, and acute depression. She was consumed with conflict. Her actions disrupted personal relationships. When people asked how she was doing, she would say, "Fine," but that was a lie. Her unresolved anger was devastating her life physically, emotionally, and spiritually.

Debbie's anger was justifiable, of course, but when she failed to see what the anger was doing to her life, when she failed to see the train coming down the tracks, she demonstrated how sin multiplies. "Do not make friends with a hot-tempered person, do not associate with one easily angered, / or you may learn their ways and get yourself ensnared" (Proverbs 22:24-25 NIV). Of course, Debbie did not associate willingly with those criminals, but she did get ensnared in the net of anger.

Again, Proverbs 29:22 (NIV) says, "An angry person stirs up conflict, and a hot-tempered person commits many sins." Unresolved anger multiplies sin.

When you get angry, there is a reason. It might be a justifiable reason, as was the case with Debbie. It might be an insignificant reason, but insignificant as it may be, you seem to be angry all the time and anything can set you off. The reason you get angry might be "out there" in the world around you. It might be within you.

Whatever sets your anger off, this natural emotion can be viewed as a tremendous gift – a potential for good. Anger is like fire. If you are careless, it will cause you no end of problems. However, if you unwrap this gift carefully, you can grow in faith toward God and in love toward others.

Anger shows that we live in a broken, sinful world. When anger wells up within you, your emotions are testifying to the fact that all is not good and pure and holy in life. The anger you feel shows that the Law of God is at work. The Bible, you may know, has two major teachings: the Law and the Gospel. The Law – those passages in the Old and New Testaments that tell us how we should be and how we should live – are like blinking lights at a railroad crossing, referring to the Potter-Ephron explanation. The blinking lights of anger call out "Danger!" They show that you and I have not lived as we ought, and trouble is coming. Now – this is important – God did not give us the Law so we would be run over. He gave it so we would stop, look, and listen for the Good News of the Savior. Galatians says, "The law was our guardian until Christ came, in order that we might be justified by faith" (Galatians 3:24).

God sent His Son Jesus to bring healing to us and our broken, sinful world. As you well know, this earthly life has a way of beating us up. Even on normal, routine days, people and pressures can get to us and make us angry. It's all the consequence of sin, our rebellion against the ways of God's Law. Jesus Christ died on the cross to pay the price for our sins. He offers complete forgiveness to all people: to Robert Lee Willie, to Joseph Vacarro, to you and me. Put your trust in this Good News, this Gospel of forgiveness, and your sins will not be held against you. In the forgiveness that flows from the cross of Jesus Christ, there is healing for you and for all of us in this broken, sinful world. Jesus said, "When I have been lifted up from the earth, I will draw all people toward me" (John 12:32 GW).

This Good News turned Debbie's life around. Once she recognized the damage being done by her unresolved anger, she unwrapped it slowly and with the forgiveness of Jesus Christ. Now the anger that had been devastating her life became an opportunity to be healed, to grow in faith and in love. Debbie wrote a book, and I recommend it to you. It's called *Forgiving the Dead Man Walking*.[4] In it, she tells how she came to forgive Robert Lee Willie and Joseph Vacarro, and others. It wasn't that she was condoning what they had done, or forgot about the hurt. No. In forgiving those who had hurt her, she was finally turning them over to God, their Creator and Judge. That's something we should all do when someone has sinfully hurt us. That's the example of Jesus on the cross. "He entrusted himself to him who judges justly" (1 Peter 2:23 NIV). When you make that effort – sometimes a very difficult effort – to forgive those who have wronged you, then you'll find, as Debbie did, that their emotional hold on you has been broken. Though they had released her years before, Debbie was finally, in the depths of her soul, escaping her tormentors. In forgiving them, she came closer to healing. But there was more.

Debbie writes in her book:

> I came to a very clear and very real understanding that I could never "get on with life," nor could I discover, or do, what God intended for my life because I had never been able to forgive the most central character in my personal drama. I'd forgiven Robert Willie and Joseph Vaccaro as best I could. I'd forgiven Robert Willie's mother. I'd forgiven my own mother. I'd even reached the point where I'd forgiven God. But I had not yet forgiven myself.
>
> I realized that before I could do that, I had to feel that God had forgiven me. Which in turn meant I needed to ask His forgiveness. Not that I still blamed myself for what happened with the kidnapping, but there was plenty I'd done wrong since. I'd made a mess of my life by doing so many things I should never have done, and not doing other things I knew I should do.[5]

Debbie had now dealt with anger the right way. Through Law and Gospel, through the Good News of forgiveness of sin, she has survived. She's healed. Jesus our Savior taught us this way: "Forgive us our debts, as we also have forgiven our debtors" (Matthew 6:12).

Psalm 32 sums up Debbie's experience, and describes the healing that can begin through the life-changing forgiveness of Jesus Christ:

> Blessed is the one whose transgression is forgiven,
>   whose sin is covered.

Blessed is the man against whom the LORD counts no iniquity,
and in whose spirit there is no deceit.

For when I kept silent, my bones wasted away
through my groaning all day long.
For day and night your hand was heavy upon me;
my strength was dried up as by the heat of summer.   *Selah*

I acknowledged my sin to you,
and I did not cover my iniquity;
I said, "I will confess my transgressions to the LORD,"
and you forgave the iniquity of my sin.   *Selah* (Psalm 32:1-5)

Anger is a gift that comes to everyone. Next time anger wells up within you, unwrap it carefully. Ask yourself, *Why am I angry? What is it in this sinful world or within me that has set me off?* Then go to God to help you use the energy of anger for good. Unwrapped with forgiveness, anger can be a gift to help you improve your relationships, your health, and many aspects of your life. Most importantly, when the gift of anger is unwrapped with the Good News of Jesus Christ, anger can become an occasion for the Spirit to work greater faith in God and new love toward others. In a memorable passage, Debbie Morris wrote, "I do know this: Justice didn't do a thing to heal me. Forgiveness did."[6]

Amen.

For Further Reflection

"You shall not murder." (Fifth Commandment)

- Put yourself in the story of anger – Genesis 4:1-7; Acts 7:1, 51-54
- "We should *fear* ... God"[7] – Matthew 5:21-22; 1 John 3:5; Matthew 6:14-15; Romans 2:4-5
- Through Jesus, God rescues us from His fearful anger at our sins – Matthew 27:46; Romans 5:6-11; 1 Peter 2:24

- Therefore, "we should fear and *love* God"[7] – Psalms 6, 32, 51

> *To Thee, omniscient Lord of all,*
> *In grief and shame I humbly call;*
> *I see my sins against Thee, Lord,*
> *The sins of thought and deed and word.*
> *They press me sore; I cry to Thee:*
> *O God, be merciful to me!*
>
> *O Lord, my God, to Thee I pray:*
> *O cast me not in wrath away!*
> *Let Thy good Spirit ne'er depart,*
> *But let Him draw to Thee my heart*
> *That truly penitent I be:*
> *O God, be merciful to me![8]*

Retrospective

I've preached about anger over the years, and watching the crowd during the sermon I've been struck by the attention of men to the topic. People are angry today, more so than we'll admit, and I include church men among them. Jesus teaches, "Out of the heart of man, come evil thoughts, sexual immorality, theft, murder, adultery, coveting, wickedness, deceit, sensuality, envy, slander, pride, foolishness" (Mark 7:21-22). A critical question every preacher should ask as he begins to think about the next sermon is, "How can I get into the hearer's heart?" In a similar way, as you sit and listen to a sermon, monitor your own heart: "How do these words touch my inmost being?" The Bible is clear that God's truth has to go down to the heart. While our Christian faith is not based upon emotions but upon the objective Word of God, emotions point to how original sin continues in our hearts. God put His Law into our hearts at creation

(Genesis 1:26). Although the fall into sin blurred that inborn Law, it's still present (Romans 2:14-15). The inborn Law stirs up original sin in order to show our brokenness and need for the Savior who reconciles us to God (Galatians 3:24). This is not only true for those who do not yet know Jesus; it continues to be true for us who believe in Him. Anger against another person is expressed in four possible ways: inner thoughts and feelings, gestures, words, and finally actual murder.[9] Anger is one example of how Jesus' forgiveness for our sins can reach deep down into our beings, how emotions explained theologically take us to the Word of our only Savior. As God forgives our confessed anger against others, He leads us to forgive and experience the emotional release of forgiving those who have sinned against us. For myself, I'm less angry than I used to be, but there are still plenty of times. God, have mercy!

Week 33 – Don't Forget!

Delivered at St. Peter's Lutheran Church, Chicago, Illinois
August 23, 1970

Text – Luke 10:27

And he answered, "You shall love the Lord your God with all your heart and with all your soul and with all your strength and with all your mind, and your neighbor as yourself."

Prayer

Lord, help us to love You more and more with all our heart, soul, strength, and mind. You haven't forgotten us but we often forget You as we go about our daily lives. Our forgetfulness shows when we don't love our neighbor according to Your commandments. Forgive us for Jesus' sake, and give us Your Holy Spirit so that we will remember You as we go about the tasks of this new week. Amen.

Grace to you and peace from God the Father, and from our Lord Jesus Christ!

Our sermon this morning is based upon both the Gospel and Epistle lessons which were read before. I call your attention especially to these words: "You shall love the Lord your God with all your heart and with all your soul and with all your strength and with all your mind, and your neighbor as yourself."

One of the most common questions in our day-to-day living begins with, "Did you forget…?" Wives ask their husbands, "Did you forget to cash your check?" "Did you forget to make a doctor's appointment?" And parents ask their son or daughter, "Did you forget what time we told you to be in last night?" This morning in our sermon, we're going to ask whether God has forgotten you and me, His children, and then we will hear His answer. May the Holy Spirit be with us in the coming minutes, that we may grow stronger in our faith and remember more and more to put our faith into practice during the week.

First, then: Has God forgotten you and me? In the hustle and bustle of modern life, it often seems just that way. We were created to live in the peaceful and green Garden of Eden, but today we live in the noise and smoke of concrete and steel cities. We were created to live at peace with all creatures, but today we can't even live at peace with ourselves. We were created above all to live as children of our heavenly Father, but today all too many people have forgotten the God who created them. It doesn't seem to make sense. The Church has always said that God is good, but look at all the troubles in the world today. Has God forgotten us?

Or perhaps we should ask: Have we forgotten God? The trouble with the world today might not be that God has forgotten us, but that you and I have forgotten God. Have you? Many times in our lives, we have made promises to remember God and His will for us. We've often thought, *Yes, I want to love the Lord my God with all my heart, with all my soul, with all my strength, and with all my mind. And I want to love my neighbor as myself.* But have we always remembered to do that? If you're like me, the answer is *no*. We forget God so many times every day. For example, do you remember yesterday when you swore? Yet God has told you, *don't forget,* "You shall not take the name of the LORD your God in vain" (Exodus 20:7). Or do you remember yesterday when you were idly gossiping about so-and-so behind her back? Yet God has told you, *don't forget,* "You shall not bear false witness against your neighbor" (Exodus 20:16). Or do you remember yesterday when an immoral thought crossed your mind? Yet God said, *don't forget,* "You shall not commit adultery" (Exodus 20:14). We could go on and on and on. It comes down to this: You and I haven't loved the Lord our God with all our heart, with all our soul, with all our strength, and with all our mind. And we haven't loved our neighbor as ourselves. Yes – all too often, we have forgotten God.

God's Law tells us that the trouble with the world today is with us, and not with God. God is still good, and He still offers His promises of life. But God's good promises of life are given in only one way – through our Savior from sin and death, Jesus Christ. This is the Good News for you and me and our troubled world. The answer to finding the fulfillment of God's promises is not by ending pollution, or stopping a war, or anything else we might come up with to solve.

The only answer for modern living is the life, death, and resurrection of our Lord and Savior Jesus Christ. He came down to earth and lived the kind of life that you and I could never live. Where we break the commandments, our Lord has kept them all. Where we deserve to die the death of sinners, Christ died for our sins so we might live as God's forgiven people. Where we should fear the grave, Christ was raised by the Father to overcome the grave. No, God has not forgotten you and me. The proof is present for all to see – the life, death, and resurrection of our Lord and Savior Jesus Christ.

God hasn't forgotten, and you and I know this by faith. We hear again and again the words of God's promise of forgiveness in Jesus Christ as they are preached and taught – and we believe. By faith we remember that God never forgets His people. No longer do we think quite so highly of ourselves, but by faith we believe the Good News that Jesus Christ lived and died for us. We need to guard and strengthen that faith. That's why we come to church each week – to strengthen our faith in our Savior. That's why we read, or should read, the Scriptures every day – to strengthen our faith in our Savior. That's why we pray, or should pray, every day – to strengthen our faith in our Savior. For the promises of God are given to those who have faith in Jesus Christ.

Now, we have said so far that God has not forgotten you and me, but has sent His Son to die for us, and by faith we remember this Good News. But what does this mean for us when we have to face a rough world every day of the week? It means: *Don't forget God this week!* Put your Sunday morning faith into practice Monday through Saturday. Our Savior tells us just how to do that: "You shall love the Lord your God with all your heart and with all your soul and with all your strength and with all your mind, and your neighbor as yourself." Don't forget your God. He suffered and died for you. Let your love for Him guide you in all you do this week, whether it be working, playing, or praying. And don't forget your neighbor. When he needs help, lend a hand. If you can cheer her up, do so. If you can share his sadness, do that. If you can tell her about your faith, do that. And who is your neighbor? Her, and him, and her, and me, and people who aren't Lutheran, and people who aren't even Christian, white people, black people, and yellow people. Our Lord tells us that everyone is our neighbor.

People often tell each other not to forget this or that. This morning, the Holy Spirit is telling you and me, *don't forget to* "love the Lord your God with all your heart and with all your soul and with all your strength and with all your mind, and your neighbor as yourself." Don't forget – because your Savior Jesus Christ didn't forget you, but loved you enough to suffer and die for your sins.

The peace of God, which passeth all understanding, keep your hearts and minds through Christ Jesus. Amen.

For Further Reflection

"You shall have no other gods." (First Commandment)

* Put yourself in the story – Genesis 17:1; Exodus 32; Isaiah 42:8; Proverbs 8:13; Matthew 4:10; Luke 16:19-31
* What God does for us – Deuteronomy 6:4; Matthew 3:13-17; Hebrews 9:14; 2 Corinthians 13:14
* Therefore, "We should fear, love, and trust in God above all things."[1] – Ecclesiastes 12:13-14; Proverbs 3:5; Psalm 139:23-24; Psalm 73:25-26.

> *Lord, Thee I love with all my heart;*
> *I pray Thee, ne'er from me depart,*
> *With tender mercy cheer me.*
> *Earth has no pleasure I would share.*
> *Yea, heaven itself were void and bare*
> *If Thou, Lord, wert not near me.*
> *And should my heart for sorrow break,*
> *My trust in Thee can nothing shake.*
> *Thou art the portion I have sought;*
> *Thy precious blood my soul has bought.*
> *Lord Jesus Christ, my God and Lord, my God and Lord,*
> *Forsake me not! I trust Thy Word.*[2]

Retrospective

Ordinarily, a seminarian preaches in churches only after having completed the first course in homiletics, a fancy word for preaching taken from the Greek word for conversation (Luke 24:14). I had that first course during the 1969-1970 academic year, and preached this sermon the following summer, just before beginning my second year at the Seminary. I'll never forget how scared I was when I first began preaching, but I got into it. I thank the pastors who gave me opportunities to substitute for them. This was one of those preaching opportunities to help me get my "pulpit legs." What students learn in preaching classes needs to be practiced, or their newfound skills and learning will slip away. So thanks to every pastor who welcomes our seminarians into his pulpit!

About to read this sermon almost 50 years later, I was anxious. What will I find? Relieved to find the doctrine correct, I also noticed several "tricks of the trade" – the preaching techniques that I learned as a young student, and still use and teach to seminarians. One example: There are many parallelisms and antitheses in this sermon. That simply means you say something positive with several similarly constructed sentences, though using slightly different wording (parallelism). Similarly, if you're saying something negative to highlight the positive, you make that contrast with several sentences, again with slightly different wording (antitheses). This device of oral style has several benefits. It makes the task of memorizing easier for the preacher because in delivery you know you're about to say the same thing in several ways, rather than several different thoughts. Most importantly, it makes it easier for the hearer to get the point. Just because I've said something once, doesn't mean you've heard it. If I say it several times in different ways, you will hear the basic point. I don't expect the people to work through the sermon with me. They pay the pastor to do the work! Our job is to be as persuasive as possible, so the Holy Spirit can plant and nurture faith in their hearts. "Tricks of the trade," used in service of the text and pastoral care of souls, can give the Spirit more room to work on hearers' hearts.

These days, students sometimes ask if I'm nervous when I'm about to preach – nervous because it's the Word of God. No, I say, that fear of God should be dealt with in my studies and devotion. I usually enter the pulpit eager to preach. My anxiety is that I've studied, outlined, written, and memorized well, and that I'll execute to the best of my ability so the Spirit can work conviction. Martin Luther said that you should never pray the Lord's Prayer when you leave the pulpit because you shouldn't pray "forgive us our trespasses" after preaching God's Word.[3] Entering and leaving the pulpit, the focus is on the audience, that they will "fear, love, and trust in God above all things."[1]

How interesting, this flower outline! (See next page.) A homiletics (preaching) professor, Andrew Weyermann, taught it to us and I still teach it to students. In school, we're taught outlining that starts at the top of the page, Roman numeral I, then II, and so on. That's fine for something to be read, but for people who are not reading but listening, and listening at the mercy of the speaker, it's important to keep bringing the hearers back to the central thought of the sermon. The flower outline does that. Each petal should relate in an obvious way to the center, the central thought. Furthermore, if one "petal" does not relate directly to the central thought, you don't need it. Take it out. These days, almost 50 years later, I usually don't draw out a flower outline for my sermons, but I'm disciplined to make sure each paragraph relates directly to the central thought. That's one of the benefits of aging in preaching or any craft; you instinctively and more efficiently do things that in earlier years took more time and work. The moral for young preachers: Do the details you've learned in seminary until they become your own instincts.

The church bulletin (p. 309) brings back memories. Rev. Weber, the pastor of St. Peter's, wouldn't have known me from the man in the moon, but he was a friend of my 3rd- and 4th-grade teacher, Mr. Clifford Braun. Hence the invitation to preach. I'm glad to know that St. Peter's is still serving its South Chicago neighborhood. Take a look at the youth car wash. $1.25 per car, but if you had whitewalls, 25 cents more! By the way, that car wash was August 29th, Diane's birthday. We would meet two years later, and the rest of the story is history!

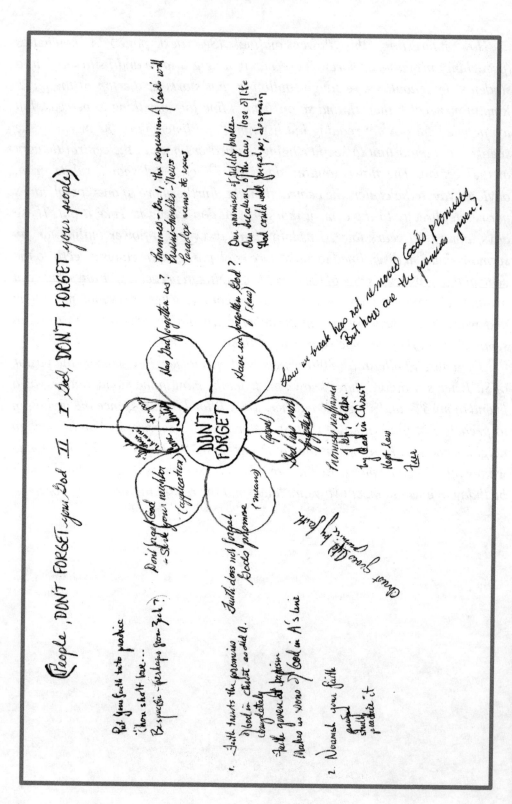

Vol. 13   SAINT PETER'S   No. 34
            EV. LUTHERAN CHURCH - MISSOURI SYNOD
            Eighty-Sixth and Kedvale Ave.
            W. M. Weber, Pastor
            P. E. Wackenhuth, Minister of Music

Parsonage: Phone: Church   - 582-0470
    8555 S. Keeler Ave.   Parsonage - 585-2912

DIVINE WORSHIP: 8:15 and 11:00 A.M.
SUNDAY SCHOOL AND BIBLE CLASS: 9:45 A.M.

THIRTEENTH SUNDAY AFTER TRINITY - August 23, 1970
Epistle, Gal. 3:15-22   Gospel, Luke 10:23-37

MUSIC FOR WORSHIP:
Prelude: "We Now Implore God the Holy Ghost"
                                          Walther
Voluntary: "Lord, Thee I Love with All My Heart"
                                          Alberti
Postlude: Finale, from Sonata VI   Mendelssohn

            8:15 and 11:00 A.M. Worship
HYMNS: 231 - 442 - 45

TODAY'S WORSHIP speaks of the covenant which God
made to Abraham. The words of the introit petition
God to remember His covenant of mercy to us. The
promises of the covenant are obtained when—in the
words of the collect—we "love that which Thou   st
command." The law which Christ gave us was to love
our neighbor, as exemplified in today's Gospel lesson of the good Samaritan. The old law, given to
Moses, was given—as Paul explains in the epistle
for today—"till the Seed should come;" now that the
Seed (Christ) has come, we are to be "Christs" to
our neighbor. For He says: "Inasmuch as ye have done
it unto one of the least of these My brethren, ye
have done it unto Me." (Today's propers are found on
page 78 in the hymnal.)

FOR YOUR MEDITATION:
  Hymns 397, 439, 440 orother hymns of consecration
  and stewardship.

OUR GUEST PREACHER today and next Sunday is Dale
  Meyer, student at Concordia Theological Seminary
  in St. Louis and member of St. Paul's Lutheran
  Church in Chicago Heights. We welcome him into
  our midst in the name of our Lord Jesus Christ.

A CAR WASH will be held on Saturday, August 29th,
  from 9:30 A.M. to 2:30 P.M., sponsored by Youth
  in Action. Proceeds will help them finance their
  retreat to Walcamp. Donation is $1.25 (25¢ extra
  for whitewalls).

Week 34 – Do Not Grumble!

Delivered at St. Salvator Lutheran Church, Venedy, Illinois
and St. Peter Lutheran Church, New Memphis, Illinois
August 26, 1979

Text – John 6:41-51

So the Jews grumbled about him, because he said, "I am the bread that came down from heaven." They said, "Is not this Jesus, the son of Joseph, whose father and mother we know? How does he now say, 'I have come down from heaven'?" Jesus answered them, "Do not grumble among yourselves. No one can come to me unless the Father who sent me draws him. And I will raise him up on the last day. It is written in the Prophets, 'And they will all be taught by God.' Everyone who has heard and learned from the Father comes to me – not that anyone has seen the Father except he who is from God; he has seen the Father. Truly, truly, I say to you, whoever believes has eternal life. I am the bread of life. Your fathers ate the manna in the wilderness, and they died. This is the bread that comes down from heaven, so that one may eat of it and not die. I am the living bread that came down from heaven. If anyone eats of this bread, he will live forever. And the bread that I will give for the life of the world is my flesh."

Prayer

Heavenly Father, You teach us to be content. We should be! You provide for our needs of body and soul. Our thankfulness to You makes a difference in how we deal with people, or it should. How often we complain about other people! Our grumbling is the old way of sinful living. It shows we're never deep enough into Your Word, the Word of Jesus that draws us to You and perfect contentment.

So when we're about to grumble, touch our hearts and soften our words to reflect our new life in Jesus. Amen.

School has started. Time to start learning things again. This morning I am going to teach you all a new word. It is a Greek word. The word is *gonguzo* (γογγύζω). *Gonguzo.* It means to grumble. Stick out your chin. Look down instead of up. Mumble about so-and-so who did such-and-such and I don't like it. I thought I should explain what *gonguzo* – what grumbling – is, since we never, ever see it here in New Memphis or Venedy among our good church people!

The Gospel lesson for today says that the Jews *"gonguzoed"* about something that Jesus had said to them. He had told them, "I am the bread of life; whoever comes to me shall not hunger, and whoever believes in me shall never thirst" (John 6:35). The Bible tells us that the Jews didn't like that. The Bible reports, "They said, 'Is not this Jesus, the son of Joseph, whose father and mother we know? How does he now say, 'I have come down from heaven'?'" (John 6:42). They *gonguzoed* because Jesus was challenging them to something new. He criticized their old way of life. These Jews were proud of their religion. They boasted that Moses and the prophets were their ancestors. They stuck their chins out with pride and said that they were God's chosen people – which they were – but then they didn't live according to what God and Moses and the prophets had told them. Jesus came to them and said, *Your old way of life is like bread that perishes. I am the living bread come down from heaven.* He was challenging them to a new way of life. They didn't like it. So, they *gonguzoed.*

Jews aren't the only ones who *gonguzo.* What if I would stand up here and say, "You ought to change your old ways of life." What if I would say that some of you men ought to spend less time at the tavern and less time at work, and more time at home with your wife and family? What if I would stand up here and say that some of you women ought to find more work to do – maybe even get a job – and spend less time busybodying over the telephone? What if I would stand up here and say that some of you children shouldn't just play, but hit the books more than you do? What if I challenge the way you have been living? You would go out of church and think, *Who does he think he is? He's got a few things to learn himself!* You would *gonguzo.* The fact is that I am not challenging your way of life. God is. It is His Word that you are hearing now. Is your life so great that you are going to *gonguzo* against God?

When the Jews *gonguzoed,* Jesus turned on them and said, "Do not grumble among yourselves. No one can come to me unless the Father who sent me draws him." Jesus is saying, *Don't grumble because I told you the truth. Your old way of living isn't going to get you to the Father. Doesn't matter if you have Moses and the prophets. Doesn't matter if you've been faithful and active in this Lutheran church a long time. No way are you going to get yourself to the Father. So stop grumbling. Stop "gonguzoing"!*

You may be familiar with a TV show called *The Gong Show*.[1] People come out and do an act. When the act gets bad, the gong is struck – like this. ... Jesus is saying, *Stop GONGuzoing against the truth. Your act needs to be changed.*

It is the Heavenly Father who takes a bad act and makes it a good one. It is the Father who changes your old way of living, with all your failures and all your *gonguzoing,* and gives you a new life. The Bible says, "No one can come to me unless the Father who sent me draws him." Notice what it says:

1) The Father draws you; you don't draw yourself. No one leads a life that moves oneself closer to God. Faith and good works are a gift from the Father, and something for which you cannot take credit.

2) The Father draws you closer to Himself by drawing you closer to Jesus. The Father sent Jesus so you have a way to get closer to God. Believing in some vague God won't save you. Believing in the God who sent Jesus will.

3) Faith is nurtured by God's Word. Jesus says in today's text: "It is written in the Prophets, 'And they will all be taught by God.' Everyone who has heard and learned from the Father comes to me." Hence it is so important for you, each week, to take the criticism that God's Word dishes out, and then go to your Savior and hear the wonderful Word of forgiveness. See what happens?

We like to grumble, *gonguzo*, against God when He tells us that our way of life isn't right. Jesus is saying, *Bong! Stop your gonguzoing! Listen to the Father who sent me! Believe in me! Then live a new life.*

So let's cut out the *gonguzoing* around here. Bong! It's part of the old way of living. Jesus calls you to live a new life each day – a new life that begins with Him.

Amen.

For Further Reflection

"Thou shalt not take the name of the LORD thy God in vain." (Second Commandment)

- The "name" of God is His entire revelation to us. On the negative side, this commandment forbids more than just cursing or swearing with words like "Jesus" or "God." God commands us not to misuse His teaching in any way, including complaining against His will and ways.
- Put yourself in the story of grumblers against God – Exodus 16:1-15
- The punishment for grumbling is reason to fear – Numbers 21:4-9; 1 Corinthians 10:1-12; James 5:9
- The Good News is that those who confess their complaining against Him are forgiven because God's Son was lifted up on the cross (John 3:14-18; John 12:31-33). From that Gospel comes a positive side to every commandment. "We should fear and love God that we ... call upon God's name in every trouble, pray, praise, and give thanks" (Martin Luther, Small Catechism).[2]
  - o The positive keeping of the commandment – Psalm 141:1-3; Psalm 142:1-2; Philippians 2:12-16; 1 Peter 4:7-9
- Your prayer for the positive – "Our Father who art in heaven, hallowed be Thy name."

Keep me from saying words
That later need recalling;
Guard me lest idle speech
May from my lips be falling;
But when within my place
I must and ought to speak,
Then to my words give grace
Lest I offend the weak.

Lord, let me win my foes
With kindly words and actions,
And let me find good friends
For counsel and correction.
Help me, as You have taught,
To love both great and small
And by Your Spirit's might
To live in peace with all.[3]

Retrospective

Here's a sermon that could have been better. Jesus used the image of bread in this Gospel text, picking up on manna in the Old Testament, but I didn't because I suspected the hearer would think, "I've heard this before. I know what's coming." By contrast, "gonguzo" would have been new to the hearers, and certainly memorable. The preacher isn't bound to the image but to the doctrine of the text. So far, so good.

But in the third paragraph, my list of how the men, women, and children in the congregations should be living more in line with God's Word was, in retrospect, a bit brash, heavy-handed Law. Reading that paragraph almost 40 years later, I see that I came across as complaining about them! I gonguzoed! Instead, I should have been inviting them to think about their lives in a Christ-centered way. His doctrine, His bread, is all sufficient; live His way and keep His command to "love your neighbor as yourself" (Matthew 22:39). I got that paragraph wrong, I think, because the illustration of "gonguzo" was taking over for the text in my mind. That happens; we preachers get so enamored with some idea or an interesting illustration that we let it push aside the text and take over the sermon. If I were writing that paragraph today, I might well address the same shortcomings, but in the spirit of Romans 2:4 – "God's kindness is meant to lead you to repentance." Seminarians, take note: The president has given you an example not to follow!

Still, the parishioners bore with me, and my affection for them continues to this day. That's one virtue of small congregations that take fresh, new pastors from the Seminary. They take him in, let him learn and grow in their midst, clip his wings when necessary, and love him and his family more than is sometimes deserved. Putting up with some flawed sermons and rookie mistakes, they honor the Word of God that makes them His people and gathers them together in worship. In retrospect, I smile and wonder if, after this sermon, the men went down to Moose's Tavern as they always did (Moose's was a family place, not disreputable), the women went home and got on the party line, and they all asked, "What was Pastor Meyer so upset about this morning?"

Week 35 – By Grace Alone, Grace in His Son

Delivered at the Chapel of St. Timothy and St. Titus
for the opening of the 178th academic year,
Concordia Seminary, St. Louis, Missouri
September 2, 2016

Text – Deuteronomy 6:5-6

You shall love the LORD your God with all your heart and with all your soul and with all your might. And these words that I command you today shall be on your heart.

Prayer

By grace God's Son, our only Savior,
Came down to earth to bear our sin.
Was it because of thine own merit
That Jesus died thy soul to win?
Nay, it was grace, and grace alone,
That bro't Him from His heav'nly throne.

By grace! This ground of faith is certain;
So long as God is true, it stands.
What saints have penned by inspiration,
What in His Word our God commands,
What our whole faith must rest upon,
Is grace alone, grace in His Son.[1]

Let me speak to you about curriculum. How boring will this be? Syllabi, assignments, tests... it's boring and a drudge only when you have a narrow understanding of curriculum. The faculty wants you to have a wide understanding of curriculum. Concordia Seminary is dedicated to your *curriculum vitae*, the curriculum – the course – of your entire life. You are, as they say, "living in the dash," the time on a grave marker between your birth and death. You already know the date of your birth and now you are living in the dash. How you understand the dash will make all the difference when your earthly course is done, when it comes time for the date of your entrance into eternity to be inscribed.

"You shall love the LORD your God." The curriculum of life is all about God. "In the beginning, God..." Not you. Not me. And then God does an amazing thing that none of us could comprehend. God – who is perfect in Himself, who has no need for anything outside of Himself – God creates something other than Himself. "In the beginning, God created the heavens and the earth" (Genesis 1:1). The first assignment in the curriculum of life under God is to stand in awe of the Creator.

We had a student last year who was into photography. One spring evening, he and his fiancée drove an hour or so into southern Illinois so he could get away from the city lights. The city lights pollute our appreciation and wonder of the heavens. When he got out there, he took pictures of the stars – pictures we use to this day. Four out of five Americans don't have that experience where they live, because of light pollution. Look up at night to be awed by the greatness of the Creator. "Lift up your eyes on high and see: who created these?" (Isaiah 40:26).

I mentioned at orientation the other day that I encourage you, I beg you, to get out of the cocoon of the Concordia campus. One of the things you ought to do is go over to Washington University, just a few blocks north. When you approach the Planetary Sciences building, you'll see bronze inlays in the sidewalk. First is Pluto, then a little farther up, to scale, is Neptune, and on and on you walk, until eventually you get to Earth, Venus, Mercury, and the Sun. The sidewalk is maybe 50 feet long – small – but you see the planets and have to be awed by the greatness of the solar system. I stand there and think, *Wow! This is just a sidewalk!* "Lift up your eyes on high and see: who created these?" Inside the Planetary Sciences building, in the lobby, you will find an exact replica of one of the Mars rovers. And around that rover are pictures of the Martian landscape. I look at that and it's *Shut up, Dale!*

Speaking of the planets, the United States has a satellite named Juno circling Jupiter in a polar orbit. Jupiter is *massive*. In reading about that mission, I learned that its diameter is 11.2 times bigger than Earth's, and it would take 1,321 Earths to fill Jupiter. Now, so what? Big planet, right? The universe is filled with hurtling objects that, every once in a while, cause the people of this world consternation. What if it would come and eliminate not only the dinosaurs but *us*? Jupiter is so big that it takes those hits so Earth is preserved. And if a hurtling object doesn't actually go into Jupiter, Jupiter's gravity gets ahold of that thing like a slingshot and sends it away from the solar system – and away from the little place you and I live. *Wow!* Who designed that protection for us?

I have a friend who says, "Hmmmm…" God thundered at Job, "Where were you [*you squirt of a president…*]," "Where were you [*you squirt seminarian…*]," "Where were you when I laid the foundation of the earth?" (Job 38:4). And even here on campus, look at the trees – the trees are like the pillars of God's cathedral of creation. Look at the herbs, look at the vegetables, and look at the flowers that are planted almost everywhere you walk. Creation is a cathedral built by God for His praise. The first assignment in the curriculum of God starts with seminarians, professors, and staff shutting up in awe at the greatness of the Creator.

"You shall love the LORD your God." That's the second assignment in the curriculum of God, and… well, it's impossible. Truly loving God is by nature impossible for us. We can stand in awe of creation, but this second assignment is why we are in trouble – and that's why we have to be in *this* cathedral, *this* building. God originally created us not only to be creatures, but to be creatures who are dependent upon Him. And in a perfect world, dependent creatures love the Creator – the One in whom they live, move, and have their being. But here's the catch. Mankind was given the terrible ability to make the decision to leave its dependence upon the Creator aside, and to opt for independence. Created to love God, mankind was given the terrible ability not to love the Creator, upon whom we are totally dependent, but rather to love something or someone else more than Him. That's what happened. God didn't create robots. Because humanity chose to act independently rather than in perfect dependence… because humanity chose to love the creature more than the Creator… because of that, our will is bound by sin. Original sin has so corrupted us that the original gift of freedom of the will only opts for independence and love *away* from God. We cannot love God as we ought. Yes, even your sanctified hearts – your hearts that want to be pastors and deaconesses in the Church – your hearts (and mine) still struggle to be independent of God. When we processed in, we sang that great hymn by Robert Robinson, "Come, Thou Fount of Every Blessing," and he captures this tendency that you and I have to strive for independence, and not to love God spontaneously because we are in captivity to sin. Robinson says, *"Prone to wander, Lord, I feel it; / Prone to leave the God I love."*[2] Our free wills are bound. Yes, "The heavens declare the glory of God, and the sky above proclaims his handiwork" (Psalm 19:1), but "I do not do the good I want, but the evil I do not want is what I keep on doing" (Romans 7:19). You and I are in captivity to sin, and as a consequence, we of ourselves cannot be captivated by the love of God. That's the second part of the assignment – and brothers and sisters, the dean has called you in. You are flunking out. I am flunking out. *Shut up, Dale.*

This brings us to the third assignment for life in God's curriculum. Your Creator is your *Re*-Creator. Although our wills are captive to sin, according to His mercy He has given us a new birth (cf. 1 Peter 1:3). "When I look at your heavens, the work of your fingers, the moon and the stars, which you have set in place, / what is man that you are mindful of him, and the son of man that you care for him?" (Psalm 8:3-4). *Wow!* If it is incomprehensible that God – a perfect being – went outside of Himself to create this cosmos, this world in which you and I live in our little corner, it is even more awesome that this Creator sends His Son into His fallen creation to re-create *you* by name. Your Creator is your loving, compassionate Re-Creator. He re-creates *you*. "Great indeed, we confess, is the mystery of godliness" (1 Timothy 3:16). The Creator re-creates us in His Son.

God's curriculum for your life is not just about what happened 20 centuries ago. That Jesus lived, died, and rose again is critically important. You're not here to become curators of congregational museums, dusty old gatherings remembering only things of long ago. It's in the dash that the Re-Creator works on hearts through the Word of His Son whom He sent here. God's re-creation through the obedience, suffering, and resurrection of Jesus Christ comes to you daily through His Word – spoken, written, and sacramental. "These words that I command you today shall be on your heart" (Deuteronomy 6:6). The Spirit of the Creator re-creates you. "If anyone is in Christ, he is a new creation" (2 Corinthians 5:17). In the cathedral of creation, we fear God. And in our little cathedrals, our churches, and this chapel, the Spirit brings us to dependence upon Him and to love for Him, through His Son.

"By Grace Alone, Grace in His Son" is the title of God's curriculum for your life. Grace means we have nothing of our own that gives us standing before God. Grace means *"Nothing in my hand I bring; / Simply to Thy cross I cling."*[3] Being totally dependent upon grace alone means that you and I freely admit, and even rejoice in, our dependence upon God. Even in the good works that we sincerely do... even in the cooperation that does occur between the believer and God in sanctified living ("We are God's fellow workers" – 1 Corinthians 3:9)... even then, we are still totally dependent upon our Creator and Re-Creator. "It is God who works in you, both to will and to work for his good pleasure" (Philippians 2:13). Being totally dependent upon grace alone means that we are to be *obedient*, obedient to His will and obedient to His words. "Search me, O God, and know my heart! Try me and know my thoughts! / And see if there be any grievous way in me, and lead me in the way everlasting!" (Psalm 139:23-24). Being in grace – being totally dependent upon grace alone – means that the capstone of this curriculum of your life is gratitude. We have nothing – *nothing!* – that we can ultimately present to Him and say, "Hey, look at me!" Before God, it is *Shut up, Dale... Shut up, Put-in-your-name*. The capstone is gratitude – gratitude for grace – now, in the dash, and into eternity. "What shall I render to the LORD for all his benefits to me? ... I will offer to you the sacrifice of thanksgiving and call on the name of the LORD" (Psalm 116:12, 17).

That's the curriculum, and it follows the three articles of the creed: the first, the creation; the second, our sin and need for a Savior; and the third, the Holy Spirit who comes through the Word to re-create you and re-create me in Jesus Christ. "You shall love the LORD your God with all your heart and with all your soul and with all your might. And these words that I command you today shall be on your heart" (Deuteronomy 6:5-6). In the name of Jesus.

Amen.

For Further Reflection

"Forgive us our trespasses." (Lord's Prayer, Fifth Petition)

- Put yourself in the story of this sincerely religious person. Read Acts 7:58 - 8:3, Acts 9:1-5, and in 1 Timothy 1:15 note the present tense, "I am," speaking of himself as a believer.
- Martin Luther: "The man who imagines that he will come to grace by doing whatever he is able to do is adding sin to sin. Therefore he becomes doubly guilty. Nor is speaking in this way giving any cause of despair; it is rather moving men to humble themselves and to see the grace of Christ. Certain it is that man must completely despair of himself in order to become fit to receive the grace of Christ."[4]
- Mull over James 2:8-12, Ezekiel 18:19-24, Romans 7:7, and Galatians 3:10-14. "If you, O LORD, should mark iniquities, O Lord, who could stand? / But with you there is forgiveness, that you may be feared" (Psalm 130:3-4). With that in mind, take to heart Psalm 19:12, John 3:16-17, Galatians 3:10-14, Romans 6:23, and Genesis 32:10.
- Dietrich Bonhoeffer: "One extreme thing must be said. To forego self-conceit and to associate with the lowly means, in all soberness and without mincing the matter, to consider oneself the greatest of sinners. This arouses all the resistance of the natural man, but also that of the self-confident Christian… If my sinfulness appears to me to be in any way smaller or less detestable in comparison with the sins of others, I am still not recognizing my sinfulness at all. My sin is of necessity the worst, the most grievous, the most reprehensible."[5]

> *Come, Thou Fount of ev'ry blessing,*
> *Tune my heart to sing Thy grace;*
> *Streams of mercy, never ceasing,*
> *Call for songs of loudest praise.*
> *While the hope of endless glory*
> *Fills my heart with joy and love,*

Teach me ever to adore Thee;
May I still Thy goodness prove.

Oh, to grace how great a debtor
Daily I'm constrained to be;
Let that grace now like a fetter
Bind my wand'ring heart to Thee:
Prone to wander, Lord, I feel it;
Prone to leave the God I love.
Here's my heart, O take and seal it,
Seal it for Thy courts above.[6]

Retrospective

Talking about "the curriculum of life" could be expected at the start of a school year, but in this sermon for the opening of Concordia Seminary's 178th academic year, the word curriculum was loaded with special meaning. For several years, the faculty had been engaged in a thorough revision of the residential curriculum. Times change, and curricula also need to change so that students are best formed for faithful life and witness in the 21st century. The faculty worked hard on the new curriculum, giving thousands and thousands of hours, hearing the best advice from teachers of education, from counselors who work with clergy, from church officials who deal with successful and struggling pastors, from alumni, and from laypeople. So when my very first sentence came out, "Let me speak to you about curriculum," I bet they rolled their eyes – "Is there no escape from curriculum?" As you read this, the new curriculum is now in place. Seminarians continue to study the Bible in depth, the Lutheran Confessions, and the skills of parish ministry, like preaching, teaching, visitation, leadership, and the like. What's new in the new curriculum is an emphasis upon wholeness, upon a pastor whose head and heart are in sync with the faith, who is as alert to his physical, emotional, and spiritual personal life as he is to his public ministry.

Might that be true for all Christians? We all have a curriculum, a course of life that is lived between the date of our birth and the date of our death. That's where the Spirit of God and His Son comes to us – body, soul, and spirit – justifying and sanctifying us to be wholly His. We know at least the basic truths – that God in grace sent Jesus to die for our sins, and through faith I have the Easter promise of heaven – but how often do our emotions and character flaws become occasions for sin? God's curriculum is not just for a seminary classroom or church Bible class. It's for all of us, for all of life, holistic – the dash that leads us by grace alone, grace in His Son, to the crown of eternal life.

Week 36 – Touching People

Broadcast on The Lutheran Hour
April 14, 1991

Text – Acts 26:16-18

[Jesus said] "I will appear to you, delivering you from your people and from the Gentiles – to whom I am sending you to open their eyes, so that they may turn from darkness to light and from the power of Satan to God, that they may receive forgiveness of sins and a place among those who are sanctified by faith in me."

Prayer

Almighty God, Your Son Jesus Christ is our Savior and the only Light of the world. Grant that we who have put our trust in Jesus may be enlightened by Your Word and Holy Sacraments. May this light of Christ then shine brightly in our lives. Give us determination to demonstrate with our actions what we profess with our lips. Let the light of Christ shine to all the ends of the earth, so people now living and worshiping in spiritual darkness may come to know the forgiveness of sins. In Jesus' name we pray. Amen.

Do you ever question why Christians try to convert people of other faiths to Christianity? I'll readily admit that doesn't set well with many people.

- "You have no business sending missionaries to Africa to change ancestral religions."

- "The people of the Far East have been served for centuries by their religions. Who do you think you are to try and change them?"

- "The Jewish people have suffered so much. How dare you insult them by trying to make them Christians?"

- "Hands off!"

And so it goes.

Maybe you get even more upset when Christians say that there is a heaven and there is a hell, and the only way to heaven is through Jesus Christ. The person who rejects Jesus Christ is destined for hell.

- "How does anyone dare to think that they have a corner on the truth?"

There was a time, before his conversion, when the man we now know as the apostle Paul was upset with Christians for promoting their faith as the only saving faith. You may remember that Paul – or Saul as he was called before his conversion – hated our Christian message. Do you know what so infuriated him? What angered Saul was that the Christians were proclaiming that the crucified Jesus Christ was the Savior promised by God in the Old Testament. Saul had been looking for the Savior. That someone from Nazareth named Jesus might be the Savior didn't anger Saul. What upset Saul was that this alleged Savior had been crucified. What kind of Savior is it who suffers and dies? In Saul's opinion, saviors are supposed to be glorious, not executed! A crucified Savior didn't fit Saul's job description for a real Christ. So Saul persecuted the Christians for saying that there is no other way to be saved than by the crucified Jesus Christ.

Trying to stop the Christian mission led Saul to Damascus. Last summer at our Lutheran Laymen's League convention, the Rev. Wallace Schulz, my faithful coworker here at *The Lutheran Hour*, preached about that trip to Damascus. He used an expression that stuck in my mind. He said, "Sometimes God has to knock you off your horse." That's what God did to Saul. As he was traveling to Damascus to stop the Christian mission, God knocked him off his horse.

Let's hear Paul's own description, as recorded in Acts chapter 26:

I journeyed to Damascus with the authority and commission of the chief priests. At midday, O king, I saw on the way a light from heaven, brighter than the sun, that shone around me and those who journeyed with me. And when we had all fallen to the ground, I heard a voice saying to me in the Hebrew language, "Saul, Saul, why are you persecuting me? It is hard for you to kick against the goads." And I said, "Who are you, Lord?" And the Lord said, "I am Jesus whom you are persecuting. But rise and stand upon your feet, for I have appeared to you for this purpose, to appoint you as a servant and witness to the things in which you have seen me and to those in which I will appear to you, delivering you from your people and from the Gentiles – to whom I am sending you to open their eyes, so that they may turn from darkness to light and from the power of Satan to God, that they may receive forgiveness of sins and a place among those who are sanctified by faith in me." (Acts 26:12-18)

When Saul got up from the ground, he opened his eyes but could not see. He had been blinded! His companions led him to Damascus. Saul remained blind for three days until God restored his physical sight (Acts 9:8-18). The restoration of his physical sight was nothing compared to the light that had now poured into Paul's soul. His hatred for the Christian mission had been based on unbelief – unbelief that a crucified man is the Christ, the Savior of the world. That is the most terrible darkness that Paul or you or any human being can ever experience.

Jesus Himself struck Paul with the blinding truth, the truth that the crucified One – yes, the crucified One – lives, and the Christian Church is His Church, the Christian mission is His mission, and opposition to that mission is opposition to God. That light of Christ drove away the darkness of Saul's misplaced religious ideas. He, who had so hated the Christian mission, had the eyes of his soul opened, and he became the greatest missionary of the early Church. The rest of Paul's life was the fulfillment of Jesus' commission to open people's eyes "so that they may turn from darkness to light and from the power of Satan to God, that they may receive forgiveness of sins and a place among those who are sanctified by faith in me" (Acts 26:18).

Every person in this world needs to have their eyes opened. I'm not talking here about physical eyesight. I'm talking about God's light coming into the darkness of our own souls. This is a world of sin. Evil, hatred, greed, betrayal, jealousy, slander, crime, destruction: these things are all about us. You are a part of this dark, sinful world. St. John says, "If we say we have no sin, we deceive ourselves, and the truth is not in us" (1 John 1:8).

Now, you may or may not know the truth. John says that truth is not automatically within us. The idea that all religions are basically true, that one world religion is ultimately no better than another, rests upon the notion that religious truth is a common property of all peoples. But John says it is possible that the truth is not in you or me. The Bible says that the truth is not in you if you do not admit to your sin. Avoid confessing your sin, and you are not in truth, not in the light; rather, you are deceived, and you are in spiritual darkness.

Paul was enlightened by the Gospel and was sent to turn people "from darkness to light and from the power of Satan to God, that they may receive forgiveness of sins" (Acts 26:18). That spiritual sight comes because of Jesus Christ, the Son of God and the Savior of sinners. On a dark Good Friday, Jesus died on a cross and endured the anger of God against our sins. Christ on the cross was punished with the fury of hell so we need never experience God's wrath. He endured the greatest darkness of all – abandonment by God who punished His Son for our sins – so we can now live in His light and be illumined by His Word.

The terrible darkness that enshrouded the world on Good Friday gave way on Easter morning to a bright light. On Easter, God raised His Son Jesus from the dead. He restored Him to life. By the resurrection of Jesus Christ, God brought life and immortality to light. By the resurrection, God showed that the crucified One truly is the Savior, who alone is the Light of the world. By raising His Son, God vindicated Jesus' words that the Christ had to suffer and rise so that repentance and forgiveness of sins will be preached throughout the world.

The message of Christians to people of other faiths, the message that we Christians continually would share with one another, the appeal I make to you now, is to trust God's Son Jesus Christ for the forgiveness of your sins. St. John says, "If we walk in the light, as he is in the light, we have fellowship with one another, and the blood of Jesus his Son cleanses us from all sin" (1 John 1:7). Although some people are offended by the missionary nature of Christianity, that's the way it is. The Bible is very clear on this. Talking about God and heaven, Jesus said, "No one comes to the Father except through me" (John 14:6). That's very clear. The apostle Peter said in a Bible reading that many churchgoing Christians will hear today, "There is salvation in no one else, for there is no other name under heaven given among men by which we must be saved" (Acts 4:12). That is also very clear.

So, yes, we are out to convert people from other world religions to Christianity. And yes, we are out to convert to Christianity people who practice no religion. And yes, we are out to convert people who think of themselves as Christians but are blind to Christian truth, nominal Christians who don't know who Jesus Christ is and what He's all about. Yes, we are a missionary religion – because Jesus told us: "Go therefore and make disciples of all nations, baptizing them in the name of the Father and of the Son and of the Holy Spirit, teaching them to observe all that I have commanded you" (Matthew 28:19-20). Some people may say "Hands off!" but we want to touch people with the story of Jesus Christ.

We want to *touch* people, not clobber them. One reason why you may advocate a "hands off" policy is because of past abuses. Over the centuries, many people became Christians (at least Christian in name) because some conquering army invited them to become Christians at the point of a sword. You can probably cite other cases where someone was bullied into Christianity but in fact their heart was never touched. I want to tell you today about some Christians who touch others with the story of Jesus Christ. There are many Christians who witness in a sensitive manner. One such organization that touches and does not clobber is Lutheran Braille Workers (LBW). Lutheran Braille Workers faithfully transcribes Gospel materials into Braille so people who live in physical darkness can bask in the light of Christ and His forgiveness. The World Health Organization says that there are 52 million blind people in the world. You may be one of these millions. Or you may know someone who is blind.

Lutheran Braille Workers traces its beginnings back to Mr. Fred Graepp of Fresno, California. In some ways, his story is like that of Paul. Fred Graepp was studying to become a pastor. He had to set that career goal aside in 1941 when he became blind. During those days of World War II, he discovered that most Braille Bibles in Germany had been destroyed. He wanted to help. So he placed an ad asking for volunteers to help transcribe the German Bible into Braille. That ad was answered by a young lady who learned to become a Braille transcriber. Her name was Helen Loewe Koehler, and soon she had quite a few other people helping her in the project. One thing led to another, and in 1954 Lutheran Braille Workers was officially incorporated.

Though LBW is headquartered in Yucaipa, California, Yucaipa is only a fraction of the story. The real story is the work centers of these Braille workers. Two hundred work centers, scattered throughout the United States, Canada, and one in Brazil, are places where volunteers regularly gather together to prepare Braille materials for the blind throughout the world. With their special paper and special machines, with devices that bind and boxes to ship, these volunteers are sending out materials to 120 countries of the world – materials that literally touch hearts with the story of God's light in Jesus Christ.

I visited Work Center 182 in Phoenix, Arizona. I was staying with some friends, Bill and Ruth Parcks. They talked about the work center where they were involved, and asked if I'd like to go see it. "Well, of course I would!" So they took me to this work center on North 43rd Ave. there in Phoenix, and I met a wonderful group of Christian people. They were busy preparing Braille materials that would be shipped to the blind.

The volunteers I met there had both zeal and sensitivity. These workers enjoyed being with one another. Most of them were retired, and they enjoyed this labor of love. That's because they were sharing Jesus through Braille. The motto of Lutheran Braille Workers is "Bringing Christ to Those in Darkness." Bill and Ruth and their 7,000 coworkers are zealous missionaries.

These 7,000 are also sensitive, touching missionaries. When I saw them at work, they weren't converting people at the point of a sword. They weren't belittling people who are not Christian – nothing haughty or arrogant as they went about their work. Nor were they condescending in their attitudes toward the blind. No, theirs was a sensitive zeal as they prepared these Gospel materials so God's Spirit could touch the hearts of people – people who read by touching.

Yes, we Christians are a missionary group. We have been commissioned by God to share His light with the world. In Luke 24, the resurrected Jesus told the disciples, "Thus it is written, that the Christ should suffer and on the third day rise from the dead, and that repentance for the forgiveness of sins should be proclaimed in his name to all nations, beginning from Jerusalem. You are witnesses of these things" (Luke 24:46-48).

Our God is not perverse; ours is not a God who takes sadistic pleasure in afflicting us or in sending anyone to hell. Yes, there is a hell, but God doesn't want anyone there, especially you. God is good, and He wants every person in the world to be saved and go to heaven. The Bible says, "God ... desires all people to be saved and to come to the knowledge of the truth" (1 Timothy 2:3-4). And God especially wants you to know His light, to enter His heaven. He wants to open your eyes as He opened Saul's. He wants all people to be touched by the light of Christ.

Amen.

For Further Reflection

"I believe in the Holy Spirit." (Apostles' Creed, Third Article)

- Put yourself in the story of people touched by Jesus – Mark 8:22-25; John 9:1-12
- These miracles are signs that Jesus is the Promised One – Isaiah 29:18; Isaiah 35:5; Isaiah 42:6-9; Luke 4:16-21; Luke 7:18-23
- "We should *fear* ... God."[1] A sobering word about basing your thoughts about God on sight – Mark 4:10-12.
- What does the Holy Spirit do? 1 Corinthians 2:9-14; 1 Corinthians 12:3; 1 Peter 2:9. "The Holy Spirit calls, gathers, *enlightens*, sanctifies, and keeps the holy Christian church by the gospel in Word and sacraments" (Martin Luther, Small Catechism).[2]
- Therefore, walking by faith, not by sight (cf. 2 Corinthians 5:7), we "fear and *love* God"[1] – 1 Peter 1:8-12

> *Spread the reign of God the Lord,*
> *Spoken, written, mighty Word;*
> *Ev'rywhere His creatures call*
> *To His heav'nly banquet hall.*
>
> *Lord of harvest, great and kind,*
> *Rouse to action heart and mind;*
> *Let the gath'ring nations all*
> *See Your light and heed Your call.*[3]

Retrospective

LBW work centers are inspiring. Over the years, I have visited several of these centers throughout the United States, and I have always been impressed by the selfless dedication of volunteers to the cause of making the Bible readable for the blind. "The LORD opens the eyes of the blind" (Psalm 146:8). In the days of St. Paul, most people in the Roman Empire could not read or write. They could make out signs in shops, sign receipts, things that enabled them to get along in daily life. To sit and read the Bible? Impossible for most ancients, even if they could see. They heard the Word with their ears. How blessed we are in our time to be able to hear and read God's Word! How blessed are people without sight to be touched by the Word prepared for them by Lutheran Braille Workers! Like many other quiet organizations of committed Christian volunteers, LBW demonstrates that the mission of Christ and His Word to the world is larger than we comprehend. Indeed, that's been one of the things I've learned in my decades of life and ministry. The Spirit of God is present and active, touching people, wherever and however the Gospel is present. Awesome!

Week 37 – Remember the Homeless

Delivered at St. Paul Lutheran Church, Shobonier, Illinois
for Mission Festival Sunday
September 16, 1984

Text – Psalm 84

How lovely is your dwelling place,
　　O LORD of hosts!
My soul longs, yes, faints
　　for the courts of the LORD;
my heart and flesh sing for joy
　　to the living God.

Even the sparrow finds a home,
　　and the swallow a nest for herself,
　　where she may lay her young,
at your altars, O LORD of hosts,
　　my King and my God.
Blessed are those who dwell in your house,
　　ever singing your praise! 　*Selah*

Blessed are those whose strength is in you,
　　in whose heart are the highways to Zion.
As they go through the Valley of Baca
　　they make it a place of springs;
　　the early rain also covers it with pools.
They go from strength to strength;
　　each one appears before God in Zion.

O LORD God of hosts, hear my prayer;
　　give ear, O God of Jacob! 　*Selah*

Behold our shield, O God;
    look on the face of your anointed!

For a day in your courts is better
    than a thousand elsewhere.
I would rather be a doorkeeper in the house of my God
    than dwell in the tents of wickedness.
For the LORD God is a sun and shield;
    the LORD bestows favor and honor.
No good thing does he withhold
    from those who walk uprightly.
O LORD of hosts,
    blessed is the one who trusts in you!

Prayer

O God, You have called us to Your house. Here You give us innumerable blessings by the Spirit of Your Son, our Savior Jesus. Here Your Word assures us You are sun and shield, sun to lighten our dark times and shield to protect us from evil. Heavenly Father, we love our church home and pray You lay on our hearts those who do not have a church home. Give us a spirit of mission in word and deed that comes from hearts grateful to You for our salvation. In Jesus' name, Amen.

Thank you, Pastor Doug Meyer, for inviting me to St. Paul today. I hope I have something worthwhile to say, something that will touch your heart and your actions. I selected Psalm 84 as my sermon text. This is a familiar Psalm. "How lovely is your dwelling place, O LORD of hosts!"

Isn't that the truth? Most of you probably love this house of the Lord – this building. Maybe you were baptized here… confirmed… married… and you very well may have your funeral here. You love this house of the Lord. My own church is in Collinsville. I love that building – that house of the Lord. "How lovely is your dwelling place, O LORD of hosts!"

Today is your Mission Festival Sunday. You have a church home. I have a church home. But how many billions of people in the world have no church? They are "homeless" people. They have babies, but do not bring them to church for Holy Baptism. They just let the child grow up. Those children don't come to the Lord's house for Sunday School or Confirmation. They are not instructed in the Word of God. They believe whatever anyone tells them. It may be right, but it may be wrong. People who live apart from the Lord's house usually have one wrong idea. They think that God is impressed with their good works. It doesn't matter if they live in Africa or America. *Look at what I did, God. I built this beautiful idol*, a pagan may say. *Look at how well I've done, God. I led an honest, moral life. Sometimes I even prayed and went to church*, says an American. These are homeless people – people who have not yet sought refuge in God and His gracious Word.

I visited a family last week. They were all raised in the church and were interested in transferring their membership to our congregation. The husband asked a very interesting question. He said, "I want to ask you something selfish. I don't go to church much – two or three times a year. The congregation I'm in now doesn't pressure me to go to church. Will you?" What would you say? I told him that I found out a long time ago that you can't force people to go to church. You and I can't force homeless people to love the Lord's house. They have to come by themselves.

What's going to make them come? What's going to make someone down the street come to St. Paul? What's going to make a native in New Guinea seek out the missionary and the little mission church? The answer is the message of the Church. That message is that God bestows great blessings upon people who need help. That's what brings people home to God's house – the message.

> For a day in your courts is better
>   than a thousand elsewhere.
> I would rather be a doorkeeper in the house of my God
>   than dwell in the tents of wickedness.
> For the LORD God is a sun and shield;
>   the LORD bestows favor and honor.

No good thing does he withhold
   from those who walk uprightly. (Psalm 84:10-11)

The message is that God is "sun and shield." He is the sun that illuminates and brightens everyone's life. When you are overburdened with grief, depression, anxiety, or fear, God is a sun who breaks through that darkness. He says, "I am the light of the world. Whoever follows me will not walk in darkness, but will have the light of life" (John 8:12). God is sun, and God is shield. A shield protects. God protects people who need protection. When you are assaulted by worry, His Word says, "Do not be anxious about your life, what you will eat or what you will drink, nor about your body, what you will put on" (Matthew 6:25). When you are tempted to sin, His Word shields you: "How then can I do this great wickedness and sin against God?" (Genesis 39:9). When the godless seem to prosper while you're having trouble, God protects you by reminding you that one thing is needful – and that shall not be taken away (cf. Luke 10:42). God is sun and shield. He illuminates the dark times in your life. He protects against the assaults of the evil one. That's a good message. That will bring people home to church.

I preached here seven or eight years ago. At that time, I was serving a little church in a town called Venedy. In the summer when the church windows were open, no air conditioning, it was not unusual for a sparrow to come in and fly around the sanctuary. Funny thing – when the service began, the sparrow would stop flying around and sit on top of an organ pipe. Just like the psalm says, "Even the sparrow finds a home, and the swallow a nest for herself, where she may lay her young, / at your altars" (v. 3). Like the sparrow, you've found your comfort here in the house of God. The Gospel of Jesus Christ comes to you here. Through that Gospel, God blesses you. "Blessed are those who dwell in your house, ever singing your praise!" (v. 4). Because this Gospel has so blessed you, you can join the psalmist and say, "I shall dwell in the house of the LORD forever" (Psalm 23:6).

Today I ask you to please remember the homeless. Remember those who do not know the Church's message of Jesus Christ. Remember them in your prayers... remember them in your contributions for mission... remember them in your words and in your actions. Remember the work of missions. You and I wouldn't be Christians today – you and I wouldn't dwell in the house of the Lord forever – were it not for some missionary who brought the Good News to our forefathers.

Amen.

For Further Reflection

"Thy kingdom come." (Lord's Prayer, Second Petition)

- Here we pray that our Father would rule and reign in our hearts by grace ("kingdom of grace") and one day take us to heaven ("kingdom of glory")
- Only us? Put yourself in the story – Zechariah 8:14-23. Those going to Jerusalem in this prophecy show true fear and love of God.
- Can we add to the throng? Matthew 5:14-16; Matthew 9:35-38; 2 Thessalonians 3:1; 1 Peter 2:9; 1 Peter 3:15
- Pray for missions – Acts 4:23-31; Revelation 22:20

> *O Christ, our true and only light,*
> *Enlighten those who sit in night;*
> *Let those afar now hear Your voice*
> *And in Your fold with us rejoice.*
>
> *O gently call those gone astray*
> *That they may find the saving way!*
> *Let ev'ry conscience sore oppressed*
> *In You find peace and heav'nly rest.*
>
> *That they with us may evermore*
> *Such grace with wond'ring thanks adore*
> *And endless praise to You be giv'n*
> *By all Your Church in earth and heav'n.*[1]

- Could it be we have forgotten the fear of God and thereby grown cold in our love of Jesus?

Retrospective

Mission festivals were common years ago. Held most often in the fall, Mission Festival Sunday would have regular morning worship and then a special mission service in the afternoon or evening. The practice has declined over the years, although some rural churches still observe an annual Mission Sunday. St. Paul in Shobonier, Illinois, is a rural congregation. There are cultural reasons for the decline in Mission Festival Sundays. For example, people have busier lives than their parents and grandparents did, so going back to church for another service is hard to squeeze into their plans.

I wonder if something else is going on. In our busy-ness, have we lost our first love (Revelation 2:4)? Have we regular church-goers forgotten that the Good News of Jesus is a radical message, that His grace alone saves us? Have we been lured into thinking of the church as another voluntary community organization? Those were the concerns on my mind when I wrote this sermon three decades ago. Today mainline denominations are in membership decline. Might it be that we need to be convicted anew that our only hope and help is Jesus? "We cannot but speak of what we have seen and heard" (Acts 4:20).

Week 38 – The Glove Compartment God

Broadcast on The Lutheran Hour
February 2, 1997

Text – Exodus 20:5-6

You shall not bow down to them or serve them, for I the LORD your God am a jealous God, visiting the iniquity of the fathers on the children to the third and the fourth generation of those who hate me, but showing steadfast love to thousands of those who love me and keep my commandments.

Prayer

Dear God, the life You have given us seems to be a constant test. How rare are the moments when nothing is whirring in our minds or weighing heavily on our hearts! All this You know, Heavenly Father, and more. We cannot comprehend the extent of humanity's alienation from You because of sin, but You know and grieve our wandering from You. We might wonder where You are in our trying times, but Your jealous love is always seeking us. Be patient with us, Heavenly Father, and for Jesus' sake bring us now and forever to the embrace of Your love and peace which passes all understanding. Amen.

Happily ever after? Maybe not for you or for some couple you know. Are you constantly bickering? Is the atmosphere in your home so tense that you can cut it with a knife? Contemplating divorce? That's the way it was for Mario and Vivian, a young married couple in Caracas, Venezuela. Their story was shared with me by a mutual friend, Mike Wakeland.

Mario and Vivian had been married for about three years. Like many young couples living in Caracas, they were faced with the pressures of job uncertainties, inflation, and the constant threat of crime. Mario's job as a radio and television announcer had him working long and irregular hours, and by his own admission led him to ignore his wife. Soon the couple had drifted apart, linked only by their two-year-old son. When they did talk, the conversation often was transformed into a shouting match, which generally ended by Mario storming out of the apartment.

Mario and Vivian decided that their marriage was finished, and they filed for a divorce. In Venezuela, a one-year separation is required before a divorce is granted, and during this year the young couple tried unsuccessfully to reconcile. It seemed that each time they got together, old wounds were reopened and the shouting returned.

Now, let's call "time out" on this marital mess. If we shared Mario and Vivian's problems with Dr. Ruth or Dr. Laura or any counselor, they would give their perspective on what this unhappy couple could do. But now you're listening to Dr. Dale, and if you've listened to this program before, you know that I take a religious perspective on life. Jesus once said, "Seek first the kingdom of God and his righteousness, and all these things will be added to you" (Matthew 6:33). That verse leads me to suspect that one big reason Mario and Vivian's marriage is on the rocks is they have nothing in their marriage that is more important than they are. Mario seeks first what Mario wants. Vivian seeks first what Vivian wants. A marriage cannot be pulled in two different directions for very long without crashing. A marital wreck is about to happen.

"Seek first the kingdom of God." How would you picture Mario and Vivian's relationship to God? Oh, they knew that God exists. That will become evident when the story continues. But, so what? God was no big deal to them. He was just existing, like a rock or a tree. Picture this: Mario and Vivian's relationship to God was like proof of insurance in the glove compartment. You know that many states and provinces require drivers to carry proof of insurance. Most of us simply stick that card or paper in the glove compartment and forget about it. You don't think about the insurance company when you get into the car to do your daily business. You can drive any way you want. You can drive any place you want. You are the driver. You're in charge. You can do what you want, whether the insurance company likes it or not. That proof of insurance simply exists, stuck away in the glove compartment. It's irrelevant until you've had an accident. That's when that irrelevant piece of paper becomes pretty important. That's the way I picture Mario and Vivian's relationship to God. For a while they were getting by. *Yeah, sure, God exists*, they might have said, *but so what? We're getting by*. Well, their individual desires and drives were in sync for a while, but they're not in sync any longer. Now their marriage is careening toward disaster – and in desperation they turn to God. Time to pull Him out of the glove compartment.

Let's pick up the story again. Each time Mario and Vivian got together, the old wounds were reopened and the shouting returned. Finally, just a few short weeks before they could finalize their divorce, they decided to give their marriage one more try and also decided to look for help. They came to El Salvador Lutheran Church one Sunday morning to see if maybe God had an answer for them. While they didn't come right out and shout their problem to the whole congregation, Pastor Mike Wakeland and his wife, Cathie, recognized that this was a young couple who needed to hear about God's forgiveness in Jesus Christ. They invited them to supper that night, and spent several hours listening to them, sharing the Gospel with them and praying with them.

Mario and Vivian found the power of forgiveness. They experienced the forgiveness of their sins, and began to learn about forgiving each other. They did not go through with their divorce, but instead recommitted themselves to their marriage. Today, their home is not filled with shouts of anger, but rather shouts of joy, as they raise their three children and rejoice at what God is able to do through faith in His Son Jesus Christ.

Now, that's the story – a happy ending! The moral of the story is this: God wants to be the driving force in your life, not just along for the ride. God doesn't want to be in the glove compartment, just existing and irrelevant to how you live and what you do. God doesn't even want to be your copilot. He wants to be the driver in your life. He wants to lead you with His great forgiveness for your sins. He wants to guide you with His Word. He wants to give you courage with His unquenchable hope. He wants to surround you with His unconditional love. Because God wants to do all of this for you, why would you relegate Him to the periphery of your life? He's not a happy camper when we stick Him in the glove compartment. That's why He says, "I the LORD your God am a jealous God" (Exodus 20:5).

When you hear that word "jealous," you may think of someone who is petty and small-minded, like some of those characters on soap operas. These characters don't have a clue about real love. Now, if God were a jealous God in a petty, soap opera sense, you could expect Him to strike you or me or Mario and Vivian down with a bolt of lightning, and say, *There, that'll show you. Don't you mess with My feelings!*

But that's not the way God wants you to understand the word "jealous." Exodus 20:5 was written in Hebrew. The Hebrew word that is translated jealous is *qanna* (קַנָּא). It's an adjective, a word that modifies a noun. Interestingly enough, *qanna,* jealous, is applied only to God in the Old Testament. It indicates that God, the Creator, demands exclusive service from us, His creatures. Not to give God His due – which is to love Him with all our heart, soul, mind, and strength (cf. Mark 12:30) – and not to give our loving devotion to the One who has made us and lavished so many mercies upon us, is to put God in the glove compartment of our daily life. All this invites His just punishment against our sins. "I the LORD your God am a jealous God, visiting the iniquity of the fathers on the children to the third and the fourth generation of those who hate me, but showing steadfast love to thousands of those who love me and keep my commandments" (Exodus 20:5-6).

This jealous God is a patient and long-suffering lover. Instead of throwing a temper tantrum because of all the times you and I stick Him in the glove compartment and forget Him, God goes along with it. He lets Himself be marginalized. He stays silent while we sinners direct our lives wherever and however we think best. He waits in silence because He wants us to discover that our independence from Him is nothing more than an invitation to trouble and eventual disaster. "God our Savior ... desires all people to be saved and to come to the knowledge of the truth" (1 Timothy 2:3-4). There is no person alive who has ignored God too much. There is no one alive who has marginalized God too many times. There is no one, especially you, whom the jealous God has written off as hopeless. Insurance companies can cancel insurance, but God has not written you off.

So, "seek first the kingdom of God" (Matthew 6:33). We all have troublesome areas in our lives. Christians have troubled spots in their lives, and so do non-Christians. For some, it's marriage. Some marriages crash; others stay together, but everyone is miserable. For others, the troubles are different. Some are careening toward disaster because of alcohol or drugs. Others are facing a ruinous bottom line in family finances. For still others, illness is the troublesome area of life. What's your troubled area? As I said, we *all* – Christians and non-Christians alike – have troublesome areas in our lives. Can you believe that your troubles can be occasions of great blessing?

Theologians call this a "time of grace," and that's what we're all in – a time of grace. The troublesome areas of our lives are opportunities to tell God we are heading toward disaster. And without His help, we will certainly bring our lives to ruin. God's grace, His kindness, comes to you in your troubled times in the forgiveness and hope that comes in the Good News of Jesus Christ. Jesus once said, "The greatest love you can show is to give your life for your friends" (John 15:13 GW), and that's what He did on the cross of Calvary. God – the just judge who could punish you and me for all the times we have failed to love Him with all our heart, soul, mind, and strength – chose instead to punish His Son Jesus in our place. In Jesus' hours upon the cross, He experienced the full measure of hell toward which we sinners have been steering our lives.

What Jesus has done for you expresses an unfathomable love. It's a love for you and for every aspect of your life, especially for those troubled areas in your life where your sin is leading you to trouble and disaster. The best thing you and I can do in this limited time of grace (limited because you don't have all eternity to get it straight – there will be a decisive and absolutely final day of judgment) is to act on Jesus' invitation to seek the kingdom of God above all else.

Let God take the driver's seat in your life. Seek Him first, and He promises that the other things will be added unto you (Matthew 6:33). When Mario and Vivian brought their marital mess into contact with the Word of God through Pastor Wakeland's ministry, they realized their need for forgiveness. From that forgiveness came the hope and the power for reconciliation.

On one of our *On Main Street*[1] television programs, the topic was how to survive adultery in marriage. A husband and wife, Steve and Kathy, were on the show. Each had been unfaithful to the other. Theirs was an awful marriage, and yet with God's help they were able to put it back together again. That's a real tribute to the restorative power of God. On that program, we also had Janel. Janel is a Christian. She was a faithful wife. Her husband cheated on her, and they were not able to put it back together again. I asked our guest expert, Dr. Donald

Harvey, "What's the difference? One couple gets together again, and the other doesn't. Why?"

Dr. Harvey said the answer is reconciliation. In both cases, there was forgiveness. Kathy and Steve forgave each other, and then worked to reconcile with one another. Janel forgave her guilty husband, but he wouldn't work with her toward reconciliation. When God comes out of the background of life, He not only gives the power to forgive but He also makes reconciliation possible. I'm glad that Kathy and Steve reconciled. And I'm glad that Mario and Vivian reconciled. How about you? Is the air so thick in your marriage that you can cut it with a knife? "Seek first the kingdom of God and his righteousness, and all these things will be added to you" (Matthew 6:33).

Until next week, glance over at your glove compartment when you get into your car. Have you shoved God off to the side of your life? "I the LORD your God am a jealous God" (Exodus 20:5). He wants out! He wants to assure you of His forgiveness. He wants to give you His hope of reconciliation. And He wants to surround you and yours with His love.

Amen.

For Further Reflection

"You shall not covet your neighbor's house. You shall not covet your neighbor's wife, workers, animals, or anything that belongs to your neighbor." (Ninth and Tenth Commandments)

- God's redeeming love moves us to love and fear Him and keep His commandments
- Read Exodus 20:1-21. See how the verses are arranged. His jealous love has redeemed His people – Exodus 20:1-6. The response to His mercies, obeying the commandments – Exodus 20:7-16. In conclusion, "You shall not covet" (Exodus 20:17).
- "You shall not covet" is a twofold challenge. First, search what's really in your heart; see Romans 7:22-25. Second, since God in Jesus has redeemed

you, live as His freed people; do not put yourself into bondage to anything or anyone – Galatians 5:1. "You shall not covet"!

- Fearing God and keeping His commandments (cf. Ecclesiastes 12:13-14) begins and ends with God's jealous, redeeming, and liberating love for His people
- Pray to walk God's way – Psalm 139:23-24

> *One thing's needful; Lord, this treasure*
> *Teach me highly to regard.*
> *All else, though it first give pleasure,*
> *Is a yoke that presses hard!*
> *Beneath it the heart is still fretting and striving,*
> *No true, lasting happiness ever deriving.*
> *This one thing is needful; all others are vain –*
> *I count all but loss that I Christ may obtain!*
>
> *Therefore You alone, my Savior,*
> *Shall be all in all to me;*
> *Search my heart and my behavior,*
> *Root out all hypocrisy.*
> *Through all my life's pilgrimage, guard and uphold me,*
> *In loving forgiveness, O Jesus, enfold me.*
> *This one thing is needful; all others are vain –*
> *I count all but loss that I Christ may obtain!*[2]

Retrospective

There were some times in our earlier years when Diane and I were strongly disagreeing about something or other, but the atmosphere always calmed by Sunday noon. Coming before God in worship every Sunday morning was a reminder that Christian marriage is three – husband, wife, and God – as Ecclesiastes tells us. When God is the third strand holding husband and wife together, the final word should always be His Word of forgiveness. As the illustrations in this sermon show, marriage is a laboratory experience; you personally feel the consequences of sin, and the importance of forgiving and being reconciled to one another.

Forgiveness and reconciliation are two different but related things. God is the start, having ordained His Son in eternity to come and take away the sins of the whole world. Jesus did that – fact, period – what we call "objective justification." But, as Paul notes, not all have believed (cf. Romans 10:16). It's faith, trusting in the promises of God, that makes the forgiveness of sins personal to you. That's what we call "subjective justification." Worked miraculously in you by the Holy Spirit, faith makes reconciliation between you and God a fact. You can think of it as a vertical relationship. You're passive; God is active in forgiving and reconciling you to Himself.

How does that play out in our horizontal relationships? It's similar to objective and subjective justification. It starts with forgiveness, trusting the promise that forgiveness is ours personally through faith, and then proceeds to forgiving those who wrong us. Forgiveness, however, does not always bring about immediate reconciliation, just as objective justification doesn't mean that everyone has received God's forgiveness through faith and is bound for heaven. Reconciliation takes two. There are times when you won't pursue reconciliation. For example, if you're the victim of a rapist, the Christian thing to do is forgive him. I'm not suggesting that is easy; it is most difficult, as the sermon about Debbie Morris shows. Forgiving a rapist does not mean that you're going to invite him into your house for brunch. The same can be said of other sins that victimize you or someone close to you. Yes, you should forgive the murderer, the robber, the embezzler, the adulterer, the perjurer, the slanderer, and the like. Forgiveness frees you from their hold on your emotions, but forgiveness does not mean, for example, inviting the robber to your dinner party.

More commonly in our day-to-day life, you'll want reconciliation in your circle of coworkers, friends, your family and marriage. Since you work and live in close associations with these people, common sense says you'll want to work toward reconciliation. It makes moving forward so much easier interpersonally. Steve and Kathy were both willing to work toward reconciliation and achieved it, but Janel's husband wasn't willing, for whatever reason. And so she went on, certainly with regrets that reconciliation didn't happen but still forgiving her ex. Sometimes you patch it up; other times not. Living in forgiveness, living in the fear and love of God who forgives and is reconciled to us, means you try. True, the sin that still clings deep in our hearts makes us resist forgiving the person who wronged us and working toward reconciliation, but Jesus said to forgive 70 times 7 (Matthew 18:22 GW) and has entrusted to us the "ministry of reconciliation." This struggle shows room for continued growth in our sanctified life in Christ, and makes us yearn deep in our hearts for heaven, where "Perfect love and friendship reign / Through all eternity."[3]

348

Week 39 – Surely the Lord Is in This Place

Delivered at St. Paul's Lutheran Church, Evansville, Indiana
for the installation of Rev. Walt Ullman
October 1, 1978

Text – Genesis 28:10-22

Jacob left Beersheba and went toward Haran. And he came to a certain place and stayed there that night, because the sun had set. Taking one of the stones of the place, he put it under his head and lay down in that place to sleep. And he dreamed, and behold, there was a ladder set up on the earth, and the top of it reached to heaven. And behold, the angels of God were ascending and descending on it! And behold, the LORD stood above it and said, "I am the LORD, the God of Abraham your father and the God of Isaac. The land on which you lie I will give to you and to your offspring. Your offspring shall be like the dust of the earth, and you shall spread abroad to the west and to the east and to the north and to the south, and in you and your offspring shall all the families of the earth be blessed. Behold, I am with you and will keep you wherever you go, and will bring you back to this land. For I will not leave you until I have done what I have promised you." Then Jacob awoke from his sleep and said, "Surely the LORD is in this place, and I did not know it." And he was afraid and said, "How awesome is this place! This is none other than the house of God, and this is the gate of heaven."

So early in the morning Jacob took the stone that he had put under his head and set it up for a pillar and poured oil on the top of it. He called the name of that place Bethel, but the name of the city was Luz at the first. Then Jacob made a vow, saying, "If God will be with me and will keep me in this way that I go, and will give me bread to eat and clothing to wear, so that I come again to my father's house in peace, then the LORD shall be my God, and this stone, which I have set up for a pillar, shall be God's house. And of all that you give me I will give a full tenth to you."

Prayer

O God, You teach us to trust You as our heavenly Father, loving and caring for us, Your children. We thank You for the pastors You raise up and call to lead our congregations: pointing us to Jesus, bringing us His lively Word and Sacraments, and being examples of living in Your love and reverent fear. Encourage them in their care and concern for the welfare of Your Church. May Your Spirit lead them to live in sincere and complete dependence upon You in their personal lives, both in godly struggles for the advance of Your kingdom and in the subtle temptations Satan uses to take them down. Hearten their families and homes with the embrace of faith, hope, and love that are in Christ Jesus. In His name we pray. Amen.

This is a good Bible story for you children, and for you adults, on any day of the week. And this is a *great* Bible story on this particular Sunday afternoon, at this time when you people of St. Paul's congregation officially welcome and install your new pastor, Rev. Walt Ullman. There are few days in the lives of Christian people that are as happy and joyous as this day, when a congregation welcomes a new shepherd into its midst. There are few things as reassuring to God's people as knowing you have a pastor, a faithful servant of the Lord Jesus Christ who will feed you with the holy Word of God and the Sacraments. What a delight it is for all of you this day to welcome not only a pastor, but to welcome the pastor's family into your congregation. His wife and his children are the ones who support him in his ministry, encourage him when he gets discouraged, humble him when Satan would tempt him to pride, and fill his life with love. This pastor's family reminds you people of St. Paul's how good and holy Christian family life is to be. And so, what a joyous and happy day this is for all of you – this day when you welcome the Ullmans!

This is also a time of apprehension. You people of St. Paul's are wondering:

Thank God, we have a pastor, but what will he be like? He certainly seems nice enough. The rumors around church are that he is a fine fellow. But what will he really be like? Will he be warm and open, showing care and concern for his people? Will he be faithful? Will he preach and teach the pure Word of God as it stands written in Holy Scripture? Will he minister faithfully to the sick, the shut-in, the troubled?

On this happy and joyous day of installation, you congregation members are not the only ones who wonder what it will be like. Pastor Ullman also wonders:

What will it be like here in Evansville? Will my ministry here be blessed? Will the people of St. Paul's work arm-in-arm with me to fulfill our Lord's command to bring the Gospel to all people? Or, instead of working arm-in-arm, will the devil tempt them to butt their heads against mine in opposition and contentiousness and strife?

Your new pastor has these concerns in his mind this day. It is only natural. It is only human nature to wonder, *What lies ahead of us?*

For that reason, I have picked the story of Jacob's Ladder as the text for this service. It is a simple story – we all learned it in Sunday School. It is a truly great story on this particular day because it tells you that the LORD is God; He will be with you, pastor and laypeople alike; He will bless and invigorate you through the Spirit of the Lord Jesus Christ; and finally, He will bring you redeemed to the eternal joy of heaven above. There are great blessings ahead of you here, Pastor Ullman. There are great blessings ahead of you, people of St. Paul's!

Jacob started out the same way you are today. He was a bit apprehensive. His father, Isaac, told Jacob to leave their home in Beersheba and to journey to the land of Haran where his uncle, Laban, lived. Before Jacob left for the new place, his father Isaac blessed him and assured him that the LORD God would accompany him in his new experiences. Yet, despite the blessing of his father, we may be sure that Jacob was a bit apprehensive. He was going to a new place: new people, new challenges. With such thoughts running through his mind, he journeyed toward Haran. On one particular evening, he laid down to sleep. The

Bible tells us that he had no pillow, so he used a stone for a pillow. You don't sleep too well when your head is on the rocks and you're apprehensive about the future. We might guess that Pastor Ullman has slept lightly these past nights, wondering what is ahead of him. So Jacob slept. God looked down in loving kindness. *We must reassure Jacob that all will be well.* And so the LORD God appeared to Jacob in a dream, the dream we call "Jacob's Ladder." Jacob dreamed that this ladder reached from earth all the way to heaven, and angels were going up and down the ladder. At the top of the ladder stood the LORD God. And He said this to Jacob:

> I am the LORD, the God of Abraham your father and the God of Isaac. The land on which you lie I will give to you and to your offspring. Your offspring shall be like the dust of the earth, and you shall spread abroad to the west and to the east and to the north and to the south, and in you and your offspring shall all the families of the earth be blessed. Behold, I am with you and will keep you wherever you go, and will bring you back to this land. For I will not leave you until I have done what I have promised you.

With these words, the LORD God reassured Jacob that it would go well for him in his new place. Today, He also reassures you – pastor and people – that it will go well for you here, if you remain faithful to this Word.

"I am the LORD God" (Genesis 28:13 KJV). That's the way God started His speech to Jacob. That is the way you – pastor and people – begin your work together this day. He is the LORD God! He is the One who stands at the top of the ladder! He is the One to whom we look up – and no other! He set the stars in the heavens. He created this world. He filled the oceans with life, and He placed mankind upon the earth. He made all things good. All was perfect. And so He expects it to be: "You shall be holy to me, for I the LORD am holy (Leviticus 20:26). The heart of holiness, the center of perfection, is to hold Him as your LORD and God alone. Put nothing else ahead of Him. He's at the top of the ladder! But ever since the fall of Adam and Eve, we try to pull Him off of His pedestal and put something else in the place of God. That's why we are sinners. We are not holy the way He says we shall be holy. The root reason for your sin, people, is your failure to keep the First Commandment – your failure to fear, love, and trust in God above all things. As you begin this new era in the history of your congregation, remember: God stands at the top of the ladder, and no one else.

The devil so often comes to us pastors and tempts us to believe that we are at the top of the church, and need not answer to anyone. The pastor does not stand at the top of the church. So it is that the first president of our Synod, Dr. C.F.W. Walther, wrote in his great *Kirche und Amt* these words: "The minister must not tyrannize the church. He has no authority to introduce new laws or arbitrarily to establish adiaphora or ceremonies. ... The minister has no right to inflict and carry out excommunication without his having first informed the whole congregation."[1] We pastors must remember that we are not sovereign kings within the congregation – God and His Word stand at the top of the ladder.

By the same token, the devil tempts you, people of the congregation, to believe that you are the boss. *We pay the light bills. We pay his salary. We hired him and we can fire him.* That is the talk of the devil. Although you as a congregation have great authority – authority that comes from God Himself – yet you the congregation are not at the top of the ladder. It is God who has given you the authority to preach the Gospel and to administer the Sacraments. It is God who has given the Church the Office of the Keys. It is God who is on top, and the congregation stands beneath Him. God spoke to Jacob, and God speaks to you today and says, "I am the LORD God." He stands over pastor and people alike.

Now God continued His speech to Jacob by promising him great blessings. God promised that the land where Jacob made his rocky bed would one day be his own possession. God promised that Jacob would have descendants as numerous as the dust of the earth – descendants reaching to the north, the south, the east, and the west.

You know what? God kept His promises to Jacob. Years later, Jacob returned to this place of his dream as a rich and wealthy man, and possessed it. Jacob had children from whom come the twelve tribes of Israel, a numerous and mighty nation. The God who is on top of us all is a God who makes promises and keeps them. As you begin this new era at St. Paul's, remember His greatest promise and His greatest fulfillment. Already in Eden He promised the Savior: "I will put enmity between you and the woman, and between your offspring and her offspring" (Genesis 3:15). To Jacob He said, "In your offspring shall all the nations of the earth be blessed" (Genesis 22:18). From the seed of Jacob, from the descendants of Israel, was born the Savior, our Lord Jesus Christ. God had made to us sinners the promise of a Savior. At the right time, God kept His promise. St. Paul writes, "But when the fullness of time had come, God sent forth his Son, born of woman, born under the law, to redeem those who were under the law, so that we might receive adoption as sons" (Galatians 4:4-5). The God who stands at the top of Jacob's Ladder is not a God who is aloof and removed from us sinners and from our problems. No, He is a God who sent His Son down into this world to live among us, to pay the terrible price of our sins upon the cross, and to rise to new and eternal life.

The promised Savior sent by God will be the focus of your life and work together. As you, Pastor Ullman, go about your daily tasks, always remember the Lord Jesus. Each Sunday morning, when you have that high honor and privilege to preach to the people from this pulpit the Holy Scripture, remember to ever direct their sight to the Lord Jesus. And you people of the congregation: Please, look to Jesus alone. Expect to hear His Word alone in this church and in your organizations. Focus your eyes on His cross, the sign that God has come down to save you. You should not have unrealistic expectations from this man, but you should expect him to show you the Lord Jesus. (Incidentally, I know Rev. Ullman very well. He will preach and teach Christ and His holy Word. You may rest assured.) Where would you be without your Savior? Where would you be in the life to come without a Savior who paid the eternal price of your sin? You know where you'd be. So, I beg you – in the months and years ahead, fix your eyes on Jesus alone.

God's speech to Jacob included another promise: "Behold, I am with you and will keep you wherever you go, and will bring you back to this land. For I will not leave you until I have done what I have promised you." God did stay with Jacob. He will be with you. To you, brother Walt, the Lord Jesus Christ promises, "And behold, I am with you always, to the end of the age" (Matthew 28:20). St. Paul says, "He who began a good work in you will bring it to completion at the day of Jesus Christ" (Philippians 1:6). So, remember His presence. Let the Word of God be your constant daily companion. Let it be your guide as you tend this flock which the Spirit has placed into your care. Let the Word support and strengthen you in the difficult days of ministry that are before you, for Satan will certainly try you. Attack the throne of God each day with your prayers, for He has commanded you to pray, and He promises to answer. At all times, remember His promise, "I am with you always."

God also promises to be with you, the people of St. Paul's. On this particular day, we especially remember that God is with you through the Office of the Holy Ministry. God in His wisdom and love has instituted the Office of the Holy Ministry for you. This is not a human institution, this pastoral ministry. It is a divine office founded by God Himself. God has instituted this office for your welfare. The prime responsibility of your pastor is to serve you with the saving Word of the Gospel and administer the Sacraments. When he does this faithfully, you owe him honor and respect. We again quote Dr. Walther's *Kirche und Amt*: "To the ministry there is due respect as well as unconditional obedience when the pastor uses God's Word."[1] God has given the Church this holy ministry. Through the work of the ministry, through the work of Gospel and Sacraments, He promises to be with you people in the months and years ahead. God will keep this promise.

God finished His speech to Jacob. The Bible says: "Then Jacob awoke from his sleep and said, 'Surely the LORD is in this place, and I did not know it.' And he was afraid and said, 'How awesome is this place! This is none other than the house of God, and this is the gate of heaven.'" I want to tell you, after God got done talking to Jacob, he woke up. He knew God was with him. And I'm telling you: When you hear God talk, when you hear how God sent you His son Jesus, when you remember that He has given you a pastor to feed you the Word of life… Wow, I'll tell you, *that* will wake up this congregation! This is the house of God! The Lord is with you! And by the grace of God and by the precious blood of Jesus, this will prove the gate to heaven, where we all – pastors and laypeople alike – shall live forever.

Amen.

For Further Reflection

"I believe in the Holy Spirit, the holy Christian Church, the communion of saints." (Apostles' Creed, Third Article)

- The fear and love of God in our life together – 1 John 4:19-21; Acts 2:42-47; Hebrews 10:25

- Can you put yourself in the story of the early Church? The sharing of holy things, "the communion of saints," makes a congregation a different kind of fellowship than other gatherings of people in our world – 1 Corinthians 10:14-17; 2 Corinthians 1:3-7; 2 Corinthians 8:15; 1 Peter 4:7-11. Is your congregation like that?
- "Our Father" (Lord's Prayer, Introduction)
    - In this prayer of our faith family, we pray with and for one another – "Our," not "My." Next time you pray "Our Father," pray it as an intercessory prayer for someone in your congregation or for the whole congregation.

Holy Spirit, ever living / As the Church's very life;
Holy Spirit, ever striving / Through us in a ceaseless strife;
Holy Spirit, ever forming / In the Church the mind of Christ:
You we praise with endless worship / For Your gifts and fruits unpriced.

Holy Spirit, ever working / Through the Church's ministry;
Quick'ning, strength'ning, and absolving, / Setting captive sinners free;
Holy Spirit, ever binding / Age to age and soul to soul
In communion never ending, / You we worship and extol.[2]

Retrospective

My denomination is not alone in experiencing a shortage of pastors, but The Lutheran Church–Missouri Synod is the church I know best. We have two seminaries that provide the church with its pastors: our Seminary in St. Louis, and Concordia Theological Seminary in Fort Wayne, Indiana. Both seminaries have been experiencing low enrollments for some years, as are 55 percent of seminaries in the Association of Theological Schools. The shortage is in their Master of Divinity programs, the bedrock of theological education for many decades. In recent years, there have not been enough graduates for all the congregations that have applied for them, and the prospects for immediate improvement are not encouraging. There are reasons for the decline, and plenty of straw bosses, people who talk but don't go to work to correct the problem. Their talk aside, this problem has profound consequences, temporally and eternally.

In my experience as a parish pastor, there are generally three groups of church members. There are the faithful parishioners who come to worship, rain or shine. Then there are those who, sadly, have become inactive in worship – not likely to come rain or shine, maybe not even at Christmas or Easter. It's with a third group, the people in the middle, where a pastor especially proves himself to be a shepherd. These are the people who come with some regularity, but are prone to get out of the habit – and weekly church attendance is a habit, a very good habit. Countless times I've met a person on Main Street, in Walmart, at a sports event, wherever, and had a conversation – just a friendly chat, no preaching about coming to church. Dependably, those little interactions resulted in keeping that parishioner coming to worship. Without pastors, those people may get out of the habit of coming to church, and – here's the profound eternal consequence – some will wander away from saving faith in Jesus. Congregations need a shepherd to seek out the sheep.

As this book comes into your hands, one of my greatest concerns is the shortage of seminary students and pastors for the mission of our Savior Jesus. Without a pastor to seek people and lead the congregation, decline can be expected, and decline in the vitality of a congregation means weaker witness to the community. Can your congregation covenant with us to raise up a new generation of pastors? Can you personally encourage someone to say, "Here am I. Send me!" (Isaiah 6:8 NIV)?

Looking at this sermon 40 years later, I notice three things. The actual manuscript you see here has only the bland title, "Installation Sermon." Today, I would give the sermon a specific title, not something generic. Having a title keeps the preacher more focused on one key theme, thus reducing the chance he'll spray many good but unconnected thoughts. If he's more focused, then the congregation will be more focused in listening and more likely to catch and remember the key thought. In preparing this book, we added the title, "Surely the Lord Is in This Place." I should have done that back when I wrote the sermon. Having a specific title helps with diction.

The ancient Greek and Roman orators divided speech-making into five parts: discovery (What will I speak about?); disposition or outline (How will I arrange my material?); diction (What words shall I use? What style shall I adopt?); memory (What imagery, rhetorical devices, and arguments will sink this into my memory? The ancients did not trust someone who delivered a written speech.); and delivery (the acting, the performance of what has been prepared). The first page of this sermon for my seminary roommate Walt Ullman shows how writing the script word for word and then committing it to memory helps diction, word selection. For example, the first sentence says "good Bible story;" the second sentence builds on that – "great Bible story." However, had I used a more specific title, like "Surely the Lord Is in This Place," I would have shaped the outline around the concept of presence and absence, and therefore chosen words that reflect God with us. In other words, the title would have improved the outline and diction of this sermon. Of course, you can select the right words without verbatim preparation, but sitting at the keyboard gives you more time to select the right word, the turn of phrase, the transitions, the punchy conclusion, and the like. When you speak off of notes or from an outline, you can indeed choose some diction ahead of delivery, but verbatim preparation gives you more time for total premeditation. It's like using GPS to guide you to your driving destination; the entire route toward the goal is known, everything thought through ahead of time. Avoid "rerouting" during delivery – follow your premeditated script!

The third thing I notice about this 40-year-old sermon? The church had gotten the fancy Selectric typewriter with the removable font balls! How else could I have typed italics?

INSTALLATION SERMON

Genesis 28
Walt Ullman, Oct. 1, 1978, Evansville, Ind.

This is a good Bible story for you children and for you
adults on any day of the week. This is a great Bible story
on this particular Sunday afternoon, at this time when you
people of St. Paul congregation officially welcome and install
your new pastor Ullman. There are few days in the lives of
Christian people that are as happy and joyous as this day when
a congregation welcomes a new shepherd into its midst. There
is nothing so reassuring to God's people as knowing that you
have a pastor, afaithful servant of the Lord Jesus Christ who
will feed you on the holy Wordof God and the Sacraments. What
a delight it is for you people this day to welcome not only a
pastor, but to welcome the pastor's family into your congregation. His wife and his children are the ones who support
him in his ministry, encourage him when he gets discouraged,
humble him when Satan would tempt him to pride, they fill his
life with love, and this pastor's family reminds you people of
St. Paul how good and holy Christian family life is to be. And
so, what a joyous and happy day this is for all ofyou, this day
when you welcome the Ullmans.
     This is also a time of apprehension. You people of St.
Paul congregation say "Thank God, we have a pastor, but what
will he be like? He certainly seems nice enough. The rumors
around church are that he is a fine fellow. But what will he
really be like? Will he be warm and open, showing care and
concern for his people? Will he befaithful? Will he preach and
teach the pure word of God as its stands written in Holy Scripture?

Week 40 – It Is Well with My Soul

*Written for the Lutheran Women's Missionary League
for LWML Sunday, 2007*

Text – Psalm 31:1-5

In you, O LORD, do I take refuge;
   let me never be put to shame;
   in your righteousness deliver me!
Incline your ear to me;
   rescue me speedily!
Be a rock of refuge for me,
   a strong fortress to save me!

For you are my rock and my fortress;
   and for your name's sake you lead me and guide me;
you take me out of the net they have hidden for me,
   for you are my refuge.
Into your hand I commit my spirit;
   you have redeemed me, O LORD, faithful God.

Prayer

Our heavenly Father, oh, the depths of hurt and sorrow we sometimes feel! We feel no hope, weighed down by despair. We might even imagine that You have left us but, no, Your Spirit is in us and is interceding on our behalf. In troubled times, guide our thoughts to the cross, to Jesus who endured an eternity of hurt and sorrow for us. Out of His desperate time, You brought new life for us. In Him and by Your Holy Spirit, recreate us from the nothingness we feel.

O all-embracing Mercy, / O ever-open Door,
What should we do without You / When heart and eye run o'er?
When all things seem against us, / To drive us to despair,
We know one gate is open, / One ear will hear our prayer.[1] Amen.

Back in the 1800s, a man named Horatio Spafford wrote a hymn, and in writing that hymn he penned a line familiar to many Christians: *"It is well, it is well with my soul."*[2] Perhaps you are familiar with Mr. Spafford's hymn, but you may not always identify with the refrain, *"It is well, it is well with my soul."* Is it really? It's not always well with my soul, and I'm sure it's not always well with your soul. Many times a soul that is well is more of a pious hope than reality. *Oh, that my soul felt well, rather than the anguish I'm now feeling!* In your private times of prayer, and when you come here for public worship, you don't always feel that it's well with your soul.

King David was right there with you, as Psalm 31 tells us: "Be gracious to me, O LORD, for I am in distress; my eye is wasted from grief; my soul and my body also" (v. 9). Things weren't so well with David's soul. Whatever the details might have been, David's enemies were strong against him: "They scheme together against me, as they plot to take my life" (v. 13). And it wasn't as simple as this – *Yes, my enemies are coming against me but at least I can count on my friends.* No, the people that should have been strong with David were waffling – or worse. "Because of all my adversaries I have become a reproach, especially to my neighbors, / and an object of dread to my acquaintances; those who see me in the street flee from me" (v. 11). Enemies without and enemies within. It was a time of intrigue. "I hear the whispering of many" (v. 13). These were some of David's problems, and you can sympathize with him.

You probably don't have enemies plotting to take your life in the same way David was targeted, but we are threatened in ways that previous generations were not. Terrorists certainly wouldn't hesitate to kill any of us, or all of us. But closer to our daily personal lives, we can identify with people being against us. David said, "Let the lying lips be mute" (v. 18), and you've heard lying lips say things against you that are not true. Many times gossipers don't have a clue what they're talking about. They slander you, harm your reputation, put the worst construction on what you've done, or what they imagine you've done. They break the Eighth Commandment, and there's not a whole lot you can do about it. Of course, there are times when you or I have given them reason to complain. We confessed our sins earlier in the service, and the truth is that our sins – even though forgiven because of Jesus Christ – our forgiven sins still tempt people to talk. Either way, this sinful world is very much with us, in our thoughts and heavy on our hearts, and so we have good reason to think: *It is* not *well with my soul. It is* not!

All that said, grousing as we do about the injustices of life, look at the wonderful thing that goes with it. "In you, O LORD, do I take refuge," David says. That's his lead line in Psalm 31. "In you, O LORD, do I take refuge." If things weren't well with his soul, David knew right where to go to make it well – and he went to God immediately. "In you, O LORD, do I take refuge," and he follows that appeal with many more expressions of his confidence in God. "For you are my rock and my fortress; and for your name's sake you lead me and guide me" (v. 3). David expressed his confidence in God because God had helped David before, and David knew that God keeps His promises to His people. As another example, David says, "Into your hand I commit my spirit," and then says what God has done: "You have redeemed me, O LORD, faithful God" (v. 5). Here's still another example of David confessing his faith that the faithful God is there for him: "You have seen my affliction; you have known the distress of my soul" (v. 7). And one more, although there are many more throughout this magnificent psalm: "I trust in you, O LORD; I say, "You are my God." / My times are in your hand" (vv. 14-15). David knew right where to go when things were not well with his soul.

Now that was David. Wouldn't it be great to have that instinctive response? When life is ganging up on you, when not only your enemies but sometimes your friends aren't there for you, what a great thing to turn immediately to God for help! You've got it too! It's in you to do the same. Actually, it's been put in you. This instinct to turn to God isn't naturally yours, but it was born into you by your baptism. When you were baptized, you were redeemed from the greatest of troubles, from the guilt of sin, from the dread of death, and from domination by evil. In Baptism, God brought you into His fortress, into His safe place of forgiveness – even if some people won't let go of your sins and shortcomings. In Baptism, God brought you into His fortress where hope abounds, especially when you're tempted to despair about your situation in life. In Baptism, God brought you into His fortress where His love for you reaches down into your soul, a welcome thing in our so-often-loveless world. What prompted David to turn to God has been put in you by your baptism into Jesus Christ. Now, "Your life is hidden with Christ in God" (Colossians 3:3). And so you turn to God as David did, and you confess as David confessed: "For you are my rock and my fortress; ... / ... you are my refuge. / Into your hand I commit my spirit; you have redeemed me, O LORD, faithful God" (Psalm 31:3-5). When the faithful God has led you again to such a confession, you say, *It is well with my soul. It is well.* "You keep him in perfect peace whose mind is stayed on you" (Isaiah 26:3). The Spirit that prompted David to go straight to God is the same Spirit that is among us in our times of trouble. *It is well with my soul. It is well.*

I mentioned Horatio Spafford at the beginning of this sermon. In the 1800s, Horatio Spafford was a successful Chicago lawyer, a rich man with many real estate holdings. But wealth is fleeting, and the great Chicago fire of 1871 wiped out much of Spafford's wealth. Not a good time for the Spafford family. Just think of the times when you weren't sure about your economic future. Anyway, Spafford and his wife needed to get away and still had sufficient resources for a good vacation. So they planned a trip to Europe. When the time came to set out on their vacation, some last-minute business detained Mr. Spafford, but he sent his wife and four daughters ahead of him on the *S.S. Ville du Havre*. Early on November 22, 1873, disaster struck. Their ship was struck by a Scottish ship and sank almost immediately. The four daughters were lost; only Mrs. Spafford survived from their family. When Horatio Spafford sailed across the Atlantic to join his grieving wife, the captain called him to the bridge and reported that they were at the place where the *Ville du Havre* had gone down. Can you imagine the feelings? I can't, but the story goes that shortly thereafter, Spafford wrote his famous words:

> *When peace, like a river, attendeth my way,*
> *When sorrows, like sea billows, roll;*
> *Whatever my lot, Thou hast taught me to say,*
> *It is well, it is well with my soul.*[2]

Dare I say that the difficult times can prove to be times of special blessing? I'm not suggesting that we should enjoy the difficult times. I don't think David got a kick out of his troubles. That said, it's the tough times – the times when the weight of the world is on your heart, the times when you're suffering unjustly, you've done nothing wrong but people are talking against you, the times when you realize that the universe doesn't revolve around you and doesn't seem to care about you – yes, it's the tough times when you experience firsthand your sinful mortality. When you're getting "crucified," you get a better appreciation for the One who really *was* crucified. Jesus Christ knew what David went through. Jesus Christ knows what you go through. Jesus Christ went through that and much more. He took our sins and the sins of those who sin against you; He took all sins upon Himself and paid for them. Our Christian faith is not about glory, at least not yet, for there is heavenly glory to come. Yes, Jesus Christ rose from the dead and ascended to glory. Someday in glory, God will wipe away every tear from our eyes (cf. Isaiah 25:8 and Revelation 7:17). But here and now, it's not about glory, not about sweetness day-in and day-out. Though it's not welcome, these times get us into the heart of Christian faith. They bring us again into the fortress of God's protection.

"Rock! Rest on Christ the King!" As David used the 31st Psalm to tell people that God is a rock and a fortress, so the LWML, the Lutheran Women in Mission, is telling people the same today. "Rock! Rest on Christ the King!" is the theme of the LWML this year. We go to God because God is faithful and cares for us; that's the heart message of the LWML. The women of the LWML do that through their meetings and conversations. I want to highlight the literature they make available to all of us. Their *Lutheran Woman's Quarterly* has interesting articles and inspiring devotions. The LWML offers devotional books: *You Make a Difference, You Are Precious, You Are Special, You Are Loved*, and *One Cup of Water*. The LWML has other devotional resources especially suited to busy people on the go: "Mug Meditations," "Noontime Nibbles," and "Mustard Seeds," just to name a few. These are resources through which God can make it well with your soul. Thank you, Lutheran Women in Mission, for all you do for us!

In an issue of the *Lutheran Woman's Quarterly,* Dr. LuJuana R. Butts tells how she learned to pray. Says Dr. Butts, "I remember learning how to pray on my knees beside my mother, saying the twenty-third Psalm, knowing that He was my Shepherd. No matter how much hunger was there, the growling, the stomach pains, or whatever, we were not going to be in want because He was there to take care of us."[3] Dr. Butts learned as a child, the troubles of life notwithstanding, that it was well with her soul. Now, she shares that as a professor at our Concordia College in Bronxville, New York. Horatio Spafford knew that in the depths of grief it was well with his soul, and he has shared that with everyone who sings his hymn. And David knew it in the midst of his troubles. His words in Psalm 31 are God's inspired words to us today. Since God has brought you and me into the fortress of His care, a safe place where we are surrounded by such a great cloud of witnesses (Hebrews 12:1), we can say an assured fact, *It is well with my soul. It is well.*

Amen.

For Further Reflection

"Lead us not into temptation, but deliver us from evil." (Lord's Prayer, Sixth and Seventh Petitions)

- The devil tempts us to sin, as he tempted the Savior – Matthew 4:1-11; 1 Peter 5:6-11
- God also tries our faith to grow our dependence upon Him. Put yourself in the story:
  - God let Job's faith be tested – Job 1:6-22
  - Jesus tries a believer's faith – Matthew 15:21-28
  - Times of testing result in filial fear – Proverbs 3:11-12
- Do you love God *despite* your problems or *because* of your problems? James 1:2-3; Romans 5:1-5; 2 Corinthians 4:16-18
- Deliver us in the time of testing! Luke 22:31-32; 2 Thessalonians 3:3-5; 2 Timothy 4:16-18; Revelation 21:4
- The fear and love of God – Psalm 31:19, fear; Psalm 31:23, love; Romans 8:31-39

> *When darkness veils His lovely face,*
> *I rest on His unchanging grace;*
> *In ev'ry high and stormy gale*

My anchor holds within the veil.
O Christ, the solid rock, I stand;
All other ground is sinking sand.

His oath, His covenant and blood
Support me in the raging flood;
When ev'ry earthly prop gives way,
He then is all my hope and stay.
On Christ, the sold rock, I stand;
All other ground is sinking sand.[4]

Retrospective

Two homiletical preaching points about using illustrations. First, I tell students if you have a great illustration – and isn't the story about Horatio Spafford amazing? – you don't have to use it all at one time. You can start with a part of the illustration, as I did here, then move into the substance of the sermon, and later share more of the illustration. Second, students often like to use a good illustration to begin their sermon. They're thinking they need to get the listener interested. Actually, no. People will listen at the outset of the sermon. It's as the sermon goes on that the preacher needs to keep them engaged. Therefore a good illustration is more effective midway or later in the sermon than at the outset.

So far I've shared my little tips, but here comes the most important thing I can write about this sermon. The active laypeople of our church are fantastic! For twelve years I had the honor of being employed by the dedicated people of Lutheran Hour Ministries, and throughout my entire ministry have had many dependably positive times with the inspiring women of The International Lutheran Women's Missionary League. The mission of our Lord Jesus is moving forward, and great thanks are due to committed laypeople who have taken the Great Commission to heart and generously give their time and talents to their congregations and to these volunteer organizations. There are some pastors who discourage full participation by laity in the life and mission of the church. Too bad, because laypeople get into places where we pastors cannot go, and their witness has credibility that the witness of a pastor lacks. It's not that a pastor is insincere; people easily discount what he says because he's paid to do what he does. Fortunately, pastors who discourage laity in this way are few. At Concordia Seminary, we urge our future pastors both to be faithful to the commands given with the institution of the pastoral office, but also to be arm-in-arm with their laypeople. "To equip the saints for the work of ministry," Paul calls it in Ephesians 4:12. I was honored to write this sermon for LWML Sunday, and I thank them for all they continue to do.

Week 41 – Jesus, Abide with Me!

Delivered at St. Paul Ev. Lutheran Church, Fort Dodge, Iowa
for their 150th anniversary
October 13, 2013

Text – Luke 19:1-10

He entered Jericho and was passing through. And behold, there was a man named Zacchaeus. He was a chief tax collector and was rich. And he was seeking to see who Jesus was, but on account of the crowd he could not, because he was small in stature. So he ran on ahead and climbed up into a sycamore tree to see him, for he was about to pass that way. And when Jesus came to the place, he looked up and said to him, "Zacchaeus, hurry and come down, for I must stay at your house today." So he hurried and came down and received him joyfully. And when they saw it, they all grumbled, "He has gone in to be the guest of a man who is a sinner." And Zacchaeus stood and said to the Lord, "Behold, Lord, the half of my goods I give to the poor. And if I have defrauded anyone of anything, I restore it fourfold." And Jesus said to him, "Today salvation has come to this house, since he also is a son of Abraham. For the Son of Man came to seek and to save the lost."

Prayer

Almighty and eternal God, we thank You for blessing our congregation through all these years. You have sustained us through good and bad times in our country, in our families, and also in our congregation. You have given us the Spirit of our Lord Jesus with Your forgiveness and hope for what is to come. Let this anniversary increase even more our yearning for Jesus to abide with us. Amen.

Let's look at today's Gospel, the story of Zacchaeus. "He entered Jericho and was passing through. And behold, there was a man named Zacchaeus. He was a chief tax collector and was rich. And he was seeking to see who Jesus was, but on account of the crowd he could not, because he was small in stature." It was like a parade. You've been to a parade, haven't you? Can you imagine yourself at this parade, this Jericho parade, this parade that is packed with people because Jesus is passing by? "So he ran on ahead and climbed up into a sycamore tree to see him, for he was about to pass that way. And when Jesus came to the place, he looked up and said to him, 'Zacchaeus, hurry and come down, for I must stay at your house today.'" Remember, imagine yourself at this parade. You know how at some parades they throw candy and all the kids scramble to get some? Are you like the kids at this parade, Jesus' parade? Jesus is saying, *Zacchaeus, I've gotta stay at your house today.* Are you scrambling? *Jesus, stay with me, too! Jesus, abide with me! No, Jesus, you come to my house! Jesus, abide with me!*

What I'm really asking is this: Is your faith tired? Have you grown up and become such an adult that you're no longer scrambling to see Jesus? "So he hurried and came down and received him joyfully." If a church anniversary does anything, it ought to put a little scramble back into our yearning for Jesus.

Jesus, abide with me!

Jesus, I've heard about all that You did in Bible times. I could use some of that in my own life. Abide with me!

Jesus, I'm not satisfied. I'm not a whole person. Zacchaeus had money but that wasn't enough. He needed You. Jesus, abide with me!

Jesus, people hurt me. They anger me. They can make me feel like I'm alone in the world – alone without help or hope. Jesus, abide with me!

And Jesus, I feel guilty. Oh, if You knew the things I've done! Some people won't let me forget. Some holier-than-thou church people make me want to stay away. And my conscience is troubled. Jesus, abide with me!

Abide with your words of forgiveness. Abide with your teaching about sinful hurting people whom You came to seek and to save.

Abide with me, just as You stayed at Zacchaeus' house, as You stayed at Peter's house, as You stayed with Mary and Martha, as You stayed in so many homes.

Jesus, abide with me!

So like I said, if a church anniversary does anything, it ought to put a little scramble back into our yearning for Jesus.

"And when they saw it, they all grumbled, 'He has gone in to be the guest of a man who is a sinner.'" They were self-righteous. Who among us doesn't have a self-righteous streak within us? "And Zacchaeus stood and said to the Lord, 'Behold, Lord, the half of my goods I give to the poor. And if I have defrauded anyone of anything, I restore it fourfold.'" When Jesus stays at your house, He changes you. When you sit with His words, when you read what He says, when you remember what He preached, when you pour out your heart to Him, His Word will change you. "And Jesus said to him, 'Today salvation has come to this house, since he also is a son of Abraham. For the Son of Man came to seek and to save the lost.'"

I came to Jesus as I was, / So weary, worn, and sad;
I found in Him a resting place, / And He has made me glad.[1]

So you celebrate 150 years as St. Paul Lutheran Church. Congratulations! You have many memories. May they all be sanctified, because God works all things to the good for those who love Him (cf. Romans 8:28). Many of you have worked hard for your church and school. Never grow weary in well-doing, for you shall reap the harvest (cf. Galatians 6:9). But remember, it's all about Jesus. He wants to abide in your heart and home.

Amen.

I need Thy presence ev'ry passing hour;
What but Thy grace can foil the tempter's pow'r?

Who like Thyself my guide and stay can be?
Through cloud and sunshine, O abide with me.

Hold Thou Thy cross before my closing eyes;
Shine through the gloom, and point me to the skies.
Heav'n's morning breaks, and earth's vain shadows flee;
In life, in death, O Lord, abide with me.[2]

For Further Reflection

"You shall love your neighbor as yourself." (Matthew 22:39)

- The religious establishment tests Jesus with a question, but in answering, He adds a flesh-and-blood example of how to show your fear and love of God – Matthew 22:34-40. What word is common to both commandments?
- Opportunities to show real-life fear and love of God:
  - "Honor your father and your mother." Fear and love of God strives for ordered life in family, community, general society, and government.
  - "You shall not murder." Fear and love of God works to preserve and protect the life of others.
  - "You shall not commit adultery." Fear and love of God promotes sexual purity and honors marriage.
  - "You shall not steal." Fear and love of God seeks to protect the property of others.
  - "You shall not give false testimony against your neighbor." Fear and love of God seeks to guard the good reputation of other people.
- "You shall not," God's Law, shows our sin. Why do we not love our neighbors as ourselves? Mark 7:14-23; Romans 3:9-20; Romans 7:7-23.
- The commandments of the Second Table show us both the sin of the world and especially our own sins against other people. Who shall rescue us? Romans 7:24.
- Hence the Second Table, showing that all people should repent, drives us to God and Christ in the First Table:

- o "You shall have no other gods"
- o "You shall not misuse the name of the Lord your God"
- o "Remember the Sabbath day by keeping it holy"
- Then true fear and love of God in the First Table drives us to show His love in all the areas of the Second Table. See Romans 12:9-21 and Romans 13:8-10. What is the fulfillment of the Law?
- Martin Luther: "Christians live not in themselves but in Christ and their neighbor. Otherwise they are not Christian. They live in Christ through faith, in their neighbor through love. By faith they are caught up beyond themselves into God. By love they descend beneath themselves into their neighbor."[3]

In your hearts enthrone Him; / There let Him subdue
All that is not holy, / All that is not true:
Crown Him as your captain / In temptation's hour;
Let His will enfold you / In its light and pow'r.

Christians, this Lord Jesus / Shall return again
In His Father's glory, / With His angel train;
For all wreaths of empire / Meet upon His brow,
And our hearts confess Him / King of glory now.[4]

Retrospective

There are different ways to lay out a sermon. The method used in this one is called "expository" because it goes through the biblical story verse by verse, commenting along the way. It's commonly used in some faith traditions but hasn't been too widely used in Lutheran circles. That's because Lutherans believe the Gospel, the Good News of what God does for us in Jesus, should be the major thrust of a sermon, and not every text in the Bible is dominated by the Gospel. The opposite of the Gospel is the Law, the "Thou shalts" and "Thou shalt nots," that God lays down for all people. God put the Law in everyone's heart (Romans 2:14-15; Ecclesiastes 3:11), with the result that we strive to do what we ought, even though sin in us makes it impossible for us to satisfy God with our own efforts. The Law is in us, natural, but the Gospel comes to us from outside ourselves, from God's revelation in the Word of Jesus. That's why the Gospel should predominate; its purpose is to overwhelm despair when we realize that we could never do enough to satisfy God.

Back to expository preaching. Some biblical passages are short on Gospel. For example, near the end of this sermon I referred to Galatians 6:9. If you read Galatians 6:1-9, you'll see that there is almost no Gospel. Paul is telling Christians how to live. That's Law, which is good when we do it as a response to what God does for us in Jesus – but doing those good things still doesn't save us. Now if the preacher were to take Galatians 6:1-9 verse by verse, the Gospel could get short-shrift. Hence Lutheran pastors tend to present the truths of God's Word in the Law-Gospel dynamic, with Gospel dominating.

Like many texts in the four Gospels, this story of Zacchaeus does lend itself to expository preaching. It was easy to prepare and memorize, and fun to preach. And in this day and age, when people are suspicious that the church is somehow replacing God's Word with church opinions, the expository style helps people follow along in their Bibles and be confident that they will go home from church having heard God's Word.

I close with a quotation about losing zeal for the life of the church – about losing the scramble Zacchaeus showed when Jesus brought salvation to his house. Gary Thies directs Mission Central, an organization in Mapleton, Iowa, with a worldwide interest in mission. Mr. Thies has visited countless congregations, some filled with zeal for mission, others not. He shares this: "The Basic Law of Congregational Life: Churches grow when they intentionally reach out instead of concentrating on their institutional needs. Churches die when they concentrate on their own needs." Jesus doesn't abide with us so we'll wall ourselves off from society! "Love your neighbor as yourself."

Week 42 – A Tattered Security Blanket

Broadcast on The Lutheran Hour
October 18, 1998

Text – Romans 4:15

For the law brings wrath, but where there is no law there is no transgression.

Prayer

Almighty and eternal God, You teach us that we are saved by grace, through faith, and not by our own works. Help us to resist the temptation to feel secure because of our own religious works, but instead, help us to trust You because of the great mercy You have shown us in our Savior, Jesus Christ. In His name we pray. Amen.

Religious people – like myself – are in the habit of laying guilt trips on others. My topic this week is guilt, something in which we are all experienced. We know guilt because we all have guilty feelings and because some people – like religious people – can lay guilt trips on us.

Thus, I have often wondered how our religious pronouncements come across to people who have done something wrong. For example, how does a woman who has had an abortion feel when she hears religious people denounce abortion as a sin? I've wondered how a divorced person feels when he or she hears preachers talk about the sanctity of marriage. I wonder how a person in jail feels when preachers denounce a growing jail population as an indication of a crumbling society. I wonder how a gay or lesbian feels when they hear Bible passages that denounce homosexuality or, more poignantly, how the parents of a homosexual feel when they hear such passages which seem to condemn their dear child.

My musing is not whether these and other conducts are wrong. The Bible says they are. My question is how do non-religious, non-churchgoing people respond to our religious pronouncements? They can deny that their conduct is wrong. They can rationalize their behavior, giving reasons why it was the thing to do. They can cover the sin with drugs or alcohol or by acting out with bizarre conduct. Whatever the outward response might be, there's one response that is true for most people. Most people are struggling with guilt.

Now, guilt is not wrong. In a strange way, guilt is good – good because it sets the stage for someone, some religious person, to say, "I know that such-and-such is bothering you. That's why God sent Jesus. Jesus came to make good for your sin. Believe it! God forgives you. Now you can put those guilty feelings behind you and get on with life – a better life, an abundant life." That's the good Word from God that we religious people should be passing along to those who feel guilty. That's what it's all about. John 3:17 says, "For God did not send his Son into the world to condemn the world, but in order that the world might be saved through him."

But we religious people don't always do that. Instead of helping to lift the load of guilt, we often lay an even heavier guilt trip on people who are already troubled by what they have done. Why do religious people do that? The answer is this: In many instances, we religious people have not come to terms with our own guilt. It's easy for us to make self-righteous pronouncements about the sins of others, but to ignore how terribly flawed we ourselves are before God. To demonstrate that, let's go back 20 centuries and look at the Pharisees.

Now, you might be thinking, *The Pharisees? Boo, hiss! Pharisees were bad guys. Why, Jesus called them hypocrites!* Well, yes, the Bible tends to picture the Pharisees as the bad guys, as the enemies of Jesus. But the fact is that the Pharisees were the most religious people of the first-century Jews. The historian Josephus tells us they had great influence over the common people. Matthew 23 tells us they were respected. They were exemplary stewards, giving 10 percent or more to religious causes. They were interested in evangelism and mission, traveling far to make a single convert. But the thing about these Pharisees that most impressed the common people was the Pharisees' knowledge of the Bible (which in that day meant the Old Testament, the only testament then in existence). The Pharisees knew the teachings of Moses, the psalms, and the prophets. And they knew the interpretations and the traditions. The traditions were the additions that their own theologians had added to the Bible over the years. You know why the Pharisees earn a *Boo, hiss*? Not because they were religious, but because they used the Bible and their man-made traditions to lay guilt trips on other people. They didn't deal with their own guilt. They were hardhearted toward hurting sinners, rather than showing compassion.

Oh, they should have known they were guilty before God. The Old Testament didn't let them off the hook simply because they were religious. Ecclesiastes 7:20 has religious people in mind when it says, "Surely there is not a righteous man on earth who does good and never sins." The Pharisees were aware of that verse. It should have shaken their self-confidence: *Hey, could it be, could it just be that I am guilty before God?* They also knew another Bible verse. Ezekiel 18:4 says, "the soul who sins shall die." *Could* be guilty? Guilty and doomed to death, Mr. Pharisee!

But no, they didn't apply such verses to themselves. When the Pharisees heard the word "sinner," they thought of other people. They thought of drug dealers, prostitutes, convicts, thieves, adulterers, and the like. *Those people are the sinners*, the Pharisees thought. *Those people have a lot to feel guilty about, but not us. We are God's righteous people because we outwardly keep the commandments and the theological traditions of our people. We're not guilty.* So they avoided dealing with their own guilt before God by trusting their outward keeping of certain Old Testament laws and their own man-made traditions. *Boo, hiss!*

Jesus went after their false sense of security. One example is in the Sermon on the Mount. First, Jesus upheld the validity of the Law. He did not come to revise the Ten Commandments into the Ten Suggestions. In Matthew 5:17 Jesus says, "Do not think that I have come to abolish the Law or the Prophets." In fact, Jesus even upped the ante. He told His listeners that God doesn't only look for an outward keeping of the Law but He also expects purity in the heart. One example is the following statement about murder: "You have heard that it was said to those of old, 'You shall not murder; and whoever murders will be liable to judgment.' But I say to you that everyone who is angry with his brother will be liable to judgment" (Matthew 5:21-22). Jesus did the same thing with several other conducts, like oaths and infidelity. It was His way, in that sermon, of pleading with us all to acknowledge our own guilt.

Finally, He zings the Pharisees and drives home the point to you and me today. In Matthew 5:20 He says, "For I tell you, unless your righteousness exceeds that of the scribes and Pharisees, you will never enter the kingdom of heaven." That is, as outwardly righteous as you strive to be, you are still as guilty as sin before God. Outward, upright conduct is important to society. Jesus doesn't deny that. I don't deny that. The moral law is still valid. The point here, however, is that in God's sight – I repeat, in God's sight, which is far more probing than our human views of one another – I am as guilty as the convicted criminal sitting on death row. And so are you.

Picture it this way: The Pharisees used the Law and the traditions like a security blanket. If you have had small children, you know how they often cling to a blanket. It makes them feel secure. Many times we use our outward acts as a security blanket. It deceives us into a false sense of security, but it won't stand the test of time. Sooner or later the security blanket becomes tattered, so tattered that Mom and Dad look for a way to get rid of the ratty old thing. Eventually, the child comes to see that, too, and gives up the blanket, that false sense of security. That is Jesus' goal in dealing with religious people. Get rid of your reliance upon religious works and find your security in believing that God forgives you, a sinner.

One of Jesus' best-known parables comes out of this controversy. It is the parable of the Pharisee and the tax collector from Luke 18:9-14. Jesus also used this illustration with some who were sure that God approved of them while they looked down on everyone else. Jesus said: "Two men went up into the temple to pray, one a Pharisee and the other a tax collector. The Pharisee, standing by himself, prayed thus: 'God, I thank you that I am not like other men, extortioners, unjust, adulterers, or even like this tax collector. I fast twice a week; I give tithes of all that I get.'"

Do you see it? That Pharisee is clinging to his tattered security blanket of good works.

Jesus continues: "But the tax collector, standing far off, would not even lift up his eyes to heaven, but beat his breast, saying, 'God, be merciful to me, a sinner!'"

No false security there. That's why guilt feelings can be so helpful. Rather than ignore them, like the Pharisees, honesty about our individual sin and guilt sets the stage for hearing God's Word of forgiveness. Jesus' death on the cross has made good for your sinful acts. You can deal with your guilty feelings by believing that God for Jesus' sake is kind and merciful to you. That's true security – not a blanket, not the commandments – but the mercy of God to you, personally.

Jesus concludes the parable: "I tell you, this man went down to his house justified, rather than the other. For everyone who exalts himself will be humbled, but the one who humbles himself will be exalted."

So, back to my earlier musing. How do we religious people make others feel? There's an important principle for us in Romans 4:15. That verse says, "For the law brings wrath." It's talking about all the "Thou shalts" and the "Thou shalt nots" of the Ten Commandments. That's God's Law. His Law is the Ten Commandments and also other passages in which God tells us what we are to do and not to do, and how we are to be and not to be.

A footnote here: God's Law does not include man-made traditions and rules. The Pharisees added their own notions to the Word of God, and religious people today are tempted to do the same. Religious people show that they are clinging to a tattered security blanket when they cannot let the Word of God stand on its own, but feel compelled to add their own opinions to God's Word.

So, St. Paul says, "The law brings wrath." After surveying the biblical use of the Greek word *orgé* (ὀργή), the word that is used in Romans 4:15, psychologists Glenn Taylor and Rod Wilson define wrath, *orgé*, this way: "*Orgé* is a settled inner attitude that may, but not necessarily, lead to revenge and personal animosity."[1]

The Law is not bad. Of course, it's not bad. It comes from God. God is good. God's Law is a good thing to obey. More and more social scientists are coming to realize that the clear teachings of the Bible are good practical guides for daily life. But the Law is no security blanket. It does not take away our sins. In fact, it exposes our sins. Romans 3:20 says, "Through the law comes knowledge of sin." And the Law doesn't give peace. Quite the contrary – the Law works wrath. As Taylor and Wilson said, it may "lead to revenge and personal animosity."

So, here's the conclusion of the matter: If you and I use the Bible (not to mention our own traditions and personal opinions) to heap more guilt upon people who are hurting because they've done wrong, we are only contributing to greater anger. Wouldn't that be tragic? You and I can share the Good News that Jesus made good for their sins, just as He has done for us. We can share that a person is acceptable to God through faith, not through works. We can share that God's forgiveness enables them to start putting their guilty feelings behind them, just as His forgiveness helps us deal with our guilty feelings. Why alienate the people who are hurting? Why?

In an often-told story, a farmer is complaining to the preacher about the lack of rain. To that, the preacher smiles and says, "I'm in sales; I'm not in management." We religious people are in sales, not management. Therefore, you and I shouldn't presume to manage the consciences of hurting sinners by laying guilt trips on them. Instead, you and I are in the great position to share with hurting people the message of faith in a God who freely forgives sins, both ours and theirs. Are you hanging onto that tattered security blanket of your own religious works? Throw it away and cling to the mercy of God who forgives us all. Throw away your reliance on works and generously share the kindness of God. That's the way God manages the world.

Amen.

For Further Reflection

"I believe in the Holy Spirit … the forgiveness of sins." (Apostles' Creed, Third Article)

- How does Scripture describe you before the Holy Spirit worked faith in you? 1 Corinthians 2:14; Romans 8:5-8; Ephesians 2:1-7
- Put yourself in the story. Now that you believe, is there something in you that merits God's grace? Read 1 Timothy 1:15, and reflect on Paul's present tense ("sinners, of whom I am the foremost"), even though he is a committed Christian. Do you, Christian reader, see yourself as the "foremost" of sinners?
- You are forgiven…
  - By grace – Ephesians 2:8-9
  - For Christ's sake – 2 Corinthians 5:17-21; Romans 8:1-4
  - Through faith – Romans 3:19-28

- Do not slip back to thinking religious works save you – Galatians 5:1-6. Instead, fear and love the God who does save you through the forgiveness of sins – Psalm 130:3-4; Revelation 1:4-6.
- Therefore, our daily, heartfelt prayer: "Forgive us our trespasses as we forgive those who trespass against us." (Lord's Prayer, Fifth Petition)

> *Thy cross, not mine, O Christ, / Has borne the crushing load*
> *Of sins that none could bear / But the incarnate God.*
> *To whom save Thee, Who canst alone / For sin atone, Lord, shall I flee?*
>
> *Thy death, not mine, O Christ, / Has paid the ransom due;*
> *Ten thousand deaths like mine / Would have been all too few.*
> *To whom save Thee, Who canst alone / For sin atone, Lord, shall I flee?*
>
> *Thy righteousness, O Christ, / Alone can cover me;*
> *No righteousness avails / Save that which is of Thee.*
> *To whom save Thee, Who canst alone / For sin atone, Lord, shall I flee?*[2]

Retrospective

This sermon tries to tackle one of the greatest challenges for preachers and people: to chisel through the "hard pan" and go deep into the heart. I learned about the "hard pan" when I served in the rural congregations of Venedy and New Memphis. Year after year, farmers would plow, turning over the top few inches of earth. Below those top inches, the hard pan developed, a layer of dirt that didn't get broken up and so became harder, even impossible for rain to penetrate. To break the hard pan, the chisel plow was developed; it knifed deeper into the soil than a conventional plow. That's the challenge of this sermon, and honestly all sermons: to break through the hard pan of Christian self-righteousness (which should be a contradiction in terms) so that each of us becomes convinced of our sins, truly repentant, and the Holy Spirit takes the Word of Jesus' forgiveness deep into our heart and life.

To think that there's something worthy in your Christian life that merits God's grace should be easy to dispel. Just think of your deepest thoughts, feelings, urges, stirrings. "Nothing is hidden except to be made manifest; nor is anything secret except to come to light" (Mark 4:22). Just imagine, what if people were to know what's way, way down, deep within you? You and I would be so ashamed, we'd hightail out of town, too embarrassed to show our face ever again. It will be revealed. "No creature is hidden from his sight, but all are naked and exposed to the eyes of him to whom we must give account" (Hebrews 4:13).

Before discovering the true meaning of grace, Martin Luther lived under the burden of thinking his religious works had merit before God. That brought him no inner peace, only a tortured conscience. When the Spirit took the true meaning of grace down into Luther's heart, he came to realize, most insightfully, that we religious people are liable to greater sin by imaging our religious life and works merit grace.[3] Scholar John Barclay:

> The achievement of Luther was to translate Paul's missionary theology of grace into an urgent and perpetual inward mission, directed to the church, but especially to the heart of each believer. ... Paul's theology of gift is re-preached to effect the perpetual conversion of believers, who need to learn over and again to receive the gift of God and to banish the false opinion that their works will merit salvation. The gospel constitutes a mission to the self and a daily return to baptism.[4]

I was blessed to grow up in a Christian home and to go to church, Sunday School, parochial grade school, Christian colleges, and Concordia Seminary. Yup, I know the feeling: There must be something in me that merits grace before God. As I've aged, studied, and become more introspective, the truth is: Nope – "Nothing in my hand I bring; / Simply to Thy cross I cling."[5] Gotta crack my self-righteous hard pan every day!

Week 43 – Freedom in Christ

Reformation
Delivered at St. Salvator Lutheran Church, Venedy, Illinois
and St. Peter Lutheran Church, New Memphis, Illinois
October 31, 1976

Text – John 8:31-36

So Jesus said to the Jews who had believed him, "If you abide in my word, you are truly my disciples, and you will know the truth, and the truth will set you free." They answered him, "We are offspring of Abraham and have never been enslaved to anyone. How is it that you say, 'You will become free'?"

Jesus answered them, "Truly, truly, I say to you, everyone who practices sin is a slave to sin. The slave does not remain in the house forever; the son remains forever. So if the Son sets you free, you will be free indeed."

Prayer

Lord Jesus, You teach us that freedom comes from abiding in Your Word. Thank You for setting Martin Luther free through Your Word and for using him to call the Church back to the Bible. The old evil foe seeks to enslave us with many false understandings of freedom. Teach us, on this Reformation Sunday, to trust that our greatest freedom is in You. Amen.

Today is Reformation Day. That means that we think about the Church, the Reformation, the "straightening out" of the Church, and the bold man – Martin Luther. Luther was the one who wrote:

A mighty fortress is our God,
A trusty shield and weapon;
He helps us free from ev'ry need
That hath us now o'ertaken.
The old evil foe
Now means deadly woe;
Deep guile and great might
Are his dread arms in fight;
On earth is not his equal.

Though devils all the world should fill,
All eager to devour us.
We tremble not, we fear no ill,
They shall not overpow'r us.[1]

That's what Luther the Reformer said. *"We tremble not, we fear no ill, / They shall not overpow'r us."* He was no timid, weak-kneed chicken, that Luther. He was bold. He was brave. He was not ashamed of the true Church or his Christian faith in the Gospel of grace. And he was that way because he was free. Luther knew freedom. He was no one's slave. That's why he wrote, *"We tremble not, we fear no ill, / They shall not overpow'r us."*

If you think about Luther's life, you wonder if he really was a free man. He was raised in a strict household. He was poor. He often had to go caroling in order to get a handout. When he decided to become a Roman Catholic monk, his father almost disowned him. As a monk, and later as a priest, he was not free. He had to take orders from the pope and his other superiors. And then, after Luther began the Reformation of the Church in 1517, after he challenged Rome and the pope, he was constantly being called on the carpet – at Leipzig, at Worms, at Augsburg. The officials of the Roman Church and the officials of the government ordered him to take back what he had said and written. He was once kidnapped. His life was always in danger. He sometimes had to travel in a disguise. You begin to wonder how free Martin Luther really was. You know how free he was? So free, that he boldly says, *"We tremble not, we fear no ill, / They shall not overpow'r us"*!

You see, the Word of God had made Luther a free man. On this Reformation Day, on this day when we think about the history of Martin Luther, I want you to remember that the Word of God still makes us free. John 8:31-32 says, "If you abide in my word, you are truly my disciples, and you will know the truth, and the truth will set you free." Those are the words of Jesus. He gives us the prescription for freedom. He tells us how to wage our own war of independence. He says, "Abide in my word." That means, abide in the Word of God, the Holy Scriptures. If you do that, Jesus says, you'll be His disciple. In other words, you won't be a fool. When you talk about your church and your faith, you can talk confidently, because you are a disciple. You have learned from Jesus and His Word. When you learn from Jesus and His Word, *then* you know the truth. See? You don't just go out and look for the truth. Jesus is saying, *If you abide in my Word, you will be my disciple, and then, only then, will you know the truth.* Finally, that truth – the truth that comes from Jesus and His Word – that truth will make you free. This is the prescription for freedom. This is the way you and I wage our war of independence. You and I study God's Word. The Word makes us disciples of Jesus. From that, and only from that, we learn the truth. And the truth sets us free. When you and I follow those steps, we won't be anyone's fool. A fool babbles on about himself. We're different. We can speak freely and boldly about the truth we know from Christ's Word.

Our worship theme this morning is "Freedom in Christ." We don't want to have any misunderstandings. When we Christians talk about freedom, we always mean the freedom that comes in Christ. That is the freedom that you and I have because of our relationship with Jesus Christ. He is the Savior who died on the cross to end the slavery of sin. Through faith, you and I are now related to Christ. He is your personal Savior. He is my personal Savior. He makes us free. But remember: Our freedom is in Christ. There are a lot of misunderstandings about true freedom. I'll give you some examples.

Tuesday is the presidential election. That's an important event. There's no excuse for not voting! God has blessed us with a democracy. We had better exercise our right to vote. But is that the greatest freedom in the world – the freedom to go and vote on Tuesday morning? No! People in communist countries vote. They have elections. Your right to vote should be very precious to you. But that is not the greatest freedom that you have. We don't want to misunderstand freedom.

There are a lot of people always talking about the truth. "The truth, the truth, the truth!" they say, "the truth is all that matters." And sometimes they even quote the Bible: "The truth will set you free" (John 8:32). And so they think that if they have the facts, and if anything seems to be true, then they are free. But the Bible doesn't say that. The Bible doesn't say that the facts will make you free. The Bible doesn't even simply say that the truth will make you free. What does it say? "If you abide in my word, you are truly my disciples, and you will know the truth, and the truth will set you free." We don't want to misunderstand freedom. Real freedom, real truth, is in Christ.

Anything else is slavery. You thought slavery was abolished, didn't you? Not according to the Word of God. There are still a lot of slaves running around. We let them vote these days. Tuesday there will be millions of slaves going to the polls. They might think that they are free because they can vote. But they are not free. The Word of God says in John 8:34: "Everyone who practices sin is a slave to sin." If there is anyone in this country, if there is anyone in this town, who does not worship the Triune God – Father, Son, and Spirit – that person is a slave, not free. Even if he or she does vote, in God's sight that person is a slave, not free. If there is anyone who despises God's Word, despises Sunday morning church services, despises my sermon – that person is a slave to sin and not free. If there is anyone who persists in hatred, anyone who tries to justify ill will because they say there is a "personality clash," that person is a slave to sin and not free. Anyone who persists in malicious, back-biting, harmful gossip is a slave and not free. See? We don't want to misunderstand freedom. God doesn't judge whether you are free because you go to the polling place Tuesday. God doesn't consider you free because you have the "facts" straight, or because you think you know the truth. No, the Word of God says, "Everyone who practices sin is a slave to sin." And we thought there were no slaves left in this country! There are *a lot* of slaves. Even in New Memphis and Venedy!

Freedom, *real* freedom, comes from the Word of God. "If you abide in my word," Jesus says, "you are truly my disciples, and you will know the truth, and the truth will set you free." What is it about this Word that makes us free? The Word of God, the Bible, points us to Jesus the Savior. He is the One who sets us free. He is the One who died on the cross to end our slavery to sin. He is the One who gave the Holy Spirit to you when you were baptized. It is that Spirit that gives you faith… not only a saving faith, but a faith that frees you. Faith in Jesus

– Jesus, who is going to return soon and take you to heaven – the Word of God points us to Jesus. He is the only One that makes us free. John 8:36 says, "If the Son sets you free, you will be free indeed."

Luther understood that. He knew that true freedom is freedom in Christ. That's why he had guts. That's why he was so bold and brave. That's why he challenged the whole Roman Church, and the governments of Europe. That's why he changed the history of the world. Luther was no fool. He didn't babble on about himself. He proclaimed Christ – Christ as he had come to know Him in the Word of God.

> *With might of ours can naught be done,*
> *Soon were our loss effected;*
> *But for us fights the Valiant One,*
> *Whom God Himself elected.*
> *Ask ye, Who is this?*
> *Jesus Christ it is.*
> *Of Sabaoth Lord,*
> *And there's none other God;*
> *He holds the field forever.*[2]

Luther was not a cowardly man. He was free. Free because he believed in Jesus Christ. "If the Son sets you free, you will be free indeed."

Amen.

For Further Reflection

"I believe ... in Jesus Christ, His only Son, our Lord." (Apostles' Creed, Second Article)

- Put yourself in the story – Luke 18:9-14
- The Reformation began when Martin Luther posted the 95 Theses in 1517. The First Thesis: "When our Lord and Master Jesus Christ said, 'Repent,' (Matt. 4:17), he willed the entire life of believers to be one of repentance."[3]

- Luther wrote about grace the next year, 1518: "The man who imagines that he will come to grace by doing whatever he is able to do is adding sin to sin. Therefore he becomes doubly guilty. Nor is speaking in this way giving any cause of despair; it is rather moving men to humble themselves and to seek the grace of Christ. Certain it is that man must completely despair of himself in order to become fit to receive the grace of Christ."[4]
- From 1529: "I believe that Jesus Christ, true God, begotten of the Father from eternity, and also true man, born of the virgin Mary, is my Lord. He has redeemed me, a lost and condemned creature, purchased and won me from all sins, from death, and from the power of the devil, not with gold or silver but with his holy, precious blood and with his innocent suffering and death. All this he did that I should be his own, and live under him in his kingdom, and serve him in everlasting righteousness, innocence, and blessedness, just as he has risen from death and lives and rules eternally. This is most certainly true."[5]

> *Rock of Ages, cleft for me, / Let me hide myself in Thee;*
> *Let the water and the blood, / From Thy riven side which flowed,*
> *Be of sin the double cure: / Cleanse me from its guilt and pow'r.*

> *Not the labors of my hands / Can fulfill Thy Law's demands;*
> *Could my zeal no respite know, / Could my tears forever flow,*
> *All for sin could not atone; / Thou must save, and Thou alone.*[6]

Retrospective

It is always helpful in a sermon to describe what something is not. In this sermon, it's what true freedom is not. Antitheses make the truth clearer, teach the hearer to be more discerning, and... here's a trade secret... make sermon-writing easier because you slow down to dwell on one point instead of galloping from new point to new point. It's easy at this time of year to bring out the standard Reformation slogans, but what do they really mean in our context? The context of the presidential election provided one antithesis when I preached this many years ago. By the way, the election that year was between Gerald Ford and Jimmy Carter. What is the context this year? Could it be slavery to self-righteousness – Pharisaic pride – the reason some Jews took offense at Jesus? Could it be the opposite – slavery to no law, do whatever you desire – Epicurean indifference?[7] Well-handled, the Law punctures those balloons. Could it be the slavery of so many people today to anger, to unforgiveness, to selfishness? We see that all the time on our screens. Do we let the Word free us from our bondage to feelings? Could it be that we have become such a social media society that we don't dedicate time to deep and extended study of the Word? Slaves to tweets and snap judgments, rather than reflection on life in light of the Word? Or might it be slavery to discovering our own identity apart from the truth of God's Word? Google "identity" and you'll be surprised by how many identities people have created trying to find out who they truly are. Martin Luther found who he was in God's Word, and also what he was not. Do you? These are different antitheses than I used some 40 years ago, but ones suited for this day and age. Antitheses help contrast the Word of God to popular assumptions and practices, what I like to call "the word of the world." Just remember, preacher, the purpose of antitheses is not to go on a tirade against something but to highlight the truth of the Word and the better way of the Gospel. And remember, hearer, when you meditate upon what you believe, think also about what you don't believe. Being discriminating with preaching, hearing, and devotion helps us see the radical nature of faith in the grace of Jesus and His Word.

By today's standards, this was written on an old clunker of a typewriter! When we started in Venedy and New Memphis in 1974, five years before this sermon, there was no desk in the pastor's study in the parsonage, no desk chair, and the typewriter was manual – the little blue portable typewriter I had used in college and seminary – a Royal, I think. Not having a desk, it sat on a wobbly TV tray table, and my chair was Grandpa Meyer's old, old rocker. It was hard to type in a rocking chair, but I liked the rocker and we didn't have many chairs. Pretty spartan pastor's study! In time, Ed and Evelyn Borrenpohl donated a real desk and chair, nice and new. Then the church got a Selectric typewriter. It had a type ball that you could change when you wanted to change the font. It wasn't just sermons that were typed there; I did the bulletin myself the first years – ran them off on the mimeograph. Diane and I folded them by hand Saturday afternoon. Some of my bulletins looked so bad that the congregation eventually paid Joyce Borrenpohl to become part-time secretary. The progress we thought we were making!

Freedom In Christ

John 8:31-36
Reformation Day
October 31, 1976
New Memphis and Venedy, Illinois

Today is Reformation Day. That means that we think about the church,
the reformation, the "straightening-out" of the church, and the man who
did it, Martin Luther. Luther was the one who wrote:

> A mighty fortress is our God,
> A trusty shield and weapon;
> He helps us free from every need
> That hath us now o'ertaken.
> The old evil Foe
> Now means dead woe;
> Deep guile and great might
> Are his dread arms in fight
> On earth is not his equal
>
> Tho' devils all the world should fill,
> All eager to devour us,
> We tremble not, we fear no ill,
> They shall not overpower us.

That's what Luther the reformer said. "We tremble not, We fear no ill,
They shall not overpower us." He was no timid, weak-kneed chicken, that
Luther. He was bold. He was brave. He was not ashamed of his church or
his Christian faith. And he was that way because he was free. Luther
knew freedom. He was nobody's slave. That's why he wrote "We tremble not,
We fear no ill, They shall not overpower us."

If you think about Luther's life, you wonder if he really was a free
man. He was raised in a strict household. He was poor. He often had to
go caroling in order to get a handout. When he decided to become a Roman

Week 44 – Live with Forever in Mind

St. Andrew Lutheran Church, Silver Spring, Maryland
November 3, 2013

Text – Philippians 3:20

But our citizenship is in heaven, and from it we await a Savior,
the Lord Jesus Christ.

Prayer

> *Come, my soul, thy suit prepare,*
> *Jesus loves to answer prayer;*
> *He Himself has bid thee pray,*
> *Therefore will not say thee nay.*
>
> *While I am a pilgrim here,*
> *Let Thy love my spirit cheer;*
> *As my Guide, my Guard, my Friend,*
> *Lead me to my journey's end.*
>
> *Show me what I have to do;*
> *Every hour my strength renew.*
> *Let me live a life of faith;*
> *Let me die Thy people's death. Amen.*[1]

Dear Jesus, these good people invited me to preach. Let me do something
different. Let me talk to You. We talk so much *about* You in church, but we talk
so little *to* You. And when we do pray to You in church, it is so often with the

formal words of old prayers. There's nothing wrong with those old formal prayers. They can be quite eloquent, but sometimes they don't adequately express our feelings. So Lord Jesus, let me tell You how I feel about this Bible passage that Pastor Hricko asked me to preach on: "But our citizenship is in heaven, and from it we await a Savior, the Lord Jesus Christ." *We await a Savior?* We're waiting for Christ's return? Are we really? Lord Jesus, did we wake up this morning hoping You would come back today? We're not very good about waiting. We used to wait for the mail to come, and when it arrived we'd open it. Sometimes we'd write a check to pay a bill or write a letter and put it in the mailbox, and a few days later it would reach its destination. We don't wait like that anymore. "How come you didn't answer the email I sent you this morning?" "Why don't you text me?" Oh, dear Jesus! Everything is so ASAP. We've lost the habit of sitting and waiting. We've lost our sense of time. That comes at a spiritual price. *Wait on the Lord?* (Psalm 28:1) *No, we've got to do something!* Could that be why our heavenly Father lets us get sick? Is that a benefit of old age – that we learn how to wait? Could it be that we are so oriented toward here and now that we don't pay much attention to heavenly things?

The Bible says, "Our citizenship is in heaven." Heaven is unseen. The only way we can know about heaven is from what You tell us in the Bible. But oh, we get so caught up in the things we see and hear. We watch shows; we watch sports; we watch news. And we hear the chimes and dings from our cell phones; we hear chatter; we hear the noise of cars and planes and trains. Dear Jesus, this world bombards our senses! So much is sensual, and sexual, and about power – who has it, who wants it. Jesus, the Bible says, "For we walk by faith, not by sight" (2 Corinthians 5:7), but I confess the things that are seen crowd out the things that are unseen: the things of faith, Your Word, heaven.

"But our citizenship is in heaven, and from it we await a Savior, … [*You,* our] Lord Jesus Christ." Dear Jesus, send us Your Spirit now. Remind us that we are *in* the world – we do deal with the things of sight here and now – but in the last analysis, we are not *of* the world (cf. John 17:16); our citizenship is in heaven. Oh, Spirit of the Lord Jesus, remind us to slow down and wait – to be still and know You are our Lord (cf. Psalm 46:10). Teach us that "In repentance and rest is your salvation, / in quietness and trust is your strength" (Isaiah 30:15 NIV). We need Your saving presence now. You were seen so long ago. Your miracles were seen. Your words were heard. Your sufferings are remembered; You paid the price for our sins. All our busyness, all our doings, all our good intentions cannot make us acceptable to our Father, much less to one another. It's only because of You that we know we are forgiven and loved by the Father. Lord Jesus, don't let us confine You to the distant past. We need Your saving presence *now*. Come, fill our hearts with more and more love and devotion for You.

And if it is true that we didn't wake up this morning hoping that today is the day You will come back to take us home, we know that You understand. You know our frame; You remember that we are dust (cf. Psalm 103:14). You have compassion on us, just as You had compassion on the crowds when You were seen and heard. That said, we pray that You will increase our desire for Your return. Life can beat us up. We don't know how to wait. Our senses are assaulted by so much that can harm us. Increase our desire for that place beyond sin.

> *From sorrow, toil, and pain,*
> *And sin we shall be free*
> *And perfect love and friendship reign*
> *Through all eternity.*[2]

We need You, our Savior, more than we know. "This Jesus, who was taken up from you into heaven, will come in the same way as you saw him go into heaven" (Acts 1:11). "Amen. Come, Lord Jesus!" (Revelation 22:20). Help us live with forever in mind.

Amen.

For Further Reflection

"From thence He will come to judge the living and the dead." (Apostles' Creed, Second Article)

- The promise – Acts 1:6-11; John 14:1-3; Hebrews 9:24-28; Matthew 24:36-44; Revelation 1:4-7
- The problem: Without the fear and love of God, you become complacent – 2 Peter 3:1-13

- Where are you in the story? Matthew 25:1-13
- In the fear and love of God, yearning to see Jesus – Luke 21:25-28; Titus 2:11-14; Revelation 22:20

> *Hark! A thrilling voice is sounding!*
> *"Christ is near," we hear it say.*
> *"Cast away the works of darkness,*
> *All you children of the day!"*
>
> *Startled at the solemn warning,*
> *Let the earthbound soul arise;*
> *Christ, its sun, all sloth dispelling,*
> *Shines upon the morning skies.*
>
> *So, when next He comes in glory*
> *And the world is wrapped in fear,*
> *He will shield us with His mercy*
> *And with words of love draw near.*[3]

Retrospective

Casting a sermon as a prayer is a form I've used several times through the years. And without making the whole sermon a prayer, more and more I find myself including short prayers in the text of normal sermons. A cynic could call this a gimmick, and preachers do use gimmicks, but this is no gimmick. Preaching now almost 50 years, I find myself more and more conscious that I'm speaking to the people for God and conversely, I'm speaking to God on behalf of the people. Speaking for God is the prophetic function of preaching; speaking to God on behalf of the people is the priestly function of preaching. This sermon attempted to voice the conflict faithful believers feel between life in the world (sight) and living with their thoughts on heaven (faith). A pastor does more than speak the correct doctrine. He also models the faith to people. Paul said, "Be imitators of me, as I am of Christ" (1 Corinthians 11:33). One part of modeling is showing people how to pray. I hope this sermon helped them. "Pray without ceasing" (1 Thessalonians 5:17) is possible, and it will show up in our conversations and even in our preaching.

I fondly recall visiting an elderly member of our church in Collinsville, Mrs. Henrietta Leonhardt. I say "fondly" because she was always very kind, especially thankful for the devotion and Holy Communion I brought to her. Henrietta was living with forever in mind. Many a time she recited to me a stanza from a hymn that was dear to her. To my delight, on one visit she gave me a copy of the stanza that she had cut out of an old church magazine, Der Lutheraner. The stanza begins, "O Lieber Heiland, hol' mich heim" – "O dear Savior, take me home."[4] Mrs. Leonhardt looked forward to seeing Jesus, and in my ministry I've seen many pious people just like her. They yearn to see their faith translated into sight. It's not that they disdain this world – oh, no! Older saints tell stories with warm remembrance of all the blessings God gave them in their lives in this beautiful world, and with beloved family and friends. The progress of time and frailties of age make very personal the hope planted in them in earlier years, the hope of heaven. "Heaven is my home."[5] This sermon, this prayer, reflects that increasing desire in me to be with the immortal, with all the saints around the throne. This may well strike many people as a strange yearning, but it is the faith of the Church. As we mature in years and in sanctification, we should be desiring more and more to see Jesus. "Whom have I in heaven but you? And there is nothing on earth that I desire besides you" (Psalm 73:25).

I wrote the dissertation for my Ph.D. on the preparation and delivery of speeches by ancient Greek and Roman orators. The consummate writer on rhetoric was Quintilian, who said he would normally write out speeches, if there was time.[6] The scan on the next page depicts a time when I didn't have a computer handy; perhaps I was on an airplane, so I wrote it out longhand. Penmanship was part of parochial grade school when I grew up, so longhand writing is something I still enjoy doing. As time permits, I write thank you letters to Seminary donors, longhand; more impact, I think, than a typed form letter. But back to this sermon – as always, title on top, to keep my writing focused on the theme. Date and place for the sermon is noted. For this sermon, I wrote out the text in Greek. Almost all of our seminarians have to learn Greek, the original language for the New Testament documents, and my Ph.D. is in Greek and Latin from Washington University in St. Louis. The original language gives the pastor insights that easily escape us when reading in English. I hasten to add, however, that you can trust English translations; the scholars who do the translations feel the burden to make the Word understandable and correct to English readers.

Having on paper those preliminaries – title, date, place, and text – my penmanship wrote the sermon. Writing longhand is slower than typing, but the slowness gives time to select carefully the words you want to use – choice words to make better impact upon hearers. The ancients called it "diction." The notes you see in the margins are additions that come from second and third read-throughs of the sermon as I was memorizing and getting ready for delivery. What this reminiscence does is highlight the many changes that have taken place during my lifetime, including the loss of disciplined memory and the art of penmanship in our schools. I'm thankful I grew up when I did!

<u>Live with Forever in Mind</u>　　　　St. Andrew, Silver Spring, MD.
November 3, 2013

Philippians 3²⁰· ἡμῶν γὰρ τὸ πολίτευμα ἐν οὐρανοῖς ὑπάρχει,

ἐξ οὗ καὶ σωτῆρα ἀπεκδεχόμεθα

κύριον Ἰησοῦν Χριστόν.

1.　Dear Jesus, these good people invited me to preach. Let me do something different. Let me talk to You. We talk so much <u>about</u> You in church but we talk so little <u>to</u> You. And when we do pray to You in church, it is so often with the formal words of old prayers. There's nothing wrong with those old formal prayers. They can be quite eloquent but sometimes they don't quite express our feelings. So Lord Jesus, let me tell You how I feel about this ~~text~~ Bible passage...

2　... about the text Pastor Hricko asked me to preach on. "For our commonwealth is in heaven, from where we also await a Savior, (our) Lord Jesus Christ." "We await a Savior?" We're waiting for Judgment Day? Are we really? Lord Jesus, did we wake up today hoping You would come back today? We're not very good about waiting. We used to wait for the mail to come. When it did, we'd open it. Sometimes we'd write a check to pay a bill or write a letter and put it in the mailbox and a few days later it would reach its destination. We don't wait like that anymore. "How come you didn't answer the e-mail I sent you yesterday?" "Why don't you text?" Oh dear Jesus! Everything is so ASAP. We've lost the habit of sitting and waiting. Could that be why our heavenly Father lets us get sick? Is that a benefit of old age, that we learn how to wait? Could it be that we are so oriented toward here-and-now that we don't pay much attention to heavenly things?

That comes at a spiritual price

We've lost our sense of time

"Wait on the Lord." No, we've got to do something.

Week 45 – "God Setteth the Solitary in Families"

Thanksgiving
Delivered at St. Salvator Lutheran Church, Venedy, Illinois
and St. Peter Lutheran Church, New Memphis, Illinois
November 27, 1980

Text – Psalm 68:5-6 (KJV)

A father of the fatherless, and a judge of the widows, is God in his holy habitation. God setteth the solitary in families: he bringeth out those which are bound with chains: but the rebellious dwell in a dry land.

Prayer

O God, our Father in heaven, Your Son teaches us to pray for our daily bread. This Thanksgiving, we thank You for daily bread and all the necessities You give us. You give generously out of fatherly love for us, Your children. Today, we especially thank You for our families, for wives and husbands, children and parents, sisters, brothers, and all whom we call our family. With the grace You give us in Your Word, help us strengthen all family ties and always offer up our thanks and praise that You have set us in family. In Jesus' name, Amen.

What are you thankful for? I hope you are thankful for many things. If you would honestly think about it, many of the things for which you are thankful are not absolutely necessary, such as a color TV, a La-Z-Boy® recliner, $1,000 in the bank, or grain exports. Some things for which we are thankful *are* necessary. I'm thinking of food, clothing, and shelter. We may not need to export grain to stay alive, we may not need a La-Z-Boy, but food for our bodies and clothing and shelter to protect us from the elements are necessary. We also need the dear Gospel of Jesus Christ. Of course, the Gospel is not necessary for earthly life. Many people live and die without ever letting the Savior of sinners into their heart. But the Gospel is necessary for a God-pleasing daily life now, and for an eternity with Him in heaven forever. Everything else could be taken away from me, and I'd still come to church today and give thanks for the Gospel. There is something else that is necessary to life – something that I want to talk about for a few minutes. It is the family. Your family. The family is far more necessary to life than a lot of people in our time think.

Psalm 68:6 (KJV) says, "God setteth the solitary in families." Who sets the solitary in families? God. God instituted the family. There are a lot of things in this life that God did not make: this building, TVs. Many laws of society have been made by man, not by God. Many things even in the church were created by man and not by God. But God did make the family. Back in the Garden of Eden, He made Adam. He let Adam live for some time in all the splendor and beauty of that place. But He saw that Adam was not happy. Adam was lonely. And so, as you know from Genesis 2, He caused a deep sleep to fall upon Adam; He took a rib, and made a woman – Eve. He brought Eve to Adam and they were the first husband and wife. They had children, including Cain and Abel and Seth. That was the first family. God made it. God instituted the family. "God setteth the solitary in families."

Today, this divine institution is under great attack. I could talk about all the evils "out there" that are attacking the family in our society, but I won't. I want to talk about the evils that are attacking *Christian* families. You and I – who are thankful for that dear Gospel – you and I find our families under attack... And often we do nothing to fight back. Look at the picture on your bulletin. In this picture, the family is eating dinner together. "God setteth the solitary in families" – but if you don't spend time together, you will become solitary lives who only sleep under the same roof. This family is also having a devotion after dinner, led by the father. This family is from before 1980, but looking at the picture, we notice some things that have changed throughout the years – and not for the better. Take, for example, the TV... A Christian family can spend an entire evening together in front of the television set, and not say ten words to one another. "God setteth the solitary in families" – but sometimes your TV makes your life solitary. The family is the basic unit of the church. Our church can be no better than the families that make it up. I am sure that many of our Christian families do not give the Word of God the place it rightfully deserves at the family altar. "God setteth the solitary in families" – but even among us, the institution of the family is under great attack.

Although your family may have its troubles, although you may not have done everything you should have through the years to strengthen your family, we give thanks today that God does not abandon the Christian family. God does not want you and the people in your house to lead solitary lives. He wants you together. He wants you to be a family. When our Savior was on this earth, one of the first things He did in His public ministry was to attend the wedding at Cana (John 2:1-11). There at Cana, two solitary lives were set into family, and the Savior of sinners was there to add His blessing. When the wine failed, He provided. When the wine fails, when the crops fail, when dollars fail – the Savior will provide for your family also. Remember what the Savior did for the widow at Zarephath (1 Kings 17:8-16)? She had only a cruse of oil and a jar of flour. She was going to eat that and die. But the Savior was there. The cruse of oil did not fail; the jar of flour did not go empty. At Zarephath, at Cana, He provided the necessary physical things for family life. When you pray in your home, "Give us this day our daily bread," He will hear, and He will answer.

Family life is not only a matter of food and drink. God designed family life so you might also feel the love that the Savior has for you. You know that the Savior died on the cross for you. He suffered the punishment of your sin. He gained for you forgiveness, life, and salvation. St. Paul tells us that husbands should love their wives, even as Christ loved the Church and gave Himself for it (Ephesians 5:25). The love that husbands and wives have for one another is to be that same, intimate love that Christ and the Church have for one another. Your family is a divine institution. The husband and wife reflect the love of Christ and the Church.

And what of the children? Are they an accident? Are they something to be avoided? Are they a bother? In our children, God shows us His love. God commanded Adam and Eve to "Be fruitful and multiply" (Genesis 1:28). Our God sent us a Savior – not in full-grown human form, but rather the Savior came as a baby. So also today, children are a gift from God Himself. If you wonder if God can live in a home, bring in a little child. Psalm 128:3-4 says,

Your wife will be like a fruitful vine
> within your house;
your children will be like olive shoots
> around your table.
Behold, thus shall the man be blessed
> who fears the LORD.

Family need not be husband and wife and children. To those who are unmarried, God provides brothers and sisters, parents, and other relatives. And He brings all of us together in the great family of the Church. The Church is His family. We are related to one another. We in the Church are blood relatives to one another. The blood of Jesus Christ has made us family.

On this Thanksgiving Day, I invite you to be discriminating as you give thanks. Give thanks for all the Lord has given you. Know that much that you have is not necessary for your daily life. Some things, however, are necessary. Without some things, life would not be worth living. First and foremost, the Gospel of our dear Christ. Then, your family. "God setteth the solitary in families."

Amen.

For Further Reflection

"I believe in God, the Father Almighty, maker of heaven and earth."
(Apostles' Creed, First Article)

- God promises that the redeemed will fear and love Him – Jeremiah 32:38-39
- Put yourself in the story; the temptations of prosperity – Deuteronomy 8:1-20
- "Man shall not live by bread alone" (Matthew 4:4) – Isaiah 55:1-3; John 6:25-35; Matthew 6:25-34
- Thanksgiving is also for family. Our Creator and Sustainer also gives "everything that we need for our bodily welfare, such as food and drink,

clothing and shoes, house and home, land and cattle, money and goods, a godly spouse, godly children" (Martin Luther, Small Catechism).[1]

- Bless this house! Proverbs 3:33; Psalm 128:1-6; John 2:1-11; Luke 19:1-10. For all these blessings we are thankful and pray, "Give us this day our daily bread." (Lord's Prayer, Fourth Petition)

Now thank we all our God
With hearts and hands and voices,
Who wondrous things has done,
In whom His world rejoices;
Who from our mothers' arms
Has blest us on our way
With countless gifts of love
And still is ours today.

Oh, may this bounteous God
Through all our life be near us,
With ever joyful hearts
And blessed peace to cheer us
And keep us in His grace
And guide us when perplexed
And free us from all ills
In this world and the next![2]

Retrospective

1980 – and I thought the family was in trouble? We've seen even more assault on the family since then: Living together outside of marriage is now accepted as normal, as are absent fathers, internet pornography, abandonment of quantity time together, and more blasé attitudes toward family attending weekly worship. Ward and June Cleaver are long gone!
   unexcited about it

Welcome, Kardashians? All this hurts people in ways we know and feel, but also in insidious ways we don't suspect. For example, if we think marriage is only about the romantic feeling of love, we've been unwittingly led into an attitude that weakens the fundamental unit of society. A friend of mine likes to say, "Complaining is not a strategy." The strategy is to hold up family as a blessing from our heavenly Father, seen especially in Christian families sanctified by the Spirit of our Savior Jesus. The strategy has to be specific – identifying the specific benefits of functional family life – and when dysfunction is present, speaking the word of forgiveness, hope, and practical help. The strategy is not just from the pulpit, but throughout all aspects of the life of the institutional church, as well as modeling Christian family life to our communities. I think people today are yearning for a culture where healthy families again become the norm, and that should happen in the church. When I was a child, the pastor of our church urged us to go beyond thanksgiving to thanks-living. A great place to start is family.

Again, this sermon is in the oral style. Short sentences, repetition of the title, and simple. I stressed the one sentence, "God setteth the solitary in families," looking at it from the perspective of the New Testament. If I were to write the sermon today, I'd say something about the content of Psalm 68 because a sermon should be both scriptural and textual. Maturing as a preacher is a long, long process! While I'll admit that this sermon is short on the textual component, I'm sure everyone went home from church thankful for family. Indeed, God's people are thankful!

Week 46 – Castles Crumble When Christ Is King

Christ the King Sunday
Delivered at Holy Cross Lutheran Church, Wichita, Kansas
November 22, 2015

Text – John 18:33-38

So Pilate entered his headquarters again and called Jesus and said to him, "Are you the King of the Jews?" Jesus answered, "Do you say this of your own accord, or did others say it to you about me?" Pilate answered, "Am I a Jew? Your own nation and the chief priests have delivered you over to me. What have you done?" Jesus answered, "My kingdom is not of this world. If my kingdom were of this world, my servants would have been fighting, that I might not be delivered over to the Jews. But my kingdom is not from the world." Then Pilate said to him, "So you are a king?" Jesus answered, "You say that I am a king. For this purpose I was born and for this purpose I have come into the world – to bear witness to the truth. Everyone who is of the truth listens to my voice." Pilate said to him, "What is truth?"

After he had said this, he went back outside to the Jews and told them, "I find no guilt in him."

Prayer

Spirit of God, put me in that room where Pilate questions Jesus. "Are you the King of the Jews?" asks the powerful governor, but Jesus' answer unsettled Pilate. I too want to feel in control; I want to be king in my own little castle. In the room of my devotion where I now stand before Jesus, shake my confidence in myself and take down the control I vainly imagine I have in life. Crumble my imaginary castle, and in place of the ruins build me body, soul, and spirit into greater devotion to the truth – Jesus Christ is King. Amen.

Our oldest grandson, Christian, is being taught to say bedtime prayers. His parents are teaching him not only to recite memorized prayers but also to make up his own prayers. Some time ago during bedtime prayers, Christian told his mother, "I don't need to ask for God's help with anything today. I've got it all under control." *I've got it all under control.* Really?

In today's Gospel lesson, Pontius Pilate's notion of being in control is challenged. Pilate is the powerful governor sent from Rome. He has an army at his command. He's in the habit of thinking that his rank, his power, and his scheming can keep him in control of his kingdom. But Pilate's kingdom is being challenged by the powerful Jewish religious establishment. Those religious leaders were savvy, too; they knew how to play hardball according to the world's rules. But you know who really challenges Pilate's notion of his kingdom? Jesus. Have you ever experienced an earthquake? You feel tremors. You get a feeling that something is happening, something that might be destructive. That's what Jesus caused in Pilate's understanding. That's what He does in your life and mine – tremors, shaking. Old ways of thinking come crashing down. They come crashing down so something new can arise out of the rubble. Castles crumble where Christ is king.

Is Christ *your* king? "So Pilate entered his headquarters again and called Jesus and said to him, 'Are you the King of the Jews?'" Jesus answered, "Do you say this of your own accord, or did others say it to you about me?'" Take that question personally. Do you say Christ is king on your own, or do you say it because the people around you are saying it? Do you say Christ is king on your own, or do you say it because everyone else is singing, *"Crown Him with many crowns,"*[1] and you're just singing along? Do I really believe Christ is my king? Am I a Christian when it is convenient, or am I a convicted follower of Jesus Christ?

"Pilate answered, 'Am I a Jew? Your own nation and the chief priests have delivered you over to me. What have you done?' Jesus answered, 'My kingdom is not of this world. If my kingdom were of this world, my servants would have been fighting, that I might not be delivered over to the Jews. But my kingdom is not from the world.'" Do I contend with life's challenges in a worldly way, with fighting and power plays, with reliance on money and resources, with career climbing and lusting after rank and prestige? Or do I meet life's challenges in a heavenly way? Yes, Christians use strength and money and position, but always under the lordship of Jesus Christ, always subordinating earthly ways to the ways of the heavenly kingdom. Romans 14:17 – "For the kingdom of God is not a matter of eating and drinking but of righteousness and peace and joy in the Holy Spirit." Galatians 5:22-23 – "But the fruit of the Spirit is love, joy, peace, patience, kindness, goodness, faithfulness, gentleness, self-control." The ways of Christ's kingdom...

"Pilate said to him, 'So you are a king?'" Pilate finds Jesus interesting, intriguing. The older I get, the more and more I find Jesus to be mysterious, larger-than-life, much bigger than my conceptions of Him. I've read a lot about Jesus over the years. No matter – He's crumbling my castle so He can be my king. I hope you feel the tremors in your life, too.

"Jesus answered, 'You say that I am a king. For this purpose I was born and for this purpose I have come into the world – to bear witness to the truth. Everyone who is of the truth listens to my voice.'" *Everyone who is of the truth listens to my voice.* This is the Good News. We are here, for whatever reason, we are here. Jesus is giving us His truth and we are listening. He crumbles our own castles so He can build us up in His truth. "I am the way, and the truth, and the life. No one comes to the Father except through me" (John 14:6). Destruction, construction at the same time.

C.S. Lewis put it this way:

> Christ says 'Give me All. I don't want so much of your time and so much of your money and so much of your work: I want You. I have not come to torment your natural self, but to kill it. No half-measures are any good. I don't want to cut off a branch here and a branch there, I want to have the whole tree down. I don't want to drill the tooth, or crown it, or stop it, but to have it out. Hand over the whole natural self ... I will give you a new self instead. In fact, I will give you Myself: my own will shall become yours.'[2]

So grandson Christian said, "I don't need to ask for God's help with anything today. I've got it all under control." Jesus teaches us a more mature prayer: *"Thy kingdom come."* That's the Good News. We're here. We're listening. The Spirit is building us in the truth of the kingdom of Christ our king.

Amen.

For Further Reflection

"Thy kingdom come." (Lord's Prayer, Second Petition)

- Pilate caved to political expedience (Matthew 27:24-26), but he wasn't done with Jesus. Imagine being in his shoes, uh, sandals – Matthew 27:62-66; Matthew 28:11-15; Revelation 1:7.
- Personal "castles" crumbling – Luke 12:13-21; Luke 16:1-9; Luke 16:19-31. Fears about your "castles" are warning flags – Who is your lord? (cf. First Commandment)
- Read Hebrews 12:1-11. Filial fear, the loving reverence of a child for a parent, is an image of the fear and love we have for our heavenly Father. *"For we know, as children should, / That the cross is for our good."*[3]
- God's kingdom will prove unstoppable – Matthew 16:18. The question to your heart: Is His reign and rule coming to you, to you now? "God's kingdom certainly comes by itself even without our prayer, but we pray in this petition that it may also come to us" (Martin Luther, Small Catechism).[4]
- Prayer for growth in His kingdom – Psalm 139:23-24

> *Ev'ry eye shall now behold Him*
> *Robed in glorious majesty;*
> *Those who set at naught and sold Him,*
> *Pierced and nailed Him to the tree,*
> *Deeply wailing, deeply wailing, deeply wailing,*
> *Shall their true Messiah see.*

Yea, amen, let all adore Thee,
High on Thine eternal throne;
Savior, take the pow'r and glory,
Claim the kingdom as Thine own.
Alleluia, alleluia, alleluia!
Thou shalt reign, and Thou alone![5]

Retrospective

Because we know that "God ... desires all people to be saved and to come to the knowledge of the truth" (1 Timothy 2:3-4), we know Jesus' motivation as He spoke with Pilate. He wanted Pilate to see the transitory nature of earthly power compared to the eternal kingdom of God. This sermon, however, wasn't written for Pilates, but for church people who have this deep feeling that there's something worthy in us before God, while we hypocritically build our own earthly "castles." Babel! (Genesis 11:1-9) This building of our own kingdoms comes out of the deep-seated and abiding original sin still within us, even among us who believe.

John Barclay is a British theologian who has written about grace, a cardinal principle of the Reformation. "In Luther's eyes, those who are especially pious are liable to a kind of super-sized sin, because they are all the more confident that their excellent works of righteousness will obtain the favor of God."[6] "God, I thank you that I am not like other men" (Luke 18:11). Here's what Luther himself wrote about grace in 1518: "The man who imagines that he will come to grace by doing whatever he is able to do is adding sin to sin. Therefore he becomes doubly guilty. Nor is speaking in this way giving any cause of despair; it is rather moving men to humble themselves and to seek the grace of Christ. Certain it is that man must completely despair of himself in order to become fit to receive the grace of Christ."[7] John Barclay again: "Paul's theology of gift [grace] is re-preached [by Luther] to effect the perpetual conversion of believers, who need to learn over and again to receive the gift of God and to banish the false opinion that their works will merit salvation. The gospel constitutes a mission to the self and a daily return to baptism."[8] *"God, be merciful to me, a sinner!" (Luke 18:13).*

Week 47 – The Darkness God Sends

Broadcast on The Lutheran Hour
December 10, 2000

Text – Micah 7:8

Rejoice not over me, O my enemy;
  when I fall, I shall rise;
when I sit in darkness,
  the LORD will be a light to me.

Prayer

O God, it's one thing to know that Jesus died for our sins. Thank You for that wonderful knowledge. We pray that in these next minutes, Your Spirit will help us bring that wonderful truth all the way home to our hearts. We all need to hear a word of affirmation and there is none more satisfying than Your Word in Jesus, "Cheer up, friend! Your sins are forgiven" (Matthew 9:2 GW). Amen.

"Dear Dr. Meyer," began a recent email. "Thank you so much for adding to my life with your prayers and messages. I always feel connected after reading your messages and look forward to each Sunday because it completes my life."

Thank you, listener, for that encouragement. Just like everyone else, I also appreciate a word of affirmation now and then.

The email continues: "I would like to request a message and prayer regarding forgiving oneself. I seem to be unable to accomplish this, even though I know Christ died for our sins. Why is this and how can I overcome this? I am 55 and I guess as we get older there is much time for reflection. If possible, before the year's end, I would love to hear this message. I definitely need help in this area."

A good suggestion! So, let's talk about forgiveness. What is it that you've done that makes it hard to forgive yourself? I'm not speaking only to my email correspondent but to everyone listening on the radio or the internet or reading this message in print or email. What is it that you have done wrong that makes it hard for you to forgive yourself?

Maybe off the top of your head you say, *Nothing*. Unlike our email writer who knows what's bothering her, you might think there's really nothing for which you need to forgive yourself. Let me try to plant some doubt in your mind. Think about your feelings – your unpleasant feelings. Think about the things that sometimes keep you awake at night. Think about the things that irritate you, that even anger you. Think about the things you'd like to do over. You'd love to turn the clock back and do whatever it is over again, but time marches on and you can't. I'm probably asking you to do more here than our airtime permits. We need to take more time and identify our feelings, our unpleasant thoughts. Those feelings are warning signs that something isn't quite right in your life. I once interviewed two counselors, Ron and Pat Potter-Ephron, who said that anger is like the flashing lights at a railroad crossing.[1] Just as those lights warn a train is coming, so your anger tells you something is going on in your soul that you need to deal with. What I'm saying to those who don't have an immediate awareness of anything that needs forgiving is that your unpleasant feelings indicate there is indeed something wrong in your life that does need to be dealt with.

Maybe it's something that's not your fault. Say, for example, you were abused as a child. You may feel guilty about it but that abuse was not your fault. Having given that as an example that not every feeling indicates you've done something wrong, let me move on to say there are other things you *have* done wrong that disturb you, if you're honest enough to acknowledge it. Maybe that one-night stand you had with a coworker. You didn't mean for it to happen, but it did because you were crying out for emotional attention. You think you've dealt with it, but every once in a while you look at your spouse and feel guilty. You haven't dealt with it all the way. Maybe that abortion you had as a teenager. That was long ago and no one knows about it now, but every once in a while the emotional pain strikes you, when you see a little baby and think about the son or daughter you aborted. You haven't dealt with it fully, have you? Maybe it's internet pornography. Oh, you've got your life together, or so you've convinced yourself. You might be active in a church and go through all the godly rituals.

And yet, if you would take the time I'm suggesting, your emotions will tell you something is terribly wrong. You're trying to hide a terrible sin. Or, since I brought up this example before, you were abused as a child. For that you are not responsible. The person who abused you is guilty; you're not. But it often happens that the abused becomes an abuser. So, you might say there is nothing in your life that needs forgiveness, but I'm telling you, "Brother, sister, there is."

About a month ago, I happened to speak to a drug counselor at a federal prison. He told me that everyone he deals with – everyone, no exception – feels he is not worthy of being loved. Feeling that way, they try to prove their unworthiness by doing things that are addictive, by engaging in conduct that lands them in jail and may even cost them their lives. This is all because they think they are unworthy of being loved! Are you worthy of being loved? Our email correspondent is having trouble forgiving herself. In other words, she doesn't feel totally affirmed in the love of God. If you, a listener, admit to nothing in your life in need of forgiveness, then take some time, more time than we have here, to examine your feelings. One way or another, your reflection upon your feelings will lead to the fact that you have sinned.

Bottom line: You and I have to get to that point where we truly acknowledge our unworthiness because of what we've done. That doesn't sound like feel-good religion, and it's not. But if you want to forgive yourself for what you've done that troubles you, this is where you have to start. There is a darkness God sends. It is the darkness of acknowledging your sin. I don't mean acknowledging your sin in a general way. Today, millions of people attend Christian churches and go through some ritual of confession that says we are all sinners. True as that is, it easily becomes routine and we can be hypocrites in mouthing the words. There is a darkness God sends, and that is to admit to yourself exactly what you have done wrong and then to say, as King David did, "Against thee, thee only, have I sinned, and done this evil in thy sight" (Psalm 51:4 KJV). This is the darkness to which God calls us, the gloom of acknowledging our sins.

God doesn't do that because He's sadistic. He doesn't do it because He's a killjoy. Quite the opposite! God doesn't want you to stay in the darkness of acknowledging your sin. He wants to lead you out into the light. "Arise, shine, for your light has come" (Isaiah 60:1), the prophet urged God's people. That's where our email correspondent is. She's in this darkness of acknowledging whatever it was that she did in the past. Now she's asking me to try and say a few words that will help her feel she's come out of that darkness into the light of God's affirming love. I think it's got to be this way – not only for her, but for us all. First the darkness, then the dawn. Without the darkness, how can you appreciate the light? Without taking time to reflect on why you have your unpleasant feelings, how can you overcome those feelings? Without acknowledging your sins before God, how can you treasure the truth that God for Jesus' sake forgives you? If you short circuit the process of confession, then the announcement that a Savior has been born will carry little meaning for you.

It is my hope and prayer that we can all realize our worthiness of being loved. Understand, however, why. It's not what you have done in the past that makes you worthy of being loved. The whole first part of my message was making the point that there are things that need to be forgiven in your life. Those things whisper to you that you may not be worthy of love. You can be sure the devil wants you to hear and believe that negative message. In the same way, it's not what you're doing now that makes you worthy of being loved. No matter how much you've got your act together – and that may include God and faith and going to church – the good things you might be doing now are not a firewall. Doubts can get in. *Am I really doing enough of the right things?* There's no certainty if you base your worthiness on what you've done or what you're doing now.

So much talk in our society about self-esteem is not helpful because people are being taught to base that esteem on themselves. Anyone with a conscience who does a little reflection will not always esteem himself very highly. Self-esteem based upon yourself is going to leave you feeling conflicted. Then there's the other side of the spectrum. Some Christians will say you are such a poor, miserable sinner that you are not worthy of being loved. Well, yes, we are sinners, but to leave it at that conflicts with something important that Jesus said: "God sent his Son into the world, not to condemn the world, but to save the world" (John 3:17 GW). We should have self-esteem – proper self-esteem.

You know why you are worthy of being loved? You are worthy of being loved because God made you. Psalm 139 says, "You alone created my inner being. You knitted me together inside my mother. ... Your eyes saw me when I was still an unborn child. Every day of my life was recorded in your book before one of them had taken place" (Psalm 139:13, 16 GW). You are worthy of being loved because God gave His Son to die for you just as Jesus died for all people.

When you acknowledge your sins and turn to Jesus Christ for forgiveness, God calls "you out of darkness into his marvelous light" (1 Peter 2:9). You are worthy of being loved because God gives His Holy Spirit to work faith in your heart. Wherever the Good News of Jesus Christ is present, there the Spirit of God is present to form the conviction that you are loved. "There is therefore now no condemnation for those who are in Christ Jesus" (Romans 8:1).

I said earlier that we all need affirmation. We need a *lot* of affirmation. Were my mother's hugs years ago enough for my whole life? Of course not. Is an occasional hug from my wife enough? No. We want to be told over and over again that we are loved by others. You and I need that continual affirmation of God's love, too. This Advent season is a reminder that – through repeated time in devotion – God sends a light into the darkness. The prophet Micah wrote, "Although I sit in the dark, the LORD is my light. / I have sinned against the LORD. So I will endure his fury until he takes up my cause and wins my case. He will bring me into the light, and I will see his victory" (Micah 7:8-9 GW).

I can't say enough about the benefits of daily devotion. My email correspondent said she gets these messages every week, and they help. There's even more help for you when you read the Good News of Jesus Christ every day in your Bible and in other devotional literature. To be effective, this daily meditation, just like Sunday worship, should have two aspects. The first is getting into the darkness God sends – the darkness of facing your sins and confessing them to God. But don't tarry there. Hear the call of the Good News out of the darkness and into God's marvelous light. God has taken up your cause. Your cause has been won by Jesus Christ. Remind yourself every day by your devotion that you are not only worthy of being loved because of all that God has done for you, but you, in fact, have His unconditional love.

This is how you learn to forgive yourself. It's not that you are God and have the power to wipe away your sins. Of course, you can't do that. But day after day you can apply yourself to the forgiving words of God. More and more you'll start to feel forgiven. More and more you'll find you can put the past behind you and press on to the glorious future God has in store for all who love Him.

One last word. Don't get too hung up on whether you feel forgiven or not. Remember what I said at the start of this message? I talked about how unpleasant feelings are signs of something else. For example, you're angry. That feeling points to something in your life that needs to be addressed. The same truth applies here. Don't condemn yourself because there are times when you don't feel forgiven. It takes a long time to get rid of guilty feelings. Some feelings may stick with you for the rest of your life. Such feelings should spur you on to think about the facts. "Although I sit in the dark," Micah said, "the LORD is my light." The fact is that Jesus died on the cross to forgive what you did wrong. The fact is that when you trust Jesus as your Savior, and believe He paid the price for your sin, you are forgiven. The fact is that God looks at you and sees you as a forgiven person since you trust in His Son Jesus. Those are facts you need to dwell on, over and over again, in daily devotion and in weekly worship. Occupy yourself with that glorious light – the Lord who forgives you – and that will start to influence your emotions. "This is how we will know that we belong to the truth," wrote the apostle John, "and how we will be reassured in his presence. Whenever our conscience condemns us, we will be reassured that God is greater than our conscience and knows everything" (1 John 3:19-20 GW).

My email writer closed by saying, "May the Lord continue to bless you." I say, "May the Lord continue to bless you, also."

Amen.

For Further Reflection

"I believe in the Holy Spirit, the holy Christian Church ... the forgiveness of sins." (Apostles' Creed, Third Article)

- In heaven, God is holy – Revelation 4:6-11. In the flesh, God's Son is holy and receives the Holy Spirit – Luke 1:35; Mark 1:9-11, 24, 34; Mark 3:11, 22-30.
- Put yourself in the story, a sinner before the holy Son of God – Luke 5:1-11. Fear!
- Bowing before the holy Judge as our Father, dread is transformed to childlike fear and love of our Father – Isaiah 57:15; 1 Peter 1:15-21
- His Word works forgiveness and holiness in us – Isaiah 6:1-7; John 17:17; 1 Peter 1:22-25. This "holy-ing" Word is our confidence, not our feelings – 2 Corinthians 5:7.

- Hence we are the "Holy Christian Church" – Exodus 19:1-6; 1 Peter 2:9-10

Creator Spirit, by whose aid
The world's foundations first were laid,
Come, visit ev'ry humble mind;
Come, pour Your joys on humankind;
From sin and sorrow set us free;
May we Your living temples be.

O Source of uncreated light,
The bearer of God's gracious might,
Thrice-holy fount, thrice-holy fire,
Our hearts with heav'nly love inspire;
Your sacred, healing message bring
To sanctify us as we sing.[2]

Retrospective

During my career, I've seen a shift from preaching characterized by talking about propositional truths to preaching that gives more time to human feelings. That is, in the previous century a minister could preach on the doctrinal truths of the Bible and be content that he had done his job. It was head knowledge, with the assumption that the heart was accepting and believing the stated truth. For many well-documented reasons, we're now living in a time when many people, practicing Christians included, don't believe in absolutes. In today's environment, the preacher who speaks only to the head is speaking past the hearer. Now the point of contact is in shared human feelings. What I've just written doesn't deny objective truth; I definitely believe there are absolutes – God's absolutes. It does say that the preacher must tend to the hearer's heart so that the objective truth of God's Word can penetrate with its healing, "holy-ing" work. When the minister identifies with the hearer's feelings, a path to the heart has been opened for the work of the Holy Spirit. By the way, it was the Greek philosopher Aristotle who first articulated the legitimate importance of emotion in public speaking.

C.F.W. Walther, the first president of Concordia Seminary, got together with students on Friday evenings to talk about Law and Gospel. In the following quotation, he talks about the proper balance of feelings and the objective truth of God's Word:

> *In your sermons you like to treat subjects like these: "The blessed state of a Christian," and the like. Well, do not forget that the blessedness of Christians does not consist in pleasant feelings, but in the assurance that in spite of the bitterest feelings imaginable they are accepted with God and in their dying hour will be received into heaven. That is indeed great blessedness.*
>
> *It is, indeed, proper that in your sermons you depict the happy moments which occasionally come to Christians when they are given a foretaste of their future bliss; but you must tell your hearers at the same time that these are merely passing moments in the lives of Christians, sun-rays which once in a while find their way into their hearts. If the description of such moments of bliss is given in a proper manner, it produces neither anguish nor grief nor doubt regarding one's being in the faith, but a heartfelt longing for an experience such as the preacher is describing. Especially such Christians who have fought their fight faithfully will feel that way. They lay prostrate in their spiritual distress and imagined that they were rejected by God, and, lo, then their Heavenly Father was pleased to pour such celestial joy into their hearts that in their ecstasy they believed they were no longer on earth, but in heaven.*[3]

Week 48 – Stir up Thy Power, O Lord!

Delivered at Faith Lutheran Church, Kirksville, Missouri
December 2, 1973

Text – Luke 3:1-6

In the fifteenth year of the reign of Tiberius Caesar, Pontius Pilate being governor of Judea, and Herod being tetrarch of Galilee, and his brother Philip tetrarch of the region of Ituraea and Trachonitis, and Lysanias tetrarch of Abilene, during the high priesthood of Annas and Caiaphas, the word of God came to John the son of Zechariah in the wilderness. And he went into all the region around the Jordan, proclaiming a baptism of repentance for the forgiveness of sins. As it is written in the book of the words of Isaiah the prophet,

"The voice of one crying in the wilderness:
'Prepare the way of the Lord,
    make his paths straight.
Every valley shall be filled,
    and every mountain and hill shall be made low,
and the crooked shall become straight,
    and the rough places shall become level ways,
    and all flesh shall see the salvation of God.'"

Prayer

"Stir up, we beseech Thee, Thy power, O Lord, and come, that by Thy protection we may be rescued from the threatening perils of our sins and saved by Thy mighty deliverance; who livest and reignest with the Father and the Holy Ghost, ever one God, world without end."[1] *Amen.*

There are a million and one things that make life what it is. One of those things is power. Power makes cars and trucks go. Power lights up our homes. Power keeps industry in business. We're having trouble finding enough power these days, however. The energy shortage confronts us on almost every hand. But there are more kinds of power than just that which comes from an oil well or an electric plant. A special kind of power is needed if a football player is to run through the defensive line to get a first down. Another kind of power is needed for the Congress and the President to do their jobs. These days, we see both Congress and the President claiming that they need power to be effective. You parents have still another kind of power which you use to keep your children in line. Power, therefore, is one of the things that makes life what it is.

Power also makes Advent what it is. Advent is the four Sundays immediately preceding Christmas, during which you and I prepare ourselves for the power which God sends into this world. Each of you has already prayed this morning for God's Advent power. Do you remember when you did it? I was standing there at the altar. I said, "The Lord be with you," and you responded, "And with thy spirit." Then I turned around and we prayed these words: "Stir up, we beseech Thee, Thy power, O Lord"![1] So you and I today are entering a season of power – a season of God's power. Do you know what that power is? Do you know how you can plug yourself into God's power? Do you know what kind of person God's power makes you? Let's take a closer look at this power for which we prayed a few minutes ago.

The power of God is Jesus Christ. We pray in Advent that Christ would come into our lives today, just as He came into the lives of people almost 2,000 years ago. The Bible makes a big point that the power of God in Jesus Christ actually came into this world so long ago. The first verses in our sermon text stress that this really happened at a definite time in history. That time was: "In the fifteenth year of the reign of Tiberius Caesar, Pontius Pilate being governor of Judea, and Herod being tetrarch of Galilee, and his brother Philip tetrarch of the region of Ituraea and Trachonitis, and Lysanias tetrarch of Abilene, during the high priesthood of Annas and Caiaphas." In other words, it was about the year 29 A.D. when Jesus Christ, the power of God, began His public ministry here on earth. In those days, His public ministry was a disappointment for many people who were looking for the power of God. Some people back then thought that when God stirred up His power, He would send a Jewish military hero who would start a civil war and drive the Roman legions of Tiberius Caesar out of Jerusalem. Others thought that when God stirred up His power, He would send lightning from heaven to strike down everyone who was a heretic. Most people just didn't think that when God stirred up His power, He would send something or someone as unspectacular as this man, Jesus Christ.

Quite a few people think the same way today. They would like to see God stir up His power and do drastic things in our world. They would like to see God send His power to dramatically eliminate poverty, discrimination, and oppression. Others would like to see God send His power now to punish those who have different ideas and lifestyles than our own. And there are even some Christians who are so eager for God to stir up His power on Judgment Day that they forget that God's power is already with us. Too many people today think that when God stirs His power, we are going to be treated to something spectacular – some flashy show such as we get on the Fourth of July. No, the power of God is already with us. The power of God is Jesus Christ. The world does not think that He is anything spectacular. A lot of people, even educated people, think of Him only as a man of ancient history, whose followers got carried away and created Christianity. But those skeptics are wrong. Jesus Christ is the power of God. He came into the world to seek and to save sinners. In Advent, we remember that He came for us. Is His coming spectacular? A lot of people don't think so, but you and I think it is pretty wonderful.

His coming is so wonderful for us sinners that we don't want it to stop. We want to plug our entire lives into this power of God. Advent is a time for plugging into that power. We can say that there are four different outlets from which we draw God's power in Jesus Christ. The first outlet is when we remember how Jesus Christ came into the world almost 2,000 years ago. We remember how He was born in Bethlehem's stable. Even though He is the power of God, He was born of a sinful woman so that He might be the Savior of sinners. We remember His public ministry. It began in 29 A.D. when John the Baptist first proclaimed the Christ. Remember what you sang?

On Jordan's bank the Baptist's cry
Announces that the Lord is nigh;

> *Come, then, and hearken, for he brings*
> *Glad tidings from the King of kings.*[2]

Those glad tidings are that Jesus Christ ministered unto sinners, He was crucified between two sinners, and He was raised again for us sinners. That's the first way that we plug into God's power in Advent – we remember what He did for us while He was on earth.

The second outlet does not involve remembering. It involves looking ahead. Advent is a time in which we look ahead to the time when Christ will return to this earth in all His glory to judge the world. Luke 21:25-28 says:

> And there will be signs in sun and moon and stars, and on the earth distress of nations in perplexity because of the roaring of the sea and the waves, people fainting with fear and with foreboding of what is coming on the world. For the powers of the heavens will be shaken. And then they will see the Son of Man coming in a cloud with power and great glory. Now when these things begin to take place, straighten up and raise your heads, because your redemption is drawing near.

That will be a spectacular sight for believers and unbelievers. But when it does happen, it will already be too late for those who have not accepted Christ as their Savior beforehand. Advent is a time for believers to confess that Jesus Christ is the power of God, and to look ahead to the day when He comes again.

You remember that the first outlet for plugging into God's power is remembering when Christ was on earth. The second outlet is looking ahead to when He comes on Judgment Day. Outlets three and four for plugging into the power of God in Jesus Christ are for the here and now. These two outlets are the Word of God and the Sacraments. The third outlet is God's Word. God stirs up His power in your life every time that you sit down and study the Bible. God stirs up His power in your life every time He speaks to you on the basis of His Word. That means now, while I'm speaking with you. That means two weeks from today, when Pastor Appold will be back to speak to you from God's Word. In fact, whenever Christians discuss their biblical faith, the power of God in Jesus Christ is being stirred up. The same thing happens at outlet number four – the Sacraments of Baptism and Communion. By being baptized and regularly receiving Christ's body and blood in Holy Communion, you people are plugging yourselves into God's power. You plug yourselves into the forgiveness of sins which Jesus Christ brings you.

Make use of these four Advent outlets and you will be a charged-up Christian. You will live the kind of life that shows forth God's power. That means you will repent. *Repent? That certainly doesn't sound like a charged-up and spectacular activity*, you may be thinking. Sure, repentance is not a spectacular activity by the world's standards. But it is the way a person who has been charged up by the power of God lives. Such a charged-up person humbles himself before God and begs, "God, be merciful to me, a sinner!" (Luke 18:13). Such a charged-up person feels genuine sorrow about his past life – sorrow for both the small failings and for the big mistakes. Finally, such a charged-up person yearns to see his Savior. He yearns to remember His life and ministry on this earth. He yearns to see Him here and now, in the Word and Sacrament. And he yearns to see Him come again in glory as judge of the living and the dead. That's the kind of life you people who have been charged up by the power of God are to live. The same kind of repentant Advent living that John the Baptist first proclaimed on Jordan's banks in 29 A.D.

Advent is one of the most blessed seasons in the Church year. I wish each of you a blessed Advent, and that God will stir up His power in your life.

Amen.

For Further Reflection

"I believe in God, the Father Almighty." (Apostles' Creed, First Article)

- Stir up Thy power? Be careful what you pray for! Job 38-39; Job 42:1-6.
- Advent is a penitential season – Isaiah 64:1-9; Leviticus 26:14-21; Psalm 5:4-5; James 4:12. We should fear God's anger.
- "I, the LORD your God, am a jealous God, punishing the children for the sin of the parents to the third and fourth generation of those who hate me, but showing love to a thousand generations of those who love me and keep my commandments" (Exodus 20:5-6 NIV).

- Penitential personally – Ezekiel 18:20. Martin Luther: "Nobody will be saved by the faith or righteousness of another, but only by his own; and on the other hand nobody will be condemned for the unbelief or sins of another, but for his own unbelief… Everyone must believe for himself."[3]
- Oh, to love God and keep His commandments! Ezekiel 18:23; 1 Timothy 2:4; 2 Peter 3:8-14; Psalm 130:4
- Penitential prayer – Psalm 119:33-40. *"Stir up, we beseech Thee, Thy power, O Lord, and come, that by Thy protection we may be rescued from the threatening perils of our sins and saved by Thy mighty deliverance"!*[1]

> *Love caused Your incarnation;*
> *Love brought You down to me.*
> *Your thirst for my salvation*
> *Procured my liberty.*
> *Oh, love beyond all telling,*
> *That led You to embrace*
> *In love, all love excelling,*
> *Our lost and fallen race.*
>
> *Sin's debt, that fearful burden,*
> *Cannot His love erase;*
> *Your guilt the Lord will pardon*
> *And cover by His grace.*
> *He comes, for you procuring*
> *The peace of sin forgiv'n,*
> *His children thus securing*
> *Eternal life in heav'n.*[4]

Retrospective

Looking back at the date and place of this sermon brought a smile. 1973 – I had graduated from Concordia Seminary, married Diane, and was doing graduate work at Washington University in St. Louis. Money was tight, so we were happy to do pulpit supply at Faith Lutheran Church in Kirksville, Missouri. Pastor Mark Appold was in Germany working on his doctor's degree. I remember Faith's lively members, active in worship and sharp in Bible class, some of whom worked at what is now known as Truman State University. Faith is about 200 miles from campus, so Diane and I would drive up Saturday afternoon in my Mercury Cougar, preach, teach, and then return home. I don't remember what the church paid me for each weekend, but I recollect that there wasn't much left after paying for gas. What I did get was practice in preaching. Someone once told me – and I've passed this on to students – "Get all the practice preaching you can." There's only so much time the curriculum can allot to preaching classes, so a student helps himself by doing pulpit supply whenever he can until he's finally in a church preaching Sunday after Sunday. Thanks to all the pastors who let seminarians into their pulpits! Thanks for sharing with them your experiences in sermon preparation and practice! You're helping prepare the next generation of pastoral leadership.

One question sometimes raised is whether a good preacher is made or born. After teaching homiletics (preaching) for about 20 years, I'm convinced every seminarian can become a good preacher, but we all have to work on it throughout the years of ministry. Yes, some do have more natural gifts for the pulpit, but those must be developed so they mature for the benefit of the people. I've seen other students, less gifted rhetorically, who have become excellent preachers because they worked at it in their passion for excellence in ministry. The key is self-discipline. We pastors can get away with throwing something together to fill the sermon time, but that will catch up with us. I remember a time when a parishioner told me that my sermons were lacking. She was a caring critic, not meaning harm. She was right. The key is self-discipline. After all, preaching preparation and practice is nothing less than sacrificial love for God's people – "that Your Word may not be bound but have free course and be preached to the joy and edifying of Christ's holy people."[5]

Week 49 – "Not a Creature Was Stirring"

Delivered at Holy Cross Lutheran Church, Collinsville, Illinois
December 4, 1985

Text – Psalm 37:7

Be still before the LORD and wait patiently for him.

Prayer

O Lord, teach us to be still before You. It's early December when we easily let ourselves slide into all the busy-ness of the season – or should I say the madness of doing everything that is expected of us? We will indeed be busy, our holiday activities will show our care for family and friends, but keep us in the calm of Your presence. Lead us to times when nothing is stirring in us except devotion and worship for Your coming. Amen.

The bulletin says that the title of this sermon is "Not a Creature was Stirring." I'm not going to be preaching about "the night before Christmas."[1] I'm going to preach on Psalm 37:7 which says "Be still before the LORD and wait patiently for him." The reason I selected the title "Not a Creature was Stirring" is that word – *stir*.

I'd like you to fix that word in your mind this Advent season. Our theme this year at Holy Cross is "Caring and Keeping." We want to care for one another. We want to keep one another close. We want Holy Cross to be a caring and keeping church. To do this, we want to fix our attention on the word *stir*. Hebrews 10:24 says, "Let us consider how to stir up one another to love and good works." The Collect for the First Sunday in Advent says, "Stir up … Thy power, O Lord."[2] Before we stir ourselves to caring and keeping, before God stirs up His power in our lives, you and I should stop our frenzied, hectic, holiday stirring. *I must go here. I must go there. I must do this. I must do that.* Slow down, Christian friend! "Be still before the LORD and wait patiently for him."

Be still and wait patiently for Him. Think about it now. How does your body feel when things are frenzied and hectic? My chest gets tight. My neck muscles get tight. I can't sleep well. I can't relax. A little bit of that is OK, but does your body need a month of it? You'll be a wreck by Christmas. *Be still and wait patiently for Him.* Your body will feel better. Remember, your body is a temple of the Holy Spirit. To save the world, God sent His Son to be flesh and blood, like you and me.

Think about it. What's your mental health like when you let yourself be pressured by too many holiday activities? You lose perspective on what's important and what's not important. You easily forget that the most important thing in Advent is that God cares for you and keeps you. You lose joy and pleasure in life when you are pressured by holiday activities. But why do we celebrate Advent and Christmas? The angel said it best: "Behold, I bring you good news of great joy that will be for all the people. For unto you is born this day in the city of David a Savior, who is Christ the Lord" (Luke 2:10-11).

Think about your relationships with family and friends when you do too much holiday stirring. The atmosphere at home and work gets tense. Something that normally wouldn't faze you becomes the start of World War III. You don't need that! Jesus came so you could care for one another, so you could keep one another close. If we can't do that now, when can we? "Be still before the LORD and wait patiently for him."

I'm going to give you the opportunity now to make a promise. Not a promise to me. Not a promise to the church. But a promise to yourself and a promise to your God. If you don't want to do this, that's your business. I'll never know. I want you to do this in your own mind.

> *I promise to myself, and I promise to God, that I will say "No" to some holiday activities. I will not let myself be overwhelmed by holiday pressures. I promise this because God the Father Himself rested on the seventh day, and blesses our rest.*

> *I promise to myself, and I promise to God, that I will spend time with my family. Not only quality time, but quantity. I promise this because Jesus cares for families.*
>
> *I promise to myself, and I promise to God, that I will spend more time in devotion and worship than I ever have before. I promise this because the Holy Spirit needs my time to bless me. He can't hit a moving target.*

To show you how important this is, especially to show you how important it is to spend more time in worship and devotion, let me close my sermon with a twist on the first lines of the famous poem:

> *'Twas the night before Jesus came, when all thro' the house*
> *Not a Christian was stirring, not even my spouse;*
> *Some stockings were hung by the chimney with care,*
> *And, yes, thoughts that Saint Nicholas soon would be there;*
> *But in our lives there was no Christmas clatter.*
> *We are still before the LORD, what else can matter?*
> *We've opened our Bibles, uplifted our hands – and what to our wondering*
> *   eyes has appeared?*
> *God stirs up His power; Jesus is here.*

Amen.

For Further Reflection

"And lead us not into temptation." (Lord's Prayer, Sixth Petition)

- Put yourself in the story – Luke 10:38-42. With whom do you identify during the holiday season?
- Who else is busy this holiday season? 1 Peter 5:8-9
- Take time to fear God. By ourselves, we cannot withstand the insidious play of Satan on our sinful nature – Romans 7:18-25. We fear God because we stand before Him as people who have given into temptation – sinners. Instead

of condemning us, He forgives and helps us resist temptation – John 3:17; James 4:5-8. *"I need Thy presence every passing hour; / What but Thy grace can foil the tempter's power?"*[3] Awareness of our sin and His help is true fear of God.

- Does God tempt us? James 1:13-14. "God surely tempts no one to sin, but we pray in this petition that God would guard and keep us, so that the devil, the world, and our flesh may not deceive us or lead us into false belief, despair, and other great and shameful sins; and though we are tempted by them, we pray that we may overcome and win the victory" (Martin Luther, Small Catechism).[4]
- Follow Jesus' example – Luke 4:1-13; Ephesians 6:11-18
- So don't just do something; sit there! Sit by your Christmas tree and meditate on the reason for the season – Psalm 46:10; Revelation 3:20. A negative example of not slowing down – Isaiah 30:15. We love God because He will sit with us.

> *Fling wide the portals of your heart;*
> *Make it a temple set apart*
> *From earthly use for Heaven's employ,*
> *Adorned with prayer and love and joy.*
> *So shall your Sovereign enter in*
> *And new and nobler life begin.*
> *To Thee, O God, be praise*
> *For word and deed and grace!*
>
> *Redeemer, come! I open wide*
> *My heart to Thee; here, Lord, abide!*
> *Let me Thy inner presence feel,*
> *Thy grace and love in me reveal;*
> *Thy Holy Spirit guide us on*
> *Until our glorious goal is won.*
> *Eternal praise and fame*
> *We offer to Thy name.*[5]

Retrospective

This sermon tries to play out the consequences of conduct. When we let ourselves get overwhelmed with holiday activities, there are undesirable results for our bodies, mental outlook, and relationships. That's true for other times of the year too, but come Christmas the consequences of losing balance are most pronounced. I've always found it very helpful when pastors, and others as well, lay out the consequences for taking this or that course of action. It's one thing to say we're sinners, but better to name specific sins and show the consequences. It's not just idleness that's the devil's workshop; busy-ness can be as well. Similarly, it's one thing to say Jesus is our Savior, but it's better to show the consequences for trusting Jesus and His promises. This is incarnational, Jesus with His skin on, and I love hearing sermons that lay out for me the blessings of going God's way by disciplining activity. The challenge, of course, becomes acting on the blessed course of action – in this sermon being still before the LORD. Now we're in sanctification, and that takes the determination of continual devotion and worship. No better time to get into that discipline than Advent!

Week 50 – The Common Things

*Delivered at St. Salvator Lutheran Church, Venedy, Illinois
and St. Peter Lutheran Church, New Memphis, Illinois
December 23, 1979*

Text – Luke 2:1-20

In those days a decree went out from Caesar Augustus that all the world should be registered. This was the first registration when Quirinius was governor of Syria. And all went to be registered, each to his own town. And Joseph also went up from Galilee, from the town of Nazareth, to Judea, to the city of David, which is called Bethlehem, because he was of the house and lineage of David, to be registered with Mary, his betrothed, who was with child. And while they were there, the time came for her to give birth. And she gave birth to her firstborn son and wrapped him in swaddling cloths and laid him in a manger, because there was no place for them in the inn.

And in the same region there were shepherds out in the field, keeping watch over their flock by night. And an angel of the Lord appeared to them, and the glory of the Lord shone around them, and they were filled with great fear. And the angel said to them, "Fear not, for behold, I bring you good news of great joy that will be for all the people. For unto you is born this day in the city of David a Savior, who is Christ the Lord. And this will be a sign for you: you will find a baby wrapped in swaddling cloths and lying in a manger." And suddenly there was with the angel a multitude of the heavenly host praising God and saying,

"Glory to God in the highest,
and on earth peace among those with whom he is pleased!"

When the angels went away from them into heaven, the shepherds said to one another, "Let us go over to Bethlehem and see this thing that has happened, which the Lord has made known to us." And they went with haste and found Mary and Joseph, and the baby lying in a manger. And when they saw it, they made known the saying that had been told them concerning this child. And all who heard it wondered at what the shepherds told them. But Mary treasured up all these things, pondering them in her heart. And the shepherds returned, glorifying and praising God for all they had heard and seen, as it had been told them.

Prayer

We're going to celebrate your birthday, Jesus! Not only that but we're going to get presents too. We're excited for Christmas to come. Help us remember how much You are like us. You came as a baby, lived in a common house in a small town. One thing is different: You came like us but You came to be our Savior. That can make us happy with our lives in our homes and here in our little town. Jesus, help us all have a merry Christmas! Amen.

What is almost here? Tomorrow night is Christmas Eve. What do we remember on Christmas Eve? You know who is very important when it comes to remembering that Christmas is Jesus' birthday? You are. Tomorrow night, all the big people are going to come to church and you are going to tell them about Jesus' birthday. You are going to be just like a pastor. You are going to take the big people and show them their Savior. That's why I wanted to have a little private talk with you today. Tomorrow night you will be very busy. Right now, you and I have a little bit of time to talk. I want to make sure that you have a happy Christmas – a happy Jesus' birthday.

Bring me that present from under the tree. … Why did you bring me the big, fancy one? Why not the little, plain one? Do you open the biggest presents first?

Do you like the fancy presents the best? The ones that cost the most money? We're all like that – big people, too. We all like the things that are bigger, fancier, richer. That is why I want to talk to you right now, before Christmas arrives. Bigger, fancier, richer: That's not the secret to a happy Christmas. No, not at all.

The things that make Jesus' birthday so wonderful are the common things. Common things like little babies. Did you ever see a baby on television news because the baby was rich and powerful and important? Is a baby ever a king or a president or a senator? Does a baby ever buy a big, important company? No, when it comes to being big and rich and important, babies don't count. They are quite common. And babies have common things, like diapers and bottles and rattles. But common little babies are the secret to a happy Christmas. Who became a common little baby, with diaper and bottle and rattle? He is the King of kings, the Lord of lords. He is the wealthiest person in the universe. He is the most powerful person to be found. But He left all of that to become a common, little baby. He did it because He loves common people like you and like me. We're pretty common, aren't we? The secret to a happy Jesus' birthday is that common little baby who came for common people like us.

Common things make Christmas wonderful. Common things like your home. Do you live in a palace? Maybe you live in a mansion? No. Do you have servants? No. Do your mom and dad have lots of money? No. I bet you they've told you that money doesn't grow on trees. You have a common home. So do I. Now, where was baby Jesus born? In a palace? In a mansion? In a barn. Pretty common, huh? Later His family moved to Nazareth and lived in a regular house. But it was common, too. Probably not even as nice as your home. But there's the secret to a happy Jesus' birthday! He wants to live in your home, even if it is just a common, plain ol' home. He likes homes like yours the best. The best way for Jesus to live in your home is for Him to live in your heart. That's why we pray:

Ah, dearest Jesus, holy Child,
Make Thee a bed, soft, undefiled,
Within my heart, that it may be
A quiet chamber kept for Thee.[1]

One more secret to a happy Christmas – a happy Jesus' birthday. One more common thing that Jesus loves: little towns. Was Jesus born in the big city of

Jerusalem, or St. Louis? No, He was born in the little town of Bethlehem. That was a common place, just like Venedy or New Memphis. The big, rich, and important people could care less about Bethlehem... or Venedy, or New Memphis. But not Jesus! He loves this common little town! He wants the people here to know what makes a happy Christmas. It's the common things. Common things like the little town of Bethlehem... or Venedy, or New Memphis. Common things like the simple home of Mary and Joseph... or your home. And, common things like a little baby who is your Savior.

Well, next time we come to church, you'll be up here leading the service! I'm glad that you and I had this chance to talk. You tell the big people, will you? Tell them that they have everything they need. Tell them to have a happy Jesus' birthday.

Amen.

For Further Reflection

"I believe." (Apostles' Creed)

- Living in the fear of God, every person accountable – 2 Corinthians 5:6-11; 1 Peter 1:13-17; Romans 3:19-20
- Now read Mark 8:27-30, Matthew 22:42, and Luke 18:8. Each person must believe for himself/herself. Infants too?
- "What is Baptism? Baptism is not just plain water, but it is water used by God's command and connected with God's Word" (Martin Luther, Small Catechism).[2]
- Reverential fear at the creative power of God's Word – Psalm 33:6-9; Mark 10:26-27; John 6:63; Romans 4:17b
- "Which is that word of God? Christ our Lord says in the last chapter of Matthew, 'Go and make disciples of all nations, baptizing them in the name of the Father and of the Son and of the Holy Spirit'" (Martin Luther, Small Catechism).[2]
- "All nations"! Jesus invites all – John 3:5-6; John 6:37, including children, Mark 10:13-16.

- "The promise is for you and for your children" – Acts 2:38-39
- Put yourself in the story – Hebrews 11:1 - 12:3
- Examples of the truth – 2 Corinthians 4:13-14
- "I believe"! – Mark 9:24

> *I know my faith is founded*
> *On Jesus Christ, my God and Lord;*
> *And this my faith confessing,*
> *Unmoved I stand on His sure Word.*
> *Our reason cannot fathom*
> *The truth of God profound;*
> *Who trusts in human wisdom*
> *Relies on shifting ground.*
> *God's Word is all sufficient,*
> *It makes divinely sure;*
> *And trusting in its wisdom,*
> *My faith shall rest secure.*
>
> *In faith, Lord, let me serve You;*
> *Though persecution, grief, and pain*
> *Should seek to overwhelm me,*
> *Let me a steadfast trust retain;*
> *And then at my departure,*
> *Lord, take me home to You,*
> *Your riches to inherit*
> *As all You said holds true.*
> *In life and death, Lord, keep me*
> *Until Your heav'n I gain,*
> *Where I by Your great mercy*
> *The end of faith attain.*[3]

Retrospective

This reads like a children's sermon but it really wasn't. Sounding like a children's message, it was actually the main sermon for the Sunday before Christmas. The adults figured out what I was up to! There are many occasions when a pastor will know that the apparent audience isn't the only audience. For example, in a wedding service, the pastor speaks to the bridal couple but it's the families and friends of the bride and groom, churched and unchurched, who are the real audience. They're reflecting on their own experiences in marriage, good and bad, while the bridal couple and party are invested more in the joyous experience than in careful listening. Similarly, in a funeral service, the grieving family is often too distraught to fully hear, but others in attendance are paying close attention. Even regular Sunday sermons have several audiences: disagreeing factions within the congregation, struggling families, white and blue collar listeners, young and old... all these and more make even the seemingly unified Sunday crowd a coming together of diverse people and interests. The great thing is that the Spirit uses the words of the sermon, the powerful Word of God, to speak to all in ways the pastor cannot fully appreciate.

So back to this "adult" sermon spoken to children. People have long observed that children's messages are often more interesting than the "adult" sermon. What does that remark tell us? That the so-called adult sermon should have more characteristics of the simpler message aimed at the children. Not simplistic but simple. Imagery, not philosophical finery. Not shallow religious fluff, but deep points made in a way that a child can understand. "Whoever does not receive the kingdom of God like a child..." (Mark 10:15). Once again, the preparation and preaching of sermons is – or should be – a practice of selfless love by the pastor. Intent upon communicating God's good work in a way the hearer can grasp, the pastor will choose a way that can be harder for a theologically educated person

— by speaking simply, forgoing the theological jargon of the clergy echo chamber — but speaking to the heart of children of every age. Do our "adult" sermons bring young and old to see Jesus?

This is the first page of my typed sermon entitled, "The Common Things." From the beginning, my preference has always been to write out the sermon word for word and memorize it verbatim. Quintilian, the encyclopedic author on ancient rhetoric, desired speeches written word for word and memorized verbatim. "Give me a reliable memory and plenty of time, and I should prefer not to permit a single syllable to escape me."[4] There are several aids to memory seen on this page. The title at the top served to keep me on the central thought as I typed. Another mnemonic aid is the limited number of paragraphs, meaning not too many thoughts to overwhelm the listener. Unlike writing for people to read, where the sentences in one paragraph will carry varied thoughts, in oral style a paragraph should carry only one thought. The sentences in that paragraph simply state and support the thought in various ways. A third memory aid is the paragraphs following one after another very logically. Transitions that change the line of thought are doable but harder for the preacher to memorize and the listener to follow. Finally, notice the hymn verse toward the end of the sermon. As I delivered the sermon from memory, I could see that verse in my mind as a "mile marker" toward the conclusion. How verbatim are my actual deliveries? I'd say about 85%. Whatever might be forgotten probably didn't need to be there in the first place.

THE COMMON THINGS   Advent IV   December 23, 1979

What is almost here? Tomorrow night is Christmas eve. What do we remember on Christmas eve? You know who is very important when it comes to remembering that Christmas is Jesus' birthday? You are. Tomorrow night all the big people are going to come to church and you are going to tell them about Jesus' birthday. You are going to be just like a pastor. You are going to take the big people and show them their Savior. That's why I wanted to have a little private talk with you today. Tomorrow night you will be very busy. Right now you and I have a little bit of time to talk. I want to make sure that you have a happy Christmas, a happy Jesus' birthday.

Bring me that present from under the tree. Why did you bring me the big, fancy one? Why not the little, plain one? Do you open the biggest presents first? Do you like the fancy presents the best? The ones that cost the most money? We're all like that, big people, too. We all like the things that are bigger, fancier, richer. That is why I want to talk to you right now, before Christmas arrives. Bigger, fancier, richer. That's not the secret to a happy Christmas. No, not at all.

The things that make Jesus' birthday so wonderful are the common things. Common things like little babies. Did you ever see a baby on television news because a baby was rich and powerful and important? Is a baby ever a king or president or senator? Does a baby ever buy a big, important company? No, when it comes to being big and rich and important, babies don't count. They are quite common. And babies have common things, like diapers and bottles and rattles. But common little babies are the secret to a happy Christmas. Who became a common little baby with diaper and bottle and rattle? He is the king of kings, the lord of lords. He is the wealthiest person in the universe. He is the most powerful person to be found. But he left all of that to become a common, little baby. He did it because he loves common people like you and like me. We're pretty common, aren't we? The secret to a happy Jesus' birthday is that common little baby that came for common people like us.

Common things make Christmas wonderful. Common things like your home. Do you live in a palace? Maybe you live in a mansion? No. Do you have servants? No. Do your mom and dad have lots of money? No. I bet you they've told you that money doesn't grow on trees. You have a common home. So do I. Now, where was baby Jesus born? In a palace? In a mansion? In a barn. Pretty common, huh? Later his family moved to Nazareth and lived in a regular house. But it was common, too. Probably not even as nice as your home. But there's the secret to a happy Jesus' birthday! He wants to live in your home, even if it is just a common, plain ol' home. He likes homes like yours the best. The best way for Jesus to live in your home is for him to live in your heart. That's why we pray:

> Ah, dearest Jesus, holy child,
> Make thee a bed, soft, undefiled,
> Within my heart, that it may be
> A quiet chamber kept for thee.

One more secret to a happy Christmas, a happy Jesus' birthday. One more common thing that Jesus loves. Little towns. Was Jesus born in the big city of Jerusalem or St. Louis? No, he was born in the little town of Bethlehem. That was a common place, just like Venedy. The big, rich, and important people could care less about Bethlehem...or Venedy. But not Jesus! He loves this common little town! He wants the people here to know what makes a happy Christmas. Its the common things. Common things like the little town of Bethlehem...or Venedy. Common things like the simple home of Mary and Joseph...or your home. And, common things like a little baby who is your Savior.

Week 51 – Company for Christmas

Christmas
Broadcast on The Lutheran Hour
December 22, 1996

Text – Matthew 1:23

"Behold, the virgin shall conceive and bear a son, and they shall call his name Immanuel" (which means, God with us).

Prayer

O God, our heavenly Father, we rejoice that You have given us a Savior! Without Jesus, our lives would lead to despair, but with Your gift at Christmas, we live in joyous hope of heaven.

O Jesus, Son of God and Son of Mary, we praise You for coming to the manger, and taking on our flesh so that You might go to the cross and redeem us from sin. In the glory of Your resurrection and ascension, pour Your Spirit into our hearts to love You more and serve others gladly.

O Holy Spirit, when the holiday passes, make every day a holy day. In this still-sinful world where problems continually come, sanctify us by Your grace so that we grow ever more dependent upon You and show the love of Christ to all.

O blest and Holy Trinity, bring us at length to You in the eternal joys of heaven. Amen.

Company's coming! Jesus, Mary, and Joseph are coming to the door of your heart and home this week. You can't avoid them. TV and radio programs, magazines and newspapers, Christmas cards and Christmas carols – Jesus, Mary, and Joseph are your company for Christmas. Let me tell you, they're not boring, like some Christmas visitors to your home. They won't be tedious. Sometimes you and I have to endure boring small talk at holiday gatherings. This might surprise you, but your company for Christmas – Jesus, Mary, and Joseph – are an engaging, relevant family.

They're not the Cleavers.[1] We all remember Ward and June, Wally, and Beaver Cleaver, that seemingly perfect family from an era long gone. White, middle class, never cheating on each other, never divorced, Ward and June had almost perfect children. No drug or alcohol or abuse problems forever scarred Wally or the Beaver. The biggest problems the fictitious Cleavers ever faced would be considered a piece of cake now! Eddie Haskell was nothing compared to the problems families face today. The name of the Cleavers has become shorthand for a style of family life that seems no longer to exist.

Someplace along the line, we picked up the notion that Jesus, Mary, and Joseph were an ancient version of the Cleavers. The manger scenes and carols and holiday greeting cards are so glazed over with sentimentality, so clouded with a longing for a simpler time, that the Holy Family seems unreal. The stable doesn't smell any more. The straw in the manger doesn't scratch the baby. The baby doesn't cry. Mary and Joseph wear clothes that look like they're fresh from the cleaners. No grime. No sweat. And therefore, no real relevance to the problems of our lives. We've turned them into the Cleavers, and they are not!

You who are women, consider Mary. She was a wonderful young woman and sincerely pious – and, I venture to add, she would have been unknown to us if a major personal situation had not developed in her life. Luke chapter one reports:

> In the sixth month the angel Gabriel was sent from God to a city of Galilee named Nazareth, to a virgin betrothed to a man whose name was Joseph … And the angel said to her, "Do not be afraid, Mary, for you have found favor with God. And behold, you will conceive in your womb and bear a son, and you shall call his name Jesus." … And Mary said to the angel, "How will this be, since I am a virgin?" And the angel answered her, "The Holy Spirit will come upon you, and the power of the Most High will overshadow you; therefore the child to be born will be called holy – the Son of God." (Luke 1:26-27, 30-31, 34-35)

Had it not been for that heavenly announcement, we wouldn't know about Mary today.

Because of that heavenly announcement, Mary faced some immediate personal problems. She had to explain her situation to Joseph. She had to tell her fiancé that she had become pregnant by God the Holy Spirit. And what would she say to her family and to people in the little (and I suspect gossipy) town of Nazareth? The conception of the child was heavenly, but the effects were earthly and real.

You men, consider Joseph. He didn't believe Mary at first. Would you? Joseph was a craftsman with a reputation for good work. Joseph also was a pious person who believed in the old morality. Therefore, he was ready to end his relationship with Mary. Listen to the story from Matthew chapter one:

> Now the birth of Jesus Christ took place in this way. When his mother Mary had been betrothed to Joseph, before they came together she was found to be with child from the Holy Spirit. And her husband Joseph, being a just man and unwilling to put her to shame, resolved to divorce her quietly. But as he considered these things, behold, an angel of the Lord appeared to him in a dream, saying, "Joseph, son of David, do not fear to take Mary as your wife, for that which is conceived in her is from the Holy Spirit. She will bear a son, and you shall call his name Jesus, for he will save his people from their sins." … When Joseph woke from sleep, he did as the angel of the Lord commanded him: he took his wife, but knew her not until she had given birth to a son. And he called his name Jesus. (Matthew 1:18-21, 24-25)

You see, this is not a script for Ward and June Cleaver! A heavenly conception, but with real-life earthly effects! Your company for Christmas knows life.

Your visitors this week – I'm getting ahead of myself, but I hope they'll become more than visitors – aren't exactly like your family or mine. Yes, they had their problems, and we have ours. But it's not the problems that make their company for Christmas so special. What's so special about this company for Christmas is the Child. No child ever born was quite like Jesus. It's not just the virgin birth that is so unique. Jesus is the only person ever born who is both True

Man and True God. Matthew 1:22-23: "All this took place to fulfill what the Lord had spoken by the prophet: 'Behold, the virgin shall conceive and bear a son, and they shall call his name Immanuel' (which means, God with us)." No other child was ever born for the purpose of going to the cross and dying for the sins of the world, but Jesus was. "You shall call his name Jesus, for he will save his people from their sins" (Matthew 1:21). No other child was ever born with a promise to live and be a king forever, but Jesus was. Luke 1:32-33 states: "He will be great and will be called the Son of the Most High. And the Lord God will give to him the throne of his father David, and he will reign over the house of Jacob forever, and of his kingdom there will be no end." Mary and Joseph were sinners, as all people are. We welcome them in song and story this week because their lives revolved around the same basic themes of our own stories – the ups and downs of life in a sinful world. But the greatest theme in their lives was the Child sent from heaven, Immanuel. He made them a Holy Family, and we welcome Him; we bid Him stay with us, so He might sanctify our hearts and home.

Jesus Christ, Immanuel, God with us, can make you and your family members holy in the sight of God. While Mary and Joseph are present to us only in our remembrance of the first Christmas, Jesus Christ came to literally be with you in every moment of life, not just now during the holidays. "I am with you always, to the end of the age," He promises in Matthew 28:20. Remember His company when you feel alone and isolated, even within your own family.

Jesus comes to meet your times of despair with His hope – Colossians 1:27: "Christ in you, the hope of glory." Remember that He keeps you company when other helpers have failed you, and His words of encouragement in the Bible can kindle hope for a better tomorrow.

Jesus comes to remove your guilt with His Word of forgiveness. In Him, "We have redemption, the forgiveness of sins" (Colossians 1:14). Who is right in your family arguments? God is, and in the Christ Child, God's Word is *I forgive you*. So when you're hurting because someone in your family has sinned against you, or when you hurt another by your sins, remember that your company for Christmas has come with forgiveness.

God with us makes for more godly living. If there is anything that will improve the quality of your family life, it is a spirit of forgiveness and an attitude to do better. Jesus once told a woman caught in adultery, "Neither do I condemn you; go, and from now on sin no more" (John 8:11). Your company for Christmas does not coerce you to keep the Ten Commandments. His forgiveness makes godly living your daily delight.

Don't let Jesus be merely a transient in your home, but make Him your constant company for yet another practical, real-life reason: He's the only One who can bring you to heaven. He says in John 14:19, "Because I live, you also will live." We need Immanuel. We need God with us in the practical, daily matters of family life. He comes that we "may have life and have it abundantly" (John 10:10). But most of all, we need Immanuel to lead us into the joys of eternal life, the life that is most abundant.

So the Christmas story is not a fictitious script from the past. It's not a sentimental TV story of an imaginary family. It is the story of a heavenly conception, a virgin birth, and God's blessings upon us all. Listen now to the sacred story of God coming to be with us:

> In those days a decree went out from Caesar Augustus that all the world should be registered. This was the first registration when Quirinius was governor of Syria. And all went to be registered, each to his own town. And Joseph also went up from Galilee, from the town of Nazareth, to Judea, to the city of David, which is called Bethlehem, because he was of the house and lineage of David, to be registered with Mary, his betrothed, who was with child. And while they were there, the time came for her to give birth. And she gave birth to her firstborn son and wrapped him in swaddling cloths and laid him in a manger, because there was no place for them in the inn. (Luke 2:1-7)

The conclusion of the matter is rather simple. As Mary and Joseph welcomed the Child into their hearts and home, as the Child accompanied them in their marriage and life, so I ask you to welcome your company for Christmas. His presence sanctifies your hearts and homes. His presence made theirs a Holy Family. Your company is coming. A blessed Christmas to you and yours!

Amen.

For Further Reflection

"What child is this, who, laid to rest, / On Mary's lap is sleeping?"[2]

"I believe ... in Jesus Christ, His only Son, our Lord, who was conceived by the Holy Spirit, born of the virgin Mary, suffered under Pontius Pilate, was crucified, died and was buried. He descended into hell. The third day He rose again from the dead. He ascended into heaven and sits at the right hand of God the Father Almighty. From thence He will come to judge the living and the dead." (Apostles' Creed, Second Article)

"This, this is Christ the king"[2]

- "Fear not"! – Revelation 1:12-18

> *Why lies He in such mean estate*
> *Where ox and ass are feeding?*
> *Good Christian, fear; for sinners here*
> *The silent Word is pleading.*
> *Nails, spear shall pierce Him through,*
> *The cross be borne for me, for you;*
> *Hail, hail the Word made flesh,*
> *The babe, the son of Mary![3]*

- We learn true fear and love of God by contemplating the incarnate Son of God – Hebrews 1:1-12
- A Christ-centered prayer for you – Colossians 1:11-20

> Great indeed, we confess, is the mystery of godliness:
> He was manifested in the flesh,
> vindicated by the Spirit,
> seen by angels,
> proclaimed among the nations,

> believed on in the world,
>
>   taken up in glory. (1 Timothy 3:16)

Retrospective

I remember the little nativity set my parents put under the Christmas tree every year. Intentional or not, its place under the tree reminded Dale, Bruce, and Pam that Christmas was Jesus' birthday. Come visit Concordia Seminary at Christmastime and you'll see nativities all over campus, but two get the most attention. One is the nativity outside the chapel: the Holy Family, shepherds, wise men, and cattle in a rude stable – rude because I built it myself! Inside the Chapel of St. Timothy and Titus are the splendid figures made by Fontanini in Italy. Diane and I love watching little children from campus and off-campus go to the nativity and straight to baby Jesus. They need none of our theologians to explain Christmas. It's Jesus' birthday!

In my later years, I'm returning to childhood fascination about the One in the manger. God comes into our world as flesh and blood – incarnation – this little baby Jesus. Immanuel, God is with us. A theologian has no advantage this season or any season over a little child. It boggles my mind that the Creator of the vast expanses of the universe comes to us in this humble way – this way we can all relate to. Here, I think, is another demonstration that our heavenly Father is intent on all people knowing His love for us. Not just that He sent Jesus, but that the baby fascinates across generations, little children and believing adults are together in awe and wonder. Truly, the fear and love of God.

> *Come hither, ye children; O come, one and all*
> *To Bethlehem haste, to the manger so small*
> *God's Son for a gift has been sent you this night*
> *To be your Redeemer, your joy and delight.*

See Mary and Joseph with love beaming eyes
Are gazing upon the rude bed where He lies
The shepherds are kneeling, with hearts full of love
While angels sing loud hallelujahs above.

Kneel down and adore Him with shepherds today
Lift up little hands now and praise Him as they
Rejoice that a Savior from sin you can boast
And join in the song of the heavenly host.[4]

Week 52 – The Old Shall Be Merry

New Year's Eve
Delivered at St. Salvator Lutheran Church, Venedy, Illinois
and St. Peter Lutheran Church, New Memphis, Illinois
December 30, 1979

Text – Luke 2:25-38

Now there was a man in Jerusalem, whose name was Simeon, and this man was righteous and devout, waiting for the consolation of Israel, and the Holy Spirit was upon him. And it had been revealed to him by the Holy Spirit that he would not see death before he had seen the Lord's Christ. And he came in the Spirit into the temple, and when the parents brought in the child Jesus, to do for him according to the custom of the Law, he took him up in his arms and blessed God and said,

> "Lord, now you are letting your servant depart in peace,
>   according to your word;
> for my eyes have seen your salvation
>   that you have prepared in the presence of all peoples,
> a light for revelation to the Gentiles,
>   and for glory to your people Israel."

And his father and his mother marveled at what was said about him. And Simeon blessed them and said to Mary his mother, "Behold, this child is appointed for the fall and rising of many in Israel, and for a sign that is opposed (and a sword will pierce through your own soul also), so that thoughts from many hearts may be revealed."

And there was a prophetess, Anna, the daughter of Phanuel, of the tribe of Asher. She was advanced in years, having lived with her husband seven years from when she was a virgin, and then as a widow until she was eighty-four. She did not depart from the temple, worshiping with fasting and prayer night and day. And coming up at that very hour she began to give thanks to God and to speak of him to all who were waiting for the redemption of Jerusalem.

Prayer

Lord, how precious the younger years of life can be when we use them to learn more of You. Trained early by Your Spirit to desire our heavenly salvation, what a wonderful time old age can be if it comes and we're holding Jesus close in faith and trusting Him for a heavenly future. Like the joy of Anna and Simeon seeing You in the temple, lift our thoughts beyond any difficulties of age to know by faith that we can depart in peace. Jesus, we are blessed to have You in our hearts. Spirit of our Savior, make us merry in our age! Amen.

I have a riddle for you this morning, an old riddle, almost 3,000 years old. It's called the Riddle of the Sphinx. What goes on four feet in the morning, two feet at noon, and three feet in the evening? … The answer is man. In the morning of his life, he crawls on all fours. In the midday of his life, he walks on his two feet. In the evening of his life, he walks with a cane.

Here, in our Sunday morning sermons, we often speak to those in the middle of life – occasionally to the children. This morning's text talks about you who are older. You may or may not use a cane. But if you are in your 60s, 70s, or older, then listen. The Old Testament lesson from Jeremiah promises that "the old shall be merry" (Jeremiah 31:13), and the Gospel story of Simeon and Anna tells you how to do it.

Obviously, I can't talk about old age from experience. But I do watch you who are further along in years. Does it ever happen that you sit at the table, look out the window, and think to yourself:

What shall I do today? I wish there was a quilt-in up at school. Well, in a couple weeks. I wonder if the children will be by Sunday. I know they are so busy, but you'd think they could stop by a little more often. It's just not the same since Hans is gone. He's gone twelve years now. Hard to believe. I should write Frieda. Hope she's feeling better. Oh, here's Johnny with the mail.

And so it goes, day after day after day. When you are older, you have more time on your hands. The work that you have to do is less, and maybe not quite as important as twenty or thirty years ago. There is loneliness – husband or wife gone, the children grown and leading their own lives. And then, of course, death. It has taken your husband or wife. It has taken friends and family, one by one. Soon it shall come for you.

Jeremiah promises that "the old shall be merry," and Simeon and Anna show you how to do it. They experienced the problems that come with old age. Anna was at least 84, and Simeon must have been in his 70s. They had plenty of time on their hands. Their working days were over – they spent a lot of time around the temple. They also seem to have given considerable thought to their death. That could all be depressing. Your old age could be depressing, unless you hold on to what God has promised you. God has made promises. Some of God's most beautiful promises are the ones He offers to you when you are in the later years of life.

He offers you comfort. The Bible describes Simeon and says, "This man was righteous and devout, waiting for the consolation of Israel, and the Holy Spirit was upon him" (Luke 2:25). Simeon was looking for comfort amidst all the problems and troubles of life. God offers you that comfort on every hand. If the Social Security check is not enough, God says, "Look at the birds of the air: they neither sow nor reap nor gather into barns, and yet your heavenly Father feeds them. Are you not of more value than they?" (Matthew 6:26). If you worry about your children or grandchildren, God says, "Call upon me in the day of trouble; I will deliver you, and you shall glorify me" (Psalm 50:15). If you wonder how you can keep going, God says, "Even to your old age I am he, and to gray hairs I will carry you. / I have made, and I will bear; I will carry and will save" (Isaiah 46:4). He offers you comfort in your advancing age.

He makes a beautiful promise to Simeon, and He makes it to you. He told Simeon "that he would not see death before he had seen the Lord's Christ." To you He says, *You will not die until I have shown you how you shall be saved.* That promise He keeps. He kept the promise to Simeon. Mary and Joseph brought the child Jesus to the temple. Simeon took the Savior in his arms and held Him close. God keeps that promise to you. He brings you the Christ child – day after day in your devotions, Sunday after Sunday in church, year after year in your life. To you, God is saying, *Here, take my Son, hold Him close to your heart. Hold your Savior.* You will not enter heaven at death because you have lived a good life. When you sit alone and think of all you have done through the years, don't fool yourself and think that your life is going to save you. It won't. There is no fool like an old fool. The only thing that saves you is the Baby you hold close to your heart. The Baby who grew up and took your sins – 60, 70, 80 years' worth – and put them to death on the cross. Then He arose and says to you, "Because I live, you also will live" (John 14:19). God's promises are many. Some of God's most beautiful promises are the ones He offers to you who are in the later years of life.

Hold His promises! Take Him at His Word! Then you can be merry. When Simeon held the Christ child, he broke out in a song. He sang:

> *Lord, now you are letting your servant depart in peace,*
> *according to your word;*
> *for my eyes have seen your salvation*
> *that you have prepared in the presence of all peoples,*
> *a light for revelation to the Gentiles,*
> *and for glory to your people Israel.* (Luke 2:29-32)

When Anna saw the Savior, she praised God and she spread the good Word. Do you see? The work doesn't stop when you get older. It changes – and it gets better. It changes from the daily occupations of this world to the joy of praising God for what He has done. It changes from physical labor to telling others about the Savior. You older people, more than anyone else, should be concerned about spreading the story of Jesus. You older people, more than anyone else, have the time and the ability to do it. I've been around in the church and synod. Do you know who some of the most influential leaders are in the LLL and LWML? Older people, retired people, people who have the time and ability to spread the story of Jesus. People like Simeon and Anna. Do you know how a lot of the work of the church gets done? Do you know how so much mission work can be accomplished? Do you know how we can train so many pastors and teachers? Because of older people – older people who made a will and took care of their estate. They provided for their children, and they also remembered the Lord and their church. If you do not have a will, you are inviting Satan to come and do all sorts of damage to your children, and even to your church.

Some of the most influential work in the world and in the Church is done in these ways by older people. Don't ever sit and look out the window and think that your work is over! It is not! Your work has changed from what it was in earlier years. Hopefully it has changed from the work of this world to the work of the Church – praising God and spreading the story of Jesus. That is a better occupation than any job this world has to offer!

Old age is no riddle. God intends it to be a beautiful time. God wants the old to be merry. All you need to do is take that Christ child into your arms and hold Him close to your heart.

Amen.

For Further Reflection

"You shall have no other gods before me." (First Commandment)

- Aging: A gift of time for reflection upon your past and future – Psalm 73; Isaiah 46:3-4; Psalm 23; John 14:1-6
- What are *your* stories? Psalm 37, especially vv. 3-26 and 40
- Sharing your stories of faith with coming generations – Psalm 145:1-7; Ephesians 3:20-21
- The righteous flourish in old age – Psalm 92
- Pray Psalm 86 – "Unite my heart to fear your name."

The Lord hath helped me hitherto
By His surpassing favor;

His mercies ev'ry morn were new,
His kindness did not waver.
God hitherto hath been my Guide,
Hath pleasures hitherto supplied,
And hitherto hath helped me.

Help me henceforth, O God of grace,
Help me on each occasion,
Help me in each and ev'ry place,
Help me thro' Jesus' Passion;
Help me in life and death, O God,
Help me thro' Jesus' dying blood;
Help me as Thou hast helped me![1]

Retrospective

This last sermon of the book gives me opportunity to compare then and now. I was 32 years old when I wrote this sermon for Venedy and New Memphis. What I knew of old age came from watching older family members, and – this is a special blessing of being in pastoral ministry – from visiting many, many older parishioners in all kinds of settings, from gatherings of active seniors to the dear people who couldn't get out anymore, as they would have liked. Mrs. Henze was like that. A member of the last congregation I served as pastor, Holy Cross in Collinsville, she sat long hours in her rocker, looking out the window and watching cars go by. Every time I visited with her and finished giving Holy Communion, she said, "Thousand, thousand thanks shall be, / Dearest Jesus, unto Thee."[2] Dependable – she never failed to witness her faith to young me. So many older people who can't get out are not distracted from the eternal questions by outside activity. They are facing eternal facts straight on.

I'm now passing the biblical "three score years and ten" and experiencing that our religious talk, sincere as it is in our younger years, gets very personal as we grow older. There are things about the years ahead that scare me: the infirmities of age, getting left behind, maybe even forgotten by those younger and on the go, and many other things that are distressing now but eternally trivial. "When we've been there ten thousand years..."[3] The positive side of all this is that I am growing greatly in my dependence upon Jesus. I'm desperate! I have nothing but His promises, but by faith His promises are everything. My purpose these years is to share my stories of faith with younger people, especially with the young seminarians whom God is raising up to minister to the "mature," as I did to Mrs. Henze. It's all coming into focus now, sweetly. Rev. Arnold Kuntz, now in glory, captured my experience in two sentences that have had a profound impact upon me. He wrote, "Life narrows down and crisis comes. And suddenly only one thing matters, and there in the narrow place stands Jesus."[4] I'd like to think I got the hearts of Simeon and Anna correct in this sermon. I pray fervently that I'll be like Simeon and Anna as my own years narrow down. "All the promises of God find their Yes in him [Jesus Christ]. That is why it is through him that we utter our Amen to God for his glory" (2 Corinthians 1:20).

Dr. Dale A. Meyer Biographical Information

Dale A. Meyer was born in Chicago Heights, Illinois. He completed a B.A. in 1969 at Concordia Senior College, Fort Wayne, Indiana. He is a 1973 graduate of Concordia Seminary, St. Louis, earning a Master of Divinity degree. He earned an M.A. (1974) and a Ph.D. (1986) in classical languages from Washington University in St. Louis. In 1993, Concordia Theological Seminary in Fort Wayne, Indiana awarded him the honorary degree of Doctor of Divinity.

Meyer began his pastoral career serving as pastor of St. Salvator Lutheran Church in Venedy, Illinois and St. Peter Lutheran Church in New Memphis, Illinois from 1974 to 1981. He served on the faculty of Concordia Seminary, St. Louis, Missouri from 1979 to 1981 as a guest instructor and 1981 to 1984 as an assistant professor teaching classes in New Testament and homiletics and as the director of Resident Field Education. From 1984 to 1988, Meyer served as senior pastor at Holy Cross Lutheran Church, Collinsville, Illinois. From 1989 to 2001, Meyer was speaker on the radio program *The Lutheran Hour* and until 2003 he was the host of the television show *On Main Street*.

Meyer joined the faculty at Concordia Seminary, St. Louis again in 2001. He occupied the Gregg H. Benidt Memorial Chair in Homiletics and Literature at Concordia from 2001-2005. He served as the interim president from 2004 to 2005 and became the tenth president of Concordia Seminary, St. Louis in 2005. He also serves as a professor of practical theology.

Meyer has served The Lutheran Church—Missouri Synod (LCMS) and the church-at-large over the years in several capacities. He served as third vice-president of the LCMS from 1995 to 1998. He was a charter board member of ALOA (Association of Lutheran Older Adults), has served as an honorary director of God's Word to the Nations Bible Society and as a member of the Standing Committee on Pastoral Ministry for the LCMS. He was pastoral adviser for the Southern Illinois District of the International Lutheran Laymen's League and has served as first vice-president, second vice-president, secretary, and circuit counselor of the LCMS Southern Illinois District. From 2001 until 2013, he served on the Board of Trustees of American Bible Society.

Meyer has written numerous sermons and columns for Lutheran Hour Ministries, including the booklets "Coping with Cancer" and "Real Men." He coauthored *The Crosses of Lent*, in-depth Bible studies of Matthew and Prophecy in the *LifeLight* series, and authored "The Place of the Sermon in the Order of Service" in *Liturgical Preaching* for Concordia Publishing House. He has contributed to the *Concordia Journal* and *Issues in Christian Education*. His articles include "A Church Caught in the Middle," "An Urban Seminary," and "Why Go to Church?" In 2014, Meyer wrote *Timely Reflections: A Minute a Day with Dale Meyer*, a compilation of 365 daily devotions from his long-running online series, *The Meyer Minute*. This book was published by Tri-Pillar Publishing in conjunction with Concordia Seminary, St. Louis. In 2015, he wrote *Calling Us Home: A Lenten Sermon Series on 1 Peter*, published by Concordia Seminary. Meyer published *Word Alive! 52 Selected Sermons by Dale A. Meyer* in 2017 through Tri-Pillar Publishing. In November 2017, he returned to the airwaves as part-time Speaker of *The Lutheran Hour*.

Meyer has been speaking and preaching on the road for over 25 years and continues to do so. His areas of interest and study include: 1 Peter, the Church in a changing culture, and the Sabbath applied to life today. He resides in St. Louis with his wife Diane. They have two grown daughters: Elizabeth (Darren) Pittman and Catharine (Charles) Bailey, and five grandsons: Christian, Connor, Drew, Jacob, and Nicholas.

Dr. Meyer's Recommended Reading List

Why do I love books? One reason is that I can read at my own pace, pausing whenever I want to make sure I'm understanding, and stopping periodically to ask the great question, "What does this mean?" Contrast this to something on video, TV, or radio. Those media have some splendid programs, but it's harder to push pause and ponder. The producer of a media program is in charge of the pace; you're not. In reading, you can digest – not be choked by too much information coming at you too fast. Second, which yields the greatest learning and retention? From watching video / listening to audio, maybe even taking some notes, or from reading and marking up a book? For me, it's the book. And when I've marked something in one book, I can go back to my markings in another book and get connections and contrasts into my thinking. A third reason I love books is that books, so much more than modern media, best bring me the wisdom of the ages, both secular and religious. In 2017, much material was put out about Luther, and some of the media productions were excellent – but in books I can read the Reformer, not just hear excerpts. In books, I can get into his thoughts more deeply than being a less-engaged spectator staring at a screen. So also for Plato, Aristotle, Cicero, and all the great figures of classical antiquity, the fathers of the early Church, the Reformers, the philosophers of the Enlightenment, post-modernism, and so much more… Who can read it all? I can't, and that's yet another reason why I love books. I have hundreds and hundreds, probably a thousand or more books, all on shelves in the attic of the President's House. My "man cave" is in the attic! Looking at them all, I'm humbled. And if what I've learned from my books goes to my head – as pastors are tempted to think we know more than we do, because we've read about God – I can walk into the Seminary's library, and see 300,000 volumes and get to where we should all be: *humble*.

Listed below are some books referred to in *Word Alive!* or books relevant to the topics we've been pondering in these 52 sermons. Oh, the list could be longer!

On Academic Theology (but also relevant!) …
The Proper Distinction Between Law and Gospel by C.F.W. Walther. This classic is required reading for all seminarians. One of my professors, Dr. Robert

Preus, encouraged us to reread it every few years in our ministries. Great advice!

Paul and the Gift by John Barclay. This is a most scholarly work that I recommend to anyone wanting a deeper understanding of the familiar word "grace." For the reader's convenience, Dr. Barclay says you can read the introduction, then go to the book's conclusion, and as you are able, read what's in between. What's in between is extremely helpful, and well worth your time.

Here I Stand: A Life of Martin Luther by Roland Bainton. Readable by all, this classic draws you into the life of Luther, both the drama and the day-to-day issues we all face.

Luther's Works, Volume 31: Career of the Reformer. This important volume includes the *Ninety-five Theses,* which, as you know, sparked the Reformation; the *Heidelberg Disputation,* in which Luther teaches about the fear of God, which is a thread through *Word Alive!;Two Kinds of Righteousness* which helps us understand the differences between justification and sanctification; *The Freedom of a Christian,* which instructs us on faith toward God and love toward our neighbor; and other significant works of the Reformer.

Exposition of the Decalogue in Martin Chemnitz's *Loci Theologici.* It's been said that Chemnitz is the second Martin who preserved the work of the first – Martin Luther. I use Chemnitz for a class I teach on Law and Gospel in preaching. You don't speed-read Chemnitz, but take the time and effort and you'll find him a treasure trove of teaching on the Bible and Lutheranism.

Concordances: Biblical study aids are part of the transitional time we're living in. In a concordance you can find all the occurrences of any given word in the Bible; then you can find the similarities and differences in how your selected word is used. *Naves Topical Bible Concordance* is one example. Some Bibles have small concordances at the back of the book. Today, Bible students are including modern technology with their books, as our next entry shows.

Logos Bible Software is a digital Bible study library application for laity and clergy to engage the Word of God. Logos is a Bible study tool that gathers information about the Bible through smart searches and helpful guides. These biblical resources can be used for sermon preparation, teaching Bible classes, and personal study. Concordia Seminary intentionally uses Logos Bible Software in its new curriculum for the formation of pastors and deaconesses. For more information go to www.logos.com.

On Christian Community ...

Inviting Community, edited by Robert Kolb and Theodore J. Hopkins. A collection of essays about the life and witness of congregations today, including "Funding the Mission in the Twenty-First Century" by Michael Merker and Dale Meyer.

Life Together by Dietrich Bonhoeffer. Written about seminary life, this classic can also be used to teach the privilege of life together as followers of Christ gathered in your local congregation. Concordia Seminary has used this book in our efforts to build intentional community on campus.

Paul & the Gift by John Barclay. Barclay shows how Paul wanted his congregations to be different than other gatherings of people in common society, because the Gospel establishes a different value system than the value systems of the law-dominated world in which people then and now live. This should promote deep reflection on how our congregations function today. Are they different than other associations and gatherings that our parishioners experience day-in and day-out?

1 Corinthians: A Shorter Exegetical and Pastoral Commentary by Anthony Thiselton. An exegete of world repute, Thiselton looks at the dysfunction of the Corinthian congregation through a scrupulous examination of the biblical text. Reading his commentary stimulates thoughts and actions toward healthy, Gospel-based congregations today.

A Door Set Open: Grounding Change in Mission and Hope by Peter Steiner. A congregation's culture is extremely important. It supports or undercuts the teaching, preaching, and mission of the church. This book can help congregations struggling with the tsunami of cultural and technological changes.

On Preaching ...

Do I Make Myself Clear? : Why Writing Well Matters by Harold Evans. Writing skills have deteriorated in recent years, also in seminarians, hurting a pastor's ability to speak incisively and with credibility. Young or old, preachers of the Word will benefit from Evan's challenge to write well.

The Witness of Preaching by Thomas Long. This is a standard text at Concordia Seminary. Looking at various metaphors for preaching, Long settles on the preacher as a witness who goes to Scripture on behalf of the congregation, and then speaks the Word and his witness back to his hearers. He provides details about the various components of a sermon. This is also a helpful review for the experienced proclaimer.

Lend Me Your Ears: Great Speeches in History, edited by William Safire. This collection of great speeches is profitable reading. From Pericles to Martin Luther King, you'll learn history by reading these memorable speeches. A pastor or anyone who speaks in public can benefit by reading these with an eye to the rhetorical approaches and devices used in these effective speeches.

The Company of Preachers: Wisdom on Preaching, Augustine to the Present, edited by Richard Lischer. A collection of essays about all the facets of preaching, demonstrating that preaching is more complex than any of us imagine, preachers included. Just like *Lend Me Your Ears*, you don't have to read the whole book but can read randomly in this collection to your benefit.

De Oratore (On Oratory) by Cicero. The greatest orator in the history of Rome, Cicero lived in a time of national transition, just as we do. In this dialogue, various views of speaking are debated, and easily applied to the speaking demands on a busy pastor today. The demand to speak often, the great importance of writing, various ways to persuade, and many other topics make this old work still very useful.

Preaching is Worship: The Sermon in Context, edited by Paul J. Grime and Dean W. Nadasdy. This collection of essays about preaching in liturgical context opens to the pastor possible sources of sermon content and approach. Dale Meyer contributed "The Place of the Sermon in the Order of Service."

Calling Us Home: A Lenten Sermon Series on 1 Peter by Dale Meyer. The short First Epistle of Peter, only 105 verses, is rich with guidance and encouragement for living in a post-church and increasingly secular society. This sermon series provides textual notes, full sermons, and orders of worship for the Wednesdays in Lent, as well as worship sermon suggestions for the Sundays in Lent based on Series B in the three-year lectionary.

On Sanctified Living ...

Luther's Small Catechism by Martin Luther. Quoted extensively throughout this book, the *Small Catechism* summarizes biblical teaching in a simple way.

My Utmost for His Highest: Selections for the Year by Oswald Chambers. Popular from generation to generation, Chambers sets you to deep thinking about your relationship to God and Jesus.

The Sabbath by Abraham Heschel is a classic. Though not a Christian, Heschel's treatment of the Sabbath provides deep insights about the Sabbath and sermon starters for pastors.

Timely Reflections: A Minute a Day with Dale Meyer. Even though I know the author, I use this book regularly for my own spiritual reflection!

Letting Go of Anger: The 11 Most Common Anger Styles & What to Do About Them by Ronald T. Potter-Ephron and Patricia S. Potter-Ephron. I interviewed these counselors for the television show *On Main Street*, the discussion program I hosted for Lutheran Hour Ministries. This book offers practical insights helpful for handling anger and for teaching/preaching on anger. Learning about emotions can help a pastor find entry points to lead listeners from being buffeted by their feelings to the surety of God's objective Word.

Devotions for the Chronologically Gifted, edited by Les Bayer, is a collection of short devotions. You don't have to be up in years to benefit from this readable volume. Pastors: As is often the case, good devotional books can give you some great ideas for sermons.

The Lazarus Life: Spiritual Transformation for Ordinary People by Stephen W. Smith. This insightful book was written by a pastor who was on the brink of burnout. What he writes can help pastors who feel they are losing their identity in the work of ministry.

Meditating on the Word by Dietrich Bonhoeffer. This includes his thoughts on meditation and a collection of his devotions and sermons – stimulating insights into the Word.

Letters and Papers from Prison by Dietrich Bonhoeffer. Written during his imprisonment ending in execution, Bonhoeffer wrote with an earnestness that will benefit every reader.

On America's Changing Culture …

Barna Trends. The Barna Group surveys the religious beliefs and practices of Americans. With tables and short narratives, *Barna Trends* offers short snippets easily read and used. An updated volume is released every year.

The American Mind Meets the Mind of Christ, edited by Robert Kolb. A collection of essays about Christians in today's American culture, including "Living in the Land of Milk and Honey" by Dale Meyer.

Thank You for Being Late: An Optimist's Guide to Thriving in the Age of Accelerations by Thomas L. Friedman. Do you feel you can't keep up with technological changes? Friedman shows that most of us can't, and the accelerations are going to increase. This is one reason why individuals and institutions feel so disoriented. Friedman finds hope in community, but his community pales in comparison to the community the Church has to offer.

Myth of the Millennial by Ted and Chelsea Doering. Chelsea and Ted, a graduate of Concordia Seminary, will encourage you about the next leaders of our congregations. This book also includes helpful hints for older Christians. Foreword by Dale Meyer.

The Fractured Republic: Renewing America's Social Contract in the Age of Individualism by Yuval Levin. Older people look back to the 20th century and often grieve what's been lost in American life and in the institutional church. Levin shows what came together after World War II to make for that exceptional time, but also shows the seeds of change that we are now experiencing. This book is not about religion, but you will easily make the connections to the life of the church then and now.

The Vanishing Neighbor: The Transformation of American Community by Mark J. Dunkelman. Neighbors used to visit over the fence – no longer. Dunkelman shows how community today is family and friends connecting via social media, but without the physical neighborhood where you live. This has implications for congregational life and outreach.

To Change the World: The Irony, Tragedy, & Possibility of Christianity in the Late Modern World by James Davison Hunter. The author shows that "Christian" America is not going to come back, at least not in our lifetimes. What the church needs is strong institutions that articulate a theology that engages today's culture. Congregations can become thought centers, discipling members to do this engagement in their daily lives.

Timelock: How Life Got So Hectic and What You Can Do About It by Ralph Keyes. Life has gotten even more hectic since this book came out in 1991, but it got us thinking about how a Christian looks at time – and today, as we can discern from reading *Thank You for Being Late*, such faithful stewardship of life is even more needed on our heavenward way.

Topical Index

Scripture Passage Index

Endnotes

Foreword
1 Herrmann, "Remembering Frederik Gabriel Hedberg (1811-1893) in vol. 37, n. 4 of *Concordia Journal* (St. Louis: Concordia Seminary, St. Louis, 2011), 272

Introduction
1 Cicero – *De Oratore*: http://www.communicationcache.com/uploads/1/0/8/8/10887248/cicero_de_oratore.pdf
2 Martin Luther, "Preface to the Epistle of St. Paul to the Romans," in *Martin Luther's Basic Theological Writings*, 2nd Ed. ed. Timothy F. Lull and William R. Russell (Minneapolis: Fortress Press, 2005), 101
3 Peggy Noonan, "What Comes After Acheson's Creation?" *The Wall Street Journal*, Feb. 9, 2017
4 *Luther's Catechism: The Small Catechism of Dr. Martin Luther and an Exposition for Children and Adults Written in Contemporary English (Revised) by Martin Luther*, David P. Kuske (Milwaukee: Northwestern Publishing House, 1998), 1-3
5 C.F.W. Walther, *Law and Gospel: How to Read and Apply the Bible*, ed. Charles P. Schaum, John P. Hellwege, Jr., and Thomas E. Manteufel, tr. Christian C. Tiews (St. Louis: Concordia Publishing House, 2010), 9
6 Oswald Chambers, "February 7," *My Utmost for His Highest: Selections for the Year* (New York: Dodd, Mead & Company, 1935)

Week 1 – Touching the Heart of Uncle Me
1 Alexander, "I Bind unto Myself Today," *Lutheran Service Book* (St. Louis: Concordia Publishing House, 2006), 604, 2

Week 2 – My Best Two Paragraphs
1 "Confession and Absolution," *Lutheran Service Book* (St. Louis: Concordia Publishing House, 2006), 184
2 Elliott, "Just as I Am, without One Plea," *Lutheran Service Book* (St. Louis: Concordia Publishing House, 2006), 570, 1
3 *Luther's Catechism: The Small Catechism of Dr. Martin Luther and an Exposition for Children and Adults Written in Contemporary English (Revised) by Martin Luther*, David P. Kuske (Milwaukee: Northwestern Publishing House, 1998), 321
4 Ibid., 13
5 Weingartner, "In God, My Faithful God," tr. Winkworth, *The Lutheran Hymnal* (St. Louis: Concordia Publishing House, 1941), 526, 2, 4
6 Philipp Melanchthon, *Loci Communes, 1543*, tr. J.A.O. Preus, (St. Louis: Concordia Publishing House, 1992). Note: *Loci Communes, 1543* © 1992 Concordia Publishing House. Used with permission. www.cph.org.

Week 3 – Send up the Balloons!
1 Italian, 18th cent. "Glory Be to Jesus," tr. Caswall, *The Lutheran Hymnal* (St. Louis: Concordia Publishing House, 1941), 158, 4, 2
2 Berg, "Children of the Heavenly Father," *Lutheran Service Book* (St. Louis: Concordia Publishing House, 2006), 725, 1

[3] *Luther's Catechism: The Small Catechism of Dr. Martin Luther and an Exposition for Children and Adults Written in Contemporary English (Revised) by Martin Luther*, David P. Kuske (Milwaukee: Northwestern Publishing House, 1998), 6

[4] Clement of Alexandria, "Shepherd of Tender Youth," tr. Henry M. Dexter, *Lutheran Service Book* (St. Louis: Concordia Publishing House, 2006), 864, 4-5

[5] *Barna Trends 2017: What's New and What's Next at the Intersection of Faith and Culture* (Grand Rapids, MI: Baker Books, 2017), 178-179

Week 4 – "In All Good Works Increasing"
[1] Richard Lischer, *Open Secrets: A Memoir of Faith and Discovery* (New York: Broadway Books, 2001), 84

[2] Martin Luther, "Sermons on the Epistle of 1 Peter," in *The Catholic Epistles*, vol. 30 of *Luther's Works*, ed. Jaroslav Pelikan and Walter A. Hansen (St. Louis: Concordia Publishing House, 1967), 33. Note: Adapted from *Luther's Works Vol. 30* © 1967 Concordia Publishing House. Used with permission. www.cph.org.

[3] Luther, "May God Bestow on Us His Grace," *Lutheran Service Book* (St. Louis: Concordia Publishing House, 2006), 823, 3

[4] Martin Luther, "Freedom of a Christian" in *Modern History Sourcebook* by Fordham University; scanned by Gabriel Caswell. Prepared for HTML by Dr. Stephen Shoemaker; https://sourcebooks.fordham.edu/mod/luther-freedomchristian.asp

[5] Thring, "O God of Mercy, God of Might," *Lutheran Service Book* (St. Louis: Concordia Publishing House, 2006), 852, 3, 5

[6] Barna Trends 2017: What's New and What's Next at the Intersection of Faith and Culture (Grand Rapids, MI: Baker Books, 2017), 136-137

Week 5 – The Flowers of Forgiveness
[1] Nancy Newfield and Barbara Nielsen, *Hummingbird Gardens,* (New York: Houghton Miffin Company, 1996), 8

[2] J. Warren Smith, "See How These Christians Love One Another," *Christian Historical Institute,* 2013, https://christianhistoryinstitute.org/magazine/article/see-how-these-christians-love

[3] Baker, "Show Me," Chet Baker Plays the Best of Lerner and Loewe, (New York City: Riverside, 1959)

[4] Copyright by Rotary International, 1984; *The Rotarian*, November 1984, "Humor in High Office," Volume 145, No. 5, 23

[5] Scriven, "What a Friend We Have in Jesus," *Lutheran Service Book* (St. Louis: Concordia Publishing House, 2006), 770, 1

[6] Nancy Newfield and Barbara Nielsen, *Hummingbird Gardens*, (New York: Houghton Miffin Company, 1996), 12

[7] Hyun Kyung Kim, "A Sellebration of God's Love," Summer, 1998

[8] Nancy Newfield and Barbara Nielsen, *Hummingbird Gardens*, (New York: Houghton Miffin Company, 1996), 68

[9] Scholtes, "They'll Know We Are Christians," 1969

[10] Wesley, "Love Divine, All Loves Excelling," *Lutheran Service Book* (St. Louis: Concordia Publishing House, 2006), 700, 1-2

Week 6 – Baseball, Hot Dogs, Apple Pie, and Chevrolet
[1] James Hartzell, "Baseball, Hot Dogs, Apple Pie and Chevrolet," 1974

[2] Neale, "Alleluia, Song of Gladness," *Lutheran Service Book* (St. Louis: Concordia Publishing House, 2006), 417, 3-4

Week 7 – Yearning for Home

[1] Meyer, "Calling Us Home: A Lenten Sermon Series on 1 Peter," (Concordia Seminary, St. Louis, 2015), https://www.csl.edu/product/calling-us-home-a-lenten-sermon-series-on-1-peter/

[2] Schalling, "Lord, Thee I Love with All My Heart," *Lutheran Service Book* (St. Louis: Concordia Publishing House, 2006), 708, 1

[3] Burial (Commital), *Book of Common Prayer* (New York, Oxford University Press, 1952), 333

[4] Public domain, "I Love to Tell the Story" (Arabella Hankey), 1866, 4

[5] Barna Trends 2017: What's New and What's Next at the Intersection of Faith and Culture (Grand Rapids, MI: Baker Books, 2017), 179

[6] Ibid., 178

[7] Martin Luther, "Preface to the Epistle of St. Paul to the Romans," in *Martin Luther's Basic Theological Writings*, 2nd Ed. ed. Timothy F. Lull and William R. Russell (Minneapolis: Fortress Press, 2005), 101

[8] Brorson, "I Walk in Danger All the Way," tr. Ditlef Ristad, *Lutheran Service Book* (St. Louis: Concordia Publishing House, 2006), 716, 6

[9] Friedman, "Thank You for Being Late: An Optimist's Guide to Thriving in the Age of Accelerations," ed. Farrar, Straus and Giroux (New York: Farrar, Straus and Giroux, 2016), 197

[10] Zinzendorf, "Jesus, Lead Thou On," tr. Jane L. Borthwick, *Lutheran Service Book* (St. Louis: Concordia Publishing House, 2006), 718, 4

Week 8 – Graced Toward Glory

[1] Meyer, "Calling Us Home: A Lenten Sermon Series on 1 Peter," (Concordia Seminary, St. Louis, 2015), https://www.csl.edu/product/calling-us-home-a-lenten-sermon-series-on-1-peter/

[2] Martin Luther, "A Mighty Fortress is Our God," *Lutheran Service Book* (St. Louis: Concordia Publishing House, 2006), 656, 1

[3] Lyte, "Abide with Me," *Lutheran Service Book* (St. Louis: Concordia Publishing House, 2006), 878, 2

[4] Arnold Kuntz, "Till Only One Thing Matters," *Devotions for the Chronologically Gifted*, ed. Les Bayer (St. Louis: Concordia Publishing House, 1999), 46. Note: *Devotions for the Chronologically Gifted* © 1999 Concordia Publishing House. Used with permission. www.cph.org.

[5] *Luther's Catechism: The Small Catechism of Dr. Martin Luther and an Exposition for Children and Adults Written in Contemporary English (Revised) by Martin Luther*, David P. Kuske (Milwaukee: Northwestern Publishing House, 1998), 322

[6] Ringwaldt, "O Holy Spirit, Grant Us Grace," tr. Oluf H. Smeby, *Lutheran Service Book* (St. Louis: Concordia Publishing House, 2006), 693, 1-2

Week 9 – The Lonely Battles of Jesus

[1] *On Main Street* content copyrighted from 1989 -2003, owned by the International Lutheran Laymen's League, content used with permission of Lutheran Hour Ministries, all rights reserved

[2] *Luther's Catechism: The Small Catechism of Dr. Martin Luther and an Exposition for Children and Adults Written in Contemporary English (Revised) by Martin Luther*, David P. Kuske (Milwaukee: Northwestern Publishing House, 1998), 6

[3] Scriven, "What a Friend We Have in Jesus," *Lutheran Service Book* (St. Louis: Concordia Publishing House, 2006), 770, 1

[4] Dietrich Bonhoeffer, *Life Together,* tr. by John W. Doberstein (London: SCM Press, Ltd., 1954), 21

[5] Pollock, "Jesus in Your Dying Woes," *Lutheran Service Book* (St. Louis: Concordia Publishing House, 2006), 447, 10-12

[6] Armstrong, "Nobody Knows the Trouble I've Seen," Louis and The Good Book (New York: MCA Records, 1958)

[7] *The Bonhoeffer Reader,* ed. Clifford J. Green and Michael Dejonge, (Minneapolis: Fortress Press, 2013), 560

Week 10 – Time, My Temple

[1] Ralph Keyes, *Timelock: How Life Got So Hectic and What You Can Do About It* (New York: Harper Collins, 1991), 123

[2] J. B. Phillips, *Your God Is Too Small* (London: The Epsworth Press, 1952)

[3] Watts [stanzas] and Lowry [refrain], "Come, We That Love the Lord," *Lutheran Service Book* (St. Louis: Concordia Publishing House, 2006), 669, 4 and refrain

[4] Monsell, "Fight the Good Fight," *Lutheran Service Book* (St. Louis: Concordia Publishing House, 2006), 664, 2

Week 11 – The Triumph Song

[1] *Works of Martin Luther with Introductions and Notes,* vol. 2 (Philadelphia: A.J. Holman, 1915), 373

[2] How, "For All the Saints," *Lutheran Service Book* (St. Louis: Concordia Publishing House, 2006), 677, 5

[3] "Proper Preface," *Lutheran Service Book* (St. Louis: Concordia Publishing House, 2006), 208

[4] "Sanctus," *Lutheran Service Book* (St. Louis: Concordia Publishing House, 2006), 195

[5] Baring-Gould, "Onward, Christian Soldiers," *Lutheran Worship* (St. Louis: Concordia Publishing House, 1986), 518, 4

[6] *Luther's Catechism: The Small Catechism of Dr. Martin Luther and an Exposition for Children and Adults Written in Contemporary English (Revised) by Martin Luther,* David P. Kuske (Milwaukee: Northwestern Publishing House, 1998), 1

[7] F.B.P., "Jerusalem, My Happy Home," *Lutheran Service Book* (St. Louis: Concordia Publishing House, 2006), 673, 1, 6

[8] William Barclay, "In the Hand of God," in *For All the Saints,* vol. II (Delhi, NY: American Lutheran Publicity Bureau, 1995), 250

[9] Herrmann, "Remembering Frederik Gabriel Hedberg (1811-1893) in vol. 37, n. 4 of *Concordia Journal* (St. Louis: Concordia Seminary, St. Louis, 2011), 272

Week 12 – Your Identity: Forgiven by the Holy Cross

[1] "Here's a List of 58 Gender Options for Facebook Users," *ABC News,* Feb. 13, 2014, http://abcnews.go.com/blogs/headlines/2014/02/heres-a-list-of-58-gender-options-for-facebook-users/

[2] Stephen W. Smith, *The Lazarus Life: Spiritual Transformation for Ordinary People* (Colorado Springs, CO: David C. Cook, 2008), 146

[3] Watts, "When I Survey the Wondrous Cross," *Lutheran Service Book* (St. Louis: Concordia Publishing House, 2006), 425, 1

[4] Dietrich Bonhoeffer, "Who Am I?" Accessed 10/22/2017, http://www.dbonhoeffer.org/who-was-db2.htm

[5] Kelly, "Stricken, Smitten, and Afflicted," *Lutheran Service Book* (St. Louis: Concordia Publishing House, 2006), 451, 3, 4

6 *Luther's Catechism: The Small Catechism of Dr. Martin Luther and an Exposition for Children and Adults Written in Contemporary English (Revised) by Martin Luther*, David P. Kuske (Milwaukee: Northwestern Publishing House, 1998), *13*

7 *"Formula of Concord, Solid Declaration, III, 6"* in *The Book of Concord*, edited by Kolb and Wengert (Minneapolis: Fortress Press, 2000), 562

Week 13 – Christ the Victor!

1 Homburg, "Christ, the Life of All the Living," tr. Winkworth, *Lutheran Service Book* (St. Louis: Concordia Publishing House, 2006), 420, 1

2 von Zinzendorf, "Jesus, Thy Blood and Righteousness," *Lutheran Service Book* (St. Louis: Concordia Publishing House, 2006), 563, 1

3 Catherine Marshall, *A Man Called Peter: The Story of Peter Marshall* (New York: McGraw-Hill Book Company, 1951), 273

4 Robert M. Herhold, *Learning to Die, Learning to Live* (Philadelphia: Fortress Press, 1976), 9

5 Oscar Hammerstein II, "I Whistle a Happy Tune," *The King and I*, 1951

6 *Luther's Catechism: The Small Catechism of Dr. Martin Luther and an Exposition for Children and Adults Written in Contemporary English (Revised) by Martin Luther*, David P. Kuske (Milwaukee: Northwestern Publishing House, 1998), 1

7 Gerhardt, "Awake, My Heart, with Gladness," tr. John Kelly, *Lutheran Service Book* (St. Louis: Concordia Publishing House, 2006), 467, 1, 3

8 Barna Trends 2017: What's New and What's Next at the Intersection of Faith and Culture (Grand Rapids, MI: Baker Books, 2017), 178-179

Week 14 – Schedule Hope

1 WA 12, 268 (Luther, Martin: *D. Martin Luthers Werke*. 120 vols. Weimar, 1883–2009)

2 Schalling, "Lord, Thee I Love with All My Heart," *Lutheran Service Book* (St. Louis: Concordia Publishing House, 2006), 708, 1, 3

3 Möller, "I am Content! My Jesus Ever Lives," tr. August Crull, *Lutheran Service Book* (St. Louis: Concordia Publishing House, 2006), 468, 1, 4

4 Plato, vol. 3 of *Plato in Twelve Volumes*, translated by W.R.M. Lamb, (London: William Heinemann Ltd. 1967), 457c

Week 15 – Happy Coping

1 Fred M. Rogers, "Won't You Be My Neighbor?" The Fred Rogers Company, 1967

2 *Luther's Catechism: The Small Catechism of Dr. Martin Luther and an Exposition for Children and Adults Written in Contemporary English (Revised) by Martin Luther*, David P. Kuske (Milwaukee: Northwestern Publishing House, 1998), 320

3 Ibid., 9

4 Ibid., 13

5 Bonar, "Here, O My Lord, I See Thee Face to Face," *Lutheran Service Book* (St. Louis: Concordia Publishing House, 2006), 631, 4-5

Week 16 – Who Is Your Hireling?

1 von Hayn, "I Am Jesus' Little Lamb" tr. *The Lutheran Hymnal, Lutheran Service Book* (St. Louis: Concordia Publishing House, 2006), 740, 1

2 *Luther's Catechism: The Small Catechism of Dr. Martin Luther and an Exposition for Children and Adults Written in Contemporary English (Revised) by Martin Luther*, David P. Kuske (Milwaukee: Northwestern Publishing House, 1998), 7

3 Ibid., 1

[4] Hymns for the Young, 4th ed., London, "Savior, Like a Shepherd Lead Us," *Lutheran Service Book* (St. Louis: Concordia Publishing House, 2006), 711, 1-2

Week 17 – When You Raise Your Heads from Prayer
[1] *Luther's Catechism: The Small Catechism of Dr. Martin Luther and an Exposition for Children and Adults Written in Contemporary English (Revised) by Martin Luther*, David P. Kuske (Milwaukee: Northwestern Publishing House, 1998), 316-317
[2] Paul V. Marshall, vol.1 of *Prayer Book Parallels* (New York: Church Publishing, 2004), 143, 1979-II

Week 18 – A Pastor's Prayer for His People
[1] Funcke, "Draw Us to Thee," tr. Crull, *Lutheran Service Book* (St. Louis: Concordia Publishing House, 2006), 701, 1

Week 19 – *"Mom!"*
[1] Medley, "I Know that My Redeemer Lives," *Lutheran Worship* (St. Louis: Concordia Publishing House, 1982), 264, 5
[2] *Luther's Catechism: The Small Catechism of Dr. Martin Luther and an Exposition for Children and Adults Written in Contemporary English (Revised) by Martin Luther*, David P. Kuske (Milwaukee: Northwestern Publishing House, 1998), 1
[3] Ibid., 7
[4] German, 16th cent., "Lo, How a Rose E'er Blooming," tr. John C. Mattes, *Lutheran Service Book* (St. Louis: Concordia Publishing House, 2006), 359, 4
[5] Rinckhart, "Now Thank We All Our God," tr. Winkworth, *Lutheran Service Book* (St. Louis: Concordia Publishing House, 2006), 895, 1
[6] Paul W. Nesper, "Mother's Day" in *Biblical Texts* 2nd ed., (Columbus, Ohio: The Wartburg Press, 1952), 113

Week 20 – Word Alive! Connections and Conversations
[1] Toplady, "Rock of Ages, Cleft for Me," *Lutheran Service Book* (St. Louis: Concordia Publishing House, 2006), 761, 3
[2] Martin Luther, "A Mighty Fortress is Our God," *Lutheran Service Book* (St. Louis: Concordia Publishing House, 2006), 656, 1
[3] *Luther's Catechism: The Small Catechism of Dr. Martin Luther and an Exposition for Children and Adults Written in Contemporary English (Revised) by Martin Luther*, David P. Kuske (Milwaukee: Northwestern Publishing House, 1998), 5
[4] Harry Y. Gamble, *Books and Readers in the Early Church: A History of Early Christian Texts,* (New Haven: Yale University Press, 1995), 4
[5] *"Smalcald Articles, XII,"* in *The Book of Concord*, edited by Kolb and Wengert, (Minneapolis: Fortress Press, 2000), 324-325
[6] *Luther's Catechism: The Small Catechism of Dr. Martin Luther and an Exposition for Children and Adults Written in Contemporary English (Revised) by Martin Luther*, David P. Kuske (Milwaukee: Northwestern Publishing House, 1998), 1
[7] "Collect for the Church," *Lutheran Service Book*, (St. Louis: Concordia Publishing House, 2006), 102
[8] Nancy T. Ammerman, "America's Changing Religious and Cultural Landscape and its Implications for Theological Education," in vol. 40, no. 1 of *Theological Education* (Pittsburgh: The Association of Theological Schools, 2014), 33
[9] Concordia Seminary, St. Louis Motto

[10] von Zinzendorf, "Jesus, Thy Blood and Righteousness," *Lutheran Service Book* (St. Louis: Concordia Publishing House, 2006), 563, 1

[11] http://www.preces-latinae.org/thesaurus/Hymni/DiesIrae.html

[12] Loy, "The Gospel Shows the Father's Grace," *Lutheran Service Book* (St. Louis: Concordia Publishing House, 2006), 580, 1, 3, 4

[13] Franzmann, "O God, O Lord of Heaven and Earth," *Lutheran Service Book* (St. Louis: Concordia Publishing House, 2006), 834, 4

Week 21 – Your God, My God

[1] *Luther's Catechism: The Small Catechism of Dr. Martin Luther and an Exposition for Children and Adults Written in Contemporary English (Revised) by Martin Luther*, David P. Kuske (Milwaukee: Northwestern Publishing House, 1998), 1

[2] Ibid., 2

[3] Ibid., 6

[4] Gramann, "My Soul, Now Praise Your Maker," tr. Catherine Winkworth, *Lutheran Service Book* (St. Louis: Concordia Publishing House, 2006), 820, 1, 4

Week 22 – You and the Centurion

[1] Scriven, "What a Friend We Have in Jesus," *The Lutheran Hymnal* (St. Louis: Concordia Publishing House, 1941), 457, 1

[2] *Luther's Catechism: The Small Catechism of Dr. Martin Luther and an Exposition for Children and Adults Written in Contemporary English (Revised) by Martin Luther*, David P. Kuske (Milwaukee: Northwestern Publishing House, 1998), 8

[3] "How Firm a Foundation," *Lutheran Service Book* (St. Louis: Concordia Publishing House, 2006), 728, 1-3

Week 23 – The Angels Laugh; the Devils Weep

[1] Roland Bainton, *Here I Stand: A Life of Martin Luther* (Peabody, MA: Hendrickson Publishers, 2012), 293

[2] Ibid., 296

[3] Ibid.

[4] Ibid., 297

[5] von Pfeil, "Oh, Blest the House, Whate'er Befall," tr. Winkworth, *The Lutheran Hymnal* (St. Louis: Concordia Publishing House, 1941), 625, 1

[6] Roland Bainton, *Here I Stand: A Life of Martin Luther* (Peabody, MA: Hendrickson Publishers, 2012), 311

[7] Ibid., 307-308

[8] Ibid., 308

[9] Ibid., 295

[10] von Pfeil, "Oh, Blest the House," tr. Winkworth, *Lutheran Service Book* (St. Louis: Concordia Publishing House, 2006), 862, 1

[11] Ellerton, "O Father, All Creating," *Lutheran Service Book* (St. Louis: Concordia Publishing House, 2006), 858, 1, 4

Week 24 – A Man and His Toys

[1] Jorge Valdés, *Coming Clean: The True Story of a Cocaine Drug Lord and His Unexpected Encounter with God* (Colorado Springs, Colorado: Waterbrook Press, 1999)

[2] *On Main Street* content copyrighted from 1989 -2003, owned by the International Lutheran Laymen's League, content used with permission of Lutheran Hour Ministries, all rights reserved

[3] *Luther's Catechism: The Small Catechism of Dr. Martin Luther and an Exposition for Children and Adults Written in Contemporary English (Revised) by Martin Luther*, David P. Kuske (Milwaukee: Northwestern Publishing House, 1998), 7

[4] Franck, "Jesus, Priceless Treasure," tr. Catherine Winkworth, *Lutheran Service Book* (St. Louis: Concordia Publishing House, 2006), 743, 3

[5] Ibid., 4

[6] Mote, "My Hope Is Built on Nothing Less," *Lutheran Service Book* (St. Louis: Concordia Publishing House, 2006), 575, 3

Week 25 – Let the Lambs Leap

[1] *Luther's Catechism: The Small Catechism of Dr. Martin Luther and an Exposition for Children and Adults Written in Contemporary English (Revised) by Martin Luther*, David P. Kuske (Milwaukee: Northwestern Publishing House, 1998), 1

[2] Schirmer, "O Holy Spirit, Enter In," tr. Catherine Winkworth, st. 1, tr. *The Lutheran Hymnal*, 1941, st. 2, *Lutheran Service Book* (St. Louis: Concordia Publishing House, 2006), 913, 1-2

[3] Aristotle, *Rhetoric*, 1356a

Week 26 – Cross and Country

[1] How, "To Thee, Our God, We Fly," *The Lutheran Hymnal* (St. Louis: Concordia Publishing House, 1941), 580, 1

[2] James Madison, "The Federalist No. 51," in Alexander Hamilton, James Madison, and John Jay, *The Federalist: A Commentary on the Constitution of the United States being a Collection of Essays Written in Support of the Constitution Agreed upon September 17, 1787, by The Federal Convention*, ed. Sherman F. Mitchell (Washington: National Home Library Foundation, 1937), 337

[3] *Luther's Catechism: The Small Catechism of Dr. Martin Luther and an Exposition for Children and Adults Written in Contemporary English (Revised) by Martin Luther*, David P. Kuske (Milwaukee: Northwestern Publishing House, 1998), 7

[4] von Löwenstern, "Lord of Our Life," tr. Philip Pusey, *Lutheran Service Book* (St. Louis: Concordia Publishing House, 2006), 659, 1, 3, 4

[5] Aristotle, *Rhetoric*, 1413b

Week 27 – Kindling the Commitment

[1] *Morgen- und Abend-segen*, Waldenburg, "With the Lord Begin Your Task," tr. Polack, *Lutheran Worship* (St. Louis: Concordia Publishing House, 1982), 483, 2

[2] *The Concordia Pulpit for 1936: Volume 7*, ed. Martin S. Sommer (St. Louis: Concordia Publishing House, 1935), 474. Note: *The Concordia Pulpit for 1936 Volume 7* © 1936 Concordia Publishing House. Used with permission. www.cph.org.

[3] Ibid., 62. Note: *The Concordia Pulpit for 1936 Volume 7* © 1936 Concordia Publishing House. Used with permission. www.cph.org.

[4] *Luther's Catechism: The Small Catechism of Dr. Martin Luther and an Exposition for Children and Adults Written in Contemporary English (Revised) by Martin Luther*, David P. Kuske (Milwaukee: Northwestern Publishing House, 1998), 5

[5] Watts, "When I Survey the Wondrous Cross," *Lutheran Service Book* (St. Louis: Concordia Publishing House, 2006), 425, 4

[6] *The Concordia Pulpit for 1936: Volume 7*, ed. Martin S. Sommer (St. Louis: Concordia Publishing House, 1935), 64. Note: *The Concordia Pulpit for 1936 Volume 7* © 1936 Concordia Publishing House. Used with permission. www.cph.org.

[7] Martin Luther, "Preface to the Epistle of St. Paul to the Romans," in *Martin Luther's Basic Theological Writings*, 2nd Ed. ed. Timothy F. Lull and William R. Russell (Minneapolis: Fortress Press, 2005), 101

[8] Bathurst, "Oh, for a Faith that Will Not Shrink," *The Lutheran Hymnal* (St. Louis: Concordia Publishing House, 1941), 396, 6

[9] *Luther's Catechism: The Small Catechism of Dr. Martin Luther and an Exposition for Children and Adults Written in Contemporary English (Revised) by Martin Luther*, David P. Kuske (Milwaukee: Northwestern Publishing House, 1998), 7

[10] Monsell, "Fight the Good Fight," *Lutheran Service Book* (St. Louis: Concordia Publishing House, 2006), 664, 3, 4

Week 28 – Nearer God's Heart
[1] Dorothy Frances Gurney, "God's Garden," in *Poems* (London: Country Life, 1913), 1
[2] *Luther's Catechism: The Small Catechism of Dr. Martin Luther and an Exposition for Children and Adults Written in Contemporary English (Revised) by Martin Luther*, David P. Kuske (Milwaukee: Northwestern Publishing House, 1998), 1
[3] Alderson, "Lord of Glory, You Have Bought Us," *Lutheran Service Book* (St. Louis: Concordia Publishing House, 2006), 851, 3
[4] Barna Trends 2017: What's New and What's Next at the Intersection of Faith and Culture (Grand Rapids, MI: Baker Books, 2017), 136

Week 29 – *Jesus, Huh?*
[1] *Münsterisch Gesangbuch*, "Beautiful Savior," tr. Seiss, *Lutheran Service Book* (St. Louis: Concordia Publishing House, 2006), 537, 4
[2] WA 40.1: 369.13-25 (Luther, Martin: *D. Martin Luthers Werke*. 120 vols. Weimar, 1883–2009)
[3] Irving Berlin, "Doin' What Comes Natur'lly," in *Annie, Get Your Gun*, 1950
[4] *Luther's Catechism: The Small Catechism of Dr. Martin Luther and an Exposition for Children and Adults Written in Contemporary English (Revised) by Martin Luther*, David P. Kuske (Milwaukee: Northwestern Publishing House, 1998), 1
[5] Bathurst, "Oh, for a Faith That Will Not Shrink," *The Lutheran Hymnal* (St. Louis: Concordia Publishing House, 1941), 396, 1, 2, 6

Week 30 – God's Mouth House
[1] Marc J. Dunkelman, *The Vanishing Neighbor: The Transformation of American Community* (New York: W.W. Norton & Company, 2014), 18
[2] WA 10.1.2, 48 (Luther, Martin: *D. Martin Luthers Werke*. 120 vols. Weimar, 1883–2009)
[3] *Luther's Catechism: The Small Catechism of Dr. Martin Luther and an Exposition for Children and Adults Written in Contemporary English (Revised) by Martin Luther*, David P. Kuske (Milwaukee: Northwestern Publishing House, 1998), 1
[4] Neumeister, "I Know My Faith Is Founded," tr. *The Lutheran Hymnal*, 1941, *Lutheran Service Book* (St. Louis: Concordia Publishing House, 2006), 587, 1

Week 31 – Come Ye Apart
[1] Bruce D Prewer, *Australian Prayers* (Adelaide: Lutheran Publishing House, 1983), 179
[2] *Luther's Catechism: The Small Catechism of Dr. Martin Luther and an Exposition for Children and Adults Written in Contemporary English (Revised) by Martin Luther*, David P. Kuske (Milwaukee: Northwestern Publishing House, 1998), 1
[3] Ibid., 7

[4] Elliott, "Just as I Am, without One Plea," *Lutheran Service Book* (St. Louis: Concordia Publishing House, 2006), 570, 1, 3, 4

Week 32 – The Gift of Anger

[1] Sister Helen Prejean, *Dead Man Walking: The Eyewitness Account of the Death Penalty That Sparked a National Debate* (New York: Random House, 1993)

[2] *On Main Street* content copyrighted from 1989 -2003, owned by the International Lutheran Laymen's League, content used with permission of Lutheran Hour Ministries, all rights reserved

[3] Ronald T. Potter-Ephron and Patricia S. Potter-Ephron, *Letting Go of Anger: The 10 Most Common Anger Styles & What to Do about Them* (Oakland, CA: New Harbinger Books, 1995), 14

[4] Debbie Morris, *Forgiving the Dead Man Walking* (Grand Rapids, MI: Zondervan, 1998)

[5] Ibid., 223

[6] Ibid., 251

[7] *Luther's Catechism: The Small Catechism of Dr. Martin Luther and an Exposition for Children and Adults Written in Contemporary English (Revised) by Martin Luther*, David P. Kuske (Milwaukee: Northwestern Publishing House, 1998), 1

[8] Landstad, "To Thee, Omniscient Lord of All," tr. Carl Döving, *Lutheran Service Book* (St. Louis: Concordia Publishing House, 2006), 613, 1-2

[9] Martin Chemnitz, *Loci Theologici*, tr. J.A.O Preus (St. Louis: Concordia Publishing House, 2008), 738-740. Note: Adapted from *Loci Theologici* © 2008 Concordia Publishing House. Used with permission. www.cph.org.

Week 33 – Don't Forget!

[1] *Luther's Catechism: The Small Catechism of Dr. Martin Luther and an Exposition for Children and Adults Written in Contemporary English (Revised) by Martin Luther*, David P. Kuske (Milwaukee: Northwestern Publishing House, 1998), 1

[2] Schalling, "Lord, Thee I Love with All My Heart," tr. Catherine Winkworth, *Lutheran Service Book* (St. Louis: Concordia Publishing House, 2006), 708, 1

[3] Martin Luther, "Against Hanswurst, 1541," in *Church and Ministry III*, ed. Eric W. Gritsch, vol. 41 of *Luther's Works* (Philadelphia: Fortress Press, 1966), 216

Week 34 – Do Not Grumble!

[1] *The Gong Show*, created by Chris Bearde, directed by John Dorsey and Terry Kyne, produced by Chuck Barris Productions, NBC, 1976-1980

[2] *Luther's Catechism: The Small Catechism of Dr. Martin Luther and an Exposition for Children and Adults Written in Contemporary English (Revised) by Martin Luther*, David P. Kuske (Milwaukee: Northwestern Publishing House, 1998), 1

[3] Heermann, "O God, My Faithful God," tr. Winkworth, *Lutheran Service Book* (St. Louis: Concordia Publishing House, 2006), 696, 3-4

Week 35 – By Grace Alone, Grace in His Son

[1] Scheidt, "By Grace I'm Saved, Grace Free and Boundless," tr. composite, *The Lutheran Hymnal* (St. Louis: Concordia Publishing House, 1941), 373, 4-5

[2] Robinson, "Come, Thou Fount of Every Blessing," *Lutheran Service Book* (St. Louis: Concordia Publishing House, 2006), 686, 3

[3] Toplady, "Rock of Ages, Cleft for Me," *Lutheran Service Book* (St. Louis: Concordia Publishing House, 2006), 761, 3

[4] Martin Luther, "Heidelberg Disputation, 1518," in *Career of the Reformer I*, ed. Harold J. Grimm, vol. 31 of *Luther's Works*, ed. Jaroslav Pelikan and Helmut T. Lehman (Philadelphia: Muhlenberg/Fortress; St. Louis: Concordia Publishing House, 1957), 40

[5] Dietrich Bonhoeffer, *Life Together,* tr. by John W. Doberstein (London: SCM Press, Ltd., 1954), 96

[6] Robinson, "Come, Thou Fount of Every Blessing," *Lutheran Service Book* (St. Louis: Concordia Publishing House, 2006), 686, 1, 3

Week 36 – Touching People

[1] *Luther's Catechism: The Small Catechism of Dr. Martin Luther and an Exposition for Children and Adults Written in Contemporary English (Revised) by Martin Luther*, David P. Kuske (Milwaukee: Northwestern Publishing House, 1998), 1

[2] Ibid., 200

[3] Bahnmaier, "Spread the Reign of God the Lord," tr. composite (St. Louis: Concordia Publishing House, 2006), 830, 1, 6

Week 37 – Remember the Homeless

[1] Heermann, "O Christ, Our True and Only Light," tr. Catherine Winkworth, *Lutheran Service Book* (St. Louis: Concordia Publishing House, 2006), 839, 1, 3, 5

Week 38 – The Glove Compartment God

[1] *On Main Street* content copyrighted from 1989 -2003, owned by the International Lutheran Laymen's League, content used with permission of Lutheran Hour Ministries, all rights reserved

[2] Schröder, "One Thing's Needful," tr. Cox, *Lutheran Service Book* (St. Louis: Concordia Publishing House, 2006), 536, 1, 5

[3] Fawcett, "Blest Be the Tie That Binds," *Lutheran Service Book* (St. Louis: Concordia Publishing House, 2006), 649, 5

Week 39 – Surely the Lord Is in This Place

[1] Walther, C.F.W. *Church and Ministry (Kirche und Amt)*. Mueller, J.T. (tr.) (St. Louis: Concordia Publishing House, 1987), 23. Note: *Church and Ministry* © 1987 Concordia Publishing House. Used with permission. www.cph.org.

[2] Rees, "Holy Spirit, Ever Dwelling," *Lutheran Service Book* (St. Louis: Concordia Publishing House, 2006), 650, 2-3

Week 40 – It Is Well with My Soul

[1] Allen, "Today Your Mercy Calls Us," *Lutheran Service Book* (St. Louis: Concordia Publishing House, 2006), 915, 4

[2] Spafford, "When Peace, like a River," *Lutheran Service Book* (St. Louis: Concordia Publishing House, 2006), 763, 1

[3] LuJuana R. Butts, *Lutheran Woman's Quarterly*, Winter 2006, 2

[4] Mote, "My Hope Is Built on Nothing Less," *Lutheran Service Book* (St. Louis: Concordia Publishing House, 2006), 575, 2-3 and refrain

Week 41 – Jesus, Abide with Me!

[1] Bonar, "I Heard the Voice of Jesus Say," *Lutheran Service Book* (St. Louis: Concordia Publishing House, 2006), 699, 1

[2] Lyte, "Abide with Me," *Lutheran Service Book* (St. Louis: Concordia Publishing House, 2006), 878, 2, 6

[3] Martin Luther, "Freedom of a Christian" in *Modern History Sourcebook* by Fordham University; scanned by Gabriel Caswell. Prepared for HTML by Dr. Stephen Shoemaker; https://sourcebooks.fordham.edu/mod/luther-freedomchristian.asp

[4] Noel, "At the Name of Jesus," *Lutheran Service Book* (St. Louis: Concordia Publishing House, 2006), 512, 5, 6

Week 42 – A Tattered Security Blanket
[1] Glenn Taylor and Rod Wilson, *Helping Angry People: A Short-term Structured Model for Pastoral Counselors* (Grand Rapids, MI: Baker Books, 1997), 38
[2] Bonar, "Thy Works, Not Mine, O Christ," *Lutheran Service Book* (St. Louis: Concordia Publishing House, 2006), 565, 3-5 and refrain
[3] Martin Luther, "Heidelberg Disputation, 1518," in *Career of the Reformer I*, ed. Harold J. Grimm, vol. 31 of *Luther's Works*, ed. Jaroslav Pelikan and Helmut T. Lehman (Philadelphia: Muhlenberg/Fortress; St. Louis: Concordia Publishing House, 1957), 40
[4] John Barclay, *Paul & the Gift* (Grand Rapids: William B. Eerdmans Publishing Company, 2015), 571
[5] Toplady, "Rock of Ages, Cleft for Me," *Lutheran Service Book* (St. Louis: Concordia Publishing House, 2006), 761, 3

Week 43 – Freedom in Christ
[1] Luther, "A Mighty Fortress Is Our God," tr. composite, *Lutheran Service Book* (St. Louis: Concordia Publishing House, 2006), 656, 1, 3
[2] Ibid., 2
[3] Martin Luther, "The First Thesis" of *Luther's Ninety-Five Theses*, tr. C.M. Jacobs (Philadelphia: Fortress Press, 1957), 7
[4] Martin Luther, "Heidelberg Disputation, 1518," in *Career of the Reformer I*, ed. Harold J. Grimm, vol. 31 of *Luther's Works*, ed. Jaroslav Pelikan and Helmut T. Lehman (Philadelphia: Muhlenberg/Fortress; St. Louis: Concordia Publishing House, 1957), 40
[5] *Luther's Catechism: The Small Catechism of Dr. Martin Luther and an Exposition for Children and Adults Written in Contemporary English (Revised) by Martin Luther*, David P. Kuske (Milwaukee: Northwestern Publishing House, 1998), 151
[6] Toplady, "Rock of Ages, Cleft for Me," *Lutheran Service Book* (St. Louis: Concordia Publishing House, 2006), 761, 1-2
[7] Philipp Melanchthon, *Loci Communes, 1543*, tr. J.A.O. Preus, (St. Louis: Concordia Publishing House, 1992). Note: *Loci Communes, 1543* © 1992 Concordia Publishing House. Used with permission. www.cph.org.

Week 44 – Live with Forever in Mind
[1] Newton, "Come, My Soul, Thy Suit Prepare," *The Lutheran Hymnal* (St. Louis: Concordia Publishing House, 1941), 459, 1, 6, 7
[2] Fawcett, "Blest Be the Tie That Binds," *Lutheran Service Book* (St. Louis: Concordia Publishing House, 2006), 649, 5
[3] "Hark! A Thrilling Voice is Sounding," tr. Edward Caswall, *Lutheran Service Book* (St. Louis: Concordia Publishing House, 2006), 345, 1, 2, 4
[4] Cesander, "A Penitential Hymn," in vol. 25, no. 1 of *The Lutheran Companion* (Rock Island, Illinois: 1917), 312, 6
[5] Taylor, "I'm But a Stranger Here," *Lutheran Service Book* (St. Louis: Concordia Publishing House, 2006), 748
[6] Institutio Oratoria, XI, 2. 44 (https://ryanfb.github.io/loebolus-data/L124N.pdf)

Week 45 – "God Setteth the Solitary in Families"
[1] *Luther's Catechism: The Small Catechism of Dr. Martin Luther and an Exposition for Children and Adults Written in Contemporary English (Revised) by Martin Luther*, David P. Kuske (Milwaukee: Northwestern Publishing House, 1998), 7
[2] Rinckhart, "Now Thank We All Our God," tr. Winkworth, *Lutheran Service Book* (St. Louis: Concordia Publishing House, 2006), 895, 1-2

Week 46 – Castles Crumble When Christ Is King
[1] Bridges, "Crown Him with Many Crowns," *Lutheran Service Book* (St. Louis: Concordia Publishing House, 2006), 525, 1
[2] C.S. Lewis, *Mere Christianity* (New York: HarperCollins Publishers, 2001), 196-197
[3] Held, "Come, Oh, Come, Thou Quickening Spirit," tr. Charles Schaeffer, *The Lutheran Hymnal* (St. Louis: Concordia Publishing House, 1941), 226, 4
[4] *Luther's Catechism: The Small Catechism of Dr. Martin Luther and an Exposition for Children and Adults Written in Contemporary English (Revised) by Martin Luther*, David P. Kuske (Milwaukee: Northwestern Publishing House, 1998), 6
[5] Wesley, "Lo! He Comes with Clouds Descending," *Lutheran Service Book* (St. Louis: Concordia Publishing House, 2006), 336, 2, 4
[6] John Barclay, *Paul & the Gift* (Grand Rapids: William B. Eerdmans Publishing Company, 2015), 104
[7] Martin Luther, "Heidelberg Disputation, 1518," in *Career of the Reformer I*, ed. Harold J. Grimm, vol. 31 of *Luther's Works*, ed. Jaroslav Pelikan and Helmut T. Lehman (Philadelphia: Muhlenberg/Fortress; St. Louis: Concordia Publishing House, 1957), 40
[8] John Barclay, *Paul & the Gift* (Grand Rapids: William B. Eerdmans Publishing Company, 2015), 571

Week 47 – The Darkness God Sends
[1] Ronald T. Potter-Ephron and Patricia S. Potter-Ephron, *Letting Go of Anger: The 10 Most Common Anger Styles & What to Do about Them* (Oakland, CA: New Harbinger Publications, 1995), 14
[2] Maurus, "Creator Spirit, by Whose Aid," tr. John Dryden, *Lutheran Service Book* (St. Louis: Concordia Publishing House, 2006), 500, 1-2
[3] C.F.W. Walther, *"The Proper Distinction Between Law and Gospel,"* (St. Louis, Concordia Publishing House, 1986), 312. Note: *The Proper Distinction Between Law and Gospel* © 1986 Concordia Publishing House. Used with permission. www.cph.org.

Week 48 – Stir up Thy Power, O Lord!
[1] "First Sunday in Advent: Collect," *The Lutheran Hymnal* (St. Louis: Concordia Publishing House, 1941), 54. Note: Collects from *The Lutheran Hymnal* © 1941 Concordia Publishing House. Used with permission. www.cph.org.
[2] Coffin, "On Jordan's Bank the Baptist's Cry," tr. Chandler *The Lutheran Hymnal* (St. Louis: Concordia Publishing House, 1941), 63, 1
[3] Martin Luther, "III. The Discussion of the Doctrine of Personal Faith and the Faith of Others; Also, of Faith and the Baptism of Children," in vol. 2 of *The Complete Sermons of Martin Luther,* (Harrington: Delmarva Publications, Inc., 2000), 63
[4] Gerhard, "O Lord, How Shall I Meet You," *Lutheran Service Book* (St. Louis: Concordia Publishing House, 2006), 334, 4, 5
[5] "Collect for the Church," *Lutheran Service Book*, (St. Louis: Concordia Publishing House, 2006), 102

Week 49 – "Not a Creature Was Stirring"
[1] Clement Clarke Moore, "A Visit from St. Nicholas," in *Poems* (New York: Bartlett and Welford), 1844
[2] "First Sunday in Advent: Collect," *The Lutheran Hymnal* (St. Louis: Concordia Publishing House, 1941), 54. Note: Collects from *The Lutheran Hymnal* © 1941 Concordia Publishing House. Used with permission. www.cph.org.
[3] Lyte, "Abide with Me," *Lutheran Service Book* (St. Louis: Concordia Publishing House, 2006), 878, 2
[4] *Luther's Catechism: The Small Catechism of Dr. Martin Luther and an Exposition for Children and Adults Written in Contemporary English (Revised) by Martin Luther*, David P. Kuske (Milwaukee: Northwestern Publishing House, 1998), 8
[5] Weissel, "Lift Up Your Heads, Ye Mighty Gates," tr. Catherine Winkworth, *The Lutheran Hymnal* (St. Louis: Concordia Publishing House, 1941), 73, 4, 5

Week 50 – The Common Things
[1] Luther, "From Heaven Above to Earth I Come," tr. Winkworth, *The Lutheran Hymnal* (St. Louis: Concordia Publishing House, 1941), 85, 13
[2] *Luther's Catechism: The Small Catechism of Dr. Martin Luther and an Exposition for Children and Adults Written in Contemporary English (Revised) by Martin Luther*, David P. Kuske (Milwaukee: Northwestern Publishing House, 1998), 9
[3] Neumeister, "I Know My Faith Is Founded," tr. *The Lutheran Hymnal*, 1941, *Lutheran Service Book* (St. Louis: Concordia Publishing House, 2006), 587, 1, 3
[4] Institutio Oratoria, XI, 2. 44 (https://ryanfb.github.io/loebolus-data/L124N.pdf)

Week 51 – Company for Christmas
[1] *Leave It to Beaver*, created by Joe Connelly, Bob Mosher, and Dick Conway, featuring Jerry Mathers, Hugh Beaumont, and Barbara Billingsley, 1957-1963
[2] Dix, "What Child Is This," *Lutheran Service Book* (St. Louis: Concordia Publishing House, 2006), 370, 1
[3] Ibid., 2
[4] "Come Hither, Ye Children," *LYRICSMODE*, accessed 10/22/2017, http://www.lyricsmode.com/lyrics/r/religious_music/come_hither_ye_children.html

Week 52 – The Old Shall Be Merry
[1] Juliane, "The Lord hath Helped Me Hitherto," tr. Crull, *The Lutheran Hymnal* (St. Louis: Concordia Publishing House, 1941), 33, 1, 3
[2] Homburg, "Christ, the Life of All the Living," tr. Winkworth, *Lutheran Service Book* (St. Louis: Concordia Publishing House, 2006), 420, 1
[3] Newton, "Amazing Grace," *Lutheran Service Book* (St. Louis: Concordia Publishing House, 2006), 744, 5
[4] Arnold Kuntz, "Till Only One Thing Matters," *Devotions for the Chronologically Gifted*, ed. Les Bayer (St. Louis: Concordia Publishing House, 1999), 46. Note: *Devotions for the Chronologically Gifted* © 1999 Concordia Publishing House. Used with permission. www.cph.org.

TIMELY REFLECTIONS

A MINUTE A DAY WITH DALE MEYER

by Dale A. Meyer

A minute's worth of reading
for a day's worth of reflection

Timely Reflections is a collection of 365 inspirational devotions from the long-running and ever-popular Meyer Minute weekday online series. Dr. Meyer aptly uses Scripture – along with his own wisdom and experience – to guide his readers through the joys and pitfalls of daily living. Insightful, uplifting, and sometimes challenging, these daily reflections will provide plenty of spiritual food for thought. Set aside a minute a day to read, reflect, savor, and share each one!

Dr. Dale A. Meyer currently serves as President of
Concordia Seminary in St. Louis, MO.

Order online at www.tripillarpublishing.com

Also from Tri-Pillar Publishing

Timely Reflections: A Minute a Day with Dale Meyer
Dale A. Meyer

Meeting Ananias and Other Eye-Opening Stories of Faith
James Tino

Missional U: Life as a Mission Trip
Jacob Youmans

Missional Too: The Trip of a Lifetime
Jacob Youmans

Shaking Scripture: Grasping More of God's Word
Mark Manning

Abba Daddy Do: Explorations in Childlike Faith
Jacob Youmans

Powerful Love: An Introduction to Christianity
Lloyd Strelow

Talking Pictures: How to Turn a Trip to the Movies into a Mission Trip
Jacob Youmans

Extraordinary News for Ordinary People
Heath Trampe

Order online at www.tripillarpublishing.com!

Bringing CHRIST *to the Nations*®
and the *Nations* to the CHURCH

Lutheran Hour Ministries is a trusted expert in global media that equips and engages a vibrant volunteer base to passionately proclaim the Gospel to over 70 million people worldwide each week. We work in areas where other organizations are not present and use local missionaries who know the language and culture.

LUTHERAN HOUR MINISTRIES
www.lhm.org

ENERGIZE, EQUIP, AND ENGAGE LAITY FOR OUTREACH

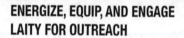

BRING THE GOSPEL TO THE UNREACHED AROUND THE WORLD

GROW GOD'S KINGDOM THROUGH EXPANDED MEDIA OUTREACH

ENGAGE COMMUNITIES IN THE DIGITAL MISSION FIELD

#WhoWillGoForUs
REFER A PROSPECTIVE STUDENT

"And I heard the voice of the Lord saying, 'Whom shall I send, and who will go for us?' Then I said, 'Here am I! Send me.'" (Is. 6:8 ESV)

Who is our next church worker? Please encourage those you know with the skills and abilities to serve as a pastor or deaconess to consider church work vocation.

Want to make a referral?
Contact Ministerial Recruitment and Admissions
at 800-822-9545 or admissions@csl.edu.

801 SEMINARY PLACE • ST. LOUIS, MO 63105 • 800-822-9545 • WWW.CSL.EDU

CPSIA information can be obtained
at www.ICGtesting.com
Printed in the USA
FSHW02n0057090618
49109FS